Naomi "Omie" V

D0503543

Naomi "Omie" Wise

Her Life, Death and Legend

HAL E. PUGH *and*
ELEANOR MINNOCK-PUGH

McFarland & Company, Inc., Publishers
Jefferson, North Carolina

ISBN (print) 978-1-4766-9013-1
ISBN (ebook) 978-1-4766-4788-3

LIBRARY OF CONGRESS AND BRITISH LIBRARY
CATALOGUING DATA ARE AVAILABLE

Library of Congress Control Number 2022038728

© 2022 Hal E. Pugh and Eleanor Minnock-Pugh. All rights reserved

*No part of this book may be reproduced or transmitted in any form
or by any means, electronic or mechanical, including photocopying
or recording, or by any information storage and retrieval system,
without permission in writing from the publisher.*

On the cover: (front to back) Adams' spring where Naomi Wise
mounted the horse and rode to the river (courtesy Randolph County
Public Library, Randolph Room); warrant signed by the coroner,
John Craven, sending Jonathan Lewis to jail without bond for the murder
of Naomi Wise, April 8, 1807 (courtesy State Archives of North Carolina);
Naomi Wise tombstone (with erroneous death date), erected in the
1940s, Providence Friends Meeting cemetery, Randolph County,
North Carolina, 2020 (the authors); "Naomi's Cooling Board,"
the rock on the east bank of Deep River where Naomi Wise's
body was laid for the coroner's inquest (the authors)

Printed in the United States of America

*McFarland & Company, Inc., Publishers
Box 611, Jefferson, North Carolina 28640
www.mcfarlandpub.com*

To Francis Howgill Julian,
who reflected on the story of Naomi Wise:
"There might be a volume wrote on this subject.
Who will undertake the task?"

—September 2, 1879, *The Asheboro Courier*

Table of Contents

Acknowledgments

More than 200 years ago Naomi Wise was murdered in the waters of Deep River in Randolph County, North Carolina. She has touched innumerable lives in life and in death.

While we investigated and wrote about the events and people surrounding the murder, the Naomi Wise story continued to ensnare a growing number of people who helped us share this piece of history. Our friend and enthusiastic supporter, folklorist Sarah Bryan, we profusely thank for assistance and encouragement. She enabled us to take a dream and make it a reality. Charles Barker and Jerry Brown, we thank for always having time to sit down and share a love and appreciation of family stories and personal mementos. To Dan and Dedra Routh with Dan Routh Photography we owe a great debt for working with us to capture the drone views and other photos of Deep River.

We would like to thank Ellen Robbins of the North Randolph Historical Society, Donna Toomes and Louise Hudson of the Randleman Library, Gwen Gosney Erickson of the Guilford College Quaker Archives, and R.S. Spencer, Jr., of the Hyde County Historical and Genealogical Society. Special thanks to L. McKay Whatley, Jr., Roberta Gavin, and Kendra Lyons of the Randolph County Public Library's Randolph Room and the fine staff at the State Archives of North Carolina. We would like to thank the City of Randleman for assisting and allowing us access to city-owned property.

We want to thank Karen Paar, director/archivist of Mars Hill University's Liston B. Ramsey Center for Regional Studies, and Lynn Cates, formerly of Duke University's Rubenstein Library, for their cooperation and help. The staff at the Clark County, Indiana, Clerk's Office, the Indiana Historical Society, the New Albany-Floyd County Public Library's Stuart Barth Wrege Indiana History Room, Vincennes University's Lewis Historical Library, the Southern Indiana Genealogical Society, and the Ohio Historical Society deserve our gratitude. Members of the

Acknowledgments

Wise family and the Lewis and Field families, we thank for sharing, and for enabling us to share, the stories of tragedy and triumph. A special thanks to Keith Fogleman and Ann Turner.

Twenty-five years have passed since we started our quest for the facts surrounding the death of Naomi Wise and we thank those good friends and family who searched before us, shared their knowledge, and are no longer with us: W. Calvin Hinshaw, Barbara Grigg, Eleanor Long-Wilgus, Virginia Hayes, W. Talmadge Hayes, Mary Dennis, Darrell Fogleman, and Ewart Pugh.

Our sincere appreciation is extended to all of the many friends and staff who assisted, simplified and joined in the search.

The musicians and vocalists that have helped perpetuate Naomi's story we thank for the music that can uniquely portray the emotion within the words. We thank all the performers for sharing the ballad and keeping Naomi's memory alive.

Preface

Our fascination with Naomi Wise has developed over many years, largely as a consequence of ties of kinship and neighborhood. We live in New Salem, a community at the edge of the town of Randleman in Randolph County, North Carolina. The 1807 murder of Naomi Wise occurred only two miles from where our home is now located. Many of the families intimately involved with the discovery of the murder and the subsequent trial lived in and around New Salem. Naomi herself lived and worked in the Adams family's household, which was scarcely a half-mile west of where we reside. Hal's ancestors settled in this area of Piedmont North Carolina in 1756, and many had connections to her. Joseph Elliott, whom Naomi's daughter served as an apprentice, was Hal's fifth great-grandfather, and his son Benjamin Elliott, who employed Jonathan Lewis, Naomi's lover and accused murderer, was a fifth great-uncle. Hettie Elliott, in whom Jonathan Lewis supposedly had a love interest, was Benjamin Elliott's sister and Hal's fifth great-aunt. The Joseph Elliott family lived on the east side of Polecat Creek, one-half mile from our residence. Hal's fourth great-grandfather, Tobias Julian, lived near Deep River where Naomi was drowned, and was a witness at the trials of Jonathan Lewis. In 1879 Tobias' son Francis Howgill Julian penned an article in *The Asheboro Courier* about Naomi's murder, contributing to the written branch of the story's path of dissemination. Hal grew up immersed in the lore of Randolph County and of the famous crime.

At the beginning of the 19th century, the land where we live was owned by William Dennis, a Quaker and a potter. (We ourselves have made our living as potters since 1972.) Dennis figures prominently in this story: he was reportedly the first neighbor Mary Adams, Naomi's employer, contacted the morning Naomi was found to be missing. It was research about William Dennis that further piqued our interest in the story of Naomi Wise and Jonathan Lewis. While researching the Dennis

1

family's involvement in the pottery-making trade, we discovered that William was subpoenaed to appear as a witness for the prosecution in Jonathan Lewis' 1807 grand jury hearing. Soon additional information concerning William's involvement with Naomi and Jonathan led us to other avenues of inquiry.

W. Calvin Hinshaw, a historian and friend, shared with us his extensive notes on the story of Naomi Wise, which he had collected over many years living in Randolph County. Calvin had the forethought to converse with people whose families had been involved in the events surrounding Naomi's death, and he passed along many of their stories to us. As luck would have it, we were also to have a providential visit by the folklorist Eleanor Long-Wilgus, who was studying the creation and history of the ballad of Naomi Wise, and had been pointed in our direction to help her get a better understanding of the story. In Long-Wilgus' possession was a narrative poem that a friend of her husband, D.K. Wilgus, professor of English, music, and folklore, and Wayland Hand, professor of Germanic literature and folklore, had found in a commonplace book in the Special Collections of UCLA's Charles E. Young Research Library. The book that was discovered had belonged to a young Quaker girl, Mary Woody, from Alamance County, North Carolina. Within the pages of this book was a narrative poem, "A true acount of Nayomy Wise," which was based on testimony of Mary Adams during the coroner's inquest. The poem contained a wealth of information: in our hands was a retelling of Mary Adams' sworn statement, in which she recounted the life of Naomi Wise. The "true acount" had found its way 2,200 miles back to Randolph County, to within two miles of the spot where the inquest was held, and where Mary Adams had stood in the presence of Naomi's dead body and given her testimony.

In the early 1970s we were also fortunate to have visited the remains of the home where Jonathan Lewis' grandfather, John Lewis, settled when he arrived in North Carolina, and the site of Richard Lewis' home near the Randolph County community of Providence, where Jonathan Lewis was born. While many of these landmarks have now vanished due to farming and development, one can still recognize the vestiges of the old roads that interconnected the homesteads during that era. Present-day New Salem Road follows the old Trading Road, and in certain locales there remains evidence of its presence, cut into the earth from the centuries of travel and erosion.

Though her own religion, if any, is unknown, Naomi Wise worked and lived in a Quaker community. Early American Quakers were required to marry within their religion, so many of the families in and around New Salem, the families who figure in this story, were interrelated. The Dennis, Elliott, Chamness, Reynolds, Norton, Woody, Watkins, Hinshaw, Beeson, Pennington, and McCollum families were all interconnected through marriage. By the beginning of the 19th century, some individuals had married outside the Quaker religion, or for other reasons were no longer members; however, there was still a strong bond, and the Quaker community continued to operate as a large extended family. Though this book is first and foremost the story of a young woman's murder, and how the accounts of her death have been rendered over the generations, it is also a portrait of a Piedmont North Carolina Quaker community in the early 19th century—a community closely bound by faith and kinship.

Introduction

In the American South, old family stories and tales of local history are often told with such fervor that, for the listener, it seems as if the events narrated happened only yesterday. Someone from outside the locale might not be able to distinguish whether the story's characters are still living or have been dead for 200 years. Such is the case in Randolph County, North Carolina, where the story of the murder of a young woman named Naomi Wise more than two centuries ago remains very much alive. Yet through the years, gossip, romanticizing, and misremembering have been interjected into that oral and documentary history, sometimes blurring reality and fiction.

The murder of Naomi Wise by her lover Jonathan Lewis has been recounted in song, story, and print since the event first happened. The tale's best-known form, a murder ballad about the killing, traveled throughout the southeastern United States, becoming embellished, amended, revised, and so entrenched in far-flung traditions that several communities claim the story as part of their own local history. It has been variously claimed that Naomi Wise was murdered at Adams's spring near Springfield, Missouri; in Indiana; in Randolph County, West Virginia; and in Georgia.[1] The murder actually occurred in northern Randolph County, North Carolina, on the night of Sunday, April 5, 1807.

The story of Naomi Wise's murder is probably best known today from western North Carolina guitarist Arthel "Doc" Watson's recording of "Omie Wise,"[2] which appeared on his self-titled first solo album in 1964. In written form, the dissemination of Naomi's story stems largely from an account published in 1851 by North Carolina writer and educator Braxton Craven.[3] However, Craven romanticized his story, made mistakes, and likely intentionally omitted some known facts. His telling nonetheless became a sensation and was copied and reprinted in the late 19th and early 20th centuries by a variety of publishers, who offered it in booklet form, as well as reprinting the story in newspapers.[4]

Introduction

The versions of the story that one hears most often in the oral tradition also draw heavily from Braxton Craven's published account. According to these renditions, Naomi Wise was a lovely young orphan girl in her teens, living with the William Adams family in what is now the village of New Salem. While working for the Adams family, Naomi met the dignified and handsome Jonathan Lewis, who lived a few miles away and passed by the Adams residence on his way to and from the nearby town of Asheboro, where he clerked for a wealthy storekeeper, Benjamin Elliott. The Adams family warned Naomi about Lewis. While dashing and good-looking, Jonathan was said to have come from an unruly, though powerful, family. His father, Richard, had earlier killed his own brother out of fear for his life. Jonathan himself was said to have a temper and was often reckless. Disregarding the Adams family's warnings, Naomi continued to see Jonathan; taken under his spell, she fell in love with him. He led her to believe that he was equally in love with her and, taking advantage of her innocence, lured her into a sexual relationship. She became pregnant.

In the meantime, the story continues, Jonathan was also courting his employer's sister, Hettie Elliott, and trying to cultivate a relationship with her. The Elliott family was well-to-do, and he saw an opportunity for advancement. But when he found out that Naomi was pregnant, Jonathan knew his chances with Hettie would likely be ruined. Falsely promising Naomi marriage and wealth, he asked her to meet him at Adams's spring late one evening. They would elope, he said, and being married, she would not be disgraced.

On that evening Naomi went to the spring, bringing a water pail with her as she did in her daily work. She met the waiting Jonathan, and, climbing onto a nearby stump, mounted the horse behind him. They began to ride toward Asheboro. Though she had at first been happy, Naomi began to have a foreboding feeling as they approached Deep River—but Jonathan assured her that all was well. They arrived at the river ford and Lewis started across, but in midstream paused. He told Naomi that she was a fool to believe that he would marry her, and with those words threw her from his horse into the water, and forcibly drowned her.

Naomi's dying screams were heard by a woman and her sons who lived nearby. Drawn outside by the commotion, they heard the sound of a horse galloping away. The next morning, one of the sons found Naomi's body below the river ford, and brought it to shore. Immediately Jonathan Lewis was suspected as the murderer. Lewis was captured and brought to the river for the coroner's inquest. He was indicted and jailed for murdering Naomi, but soon escaped and fled westward. Several years later he was found and brought back to stand trial. By that time many of the witnesses in the case had either died or moved away, so there was not sufficient evidence to convict him. Tried and released, Lewis moved to Kentucky, where he died a short while later. On his deathbed, Jonathan said that he saw Naomi ever before him, and before his last breath, he confessed to her murder.

So the story often goes. But this version, originating largely with Braxton Craven, contains both facts and errors, which would affect later retellings.

Using the pseudonym of Charlie Vernon, Braxton Craven published a serialized account in four separate Wednesday editions of *The Greensboro Patriot* newspaper, from April 8 through April 29, 1874, giving the story wide exposure.[5] Numerous booklets were published over the coming decades, spreading Craven's story further. In 1911, for example, the King Novelty Company in King, North Carolina, advertised their edition of *Naomi Wise or the Wrongs of a Beautiful Girl* for 12 cents postpaid.[6] Newspapers continued to publish articles about the tragedy, and to reprint the ballad.

In the 1930s Laura Stimson Worth (1874–1974), Randolph County historian and librarian, became interested in the Naomi Wise story and collected information and examined court records to verify that the event occurred in Randolph County, North Carolina. Worth furnished information to the Randleman Rotary Club when it reprinted Craven's story, published alongside a history of the town of Randleman. Court records and other information provided proof the event had occurred in Randolph County. However, there were also errors in the accompanying court record transcriptions, and in Naomi's reported death date. The Randleman Rotary Club's republication of the Naomi Wise story led to the creation of several articles and publications through the years that attempted to offer a more historically accurate account of what transpired. However, erroneous dates and locations, as well as transcription errors, were carried forward.

Once a story is at large in the oral tradition or in print, mistakes can be repeated so consistently that their accuracy ceases to be questioned. It has therefore been our purpose to reexamine articles, state and county court records, and other documents to correct the errors that have been made, as well as to add new information. This re-investigation has brought to light aspects of the story that had previously been ignored or unknown. Two of the most fundamental errors in popular retellings of Naomi's story have to do with her age and death date. Though she was murdered in 1807, many sources claim that her death was in 1808—so many, in fact, that even her modern tombstone, carved and placed in the 1940s, bears the incorrect date. Naomi's birthdate of 1789 is also in error; she was likely born several years prior to that date. Rather than being hardly more than a child, as she was portrayed by Braxton Craven, Naomi Wise was in fact a grown woman with two children of her own and a third on the way. (Braxton Craven's own life story sheds light on possible reasons for his romantically innocent portrayal of Naomi.)

In the 1851 *The Evergreen*, Craven placed the time of his story as happening "about forty years ago," which would have been 1811 but did not specifically mention when Naomi died. Francis Howgill Julian writing in *The Asheboro Courier* in 1879 thought her death occurred around 1809. J.A. Blair placed the date of Naomi's death as "about the year 1808" in his book *Reminiscences of Randolph County* published in 1890. A 1925 edition of the *Greensboro Daily News* stated Naomi died during the year 1808. Bascom Lamar Lunsford writing in *Stand By Magazine*, May 29, 1937, placed her death in 1808. Randolph County historian and librarian Laura Worth in 1938 incorrectly assigned the death as occurring in 1808 based on court records. She stated, "This fixes the fact of 1808 being the date & not 1800." In 1944 *The Story of Naomi Wise* also quoted Naomi's death year as 1808. The 1952 edition of *The Frank C. Brown Collection of the North Carolina Folklore: Vol. II: Folk Ballads from North Carolina* reprinted the 1808 death date from *The Story of Naomi Wise*. In 1954 Manley Wade Wellman in *Dead and Gone: Classic Crimes in North Carolina* placed her death as 1808. In 1974 Robert Roote in "The Historical Events Behind the Celebrated Ballad 'Naomi Wise'" using court records finally corrected Naomi's death year as 1807.

More broadly, the community of Quakers living in the area during the late 18th and early 19th centuries played a more important role in this story than is commonly known. Many of the figures in this story were Quakers or had Quaker neighbors and relatives. Therefore, Quaker beliefs regarding care of orphans and the oppressed had a direct bearing on Naomi Wise's life and the reactions to her death. In his version of the story of Naomi Wise, Braxton Craven chose to omit all information regarding Quakers and their involvement. As a result, that element has largely been forgotten in the years since.

This is also a story about gender relations—about a woman who died, like many women do today, at the hands of a romantic partner, and about what life was like for many women in a male-dominated society in which they possessed limited agency. Thanks to the discovery of the early 19th-century narrative poem "A true acount of Nayomy Wise," we are able to introduce the perspective of a woman, Naomi's employer, Mary Adams. Adams' testimony, preserved in the poem, offers an account of Naomi's relationship with Jonathan Lewis in a woman's own words, an opportunity all too rare for researchers studying this era.

In the following pages, we recount the historical facts of the murder of Naomi Wise as we have been able to establish them. We then discuss how the story lived on through written accounts, song, and oral history. In so doing, we address some of the many errors that have been introduced and perpetuated through these accounts. Despite the inaccuracies of the popular versions of the story, nearly inevitable when a story has been transmitted largely orally for so many generations, the folklore of Naomi Wise has accomplished something remarkable: it has kept her memory alive. Even in modern times, when a woman is murdered by a man, or someone from the lower rungs of society is put out of the way by a person of power and privilege, the victim is rarely remembered for long. The ballad of Naomi Wise, the published accounts of her life, and the oral tradition surrounding her death have served to ensure that a vulnerable, indigent, likely uneducated woman—someone who would otherwise almost certainly have been forgotten by history—is remembered more than 200 years after her murder.

Abbreviations

RCPL, RR: Randolph County Public Library, Randolph Room, Asheboro, North Carolina
RCRD: Randolph County Register of Deeds
SANC: State Archives of North Carolina, Raleigh, North Carolina

CHAPTER 1

The Quaker Community

At the beginning of the 19th century, Randolph County, near the geographical center of North Carolina, was a largely agrarian landscape.[1] In the north-central part of the county there lived a sizable population of members of the Society of Friends, or Quakers. Although neither Naomi Wise nor Jonathan Lewis, her accused murderer, was a Quaker, it was in this community of Quakers and non–Quakers that their story unfolded. Jonathan's grandfather John Lewis and grandmother Priscilla Lewis were not Quakers, but they were buried at Centre Friends Meeting. The Quakers would allow non–Quakers to be buried in their cemeteries, however, with the stipulation that grave markers were to be simple in design, so their interment at Centre Friends Meeting is not necessarily an indication of their own religion.

Quakers had migrated into the area in the mid to late 18th century from the Mid-Atlantic and New England states, as well as from eastern North Carolina. Many local residents attended Centre Friends Meeting, organized in 1757 and located on the Centre Road, which ran south and intersected with the Trading Road. Twelve years after the establishment of Centre Friends Meeting, land was purchased for Providence Friends Meeting located five miles to the southeast. Providence Meeting House was nearer the Trading Road, offering a closer and more convenient location for the large number of Quakers who had recently settled in the area. The Trading Road was one of the first major roads in the backcountry of North Carolina, leading from Petersburg, Virginia, diagonally through North Carolina, and into South Carolina and Georgia.

Naomi Wise's life in Randolph County was intertwined with that of the area's Quaker community. Many of these families were interrelated, due to the requirement that Quakers marry within their religion.

The Dennis family, who would become closely involved in Naomi's story, had moved from Chester County, Pennsylvania, and settled on the Trading Road in Randolph County in 1766. Adjoining the Dennis

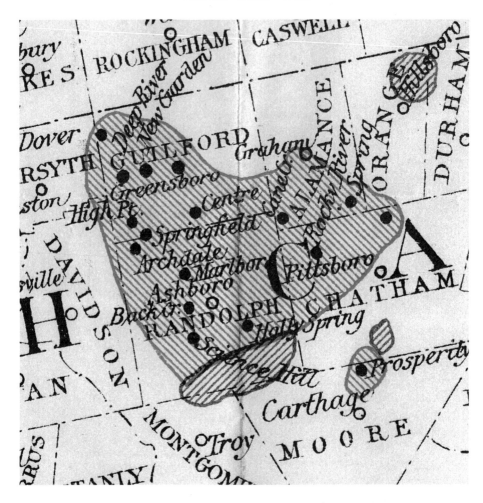

Map showing Quaker communities in the North Carolina Piedmont. Reproduced from Stephen B. Weeks, "Southern Quakers and Slavery: A Study in Institutional History" (Baltimore: Johns Hopkins University Press, 1896) (Guilford College's Quaker Archives).

property to the west was the land of William Adams and his family, who had purchased the tract in 1803. (Part of the Adams' land would later become the town of New Salem, laid out in 1816.[2]) The Adams family history has proven to be elusive. William Adams had lived in Maryland before the American Revolution and may have also lived in Hyde County, North Carolina. He first appeared in Randolph County, North Carolina, in 1801, when he purchased a 200-acre tract of land from

12

Thomas Saxton on the Polecat Creek watershed. William purchased a tract of land in 1803 from the Quaker Ebenezer Whitney, where he made his residence. Whitney, originally from Wayne County, North Carolina, had acquired two state land grants in 1799 and 1801 for 180 acres of land close to where the Colonial Trading Road and the Centre Road intersected. Braxton Craven made reference that William Adams was a farmer, which appears correct, as he owned approximately 330 acres of land in 1807. William and his family lived for 11 years on the property purchased in 1803. In 1814 he sold the property to Benjamin Marmon and it appears the family had left Randolph County by 1815 as William is not listed on the Randolph County tax list for that year. Unfortunately, no family information could be gleaned concerning Mary Adams, the wife of William.

William had a brother, Lanier [Lenoir] Adams, documented in Hyde County, North Carolina, who served as a private while in the Continental Army of the American Revolution. He had died and as a result, William had filed a Revolutionary War claim for the monies and land warrant associated with Lanier's service. There was a problem as William's sister Rachel Taylor, living in Wake County, had previously applied for and been given the claim. She passed it to Daffron [Daferon] Davis (1770–1826), who was residing in Randolph County on a 100-acre tract near William Adams' residence. While Daffron Davis was listed as an heir to Lanier Adams, his kinship could not definitively be determined.

A spring on the Adams' property near the intersection of the Trading Road and the River Road that led to Asheboro provided water for local residents and travelers. The Centre Road, later referred to as the Greensboro Road, ran north from its intersection with the Trading Road following what is now called Old Greensboro Road, and went northward toward Centre Friends Meeting House in southern Guilford County. The road to the south of the Trading Road was referred to as the River Road or River Way, as mentioned in the Woody poem. It followed modern-day Brown Oaks Road to Fox Street to East Naomi Street, where it forded Deep River near the modern bridge in Randleman. This southern route would have been the usual and nearest road for inhabitants in the northeastern area of Randolph County to travel to Asheboro, which was located approximately nine miles from the Adams property. The eastern boundary of the Dennis property adjoined Polecat Creek and the property of Richard and Elizabeth Dennis Norton. Also to the east lived the Elliott family, Quakers who had arrived from York

Naomi "Omie" Wise

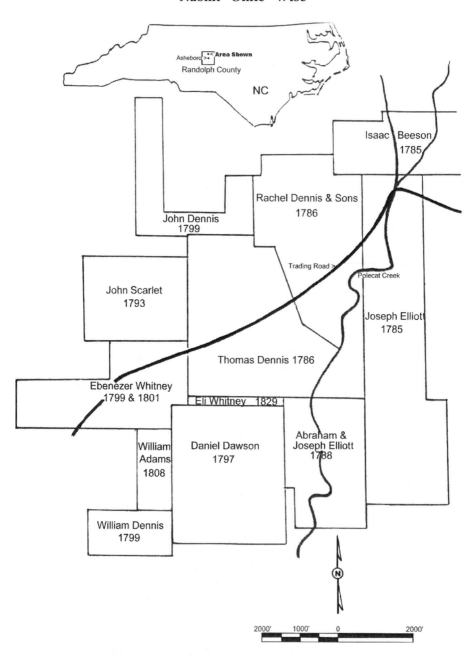

Land grants issued in northern Randolph County. William Adams purchased 125 acres of the Ebenezer Whitney land grant in 1803 (map by the authors).

County, Pennsylvania, in 1764. Approximately four miles to the northeast, along Little Polecat Creek, lived the families of John, Stephen and Richard Lewis, father of Jonathan. These Lewises, who were not Quakers, were known for ferocity, both in wartime and as civilians.

Very little is known about the background of Naomi Wise before she came to this Randolph County community. The opening lines of the poem found in Mary Woody's commonplace book—referred to throughout the coming chapters as the "Woody poem"—offer a hint about when she came to the area and where she had been living prior to her arrival.[3]

> *To Such as here and Wants to know*
> *A woman Came Some years ago*
> *Then from a Cuntry namd by hide*
> *In Randolph after did reside.*

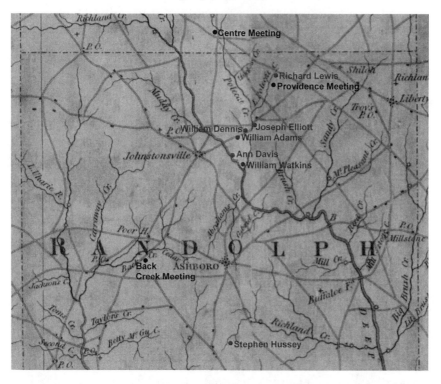

Detail of a map identifying the residence locations of Richard Lewis, William Dennis, Joseph Elliott, William Adams, William Watkins, Ann Davis, Stephen Hussey and the Quaker Meetings of Providence, Centre, and Back Creek. From "A New Map of the State of North Carolina" by Robert H.B. Brazier, 1833 (Library of Congress).

The Woody poem would seem to indicate that Naomi came from Hyde County, North Carolina; legal records suggest that she had made the move to Randolph County approximately five years prior to her murder. This evidence is supported by a November 19, 1802, Randolph County bastardy bond in which she identified Benjamin Sanders as the father of her child.

Hyde County is located in the coastal plain of eastern North Carolina and includes a portion of Pamlico Sound. In the late 18th century, it encompassed a larger area than it does today, including parts of modern Tyrell, Beaufort, and Dare counties. At least one Wise family lived in Capt. Cason Gibbs' District of Hyde County around the time of Naomi's childhood, the household headed by Andrew Wise, in which there lived "5 white females [of] all ages." Though no family relationship can be confirmed with certainty, due to the scarcity of early vital records in Hyde County, one of those five females may have been Naomi.[4] According to 20th-century Randolph County historian Laura Worth, "the Wise Family were people of good standing, upper class in the section." For reasons unknown, Naomi was left a poor orphan. Laura Worth did not leave any notes and no records have been located to substantiate the prominence and wealth of the Wise family and their relationship with Naomi, which Worth says she had heard from "old people" 25 years before.[5] The Andrew Wise family were freeholders. Andrew had purchased a 100-acre tract on the south side of Lake Mattamuskeet from Thomas Gibbs in 1779. Eight years later in September 1787, he sold the tract to Willis Wilson, Jr., from Norfolk County, Virginia.[6]

In his account of Naomi's life and death, Braxton Craven placed heavy emphasis on her identity as an orphan. In this era, a child could be labeled an "orphan" if he or she lacked the protection and support of a father, even if the mother was living, because of his death or desertion, or the child's "bastardy." In this male-dominated society, the lack of a male patron left female orphans with limited options for self-support, relegating many to the lower echelons of society. Such a girl might learn the skills associated with unmarried women, such as the trade of spinning or keeping house for a living, through apprenticeship or informally.[7] There is no documentation of Naomi being placed in a court-ordered apprenticeship, so it would seem that any work training she obtained would likely have been voluntary or informal.

In the spring of 1807, Naomi Wise was residing at the William Adams household in northern Randolph County, and working as a servant. For an unmarried woman—one who by now had two small children of her own—with no parents to aid her, domestic service would have been one of the few options available for supporting her family. The Woody poem describes her plight:

> *And Being poor and Credit low*
> *From hous to hous She had to go*
> *And labors hard in tiol and pain*
> *Herself and babes for to maintain*

Naomi was not mentioned in any of the Wardens of the Poor minutes for Randolph County. This indicates that she was making adequate income, or being sufficiently provided for, and was not considered a pauper. Under North Carolina law of the time, had she been designated a pauper, the county could have auctioned her off annually by paying the lowest bidder for her upkeep. Low bidders gained nearly free labor from the poor, as long as they promised to keep the pauper in their charge fed, clothed, and healthy. This system had the effect of forcing the destitute into a pattern of involuntary servitude, renewed on an annual basis.[8]

The Woody poem mentions that Naomi had been working at various other households prior to arriving at William Adams' home. Local oral history agrees, suggesting that she had earlier worked for other families in the community, and near the Quaker Providence Meeting.

Braxton Craven describes Naomi as "a lovely girl, just blooming in all the attractiveness of nineteen." But scholar Eleanor Long-Wilgus disagreed, writing that Naomi was "said to be somewhat older than Jonathan Lewis, and rather unattractive."[9] Long-Wilgus' source for this characterization may have been a 1925 *Greensboro Daily News* article by J.W. Cannon, which stated that "an old woman who died not so many years ago who said that she has seen Naomi, told a certain Asheboro citizen that Naomi Wise was not pretty."[10] With these contradictory accounts and the lack of verifiable descriptive records, any characterization of Naomi's appearance would be highly speculative.

Long-Wilgus' claim that Naomi was older than Jonathan Lewis does have some documentary basis. Jonathan was born in April 1783, and would have been 23 years old in 1806 when their child was conceived. The Woody poem emphasizes Lewis' youth: "She by a youngster was beguild."

Naomi's exact age is unrecorded, but circumstantial evidence suggests that she was in fact at least as old as, if not older than, Jonathan. The Woody poem refers to Naomi as a woman in the opening lines, but then identifies her as a girl in a later verse. Since Naomi was a servant, the use of the word "girl" may have had more to do with her employment and societal place than with her age.[11] A letter written in 1807 by Richard and Abigail Beeson makes reference to her as an "orfan young Lady" which would seem to indicate she was perhaps not much older than Jonathan.[12]

Counting backwards from the birth of Naomi's oldest child in 1798 to the average age a female reached puberty in the fourth quarter of the 18th century, it appears likely that she was at least 23 to 26 years old in 1806. According to Joan Brumberg, the average age of menarche in 1780 was 17 and by 1877 was near 15.[13] Moreover, North Carolina law specified that unlanded (non-landowning) and poor orphans be bound out as apprentices until the age of 18 years.[14] The fact that Naomi worked successively in several households in Randolph County suggests that her apprenticeship, had it been a formal one, was over before she arrived in the county. She can therefore be presumed to have been no younger than 18 when she came to Randolph County, about five years prior to her death, suggesting an age of at least 23 when she died.

Braxton Craven portrayed Naomi as being 19 years old when she became entangled with Jonathan Lewis. Though Naomi could not have been so young, Braxton Craven did know another unmarried woman who had become pregnant at the age of 19—his own mother. This raises intriguing questions about Craven's psychological motivations for romanticizing Naomi's purported youth and innocence. (Those questions are discussed at greater length in Chapter 8.)

As a servant and an orphan, Naomi was certainly vulnerable, and caught in a vicious cycle that placed her at the bottom of the social order. But if she was Jonathan's age or older, the suggestion that he was preying on a young girl becomes complicated. By portraying Jonathan as a "youngster," the author of the Woody poem may be signaling that he did not fit the stereotypical role of the predatory older man.

In what was, comparisons aside, a short life, Naomi Wise bore two children. Her first child, Nancy, was born in March of 1798.[15] Nancy's father and birthplace are unknown. The Woody poem tells that "and by Some person [Naomi] was defild/And So brought forth a basturd Child." Her second child, Henry, was born in 1803.

Notwithstanding the social stigma of being born outside of wedlock, the derogatory-sounding term "bastard" was in fact the standard legal terminology in North Carolina law, as in other states. When a court was notified of the impending birth of a bastard child, a legal process was set into motion which required the mother to appear before two Justices of the Peace to report the child's paternity. If necessary, a writ or warrant (often referred to as a precept) was issued for the mother, and usually enforced by a constable. The North Carolina law stated,

> Two Justices of the Peace upon their own knowledge, or information made to them, that any single woman within their county is big with child, or delivered of a child or children, may cause such woman to be brought before them, and examine her upon oath concerning the father; and if she shall refuse to declare the father, she shall pay the sum of fifty shillings, and give sufficient security to keep such child or children from being chargeable to the parish, or shall be committed to prison until she shall declare the same, or pay the sum aforesaid and give security as aforesaid: but in case such woman shall upon oath, before the said Justices, accuse any man of being the father of a bastard child or children begotten of her body, such person so accused shall be judged the reputed father, and stand charged with the maintenance of the same as the county court shall order, and give security to the Justices of the said court to perform the said order, and to indemnify the county where such child or children shall be born, free from charges for his, her or their maintenance; and may be committed to prison until he find securities for the same, if such security is not by the woman before given.[16]

It is significant that the law specified that the two justices "*may* [emphasis added] cause such a woman to be brought before them." This phrasing created a loophole, allowing the authorities the option of not pursuing the matter of the child's paternity.[17] The justices' decision about whether to pursue financial support from the father might be influenced by his social standing in the community, including such factors as economic affluence, family relationships, and political persuasion. The accused father could also avoid public identification if he made arrangements for the bond to be paid. To ensure honesty on the part of the expectant mother, the punishment for lying under oath could include a fine or prison sentence. The terminology "big with child" was intentional, as it was thought that a woman would be more vulnerable, and therefore likely to be honest about the identity of the father, if she was questioned under oath when visibly pregnant. Likewise, the requirement of visual appearance of pregnancy may have been intended as a deterrent to women who might bring false claims of paternity when not actually pregnant.

If the father of the child was named, a warrant would be issued for his appearance before two Justices of the Peace, at which time the accused was required to post a bond for appearance in the county court. The determination and ruling of paternity culminated in the issuance of a bastardy bond, which obliged the father to support and to maintain the child. Randolph County required the issuance of a bastardy bond in the amount of £100. This bond not only spared the county from having to bear the upkeep of the child, but it also acted as a disincentive to keep women from being sexually active outside of marriage.

The Woody poem mentions the birth of Henry, Naomi's second child.

> *The Second Child neomy bore think she*
> *Into a neighbors man Ben Sanders Swore.*

On the 19th of November 1802, Naomi appeared before two Justices of the Peace, Zebedee Wood and Daniel Dawson, Sr., and confirmed

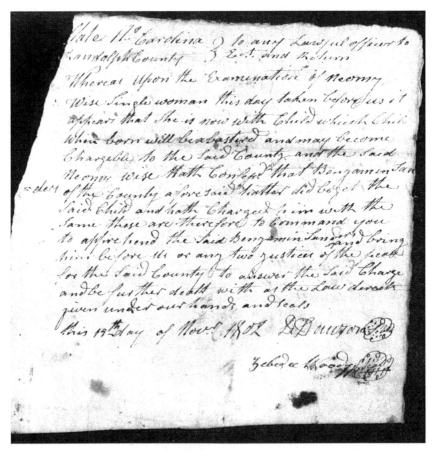

Naomi Wise bastardy bond naming Benjamin Sanders as the father of her child. November 19, 1802 (authors' collection).

Reverse of Naomi Wise bastardy bond with signatures of Benjamin Sanders who provided £50 for his appearance, and cosigners James Winningham and Thomas Saxton for £25 each on Sanders' bond. William Adams, the clerk of court, was not the husband of Mary Adams. Her husband, William Adams, signed his name with a mark (authors' collection).

that she was pregnant. She identified Benjamin Sanders, a hatter, as the father. Her son was born in 1803, prior to Benjamin Sanders' court hearing. Sanders was brought before Justices at the May 1803 Session of Court, and, pursuant to North Carolina law, posted the bond of £100 and took responsibility for Henry's maintenance and upkeep.[18]

Nine months later, Randolph County determined that Naomi, now with two children, could not adequately support her five-year-old daughter Nancy. In February of 1804, one month before her sixth birthday, Nancy

Bond signed by Benjamin Sanders with cosigners James Winningham and Thomas Saxton taking responsibility for the maintenance of Benjamin Sanders' and Naomi Wise's child, May 11, 1803 (State Archives of North Carolina).

Wise was taken from Naomi and indentured to Joseph Elliott.[19] Nancy was to learn the art of spinning, converting various fibers into yarn or thread. Joseph Elliott and his family were prominent residents of the county and considered to be of good character. Because Naomi was employed at the William Adams residence, approximately a mile away, it would have been relatively easy for her to visit her daughter. It is assumed that Henry, who was less than a year old when his sister was bound as an apprentice, remained with their mother; indeed, at least one ballad indicates that he was living with Naomi in the Adams household at the time of her death.[20]

Jonathan Lewis, born April 25, 1783, was the son of Richard Lewis (1759–1826) and Lydia Field Lewis (1762–1852). He was the oldest son in a family of seven brothers and four sisters.

The large Lewis and Field families settled in the area of northern Randolph and southern Guilford counties early, some members having arrived by 1756, and they were actively involved in the American Revolution. Craven mentions "old David Lewis" as being the patriarch of the Lewis family living in North Carolina. David Lewis was Jonathan's great-grandfather and he settled in Carteret County in eastern North Carolina, where he died in 1773. In actuality, it was Jonathan's grandfather, John Lewis, Sr. (1720–1802), born in Frederick County, Virginia, who first settled in the Piedmont. Jonathan's mother, Lydia Field (1762–1852), was the daughter of William Field and Lydia Elswick, and the granddaughter of Jane Field. The beginning of the Field dynasty in North Carolina was in 1756, when a warrant was drawn up for a 640-acre tract of property to Jane Field who arrived from Pennsylvania. The property

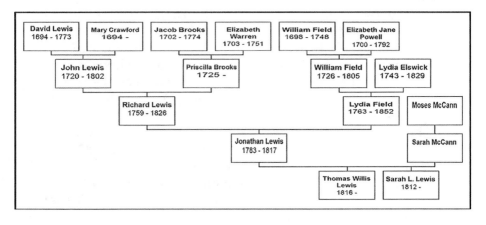

Jonathan Lewis family tree.

was situated in what would later become southern Guilford County near the edge of northern Randolph County. Jane Field's five sons purchased land in this same vicinity. In 1761, Jane's son and Lydia's father, William Field, received a land grant for 200 acres north of the Richard Lewis property near the modern-day northern Randolph County line.[21] As the Field and Lewis estates grew, so did the families' discontent with local British land agents. In the late 1760s, the Regulator movement opposed the fee system and taxation imposed by the colonial officials. William Field, Jonathan Lewis' maternal grandfather, joined the Regulators, but after their defeat at the Battle of Alamance, he took an oath of allegiance to the British Crown. This oath enabled William to serve in public office, which he would do, as an elected member of the House of the General Assembly from Guilford County, from 1771 to 1774. Soon thereafter, William served with the British as a lieutenant colonel in the Revolutionary War. His land was confiscated by the North Carolina General Assembly, and it took years for him to regain his property after the war.[22] Jonathan's father, Richard, his uncle David, and grandfather John Lewis also served in the Revolution, fighting with the 10th North Carolina Regiment. Another uncle, Stephen Lewis, sided with the British and was a member of the notorious Fanning Corps.[23]

Braxton Craven stated that the Lewises were "peculiar in appearance," being "tall, broad, muscular and very powerful men." Craven goes on to state the Lewis family were the "lions of the country" and their "character was eminently pugnacious."[24] Some family members did have many run-ins with the law, particularly Jonathan's uncles Stephen and John.

Stephen's affinity for violence and his reputation for seeking reprisal were among the reasons for the Lewis family's bad reputation. Craven claims that Stephen beat and abused his wife, circumstances which eventually led to his death at the hand of his brother, Richard.[25] The early Piedmont historian the Reverend E.W. Caruthers described Stephen Lewis as "the most reckless and daring [of the family]. Of a muscular frame and a vigorous constitution, destitute of religious culture or moral principle, and enured for years to scenes of blood and cruelty, he was a disgrace to humanity, and a terror to the neighborhood."[26]

Court records seem to substantiate the Rev. Caruthers' account, and show that both Stephen and John had continuing altercations with some of their neighbors, particularly John Allred. John Lewis was charged with assault on John Allred in 1786.[27] In 1786, Stephen was indicted for beating and raping Allred's 16-year-old daughter Lydia.

Chapter 1. The Quaker Community

According to the indictment, he "did beat, Wound and ill treat with an intent her the said Lidia against her Will then and there feloniously to Ravish and Carnally Know and other Wrongs then and there did the great damage of the said Lidia and against the peace and Dignity of said State."[28] His punishment for the violent assault was to pay court costs plus five shillings—at the time, approximately two days' wages for a laborer such as Stephen.[29] Stephen Lewis had a capias issued 1787 for assault on John Allred and had to make bond to preserve the peace as Allred was afraid Lewis would "Beat, Wound, Maim, or kill him" before the next court session. Two years later in 1789, Stephen Lewis assaulted John and broke his jaw.[30] Over the course of several years in the 1780s and early '90s, a multitude of allegations and indictments were brought against both Stephen and John, but their trials were repeatedly postponed, or, when they were found guilty of breaking the law, the brothers paid only small fines and court costs. Stephen Lewis was charged with the theft of a silver coin valued at six pence from Robert Hodgin; theft of a mill pick from Abraham Elliott; assault on his brother John Lewis; assault on members of the Cox family; and theft of a cow from Thomas Dougan. John Lewis was charged with assault on Samuel Allen; assault on Herman Cox; and assault on John Hudson.[31] This pattern of leniency suggests the possibility that the Lewises relied on influence and intimidation to avoid legal and criminal accountability.

The Lewis family's tenacity was in some instances looked on in a positive way, as witnessed by an account in the *History of the Ohio Falls Cities 2*. It tells of Jonathan's father, Richard Lewis, fortifying his cabin for a defense against Native Americans a few years after moving into the Indiana Territory from North Carolina in 1809. "Mr. Lewis had at this time lived some years on the farm where the family yet reside, and although urged by his neighbors to go to the block-house, refused to do so; at the same time preparing his cabin for defense by barricading and chaining the doors and windows, and making loop-holes for guns, etc. His son Richard was then a man grown, and his oldest daughter, Jane, could handle a rifle equal to almost any one. Accordingly they determined that, with the help of the dogs as sentinels, they would fight it out with the savages if they came that way; and without doubt they could have made a vigorous defense."

The *History of Wayne and Clay Counties, Illinois* described the temperament of some of Richard Lewis' sons after they moved from Indiana to Clay County, Illinois. They became involved in a continuous range war around 1830 concerning the ownership of half-wild hogs roaming the woods. This took place between the Lewis family and their friends and John McCawley and his friends. It was said, "all new-comers had to take sides; neutrality or indifference was not allowed ... the Lewises were fighters from the word go. They never hesitated to open the battle or attack the opposite bullies; and in the matter of rough-and-tumble-knock-down-and-drag-out, they were holy terrors from long-taw."[32]

In April of 1783, Jonathan Lewis was born into this family legacy. He grew up with his parents and siblings approximately five miles southeast of Centre Friends Meeting on Little Polecat Creek, near Providence Friends Meeting, in northern Randolph County.[33] Little is known of his youth.

Craven stated that Jonathan Lewis "was a large, well built, dignified looking man."

This is supported by Randolph County sheriff Isaac Lane who described Lewis as "a man between 25 and 30 years of age, tall slim man five feet 10 or 12 inchis high black hair and Reather of Dark skin."[34]

In May of 1805 when he was 22 years old, and again in 1806 and 1807, the Randolph County Pleas and Quarter Sessions appointed Jonathan Lewis to the post of constable. Lieutenant Colonel Alexander Gray and John Brower provided securities for his £200 legally required bond in 1807.[35] The Lewis family's reputation for toughness, as well as political alliances, likely helped Jonathan obtain this position. As constable, a job that had changed little since colonial times, Jonathan was a bonded public representative, conservator of the peace, and minister of justice for the part of Randolph County where his family lived, referred to as Captain Lewis' District. The Captain Lewis District encompassed the Providence Meeting area, where the Lewis and Field families resided, as well as sections of the Polecat Creek and Deep River watersheds, including the area where the families of William Adams and Joseph Elliott lived. Jonathan also had administrative duties, such as issuing summonses and precepts for the courts, collecting taxes, and maintaining order at the county courts.[36] By 1807 he had embarked on a secondary career, clerking for Asheboro attorney, Justice of the Peace, and businessman Benjamin Elliott. Benjamin Elliott was the son of Joseph Elliott, who had apprenticed Naomi's daughter Nancy as a spinster. Craven states, "The Elliotts were wealthy, honorable and in high repute." Joseph Elliott, Sr., was a prosperous surveyor and owned more than 1000 acres including one town lot in Asheboro.[37] His son Benjamin owned a business in Asheboro and was involved in governmental and civic duties, and was an attorney and Justice of the Peace.[38]

Chapter 1. The Quaker Community

Appointment as a constable in North Carolina was of questionable desirability. The requirements to complete the job necessitated physical strength and tenacity and some knowledge of the law. The district constable was categorized as the lowest position in the county's legal enforcement system, subjecting the appointee to possible threats of physical violence. But such an appointment may have held allure as the first stop on a path to political gain.[39]

The duties of Jonathan Lewis' two jobs would have required frequent trips from his home in the Providence community to Asheboro, a journey of about 13 miles. Craven was mistaken when he mentioned that the Lewis family was living near Centre Friends Meeting in Southern Guilford County. In actuality Jonathan lived with his parents and siblings approximately five miles southeast from Centre Friends Meeting on Little Polecat Creek, near Providence Friends Meeting in northern Randolph County.[40] The road he traveled from his home near Providence Meeting would have brought him to the Trading Road east of Polecat Creek, where he would have passed near the Joseph Elliott family homestead. Crossing the ford at Polecat Creek, he would have continued by the William Dennis property, and proceeded south on the River Road, passing the Adams's spring on his way to Asheboro. Jonathan's employment with Benjamin Elliott, and his route to and from Asheboro, would have made the home of Joseph Elliott, Benjamin's father, a convenient stop for business dealings and social visits. Joseph lived with his wife Sarah, their children, Naomi's young daughter Nancy Wise, and one or two other household members.[41] It may have been in that home that Jonathan met Naomi Wise, while she was visiting Nancy. Local oral tradition suggests that Naomi may have been working for families in the Providence Meeting area, which would also have allowed opportunities for the couple to meet. An affair began.

Few details survive, either in the written record or oral history, about the nature of Naomi and Jonathan's relationship prior to her pregnancy. The only indication of Naomi's feelings towards Jonathan are found in the testimony of Mary Adams, who reported that Naomi had told her that she was not afraid of her lover, and in fact believed him to be tender-hearted. Craven asserts that Jonathan loved Naomi early on in their romance, but his later actions bring this into doubt. (The suggestion of love may have been part of Craven's projecting his own mother's experience, or what he wished his mother's experience to have been, onto Naomi's.)

As one historian has written, though, privileged "men considered lower class women ... a sexual proving ground."[42] It seems more likely that Naomi was, for Jonathan, simply sport.

CHAPTER 2

Naomi's Pregnancy

During the second half of 1806, Naomi discovered that she was pregnant with Lewis' child. According to the Braxton Craven narrative, she became pregnant when she was working in the Adams household. The news of the pregnancy was disastrous for Lewis. It placed his career in jeopardy: depending on how he handled the situation, it might have cost him his job as constable, incurred a fine, even ruined his chances of moving forward in politics. There was also the stigma of being associated with a bastard child, even though the child would have been given its mother's name. In addition, he would have to pay for the child's maintenance, which, bastardy records suggest, he may have already been doing for another woman's child conceived out of wedlock.[1]

Constables were subject to loss of their titles and the bonds they had posted, as well as being imprisoned and fined, for infractions they might commit while serving in their position. A constable could be indicted and fined or imprisoned for refusing to keep the peace, not apprehending a felon, failure to pursue someone, or allowing a prisoner to escape or to injure themselves. They were also liable for refusing to execute a Justice's lawful command or warrant, or showing any contempt for their authority or negligence in office.[2]

Oral tradition and the Craven narrative suggest yet another reason for Jonathan to have received Naomi's news with alarm. While already in a relationship with Naomi, he was simultaneously spending time with—and presumably courting—Hettie Elliott, Benjamin's sister, then in her late teens or early 20s. Craven suggests that Jonathan's mother, Lydia Field Lewis, encouraged him to become more involved with Hettie, even referring to Lydia as an "evil genius." It seems plausible, and not necessarily evil, that Lydia would have encouraged her son to pursue Hettie. The Elliott family's affluence and social standing could only serve to increase Jonathan's interest. Marrying Benjamin's sister would have put him in an excellent position to further his career.

Chapter 2. Naomi's Pregnancy

Hettie's father, Joseph Elliott, Sr., was the county surveyor for Randolph County, having renewed his bond for £2000 in the May 1806 session of the Randolph County court.[3] It should be noted that Lydia Lewis was still alive in 1851 when Braxton wrote "Naomi Wise, or the Victim," in which he mentioned her.[4]

There is no direct information concerning Hettie's feelings towards Jonathan, but it would seem that they were complicated. Hettie's involvement with Lewis, romantic or not, is confirmed by the fact she was listed as a witness for the prosecution in the 1812 murder trial. Craven wrote that when Jonathan brought up the subject of marriage, Hettie "baffled him on every tack, and though she encouraged him, gave him but little hope of succeeding immediately."[5] Neither is there a record of how Hettie Elliott felt towards Naomi.

For all of these reasons, it was imperative to Jonathan that the news of Naomi's pregnancy not be revealed. According to the Woody poem,

> To keep it Secret then Lewis Chose
> And not the matter to expose
> To his disgrace and open Shame
> Nor bring dishonor to his name.

But Naomi thwarted his efforts by letting it become widely known that Jonathan was the unborn child's father.

> She Seemd rejoiced and likd it well
> And bold Enough the Sin to tell
> And with the Scandel So Content
> She told it mostly Where She went.

When the Elliott family became aware of Naomi's pregnancy, Jonathan assured Hettie that the rumor of his paternity "was a base, malicious slander, circulated by the enemies of the Lewis family, to ruin his character."[6]

Then, the Woody poem explains, Jonathan tried to buy Naomi's silence.

> For his own Credit Such Regard
> he promist her a grate Reward
> If She Would keep it quite Conceald
> And never let it be Reveald.

During the 19th century, men were known to use financial coercion to keep their identity from being revealed on bastardy bonds.[7] Jonathan's bribe would likely include sufficient funds to pay the 50-shilling fine she would incur by refusing to name the father in court, plus the amount necessary to cover the bastardy bond, and, presumably, an additional "reward." However, the poem goes on to say that Naomi did not take the money, but instead told everyone about the offer Jonathan had made to keep her quiet. This supports the idea that Naomi was truly enamored with Lewis, and not simply angling for money. For a woman of Naomi's low rung in society, it would have been cause for pride that someone of Lewis' social stature had become involved with her, and that she was carrying his child. Craven mentions that Naomi was putting pressure on Jonathan to "marry her forthwith, seconded by the power of tears and prayers." When this failed, she invoked the law.[8]

With no intention of marrying her, Jonathan responded by threatening Naomi with murder. Yet Craven and the Woody poem agree that Naomi seemed not to be afraid of Jonathan, even after he had menaced her life.

> He threatened that he would her kill
> She disregarded what he said
> And of his threats Seemd not afraid
> She liked her State So very well
> She Still inclind of it to tell
> And Lewis then with anger filled
> We guis he Thought She must be Killed

Jonathan tried one more tactic to keep Naomi quiet: false promises. Craven asserts that he even offered to be married by the magistrate. It seems unlikely that Jonathan could ever have been sincere in any talk of marriage. Naomi should have known, given societal norms, that the best she could hope for was that Lewis might sign the bastardy bond acknowledging his paternity, or pay her for the upkeep of the child in exchange for her silence.

As a constable, Jonathan was charged with a legal duty to take Naomi before two Justices, before whom she would be expected to name the father of her child. We can assume that, at this point, Naomi's pregnancy was advanced enough to show, forcing Lewis' hand in drawing up the precept or warrant. Should Naomi suggest to the Justices that it was Lewis who had impregnated her, and that he had tried to coerce her not to name him, Lewis would have faced not only losing the £200 bond put up as surety when he became constable, but he would have risked losing his appointment as constable. In Jonathan's later indictment by the Randolph County Grand Jury, he is specifically mentioned as being a constable.[9]

Jonathan's social position, like his career, was at great risk should it become generally known that he had had relations with someone of

Naomi's low standing. Perhaps more importantly, his self-esteem, and no doubt the esteem of others, would have been threatened by his inability to keep Naomi under control, bringing his manhood into question.[10]

There is no record of what Naomi's mental state was by this time, or whether she was truly gullible enough to believe that Jonathan might marry her. If she was that naïve, and he had murder in mind, what better way to entice her to ride off with him after dark than to promise her marriage? Plans were made for a rendezvous.

Craven states that Jonathan arranged to meet Naomi at Adams's spring, but the Woody poem maintains that he actually agreed to meet her at the schoolhouse that sat approximately 500 feet south of the spring. The simple structure was used as a school by the Quakers in the community to educate their children.[11] Later, New Salem Public School was built on the site.[12] Jonathan chose the location carefully. The schoolhouse sat on a knoll overlooking not only the spring but also the Adams family's house. Hiding behind the building, he would have had a clear view as Naomi left to meet him—and he could be sure that no one was following her. Near an intersection of the River Road and two less-traveled roads, the location also provided multiple escape routes, should he have to leave quickly on someone else's approach. The alternatives to using the River Road included one road leading east from the schoolhouse crossing Polecat Creek approximately one mile south of where the Trading Road forded the creek, and another road running south toward the William Watkins residence between the fork of Polecat Creek and Deep River.

According to the Woody poem, Jonathan and Naomi were unable to meet on the night planned, and had to attempt the rendezvous again the next week.

> Next day he Came a gain its said
> And then a new appointment made
> He told her then he thought he might
> Apoint to meet next Sunday night
> And Chargd her that She might Conceal
> The mater unto none reveal

But contrary to Jonathan's instructions, Naomi had in fact divulged the plan to Mary Adams. The secret arrangement to meet after dark, away from the house, confirmed Mary's worst suspicions about Jonathan's moral and social impropriety. Further, knowing the Lewis family's reputation for using violence to remedy disagreeable situations in which they found themselves, Mary had cause to fear for Naomi's life.

Abandoned New Salem Public School building built on the site of the school house mentioned in the Mary Woody manuscript. Photograph ca. 1930 (authors' collection).

Her fears would have been further exacerbated by Jonathan's continued demand that Naomi not mention the plans to anyone.

> *To mary Adams Soon She told*
> *And mary told her not to go*
> *Least that he might some mischief do*
> *He out of fury rage and spite*
> *To her some private mischief might*

On the evening of Sunday, April 5, Jonathan Lewis left William Watkins' house two miles south of the school, between the forks of Polecat Creek and Deep River. It was near sunset, which was at 6:47 that evening.[13] The moon was waning, so visibility would have been limited.[14] It took Lewis half an hour or less to ride the two miles to his chosen

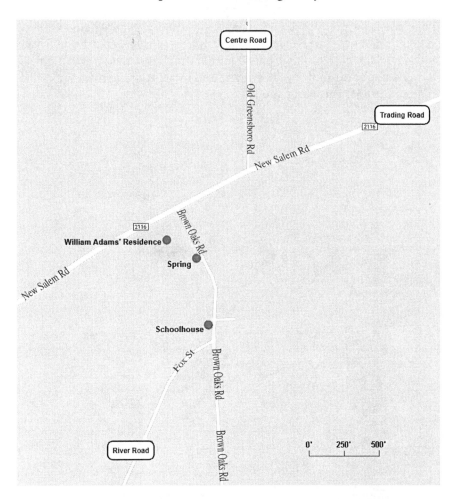

Map showing location of William Adams' residence in relationship to Adams' spring and the schoolhouse where Jonathan Lewis waited for Naomi (map by the authors).

position at the schoolhouse.[15] As planned, Naomi left the Adams' house with pail in hand. Based on horse tracks found later, it seems Lewis had been waiting behind the schoolhouse, and rode down to the spring to meet her. Craven's account mentions the horse tracks and adds that it was discovered that Naomi used a stump near the spring to mount Lewis' horse. They rode away down the River Road toward the ford at Deep River—on their way to Asheboro, Naomi perhaps believed, to be married by a Justice of the Peace. Crossing the Deep River ford would have been the first obstacle as they made their way south in the waning light. Craven embellishes his description of the ford at Deep River, talking of the high bluff with its commanding view, a blue crane slowly flying down the middle of the stream, and ravens cawing from the dwarf pines and cedars growing upon the crags.

CHAPTER 3

Death and Discovery

On Monday morning, Naomi had been missing for approximately 12 hours, since leaving for the spring. Concerned, Mary Adams consulted with neighbor William Dennis about where Naomi might be.

Mary suggested checking for Naomi at Joseph Elliott's home, in case she was there visiting her daughter Nancy—if, Mary is quoted in the poem as adding ominously, she "lives above the ground." William Dennis was less alarmed; he did not think that Lewis would murder Naomi, but thought that they had gone to Asheboro to get the bastardy bond signed, and would return. Yet he followed Mary's suggestion and traveled the few minutes to the Elliott residence, and learned that Naomi had not been there. William relayed Mary's account of what Naomi had told her about her assignation. He and Joseph Elliott resolved to go to the schoolhouse and look for signs of Jonathan and Naomi.

> *Then to the schoolhouse Both Repair*
> *And found his hors tracks plenty thare*
> *Not many Sises grat and Small*
> *The thought one hors had made them all*
> *He Came and went plain to their Sight*
> *And had Been there in both the nights*
> *Or its to travel took the day*
> *And one towards the River Way*
> *He did Conclude and did agree*
> *That She away must taken be*

Dennis and Elliott deduced that Jonathan and Naomi had disappeared together. They decided to go the next day to Colonel Alexander Gray, who was head of the militia, tell him what they believed had transpired, and let him decide what to do. A reasonable next step would have been to continue searching for Naomi and Jonathan by following the route to Asheboro and tracing any tracks. But it was then that members of the Davis family, who lived near the ford in the Deep River, came forward and reported that they had heard screams during the night.

Based on this new information, the search party changed their plan, and proceeded instead to the river. Within a short time, Ann Davis' son Joshua found Naomi's body, in the river downstream of the ford, caught against a rock outcropping.[1] Craven mentioned there were small turf islands below the ford at Deep River and an 1879 article in *The Asheboro Courier* by Howgill Julian stated that Naomi's body was found lodged against a rock. The rock where her body was found occasionally had debris and flotsam washed against it after heavy rains, so Craven's description of turf islands may have been factual, as there had been rain upriver in the six days earlier.[2] Julian also said you could see the rocks anytime when the water was low below the ford. The searchers pulled Naomi's body to the bank and laid her on a rectangular flat rock at the outcropping.

That same day, a company of men were dispatched to find Jonathan Lewis. Craven specifies that Robert Murdock, who, like Jonathan Lewis, was an employee of Benjamin Elliott, was the "brave officer" sent to lead the pursuit.[3]

View from the Naomi Street bridge looking downstream showing the outcropping of rocks extending into the center of Deep River where Naomi's body was found by Ann Davis' son, Joshua. The rock outcroppings were approximately 250 feet below the ford where Naomi was drowned. Randleman, North Carolina (courtesy Dan Routh Photography).

Chapter 3. Death and Discovery

Early that morning, Lewis had ridden to the house of Colonel Joshua Craven in Asheboro. It is not clear why Lewis chose to drop by the Craven residence, but Colonel Craven was the jailer for Randolph County, someone with whom Lewis would often have consulted in his work as constable. He may simply have wished to be seen going about his regular business so as not to raise observers' suspicions.

After leaving the Craven residence, Lewis proceeded to a sale at the Hancock family's property, located approximately five miles south of Asheboro and 13 miles south of the ford at Deep River. Vachel Hancock was preparing to move to the Indiana Territory, and would have been selling what could not be taken on the trip.[4] At the sale, Jonathan reportedly met a young woman named Martha, daughter of Stephen Huzza [Hussey], and began to court her. He went home with her family that evening.

Jonathan may have been interested in Martha, but he probably had an ulterior motive for being at the Hussey household. Jonathan and his family were friends and neighbors of Martha's mother's people, who lived near Providence Meeting, and so he would have known that, like the Hancocks, the Husseys were preparing to leave North Carolina imminently. Stephen Hussey had sold his land two days prior on April 4, to his son William, and was making preparations for his family to move to Ohio. The party at the Hussey house appears to have been related to those events. Their departure to Ohio is supported by a reminiscence of Stephen and Martha's niece in an issue of an Ohio newspaper, the *New Vienna Reporter,* in 1912. She stated the Hussey family had left North Carolina in the spring of 1807 and settled later that year in New Vienna, Ohio.[5]

Martha Hussey (1787–1845) was the daughter of Stephen Hussey (1739–1812) and Martha Chamness (1746–1830). Martha Chamness was the daughter of Anthony Chamness (1713–1777) and the aunt of Ebenezer Reynolds. The Chamness and the Reynolds families were friends and neighbors of Jonathan and the Lewis family. Ebenezer Reynolds was one of the co-conspirators indicted and found guilty of aiding the escape of Jonathan when he broke out of jail in October of 1807. Another nephew of Martha Chamness, Anthony Chamness (1773–1858), the son of her brother Joseph (1740–1818), testified on Jonathan's behalf at his later Grand Jury hearing. Lewis' final destination after the October escape was within eight miles of the route taken by the Vachel Hancock family as they crossed the Falls of the Ohio on their way to the Indiana Territory earlier in 1807. He may have planned to disappear from North Carolina by accompanying the party on its move northwestward.

Craven's version of the story relates that, after her parents had retired, Jonathan pulled Martha into his lap, and it was in this attitude, about 24 hours after Naomi's death, that they were found by Robert Murdock. Jonathan Lewis was "overawed" and arrested.[6] An article in the 1912 *The Asheboro Courier* differs from the Craven account, stating that Robert Murdock had heard that Lewis was attending a party at the Hussey house. Murdock had taken several men with him and when there, made a gentle rap at the door, and as the door opened, stepped in and arrested Lewis without any trouble. (No mention is made in that version of Martha sitting in Lewis' lap.) By the next morning, Murdock's men had brought him back to the Deep River.[7]

After Naomi's body was discovered, someone would have been dispatched to Lieutenant Colonel Alexander Gray to inform him of the murder. The commander of the militia would have had the responsibility to authorize Murdock and his company of men to locate Lewis. Gray had posted part of Lewis' £200 bond to serve as constable, and he would have likely been dismayed to hear that Lewis was thought to be involved in the death of Naomi.

Craven's story recounts that Lewis was brought from the Hussey household to the banks of Deep River. The Woody poem provides corroborating support of Craven's account that Lewis was apprehended and brought to the ford area of Deep River where Naomi was drowned, and held there until the next day for the coroner's inquest. Lewis was arrested in the company of the Hussey family on Monday night approximately 24 hours after the murder. Time constraints and 1807 legal process would have had the company of men sent to capture Lewis bring him to the ford where Naomi was drowned on Tuesday morning, less than 12 hours after his arrest.

The discovery of Naomi's body would have set in motion a forensic process that began with the notification of John Craven, Randolph County's coroner. When a corpse was found, it was the coroner's responsibility to hasten to the scene and examine any evidence to determine the cause of death. North Carolina law required that if there was any suspicion of an unnatural or violent death the coroner was obliged immediately to issue a precept to summon a coroner's jury to the scene. The testimony concerning the screams heard by the Davis family and an examination of the victim would have justified the summons for a competent number of lawful men, usually 24, to appear before him for an inquest in the presence of the body.[8] A jury of 12 was chosen from the initial group, with the coroner appointing and swearing in one man as foreman. The 11 remaining jurors were given the oath immediately after the foreman, and charged by the coroner to view the body and come to a conclusion of how the person came to their death.[9] The coroner's inquest into the death of Naomi Wise took place, and the indictment was issued, on Wednesday, April 8. The date coincides with signed and dated documentation by John Craven which gave the order to jail Jonathan Lewis on a charge of murder according to the inquest's findings. North Carolina laws stated that the coroner had the right to delay the inquest until all available witnesses could be called and gathered in front of the corpse. It may have taken two days for the coroner's inquest to be completed. A delay in completing the inquest until Wednesday morning would mean it had been approximately 60 hours since Naomi's death, and her body would have been lying on the rock for close to 48 hours. Craven and several ballads suggest that the inquest was held Tuesday morning, and it may have occurred at that time. The Woody account specifies that Lewis was brought to the location of Naomi's drowning after his capture but not brought to the area where her body had been laid until the next day.

When someone fell victim to an apparent homicide, the law directed that the body was to remain near where the crime occurred until the conclusion of the coroner's inquest. "If the body was interred it was to be dug up within any convenient time, as in fourteen days."[10] Fortunately there was only a brief period of time between the discovery of Naomi's body and the inquest. Her corpse was left lying on the large, flat rock at the edge of the river bank, where it could be viewed by the jurors. The eight-and-one-half-by-15-foot rock, later referred to by local residents as "Naomi's Cooling Board," was part of an outcropping of rocks extending out into the center of Deep River from the east bank.[11]

After determining that Naomi's death had not occurred by natural causes, legal process required an investigation into how it did come about. The coroner issued warrants for witnesses to appear at the river in the presence of the body and their examination be taken in sworn testimony. The bruising on Naomi's neck would have provided sufficient evidence to reach a determination that she had been murdered.

Rather than convening indoors, the coroner held the inquest on the riverbank, with the corpse still displayed on the flat rock which jutted out into the river, only inches above the water. There was so little flat ground on the riverbank that there was only room for the jury, coroner,

View of Deep River looking upstream. Shown in the foreground is the outcropping of rocks where Naomi Wise was found and the rectangular rock where her body was laid for the coroner's inquest. The modern bridge crosses near the original ford, and remnants of the dams mentioned in story and ballads can be seen above the bridge, with Naomi Falls Manufacturing Plant on the left. In the upper right of the image near the white house was the site of the Ann Davis residence where her family heard the screams the night of Naomi's drowning (courtesy Dan Routh Photography).

and witnesses. Spectators gathered on the steep bank, looking down on the proceedings as if in a theater. The assembled crowd would have had an unobstructed view as Jonathan Lewis was brought forward and ordered to touch the corpse.

The ritual of requiring an accused murderer to touch the victim's body was a practice referred to as cruentation, or the "ordeal by touch."[12] The word cruentation is derived from the Latin *cruentare*, meaning to

"Naomi's Cooling Board," the eight-and-one-half-by-15-foot flat rock on the east bank of Deep River where Naomi Wise's body was laid for the coroner's inquest. This outcropping of rocks was where Naomi's body was found by Joshua Davis, the son of Ann Davis. Eleanor Minnock-Pugh shown in photo. Randleman, North Carolina (authors' collection).

spot with blood. The centuries-old practice, used especially in cases in which there was only circumstantial evidence, was based on the belief that a suspect's guilt could be confirmed by his reaction to the corpse—and by how the corpse responded to his touch. In a manifestation of God's judgment, it was believed, if a murderer passed before or touched his victim's corpse, the victim's spirit would feel such indignation that the corpse would react, either by moving or by manifesting bodily fluids. The jurors and witnesses would watch the corpse for any movement, the appearance of fresh blood, or foam appearing from the victim's nostrils or mouth. At the same time, the accused would be observed closely in case his own reactions betrayed guilt.[13]

There is no documentation to suggest that Naomi's body was thought to exhibit reaction to Jonathan's touch, but sources differ on how Lewis himself reacted. The poem says he touched her "with a pale face and a trimbling hand." Craven, however, wrote that Lewis "put his hand upon her face, and smoothed her hair, apparently unmoved." He goes on to add, "So greatly was the crowd incensed at this hard hearted audacity, that the authority of the officer was scarcely sufficient to prevent the villain's being killed upon the spot."[14] Though possibly invented by Craven for dramatic effect, this action, if it happened, could have been misinterpreted by the spectators watching from above the riverbank. In actuality, Jonathan may have been explicitly told where to touch Naomi.

Some accounts of the murder suggest that Naomi's clothing was pulled over her head and tied, to hasten her drowning or suppress her cries. This idea came from Craven's account of Jonathan grasping Naomi by the throat and holding her above the water, while tying her dress above her head and then holding her under with his foot. The grand jury indictment does not mention her dress being tied over her head but instead says that Jonathan choked her and held her under the water with both hands. The tremendous strength, amount of effort, and time it would take to hold Naomi up and tie her dress over her head while she struggled and screamed make the idea seem unrealistic. With the waning moon, only two days before a dark moon, April 5, 1807, there would have been very little light and the water in Deep River would have been cold. The loud screams of Naomi while being beaten, choked, and strangled, as reported by Ann Davis who lived near the ford, would have been an impetus for Lewis to make a hasty escape before being discovered. Craven mentions her "body still muffled in the clothing" when she was found. The steady current of Deep River would account for any disarrangement of Naomi's clothes.

Chapter 3. Death and Discovery

A remarkable survival, the Mary Woody poem preserves what is essentially a transcription of the coroner's inquest, as it occurred on the banks of Deep River that day in April of 1807.

Mary Adams was sworn in, according to the poem, and testified to the facts she knew.

> The Crowner [coroner] then a Jury had
> To try the mater which was sad
> And divers people furder more
> To what the knew the also Swore
> And Mary adams did begin
> And Swore to what is within

Certainly, Mary Adams thought Lewis not only had the motive for murder but was capable of it.

> There had been two apointments made
> To meet there With Some intent
> I realy think for mischief bent
> And further more She also Said
> He has murderd her I am afraid

The Woody poem also recounts that William Watkins testified. Watkins lived between the fork of the Deep River and Polecat Creek, approximately two miles south of the schoolhouse and Adams's spring. Watkins had purchased the property from the heirs of Levi Pennington two years earlier in 1805.[15]

> And William Wadkins did declare
> That Lewis had been Surely thare
> At his own house that very day
> And in the evening went a Way
> After the seting of the Sun
> And he towards the Schoolhouse run
> And also Wadkins did declare
> That it was not two miles from thare

Another witness called to the coroner's inquest was Ann Davis. She gave evidence about hearing the "shrieking and a dofful [doleful] sound" originating at Deep River on the night of the murder.

> In that Same night that She Was drownd
> Shrieks was awful two or three
> A moaning then it Seemd to be
> Supprising Shrieks a Shocking Crying
> As if Some Woman might by dying
> Which people Recond Was not more
> That fifty perches from the dore

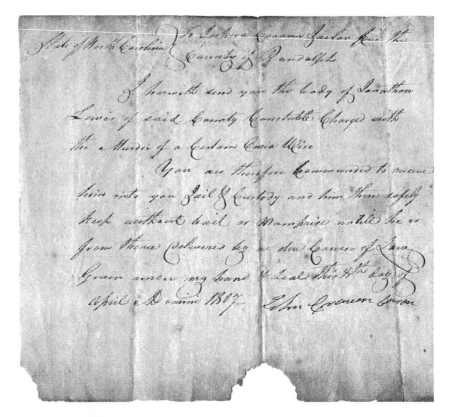

Warrant signed by the coroner, John Craven, sending Jonathan Lewis to jail without bond or mainprize for the murder of Naomi Wise, April 8, 1807 (State Archives of North Carolina).

Craven inflated the drama of Ann Davis' testimony by interpreting the noises as a "startling cry," a "wild wail," and "stifled sobs" (suggesting, presumably, that the sound was stifled by Naomi's skirts, thought by some to have been tied around her head).[16] Ann Davis' house was said to be 50 perches from Deep River—a perch was a surveying term indicating a unit of 16.5 feet—a distance of 825 feet from which Naomi's cries might easily have been heard.

The coroner's jury weighed all the physical evidence presented to them, and the testimonies of witnesses, and made the determination that Naomi Wise had been murdered by Jonathan Lewis. The coroner's inquest was closed, and Naomi's body was removed for burial.[17] Lewis was sent to the Randolph County jail on Wednesday, April 8, 1807, charged with murder.[18]

Chapter 3. Death and Discovery

State of North Carolina} To Joshua Craven Jailor for the County of Randolph

I herewith send you the body of Jonathan Lewis of said County Constable Charged with the Murder of a Certain Omia Wise.

You are therefore Commanded to receive him into you Jail & Custody and him there safely keep without bail or Mainprise untill he is from thence delivered by a due Course of Law.

> *Given under my hand & seal this*
> *8th day of April Domini 1807*
> *—John Craven Coroner*

The order to keep Lewis "without bail or Mainprise" meant that he could not be released on the permission of obtaining sureties. Some ballads about the murder include the line "no friends or relations would go on his bail." In reality, no friends or relations would have been allowed to pay his bail even if they had been willing to do so, as bail was not permitted.[19]

In another example of romanticizing the facts, Craven states that "Lewis was confined in the strong jail, that then towered in Asheboro as a terror to evil doers."[20] A new two-story brick jail built in 1850 by Randolph County may have suggested to Braxton Craven his imagery of a "towering jail." However, in the same month that the second part of Craven's story was published, February 1851, the jail burned to the ground, leaving only the cracked brick shell standing.[21] In fact, the 1807 jail was dilapidated and remote, and questions arose as to whether it was a safe and appropriate place to hold Lewis. Sheriff Isaac Lane warned that he was "apprehensive that there may be some danger of the said Prisoner's being spirited by some persons to make his escape from the said Goal [jail] it being remote from any Dwelling." Lane commanded three Justices of the Peace—John Craven, Benjamin Elliott, and Michael Harvey—to inspect the jail.[22] After visiting, they recommended the engagement of "five able bodied men well armed to serve as a Guard." On April 18, 1807, Lieutenant Colonel Alexander Gray issued an order to Benjamin Elliott, who was also Captain of the militia, mandating that he and five other men keep Lewis safely confined in jail until the May Court session.[23]

On May 5, 1807, the court appointed another committee, this time of seven members, to examine the jail and to return a report on its condition and make any recommendations for repairs. The committee determined the jail was "through decay & from being repeatedly broken in such a situation as to render it unsafe to Confine any State prisoner therein."[24] The disrepair was partially attributable to the materials used in its construction. It had been built from reclaimed timbers of the old courthouse that had stood at the town of Johnstonville.[25] Johnstonville was laid off in 1786 as the county seat for Randolph County. It was located at the intersection of the Trading Road and the Cross Creek [Fayetteville] to Salem road, approximately two miles west of the present town of Randleman. Six years later a new county seat was located near the geographic center of the county for convenience. First named Randolph Courthouse in 1793, the town was later renamed Asheborough, in 1796.

The commissioners recommended repairs be made to strengthen the jail, but after his having been incarcerated in the Randolph County jail for over one month, Lewis, it was decided, should be transported the approximately 60 miles to Hillsborough in Orange County, where there was a stronger jail, around May 10, 1807. He was to remain in the Hillsborough jail until October 3 when he would be transferred back to Randolph County in preparation for his Grand Jury hearing.[26] Preparations for the October hearing continued with the issuing of summons for prosecution and defense witnesses.

The Grand Jury convening was the subject of great public interest, not to mention gossip. A local constable being charged with the murder of his pregnant lover would be a sensational story anywhere, but the spectacle was magnified by Lewis' network of personal and professional connections. An indication of the impact of the murder on the community and the emotion it stirred can be found in a personal letter sent September of 1807 from Randolph County by Richard and Abigail Beeson. Written to their son and daughter in Ohio, it said,

> *Also another Miss hap happined that___ our constable in our County Gained favour of a orfan young Lady So Much as to get her With Child and before the Child Delivered Lover persuaded her With him & is soposed that he drounded her and at Least is Committed to hilsborough Likely you New them both Jonathan Lewis is the man & Neomi Wise....*[27]

Adding to the spectacle, this was the first time a Superior Court had met in Asheboro. (Prior to the October hearing the Superior Court had met in Hillsborough, in Orange County.) On the 3rd of October 1807, Jonathan was brought back to Randolph County from Hillsborough and placed in the county jail to await trial. The dilapidated facility had yet to be repaired and Isaac Lane sent word to three Justices of the Peace that he was again apprehensive that there might be a danger of Lewis escaping. Lieutenant Colonel Gray ordered a guard of five well-armed men from the militia to watch over Lewis and keep him confined within the jail. Once again, Benjamin Elliott, the Captain of the militia, was chosen to command the other four men.[28]

The first Superior Court was in session for Asheboro on October 6, with the Honorable Francis Locke, Jr. (1776–1823) presiding as judge. A Grand Jury was charged and seated for the hearing of the *State vs. Jonathan Lewis* on a charge of murder. Eighteen members of the grand jury were impaneled, with Elisha Mendenhall as the foreman. The other jurors were William Wilkeson, Joseph Windslow, Whitlock Arnold, Jonathan Lewallen, Peter Voncannon, Francis Sanders, John Vernon, John Spoon, John Beard, John Lawrence, Edmund York, Isaac Carns, Enoch Barker, William McCrackin, Joshua Cox, William Allred, and Jonathan Edwards.[29]

Solicitor General Edward Jones (1762–1841) of the Eleventh Circuit represented the state. Jones was born in Lisburn, Ireland, and was elected in 1791 as Solicitor General, a position created to assist the Attorney General in prosecuting Superior Court cases in North Carolina. Jones had a reputation for honor and was respected by his contemporaries as a meticulous and fair criminal lawyer.[30]

On the second day of the hearing, October 7, the Grand Jury took statements from the witnesses who had been called to give testimony for and against Jonathan Lewis. Surviving summonses indicate that witnesses who were called in Lewis' defense included Sally Shofner, William Maples, Catherine Maples, Archibald Harrison, Jeremiah Field, Anthony Chamness, and Stephen Emery and his wife Jinny Emery.[31] Catharine Maples was the wife of Marmaduke Maples, and William was Marmaduke's son. William Maples was Jonathan's cousin, Jeremiah Field his uncle, and the Quaker cabinetmaker Anthony Chamness a neighbor of the Lewis family.

Some of Lewis' defenders were themselves of questionable character. In 1807, a year after marrying, Archibald Harrison was named in a bastardy bond by an unmarried woman as the father of her recently born child.[32] Sally Shofner's husband Micheal filed for a divorce in 1811, citing as the reason that Sally "gave a look to the barest sensuality and Guilty passions, throughing off all appearance of modesty she sought criminal intercourse with every man who was wicked enough to perpratrate the crime of adultery with her." Micheal Shofner was rejected the divorce by the General Assembly, likely because it would have been considered his own failure to keep his "unruly" wife under control.[33] In 1813 Jinny Emery petitioned the North Carolina General Assembly for, and was granted, a divorce from Stephen Emery because he had "Committed a Rape on the body of a poor old decripted Woman" and then fled the country, deserting his wife and leaving Jinny to provide for herself and their "two small Children in a truely deplorable situation."[34]

William Dennis, Eli Powell, and Mary Vickery were ordered to appear as witnesses on behalf of the state.[35] William Dennis, the first person Mary Adams had solicited for help the morning after Naomi's disappearance, knew of the existence of a precept Jonathan claimed to possess, to take Naomi before the Justices of the Peace in regard to issuance of a bastardy bond. In addition, Dennis had helped Mary initiate the search for Naomi. Eli Powell was a major in the Randolph County militia and owned land near Deep River not a great distance from the ford. Additional witnesses were summoned but any official documents that would elaborate on their testimony have been lost or destroyed.

Although Mary Lowe Vickory, Christopher Vickory's wife, was among those summoned to give testimony against Lewis, she failed to appear at the Grand Jury hearing. Edward Jones ordered the court to issue a capias to have her physically taken to appear at trial in Guilford County to give evidence for the state against Jonathan Lewis.[36] Sheriff Isaac Lane documented that she had not been found.[37] Mary's reluctance to appear and give testimony against Jonathan could have been due to the fact that her step-daughters Ruhamah and Charlotte were both married to cousins of his.[38] Faced with the choice of testifying against family, she evidently decided to stay hidden until the trial was over.

By the end of the day on October 8, the Grand Jury had reached a decision on an indictment.[39]

The Jurors for the State, upon their Oath presents

That Jonathan Lewis late of the County of Randolph aforesaid constable, not having the fear of God before his eyes, but being moved and seduced by the sin begotten of the Devil, on the fifth day of April in the year of our lord one thousand eight hundred and seven, with force and arms, in Deep River, in the County aforesaid, in and upon one Omia Wise Single Woman, in the peace of God, & the State, then and there being feloniously, wilfully, and of his malice aforethought, did make an assault, and that the said Jonathan Lewis, with both his hands; the said Omia Wise in and under the waters of said river then and there feloniously wilfully and of his Malice afore thought did cast and throw, and the same Omia Wise is in and under the waters of said river He the said Jonathan Lewis with both the hands of him the said Jonathan Lewis, the said Omia Wise, then and there feloniously, wilfully, and of his Malice aforethought did press down, and hold, of which pressing down and holding in and under the waters of said river the said Omia Wise then and there was suffocated and drowned and then and there instantly died and as the Jurors

aforesaid upon their oath aforesaid do say that the said Jonathan Lewis the said
Omia Wise in manner and form aforesand feloniously wilfully and of his Malice
aforethought did kill and murder against the peace and dignity of the State.

Ed: Jones SolGl

On October 8 Solicitor General Edward Jones attested that, in his opinion, justice could not be served in Randolph County, and so along with the indictment he sent orders for the trial, and the suspect, to be moved to neighboring Guilford County. Jones did not make specific allegations as to why he felt that Randolph County would be an unsuitable place for the trial. As prosecuting attorney, though, he would have had knowledge of the intertwining relationships between family, witnesses, militia guards, and the county justice system—including the fact that the Captain of the militia, Benjamin Elliott, who had been ordered to guard the jail during Jonathan's incarceration, was the prisoner's former employer. According to North Carolina law, the witnesses who had testified at the coroner's inquest were obligated to appear at the trial in Guilford County.[40]

The trial date was set for October 26, 1807. Lewis was returned to the Randolph County jail after his Grand Jury indictment to await transfer to Guilford County. Lieutenant Colonel Alexander Gray again ordered Captain Benjamin Elliott and four well-armed privates from the militia to guard the jail and keep Lewis from escaping.

But late Friday night of October 9 or early Saturday morning, October 10, after the Grand Jury returned their bill of indictment, and while under the guard of the assigned militia, Jonathan Lewis broke out of jail. He fled in the company of Moses Smith, a fellow prisoner who had been indicted for horse stealing.[41] The direction Moses Smith took after his escape from the jail is unknown. The four guards would later be charged with providing the tools—a knife and sword—which Lewis and Smith used to pry open the prison doors.[42]

John Craven issued warrants for the arrest of the four who had "made themselves accessories to the said Crime of Murder after the fact by assisting the said Jonathan Lewis to break Gaol and make his escape."[43] (Benjamin Elliott was not among those charged.) The four accomplices were placed under a £50 bond each until their appearance at the next session of Superior Court in April 1808.[44] A witness for the state, Joseph Bulla, was bound in the sum of £50 to ensure his appearance in Superior Court to testify against the guards.[45]

Private Daniel Dawson, Jr., of the militia was the only one of the four charged by Edward Jones with conspiring to aid Lewis' escape from jail by providing the knife and sword, "with the Intent and purpose that the said Jonathan Lewis might and should thereby be enabled to make his Escape out of the said Jail."[46] Dawson, the son of Daniel Dawson, Sr., a Justice of the Peace for Randolph County, was bound over to the next Superior Court for trial in October 1808. The Randolph County court ruled there was "negligence, no Evidence of puting the knife in, showing the sword at the window—Escape not made by means of these weapons, The prisoners were there when they mounted guard." Dawson was charged only for allowing the prisoner to escape through negligence, and he plead not guilty.[47]

The following year in April 1809, Daniel Dawson would be tried in the Randolph County Superior Court, and was found innocent.[48] One of the jurors was Christopher Vickory, the husband of Mary Lowe Vickory, who had refused to appear and testify for the state against Jonathan Lewis at his Grand Jury hearing. Christopher's daughters Ruhamah and Charlotte were married to Jonathan's mother's first cousins. The guards' exoneration would seem to vindicate Edward Jones' earlier decision to transfer the trial to Guilford County because a conviction would not be attainable in Randolph County.

CHAPTER 4

Escape to the Indiana Territory

Jonathan's escape from jail was the beginning of a long flight that would end in the Indiana Territory. For a fugitive from justice to make the complex journey that this would have entailed, it is likely that he had accomplices and a pre-laid plan. Jonathan's younger brother William (1787–1844) had moved to the Indiana Territory as a young man and established a livelihood by hunting and trapping. He and other hunters followed the game, building temporary dwellings and never remaining long in one area.[1] William maintained this nomadic lifestyle, then squatted approximately eight miles from the Falls of the Ohio near a place called the Knobs, where he settled. William's knowledge of the area and its residents would have provided Jonathan with an ideal opportunity to evade the reach of North Carolina authorities. It was to this region that he fled.

The Knobs are part of the Knobstone Escarpment which rise southwest of Louisville, Kentucky, and run northward 150 miles through what was then the Indiana Territory, forming a rugged hilly terrain that rises to 600 feet above the Ohio River floodplain.[2] The southern section of the escarpment rises vertically, creating a wall-like appearance, then runs northward into present-day Clark County, Indiana. Streams dissect the escarpment, causing spurs and forming the conical hills known as the Knobs.[3] Nearby is the Falls of the Ohio, where the Ohio River drops more than 26 feet in two and a half miles, creating a series of falls and strong rapids over a limestone bedrock reef that was formed millions of years ago.[4] One early traveler observed that the roaring of the falls could be heard from as far as 15 miles away.[5] During times of low water, boaters were forced to portage around the falls or hire guides who knew the rapids, to get the boats through the channels unscathed. At the falls was the crossing of the Buffalo Trace, an ancient buffalo trail that had been used by Native Americans and by settlers moving into that area.[6]

Location of the Jonathan Lewis and Vachel Hancock residences in 1811. "A Map of the State of Kentucky: from Actual Survey, also Part of Indiana and Illinois" by Luke Munsell and Hugh Anderson, 1818 (Library of Congress).

The Indiana Territory had been created by an act of the U.S. Congress in 1800, carved from the Northwest Territory.[7] In 1800 William Henry Harrison, then Governor of the Indiana Territory, was part of a committee organized to study the defects in the administration of justice in the region. The committee declared that "the territory was an asylum for 'the most vile and abandoned criminals.'"[8] In an address to Congress in 1803, Governor Harrison stated the ruggedness and poverty of the territory aided criminals, which made impossible "the Apprehension and prosecution of the most notorious offenders against the laws."[9] In 1806 an Englishman, Thomas Ashe, explored the Falls of the Ohio area. He noted that above the falls the area along the Ohio River was "enlivened" with villages, towns, and plantations. His description of the area below the Falls was not as flattering. "Most of the settlers on the lower parts of the waters are criminals who either escaped from, or were apprehensive of, public justice."[10] In 1807 the steep and rugged region of the Indiana Territory north of the Falls of the Ohio and town of Clarksville was unsettled.[11] The Knobstone Escarpment's hills and ravines provided a livelihood for a hunter and trapper such as William Lewis—and a secure location for Jonathan Lewis to hide. Braxton Craven's account made note that "most of the Lewis family had migrated to the same region, and one Lewis was not to be trifled with, much less a community of such personages."[12]

Back in North Carolina, prosecutor Edward Jones faced obstacles in securing Jonathan Lewis' extradition from the Indiana Territory. Questions and disputes over territorial boundaries, combined with a lack of knowledge of extradition policies, all hindered legal procedures.[13]

In correspondence with North Carolina Governor David Stone, Sheriff Isaac Lane reported that visitors to and residents of the Falls area in the Indiana Territory knew where Jonathan Lewis and another escapee from Randolph County, William Aston, were staying, and had communicated this information back to the authorities in Randolph County.[14]

Meanwhile, according to Braxton Craven, folk ballads about Naomi Wise's murder were already in circulation, keeping the story from fading into oblivion.[15] One early chronicler, Colonel I.J. Brittain, wrote that someone once sang such a ballad in Jonathan Lewis' presence while he was living near the Falls of the Ohio area. His "very much excited" behavior on hearing the song made bystanders suspicious. According to this account, witnesses contacted a local schoolteacher, who then wrote to officials in Randolph County.[16] The validity of Brittain's version of events cannot be confirmed, and only circumstantial evidence has surfaced of the ballad existing at that early date, or of its having traveled that far so soon.

Certain Naomi Wise ballads thought to be of Kentucky origin contain some version of the line "He [Jonathan Lewis] has gone to Elk River, so I understand."[17] There was in fact a stream called Elk Run in Clark County, Indiana Territory, located approximately one mile north of what came to be known as Lewis Branch, at the base of the Knobs, where Jonathan was living.[18]

In 1809 Jonathan's father, Richard Lewis, sold his 259-acre farm in North Carolina, and with his wife Lydia and several of their children joined their sons in Indiana Territory, settling north of Clarksville on the west side of Silver Creek.[19] Richard Lewis' move aroused suspicions back home in Randolph County, but it would be two years before North Carolina authorities verified the location of the Lewis family members and pursued the escaped fugitive.

The Lewis family would play a significant role in the settlement of the Indiana Territory.

William Lewis, along with other hunters and trappers, had been squatting at the base of the Knobs before any permanent settlers had located there.[20] The Lewis family became well known in the county, and in 1816 the first elections in the State of Indiana were held at Richard Lewis' house.[21]

During his years of living in the Indiana Territory, Jonathan Lewis was surrounded by family. On March 30, 1811, he married Sarah McCann.[22] Sarah's father Moses McCann had been a frontier scout and trader with Native Americans during the late 18th century in the area north of the Ohio River, and his wife, Sarah's mother, may have been Native American.[23] McCann was one of the first ferryboat operators near the Falls of the Ohio at Clarksville, which for many years was the only crossing.[24] He was one of the original settlers of the town of Clarksville, having bought his first lot there in 1784.[25]

Jonathan's father-in-law was a tough man. A 1780 deposition recounts that he and another scout had a confrontation with river pirates and Native Americans near Vincennes, Indiana, in which knives were drawn.[26] In 1802 he was convicted of murdering a Shawnee man near Clarksville.

> ...being moved and seduced by the instigation of the devil, ... with force and arms ... in and upon an Indian man of the Shawnee tribe, in the peace of God and the United States then and there (the said Indian not having any weapon drawn, nor the aforesaid Indian not having first stricken the said Moses McCan) feloniously, maliciously, and of his malice aforethought did make an assault, and that the aforesaid Moses McCan, with a certain tomahawk made of iron, of the value of $2, which the said Moses McCan in his right hand then and there had and held, in and upon the head of the said Indian strike, giving to the said Indian one mortal wound of the breadth of two inches and of the depth of one inch, of which said mortal wound he, the said Indian, on the day aforesaid died....[27]

McCann's sentence for this crime was to be bound in the sum of $100 to keep the peace for one year.[28] In October of the next year, Moses married Margaret Fleehart, the widow of Joshua Fleehart, another well-known scout and hunter.[29]

The second home of Richard Lewis located near New Albany, Indiana. His first house that was built when he arrived in the Indiana Territory was said to have been lost in a title dispute (courtesy Nancy Lynn Smith, photograph taken by her father Milburn Leon Smith in the 1970s).

Before Indiana's statehood, McCann took a strong stand against slavery. In 1810 he signed a petition to the President and Congress of the United States requesting that someone other than the Governor—William Henry Harrison, who supported slavery—represent the citizens of the Indiana Territory. The petition requested an appointment of a

CHAPTER 5

The Capture of Lewis

On April 6, 1810, three years and one day after the murder of Naomi Wise, Edward Jones, the prosecuting attorney, learned of Jonathan Lewis' location from Sheriff Isaac Lane. Jones wrote immediately to North Carolina Governor David Stone, and requested his intercession in pursuit of the perpetrator of "the worst murder I ever heard of," implying in his letter that he suspected Randolph County officials were not sufficiently committed to Lewis' apprehension—"for reasons I cannot now commit to paper."[1]

Those reasons may have had to do with the Lewis family's considerable influence in local politics and civic affairs. They may also have stemmed from simple indifference to the victim, a single woman of low social standing. Perhaps due to such indifference, the militia guards who were accused of aiding Lewis' escape were acquitted of the charges. According to Braxton Craven, "indignation cried, shame to the lingering servants of law."[2]

In the spring and summer of 1810, Edward Jones pressed authorities to set in motion the process of extradition. This required that Randolph County Coroner John Craven write to North Carolina Governor David Stone, requesting that Jonathan Lewis be declared a fugitive from justice. In May, the Governor wrote to Jones, in response to his pleas, that he had received no such communication from Craven—"Indeed I have never heard any of the case besides what is contained in your letter." That same day, Governor Stone wrote to Craven about the case, which achieved the desired results.[3] The process of extradition was underway.

September of 1810 saw Randolph County authorities working to confirm Lewis' location.[4] To aid in identification, Isaac Lane sent the governor a description of Jonathan Lewis, to be forwarded on to authorities in the Indiana Territory. He also included a description of William Aston, another fugitive from Randolph County. Charged with housebreaking, Aston had fled North Carolina in 1809, and he was thought to be living with his father Richard Aston, near the Lewis family.

Several months passed, during which time the paperwork was apparently delayed because of errors. Frustrated, Isaac Lane wrote to the new governor, Benjamin Smith, apprising him of the situation to date. While Isaac Lane placed Lewis' location at "about 20 miles from the falls," the distance was actually approximately eight miles. Lane's request that the governor appeal to his counterpart in Ohio, rather than the Indiana Territory, appears to be an error in his and prior

Governor Stone's understanding of the region where the Lewises had settled, perhaps due to their reported proximity to the Ohio River.

> *Randolph County 4th March 1811,*
>
> *Sir*
>
> *I take the Liberty of enclosing a Copey of a bill of inditement against Jonathan Lewis who was Comitted to the jail of said County in year 1807 on a Charg of murder Comitted on Ome Wiyse and in october 1807 he broke Jail and escaped & I have not had it in my power to Retake him since I have found out whare he is and I got a Copey of the bill of inditement & applied to Governer Stone to make a Demand of him from the Governer of State of Ohiho and on Examination it was found impurfick & I have got a nother drawn by Archobl Murpy esqr which is wright[.] [...]For procklemation after him I will inform you whare he is he is at this time at his fathers about 20 miles from the falls of the Ohiho on the other sid he is a man between 25 and 30 years of age tall slim man five feet 10 or 12 inchis high black hair and Reather of Dark skin his father is a large man six feet high & his name is Richard which may be well to menshen that the governer may Direct the officer how to find him[.] Governer Stone told me that the proper method to git him was to Ishue a prockalemation to the Governer of* <u>State of Ohiho</u> *& that he wod ishue his orders to a officer & a gard to go and take him & confine him in jail till he Cud wright on to Inceptiture of this State to appoint a agint for the State of North Carolina to go with a guard after him & if he shud be taken you can apply to me or som other Gentelman in our County to Recomend a agint for that purpus I trust you not fail-*
>
> > *I remain with Sentiments of Esteem I Lane B the Reason that the copey of the bill of inditement Comes from the Clerke of Gilford County Edward Jones atty general moved the trial from Randolph. IL*

Weeks passed, but at last on June 3, Governor Smith responded to Isaac Lane and reported that he had taken the steps necessary to begin the process of apprehending Jonathan Lewis and extraditing him back to North Carolina.

Chapter 5. The Capture of Lewis

Viz

Yours of the 28 of March was received as also the previous letter inclosing a copy of the file of murder found against Lewis-
I deferred taking any procedure or replying to your letter untill I could see or hear from a particular gentleman who I wrote to consult on the Subject but having been disappointed I now send the answers requested & have taken such steps as appeared proper to cause Lewis's apprehension

your very obd s
BS

Governor Smith acted under the provisions of a 1793 Act of Congress, which gave executive authority to request the extradition of any fugitive from any state or any of the territories northwest or south of the Ohio River, when a copy of an indictment for a felony or other crime was certified by a governor or chief magistrate of that state or territory. According to the Act, the executive authority of the state or territory where the fugitive fled then had jurisdiction to cause the apprehension of the individual and turn them over to an agent of such authority from the requesting state. The costs of apprehending the fugitive fell to the state making the demand.[5] William Henry Harrison had been the Governor of the Indiana Territory since 1800. Governor Harrison believed there was a lot of confusion when it came to extraditing someone from the Territory. Return J. Meigs was the governor of Ohio and stayed in contact with William Henry Harrison, suggesting the paperwork for Lewis' extradition could have passed between them. A fire in 1951 destroyed a portion of the Meigs' records stored at the Ohio Historical Society Manuscript Collections, and it appears that information regarding the Jonathan Lewis case was lost at that time.[6] It is not known if Governor Harrison received any information from Governor Smith concerning Lewis' extradition by late fall of 1811.

According to Braxton Craven, the officers Isaac Lane, Joshua Craven, and George Swearingen traveled to the Falls of the Ohio area to retrieve Jonathan Lewis.[7] (He does not mention Sheriff Lane receiving any authorization from the Governor of Ohio, the Indiana Territory, or North Carolina for Lewis' extradition.) The trip from Randolph County would have been an arduous 500- to 550-mile journey for the three men. Upon arriving at their destination at the Falls of the Ohio, they reportedly located and hired hunters to extract Lewis from the locale where he was living. Braxton Craven stated that the hunters were hired because if Lane, Craven, and Swearingen "appeared in person, their object would be defeated."[8] Assuming Lane, Craven, and Swearingen traveled the most direct route to apprehend Lewis, upon their arrival at the Falls of the Ohio they would have likely stayed at either Louisville or Shippingport, Kentucky, across the Ohio River from Clarksville in the Indiana Territory, while the hunters crossed the river. Had Lane, Craven, and Swearingen themselves crossed into the Indiana Territory, they would almost certainly have been recognized immediately, as the nearest ferries were operated by close associates of Jonathan Lewis.

In the late fall of 1811, travelers crossing this part of the Ohio River would have had to travel by ferry. Jonathan Lewis' father-in-law, Moses McCann, had operated the ferry below the falls at Clarksville for many years.[9] McCann, who died early in 1811, had owned several lots and houses in Clarksville and, like his son-in-law Jonathan Lewis, would have been well known in the town. After McCann's death, the ferry was operated by John Carson and Richard Aston, Jr., a relative of Randolph County fugitive William Aston.[10] Richard Aston, Jr., married Mary Carson, daughter of the ferryman John Carson, an early settler in the Clarksville area.[11] By 1811 there was also another ferry crossing farther west below Clarksville, near New Albany. One of the owners of that ferry operation was none other than Vachel Hancock, formerly of Randolph County, North Carolina, who had moved to the Falls of the Ohio in April 1807, and whose sale Jonathan had attended the day after Naomi Wise's death.[12] Vachel Hancock had become part-owner of the ferry in 1809, the year his daughter Patsy married ferryman Caleb Newman.[13]

Two additional ferry crossings operated above the falls at Jeffersonville and Utica, but it is doubtful they were used by the party, as they

A view of Louisville, Kentucky, and the Falls of the Ohio River from near Clarksville, Indiana Territory, from "A Map of the Rapids of the Ohio River and of the Countries on Each Side Thereof…," 1806 (Library of Congress).

were farther upstream than would have been practical. It seems most probable that the hunters crossed the river via the Clarksville ferry, as this passage joined the Buffalo Trace, also known as the Indian Path, the easiest route to the Lewis family homesteads. After crossing the Ohio River they would have followed the Buffalo Trace up the east side of Silver Creek, which drained into the river between the towns of New Albany and Clarksville. Because of the nearly perpendicular shale and limestone outcroppings along the west bank, the hunters probably traveled upstream to find an area suitable for crossing the creek. At normal water levels, this would involve fording Silver Creek at a place called the Gut—a natural gorge which had formed through a solid rock wall just wide enough for a wagon to pass through.[14] During high water the Gut Ford was a dangerous crossing, forcing travelers to wait until the water lowered, or to return downstream and take the ferry crossing near the mouth of the creek at the Ohio River.

After traversing Silver Creek the hunters would have continued northward from the Buffalo Trace through the rolling hills to the base of the Knobs, where the Lewis family was living. Anyone unfamiliar with the wild terrain would have had difficulty getting into and out of the area. The hunters chosen to extract Lewis must have been familiar with the surroundings.

Braxton Craven weaves a fanciful version of what may have happened while the hunters secured Lewis' capture, but his habitual use of poetic license and lack of any corroborating records make the accuracy of the account questionable. "The three officers went to the town to await the issue; and if it failed, to collect if possible, such a force, as might be necessary to wage civil war upon the whole offending tribe."[15] The large number of Lewis and Aston family members, and people who knew the McCanns, did create a dangerous environment and mission for the hunters. The Lewis family was also known to keep dogs, which would have alerted the clan to unfamiliar visitors. Richard Lewis is reported to have used his dogs as sentinels, while William Lewis kept as many as 25 to 30 hunting dogs during the years.[16]

Craven refers to the men sent to extract Lewis merely as hunters, but they might more accurately be described as bounty hunters. He writes that the hunters were paid $75 to remove Jonathan, "dead or alive."[17] If that account is accurate and the bounty hunters were hired to extract Jonathan Lewis from within the Indiana Territory, they may have been breaking the law, if Lewis was spirited away without the governor's or a magistrate's consent. Legally the hunters should have been chosen by the authorities in the Indiana Territory. After being taken into custody, the fugitive would have been released to the three North Carolina officers near the Ohio River boundary and the hunters paid for their effort. This may indeed have occurred, but the evidence is lacking.

If Lewis was legally apprehended in the Indiana Territory, legal protection existed for the bounty hunters and the three North Carolina officers in the execution of their jobs. Further, Lewis' family and friends would have been discouraged from any attempt to thwart or overpower those transporting Lewis back to North Carolina, because under federal law, anyone trying to rescue a fugitive from justice was subject to a fine of up to $500, and a year in jail.[18] Craven's presumably unreliable account of the capture is the only extant record of what happened. All that can be said with certainty is that Lewis was successfully apprehended.

The 500-mile trip home from the Falls of the Ohio would have been onerous, especially as the group was traveling in December. According to Braxton Craven, Lewis was bound with strong cord, but at one point on the return journey he escaped, and was recaptured by Joshua Craven and Swearingen. (As with other aspects of Braxton Craven's account, no historical records are cited to verify his version of events.[19])

By the last day of December 1811, the party was back in North Carolina. Lewis was brought to and temporarily detained in Randolph County. Because the jail was still in a state of disrepair, Lewis was again transferred to the more secure facility in Hillsborough.[20]

While efforts to recapture Lewis were underway in the fall of 1811, courts in Randolph County returned to the matter of John Lewis, Jr., John Green, Ebenezer Reynolds, and William Field—accused of aiding Lewis in his 1807 escape. After Lewis escaped from jail in 1807, his flight sent him to the Providence Friends Meeting community in northern Randolph County where he was aided by family members and neighbors. Within days of Jonathan's escape, on October 13, 1807, jailer Joshua Craven issued a Bill of Complaint against John Lewis Sr., John Lewis Jr., Richard Lewis Sr., William Field, John Green, and Ebenezer Reynolds for conspiring to aid and abet Lewis after he broke out of jail. Charges were dropped against Jonathan's father, Richard Lewis, and John Lewis Sr. (who was deceased). John Lewis, Jr., William Field, and two neighbors, John Green and Ebenezer Reynolds, were indicted for harboring, aiding, and assisting in the out-of-state flight of the accused. They were placed on bond after their appearance at the April term of 1809 Randolph County Superior Court. Isaac Lane and Richard Richardson were the state witnesses at the hearing.[21] The indictment against the four had specified that they had knowledge that Jonathan Lewis had broken out of jail and provided aid to allow the fugitive to flee out of state beyond the reach of the sheriff. They were placed under a £75 bond to ensure they would appear at their trial in October 1809. Green, Reynolds, and Lewis paid £50 on their bond while William Field supplied the additional £25 required for each of them and for his own bond.[22] The April 1809 court records indicate that it was known that Lewis was no longer in North Carolina, suggesting someone may have had knowledge of the direction and location of his flight. The jury trial for the four accomplices, originally scheduled for October 1809, was delayed and continually postponed.

The intertwining relationships of family and neighbors further complicated the course of justice. William Field was Jonathan Lewis' uncle, as was John Lewis, Jr. Ebenezer Reynolds and John Green were neighbors of the Lewis and Field families. John Green was the brother-in-law of Ebenezer Reynolds, who was married to John's sister, Rachel Green. Ebenezer's sister Amy was married to Anthony Chamness, who had testified on Jonathan's behalf at the Grand Jury hearing in October 1807.

Lewis, Green, Reynolds, and Field were tried and found guilty as charged in 1809; the first three were fined £5 each, and Field was fined £20. All four were to be imprisoned for two months in the Hillsborough jail in Orange County; however, "on motion this judgment of the court" was suspended until the spring session of the Randolph County Superior Court in March 1812.[23]

In March of 1812 the defendants appeared for sentencing. In an unusual maneuver, the four entered a guilty plea and then produced a pardon from William Hawkins, the new governor of North Carolina who had been sworn on December 11, 1811.[24] The pardon was signed during the governor's first week in office.[25]

State of North Carolina

His Excellency William Hawkins Esquire
Governor, Captain General & Commander in Chief
To All to whom these presents shall come

Greeting

Whereas it has been represented to me that at a Superior Court of Law held for Randolph County, William Fields, John Lewis, Ebenezer Reynolds and John Green, were convicted of having aided and assisted, a certain Jonathan Lewis, (charged with the murder of Omie Wise,) to make his escape from Justice, and were sentenced to imprisonment and fined; And whereas, I have received sundry petitions, signed by many respectable persons, recommending the said convicts to Executive clemency:

Now therefore be it Known, that by virtue of the authority vested in me by the constitution of the state, and for many good reasons, I have pardoned and remitted, and by these presents do pardon, the said William Fields, John Lewis, Ebenezer Reynolds, and John Green, of the crime for which they stand convicted, and remit their fine and imprisonment.

Of which the Sheriff of Randolph County and all others concerned are hereby required and commanded to take especial notice.

In testimony whereof I have caused the Great Seal of the State to be affixed to these presents and signed the same at Raleigh this seventeenth day of December in the year of Our Lord One thousand eight hundred and eleven and thirty sixth year of the Independence of the United States.

> *William Hawkins*
> *By the Governor*
> *A. G. Glynn*
> *Private Secretary*

During the 1812 Spring Term of Randolph County Superior Court Isaac Lane, the sheriff of Randolph County, was himself brought before the Court for allowing Jonathan Lewis to escape from the county jail while in his custody. Lewis' apprehension and incarceration in the Orange County jail allowed the prosecutor to enter a *nolle prosequi*, a motion to proceed no further in the cause, against Lane. The motion was not an acquittal, but relieved the sheriff of immediate prosecution, and the charges were never refiled.[26]

Throughout most of 1812, preparations for Jonathan Lewis' murder trial were underway. The first order for Lewis' transfer to Guilford County was filed in April 1812. Thomas Caldwell, the Guilford County Clerk of Court, wrote an order "...that [Orange County Sheriff] Samuel Turrentine Esq. be and is hereby Authorized to remove the Body of Jonathan Lewis from Hillsborough Jail in which he is now confined to this Court unless Isaac Lane Sheriff of Randolph should apply and remove such prisoner accordingly."[27]

After a postponement of the trial to the fall term of the Superior Court in Guilford County, Lewis was transported by Orange County Sheriff Samuel Turrentine to the Guilford County jail. Turrentine was determined to assure timely delivery of Lewis and avoid the complication of another escape. Financial records mention "the hire of a chair" with which to restrain Lewis in irons—the chair referred to would have been a riding chair, usually a two-wheeled cart with a seat, which enabled authorities to transport a prisoner without removing his shackles—and a group of armed men to guard him during the 40-mile trip.[28] Lewis was delivered to Guilford County on October 21, 1812.

CHAPTER 6

The Trials

Murder and Escape

The Guilford County Superior Court convened on Monday, October 26, 1812, to try Jonathan Lewis for the murder of Naomi Wise. Local authorities were careful not to afford Lewis any chances for escape while he stood trial in Greensboro. According to early chronicler I. J. Brittain, "The sheriff of Guilford County, knowing that Lewis was such a terrible man, summoned the Greensboro Guards, with loaded muskets and fixed bayonets, to guard him to and from jail."[1]

Edward Jones, who had procured Lewis' indictment during the Grand Jury hearing in 1807, continued the search for justice, serving as the prosecuting attorney for the state in the 1812 trial.[2] Most of the 1807 state's witnesses were available to testify again in October of 1812. While the 1812 Guilford County court records are lost, an 1815 Randolph County court document lists the state witnesses and the amount paid for expenses.[3]

February Term 1815

Ordered by the Court that the County Trustee pay the costs & charges Attending the prosecution of Jonathan Lewis for Felony when trial was removed to the County of Guilford & the said Jonathan there acquited, and since discharged from Jail under the Insolvent Debtors Act. The Claim for the said costs & charges appearing to be in the manner prescribed by the Act of Assembly to wit -

To Edward Jones Sol. Genl.	£ 1.6.8			
To Admr's of Reubin Wood }	3.2.0			
former Clerk of R. Sup. Court				
To Isaac Lane Sheriff	6.0.0			
To Clerk of Guilford Sup. Court	7.2.9			
	17.9.5			
To Witnesses				
Elizabeth Craven	5.16.0		*Obed Anthony*	16.8

William Dennis	4.18.8		William Dobson	18.1
William Davis	4.5.0		Ann Davis	1.17.4
Joseph Davis	1.14.0		Hettie Ramsower	1.0.8
Amos Davis	1.14.0		Joseph Dougan	1.14.0
Eli Powell	4.8.4	22.16.0	Elz. Pennington	1.2.0
			Tobias Julian	2.4.0
William Watkins	5.4.6		Robert Murdock	3.7.2
Mary Adams	4.5.0		George Adams	1.12.0
John Craven	6.18.10		Samuel Elliott	1.12.8
William Adams	3.15.6			16.3.11
Bob Wall	3.1.4			75.9.9
Joshua Davis	2.18.1			£ 91.13.8
Joshua Craven	2.0.8			
Ann Carney	3.7.1			
Benjamin Elliott	1.18.8			
Joseph Elliott	1.12.8	35.2. 4		
		£ 75.9.9s		

The 1815 document identifies 26 witnesses who were summoned and paid for providing testimony for the prosecution of Lewis. Based on what we know of their testimony in the earlier coroner's inquest and Grand Jury hearing, it's probably apparent what they would have testified in 1812. Mary Adams clearly believed Lewis capable of murder, and she had known Naomi well. William Watkins would have provided testimony about Jonathan's proximity to the rendezvous location on the night of the murder. He knew Lewis had departed his property at sunset, and traveled the road that led to the schoolhouse and Adams's spring. Also listed among the witnesses was Elizabeth Pennington, formerly Elizabeth Pennington Beeson, who had been granted a divorce from her husband Asahel Beeson, in 1804. She may have testified to seeing Lewis on the night of the murder, as she was living near the William Watkins residence at the time.

Ann Davis and her sons also attended the murder trial. Their testimony would have described hearing a woman screaming that night. Ann's son Joshua would have told of his discovery of Naomi's body the next day, washed against the rocks downstream from the ford. Joseph Elliott, who was apprenticing Naomi's daughter, appeared at the trial, as did his brother Samuel. Joseph would have testified about searching

1815 Randolph County court record itemizing expenses for the October 1812 murder trial of Jonathan Lewis in Guilford County, North Carolina (State Archives of North Carolina).

for Naomi with William Dennis, and their discovery of the horse tracks that led from William Watkins' house to the school, and down the River Way toward the ford of Deep River.

A Quaker and a well-respected citizen in the community, William Dennis had, according to the Woody poem, initially insisted that Jonathan Lewis "would not kill." Dennis would have testified about his belief at the time that Lewis had a precept prepared for Naomi to swear the child to someone else. He would also have corroborated Joseph Elliott's testimony of seeing the horse tracks, and described following the Davis family back to the river where Naomi's body was located by Joshua Davis.

Very little has been discovered about Ann Carney, who also appeared on the prosecution's witness list, except that she is mentioned in a bastardy bond as having had a child out of wedlock in 1802, and instead of naming the father, agreeing to pay the bond for the child.[4] Her situation was similar to Naomi's. Oral tradition suggests that Lewis had been romantically involved with more than one woman (according to the Woody poem, "He held himself of high degree, But too fond of Carnality," and in the words of a local ballad, "...to many women his promise he gave"), and the fact that she was a witness for the prosecution suggests that Ann may have been one of those women, or had personal knowledge about Naomi and Jonathan's relationship.[5]

Hettie Elliott, now Hettie Ramsower, and Elizabeth Ramsower Craven, jailer Joshua Craven's wife, attended the trial as witnesses for the prosecution. It appears that by 1812 Hettie and Elizabeth had become sisters-in-law.[6] It is thought Hettie Elliott married John Ramsower. While no direct evidence could be found, circumstantial evidence lends support.[7] It was Elizabeth and Joshua Craven's home that Lewis had reportedly visited early on the morning after the murder—possibly to establish an alibi—and Elizabeth who came to the door when he arrived. The possibility also exists that Elizabeth was Jonathan's intended contact, or that Lewis was checking on the whereabouts of her future sister-in-law, Hettie Elliott.[8]

Eli Powell, George Adams, and Robert Murdock, members of the militia who were involved with Lewis' capture, gave testimony. John Craven, the coroner, was at the trial, and would certainly have testified, as he officiated the inquest, and would have given details about the examination of Naomi's body. He would have told of the results of Jonathan's "trial by touch," when he was made to touch Naomi's corpse on the bank of Deep River.

Conspicuously absent from the prosecution witness list was Mary Lowe Vickory. Mary had refused to appear at the Randolph County Grand Jury hearing in 1807, and had been placed under a £50 bond to insure her attendance at the trial in Guilford County, before Lewis' escape. Possibly influenced by her husband's family connections to the Lewis family, she evidently chose again not to appear in 1812.

Other witnesses who did not appear include members of the Vachel Hancock and Stephen Hussey families, who could have provided valuable testimony for the prosecution, as Jonathan had been attending the Hancock sale and later the Husseys' party when he was captured. It would have been difficult and expensive, though, to summon members of those families for the trial: the Husseys had moved to Ohio and the Hancocks to the Indiana Territory, both in the spring of 1807.

Neither a list of the defense witnesses attending the trial, nor a record of who defended Lewis, have been found. The state of North Carolina was not required or obliged to pay for defense expenses, as it was for the prosecution's witnesses, so no equivalent financial accounting exists in Randolph County records. We do know that at least one of the 1807 witnesses, Stephen Emery, could not testify at the 1812 trial, as he had been indicted the year before for "having Committed a Rape on the body of a poor Old decripted Woman" and had subsequently "fled his Country and has not been heard of since."[9] Sally Shofner may not have been called again as a defense witness, if the attorneys had known about the petition for divorce that had been filed against her, in which her then-husband Micheal accused her of seeking "Criminal intercourse with every man who was wicked enough to perpratrate the crime of adultry with her" and "...also desirous to be secured against the fruits of her criminal connections with other men."[10]

Regardless of the state attorney's prestige, and the long list of witnesses who did testify, the evidence against Jonathan Lewis was circumstantial. The Woody poem and Craven's account support the conclusion that no one actually saw Jonathan Lewis with Naomi the night of the murder. Five years had passed since the murder, and a suggestion was made that the most damning evidence against Lewis had been lost by the time of the trial.[11] According to Braxton Craven there had been evidence of "footprints from the stump to the river [that] exactly fitted his horse; hairs upon the skirt on which she rode, were found to fit in color; a small piece torn from Lewis's accoutrements, fitted both rent and texture ... all conspired to the same point."[12]

Braxton Craven and the Woody poem suggest that Lewis made his defense by inferring that he himself was the victim. According to Craven, Lewis was explicit that the rumor that he had impregnated or had anything to do with Naomi was a base and malicious slander propagated to ruin his character by enemies of the Lewis family. Lewis used a similar explanation when telling William Dennis that, with the precept or bastardy bond he had prepared, Naomi was not going to name the father, or that she would swear her child was fathered by someone else. His name would be cleared.

Jonathan's defense probably also used the tactic of calling into question Naomi's character, exploiting her socially inferior status and suggesting moral weakness for having already given birth to two children out of wedlock. The fact that Naomi was said to be carrying Lewis' child when murdered would have had a greater impact on the local Randolph County jurors at the time of the murder. By 1812, five years after Naomi's murder, sympathy for a pregnant victim of lower social standing would have dimmed with the passage of time. The Guilford County jury may not have been familiar with Naomi's story or the Lewis family's reputation. From the beginning, Lewis had endeavored to distance himself from rumors that he was the father of Naomi's child—"Or that it might tend to his honor, to have the Crime laid all upon her."

The length of the trial and deliberation are not known, but in October 1812, Jonathan Lewis was acquitted of the murder of Naomi Wise.[13] In "The Historical Events Behind the Celebrated Ballad 'Naomi Wise,'" the author, Robert Roote, incorrectly stated that "nowhere in the court records is the trial mentioned."[14] He based part of that information on his reference to a transcribed copy of an October 1815 court record shown in the 1944 Randleman Rotary Club publication *The Story of Naomi Wise*. It stated that the record shown was the court procedure concerning Jonathan Lewis' 1815 murder trial. The record as transcribed in that publication read, "Ordered of the Court that the County Trustees pay the cost and charges of attorneys. The prosecution of Jonathan Lewis for Felony when trial is removed to the County of Guilford to the said Jonathan Lewis there requested and said discharged from jail under the ensolvent Debtors Act."[15] Roote said the information presented in the court record was misrepresented in the article and did not refer to the murder trial but was a reference to the trial of Lewis for jailbreak, where he had served time and was released.[16] Roote was correct that the information seemed to indicate there was not a murder trial. However, the person responsible for transcribing the information from the court records made several errors, including changing one word that altered the meaning of the entire document. The court record actually stated, "Ordered by the Court that the County Trustee pay the costs & charges Attending the prosecution of Jonathan Lewis for Felony when Trial was removed to the County of Guilford, & the said Jonathan there acquited [*sic*], and since discharged from Jail under the Insolvent Debtors Act." Someone misread and changed the word "acquited" to "requested" in the transcription process.[17]

There are other mistakes in *The Story of Naomi Wise*, concerning the dates of Lewis' trials. Jonathan was not prosecuted for any crimes in 1815, rather the transcript shown was for the cost of the attorneys, witnesses, etc., for the trial which had occurred earlier in 1812. The expenses were billed to the county in the February term of the Randolph County Court of Pleas and Quarter Sessions in 1815. Lewis was tried for murder at the Superior Court in Guilford County in October 1812 and he was acquitted. There is another bill shown in the minutes of the May 1815 term of the Randolph County Court of Pleas and Quarter Sessions showing the costs and charges for the prosecution of Jonathan Lewis for his 1813 trial for escape from jail.[18]

Jonathan's acquittal did not free him from the North Carolina legal system. He was bound over on the condition of bail until the next Superior Court Session to be held in Randolph County in March 1813, to stand trial for breaking out of jail, and assisting Moses Smith in his jailbreak.[19] Almost six years had passed since his murder indictment, but at least one person remained steadfast in his low opinion of the accused. Edward Jones, Solicitor General, took the opportunity of drafting the indictment to describe Lewis as "a person of an evil mind and wicked disposition."[20]

According to North Carolina law, if a prisoner accused of flight from jail was "afterwards arrested and tried for the [original] felony for which he was imprisoned, and be acquitted thereof, that will discharge him from being found guilty of felony in breaking the prison."[21] Because of this legal precedent, Jonathan was not charged with felony escape but a lesser misdemeanor. After the indictment he was released from jail conditional on his having posted a £500 bond, which in the present day would be the equivalent of approximately $45,000.[22] His uncle Jeremiah Field, who had testified on Jonathan's behalf at the Grand Jury hearing in 1807, and Thomas Kirkman, Jonathan's uncle who had earlier in the year been commissioned as Justice of the Peace for Randolph County by Governor William Hawkins in May 1812, posted his bond. Governor Hawkins had previously pardoned Kirkman's brother-in-law William

Field for aiding in Lewis' escape. Field and Kirkman each posted £250 of the bail.[23]

After a postponement, the trial was held in October of 1813.[24] Among the witnesses for the state was Jonathan's former employer Benjamin Elliott, who, as captain of the militia, was in charge of the guards when Lewis escaped. The jury found Lewis "Guilty of breaking the jail & rescuing himself as charged in the bill of Indictment, but not Guilty as to the rescuing of Moses Smith from legal confinement: Judgement of the Court that the Defendant pay a fine of Ten pounds & costs, & be imprisoned thirty days."[25]

Once again confined in the Randolph County jail, Lewis remained incarcerated after his 30-day sentence was served because he could not or would not pay his fine and court costs. After intervention in late November by Justices of the Peace William Allred and Thomas Kirkman (Lewis' uncle), Lewis swore to the Oath of Insolvent Debtor, attesting that he was not worth 40 shillings sterling and thus was too poor to pay his fines and debt.[26] He declared what assets he had: "besides my wearing apparel Working Tools Arms for Muster One Bed of furniture One Loom One Wheel & One pr of Chards [cards]." At the conclusion of the process, Lewis was absolved of financial responsibility for his fine and court costs, and released.[27] Between the time of his 1807 arrest on suspicion of murder and his 1813 release following the sentence for jailbreak, he had spent approximately 533 days in jail, in Randolph, Guilford, and Orange Counties.[28]

Jonathan Lewis would have begun his long trip back to his home in the Indiana Territory as soon as it could be arranged. He had a daughter, Priscilla, now more than a year and a half old, whom he had presumably never met, the journey to North Carolina likely being too difficult for his wife Sarah to make with an infant. According to one account, Jonathan was last seen in North Carolina by a Mr. John Archer as he was passing through the western Guilford County village of Friendship, as he started to make his way home.[29] By the time he arrived in the Indiana Territory, it would have been almost two years since his capture.

Little is known about Jonathan Lewis' life after he returned to Indiana. Records from that time and place are sparse or lost. He is mentioned in an 1814 record as purchasing a gray horse in Clark County, a notable purchase considering that the year before in North Carolina he had attested to having less than $5 to his name.[30] In April 1816 he administered the estate of his brother-in-law Thomas McCann. Thomas had been the heir to his father Moses McCann's extensive estate, but by the 1816 inventory that followed his own death, the estate had dwindled to a ten-dollar saddle, clothing worth $12, and an unspecified amount of cash.[31] Sarah and Jonathan's second child, Thomas Willis, was born in the fall of 1816.

On April 24, 1817, five days short of his 34th birthday, Jonathan Lewis died. Braxton Craven placed the death in Kentucky, but this was likely based on inaccurate information; it seems likely that he died in Clark County, Indiana, where he and his family were then residing.[32] Craven romantically imagined Jonathan's death to be an agonizing one in which he relived his transgressions: "Naomi was ever before him; his sleep was broken by her cries for mercy, and in the dim twilight her shadowy form was ever before him, holding up her imploring hands."[33]

Craven's account of Jonathan's agonizing death may have some truth. Information handed down through members of the Lewis family posited that he died as the result of being bitten by a poisonous snake.[34] While this family lore cannot be proven, it is feasible that Lewis could have been bitten. There were two types of poisonous snakes residing in Floyd and Clark County, copperheads and timber rattlesnakes. While it is doubtful a copperhead would have killed Jonathan as their bite is rarely lethal, a timber rattlesnake (Crotalus horridus) could have been responsible, especially if Lewis was envenomated more than once. In the *History of the Ohio Falls Cities and Their Counties with Illustrations and Biographical Sketches* published in 1882, rattlesnakes are mentioned as being in the knobs area where the Lewis family lived "there were also great numbers of snakes of all kinds known to this climate and soil. These were especially plenty along the knobs, among the rock, even yet rattlesnakes and other serpents are occasionally killed there."[35] Lewis died the 28th of April 1817. The month of April is usually the time timber rattlesnakes come out of hibernation and become active. A snakebite could explain the death of Lewis at such a young age and the folklore surrounding his suffering. Craven makes mention of Jonathan's suffering: "After all hope of his recovery was given up, and his friends watched round his couch only to perform the last sad offices of life, he still lingered. He seemed to suffer beyond human conception; the contortions of his face were too horrid for human gaze; his groans were appalling to the ear. For two days the death rattle had been in his throat, and yet he retained his reason and speech." While Craven was prone to exaggeration, severe envenomation from a timber rattlesnake can cause similar reactions such as intense pain, swelling, involuntary quivering of muscles, unstable blood pressure, and renal failure.

Jonathan left his widow Sarah with a five-year-old daughter and a seven-month-old son.[36] She did not remain a widow for long. She married Hugh K. Howell a little over six months after Jonathan's death.[37] Hugh and Sarah Lewis Howell had one son, Tilman Clarke Howell, born about 1819. In 1870 Tilman was unmarried and living in Chariton County, Missouri.[38] Jonathan and Sarah's daughter Priscilla married A.C. Johnson in 1835 in Floyd County, Indiana.[39] Their son Thomas Willis Lewis married and had at least four children. By 1850 Thomas, his wife Jane, and children were living in Clay County, Illinois.[40]

The location of Jonathan Lewis' grave remains unknown.

CHAPTER 7

Family Hardship

The 1807 murder of Naomi Wise and the subsequent death of Jonathan Lewis in 1817 did not mark the end of their saga. Jonathan's fate was to leave behind a wife and two children, and the legacy of escaping justice after committing a murder. Naomi Wise died never having risen from the shadows of poverty, orphanhood, or the reputation of being an unruly woman for having had two children outside of marriage. Even in death, Naomi remained on the fringes of society: despite the notoriety of her murder, for generations afterwards there was uncertainty as to the location of her grave.

In the late 19th and early 20th centuries, it was widely believed that Naomi had been buried very near the site of her drowning. An 1884 pamphlet, *Naomi Wise or the Wrongs of a Beautiful Girl*, by M. Penny, makes mention of this.

> On July 7th, 1879, Mr. J.B. Randleman and the present Naomi Falls Company commenced building a cotton factory, ... within less than 200 yards of the ford where the tragedy referred to in this book was enacted. This place was named in honor of Naomi, who was buried on the plantation upon which Calvin Swim [Swaim] now lives, in sight of Naomi Falls Factory.[1]

On January 30, 1908, the *Randolph Bulletin* newspaper published a story about Naomi Wise, which referred to the Swaim plantation as her resting place, citing M. Penny's booklet as its source.[2] A subscriber, Mrs. E.L. Cox from Climax, a few miles northeast of Randleman in Guilford County, wrote in to set the record straight. Naomi Wise was, she wrote, "without a doubt buried in the cemetery at Providence (Meeting); which was attended by the old Chamness and Lamb families of this immediate neighborhood of whom I am a descendant. I have heard them speak of the occasion numbers of times, and the grave can be located within a few yards."[3]

Mrs. E.L. Cox was Emily Chamness Cox (1857–1924), great-granddaughter of Anthony Chamness, the Quaker cabinetmaker who had been a neighbor of the Richard Lewis family, and had testified on Jonathan Lewis' behalf at the Grand Jury hearing in 1807. Anthony Chamness was a well-known and skilled craftsman. A rectangular table with a sulfur-inlayed drawer attributed to him is in the collection of the Museum of Early Southern Decorative Arts in Winston-Salem, North Carolina.[4] Another family member, Vera King, cited family tradition that Anthony Chamness had even made Naomi's coffin.[5] He himself is buried at the Providence Meeting cemetery.[6]

Further compelling evidence of Providence as Naomi's burial place is found in the 1880 commonplace book of Elma Barker, who served as the clerk of Providence Meeting.[7] Barker had written down the words to a ballad she called "Poor Naomi," and above the verses wrote the note, "Naomi Wise was buried at Providence. A factory is now standing near the place where she was drowned by the name of Naomi Falls."[8]

In the absence of more official documentation, circumstantial evidence supports Barker's note and the oral history that the Quaker community of Providence Meeting would have taken care of Naomi's body in death and buried her at Providence. Some members of the Elliott family, to whom Naomi's daughter Nancy was apprenticed, were Quakers and because of the connection through Nancy they may have stepped in and assumed the funerary duties that would normally have been the responsibility of the deceased's family.[9] According to Society of Friends records, individuals who were not Quakers could be buried in the cemetery as long as it was agreed to by one or more appointed members from that meeting.[10] Naomi might have been buried near where she died if her body had laid out for several warm days during the coroner's inquest. Because the early April weather would have been cool, though, even if her body had remained at the riverside for approximately 48 to

An entry by Elma Barker, above the Naomi Wise ballad, specifying the location of Naomi's grave. Elma Barker's Commonplace book, 1880 (courtesy C. Barker Collection).

60 hours, it would still have been reasonable to move her to the cemetery at Providence Meeting following the inquest.

In 1929, the folklorist and musician Bascom Lamar Lunsford visited Randolph County to research the story of Naomi Wise. Schoolteacher Lalah Cox (1903–1992) took him to Providence Friends Meeting, and showed him a plain rough stone marker indicating Naomi's burial place.[11] He wrote, "Miss Cox stated that she, herself, had erected the marker to the grave which had been pointed out to her often since childhood as being Naomi's grave."[12] Lunsford did not specify where in the cemetery the marker was located; however, according to Allen Chamness (1868–1942), her grave was situated close to the highway.[13] Allen was the uncle of Lalah Cox and the brother of Alva (1862–1931) who sang the Naomi Wise ballad for Lunsford.

It is possible Naomi's burial had never been marked until Lalah Cox did so. If there had been an earlier marker, it may have been among a group of tombstones that were removed in the 1830s, when meetinghouse members decided that some of the memorials in the cemetery didn't meet Society of Friends guidelines and should be removed.[14]

In the late 1940s, a local civic club replaced a plain stone, presumably the one that Lalah Cox had placed, with a commercially made tombstone.[15] This is the marker that stands today, approximately 200 feet from the edge of Providence Church Road. As stated elsewhere in this book, the birth and death dates on the 20th-century tombstone are incorrect.

While the ballads and tombstone commemorate

Naomi Wise tombstone, erected in the 1940s, Providence Friends Meeting cemetery, Randolph County, North Carolina, 2020 (authors' collection).

Naomi Wise's death, she left a living legacy as well, in her descendants, some of whom are alive today.

After her death, Naomi's children continued to live in the community of Quakers who, by their own religious tenets, had made it their responsibility to help orphans and the poor. The Quakers felt an obligation to look after white orphan and African American children, advising that orphans' rights and poor Friends' necessities be looked after. Their Yearly Meetings took this under consideration and said, "it is worthy of serious consideration whether there is any object of beneficence more deserving attention, than that of training up the youth of this injured part of the human family in such virtuous principles and habits, as may render them useful and respectable members of the community."[16]

Of the fate of Naomi's son, Henry, little is known. He was about four years old at the time of Naomi's death in 1807, and for six years thereafter evidence of his caregivers is elusive. He may have had an early apprenticeship, or been in the care of William and Mary Adams.

Randolph County court records and an apprentice bond indicate that in 1813 Henry was indentured as an apprentice to Seth Hinshaw. "The court ordered that Henry Wise of the age of nine years be bound to Seth Hinshaw who agrees to learn him the Hatters trade and give him a freedom suit and learn to Cypher through the rule of three."[17] Henry's father, Benjamin Sanders, was also a hatter, but there is no indication that he had any influence on his son, or whether he even acknowledged him.

Henry's apprenticeship to Hinshaw was canceled in 1821. No explanation was recorded. However, another apprentice had been released from his bond with Hinshaw in the same year. Joseph Watkins had an apprenticeship to Hinshaw in the hatter's trade. His apprenticeship was also canceled in 1821 when he was then apprenticed to the potter's trade to his older brother, Henry Watkins. At the age of 18, Henry Wise was issued a new indenture by the court.[18] "On motion of B. Elliott Esquire, It is ordered that the Indentures for Henry Wise as an apprentice to Seth Hinshaw be cancelled. And the said Orphan Henry Wise Now of the age of eighteen years, be bound to Simion [Simeon] McCollum to learn the art of Farming. He also agrees to give the said Henry six Months schooling and when free a horse, saddle & bridle worth sixty Dollars."[19] It was Simeon McCollum's father Stephen who took on Nancy Wise as an apprentice after she left the home of Joseph Elliott.

Nothing is known of Henry Wise's life after the age of 18. He seems to disappear from the written records.

State of North-Carolina,
Randolph **County.** } ss.

THIS INDENTURE, made the _second_ day of _August_ in the year of our Lord one thousand eight hundred and _thirteen_ between _Benjamin Marmon_ Chairman of the County Court of _Randolph_ County, and State aforesaid, on behalf of the Justices of the said County and their successors, of the one part, and, _Seth Hinshaw_ of the other part, WITNESSETH, That the said _Benjamin Marmon_ in pursuance of an order of said County Court, made the _3rd_ day of _August_ and, according to the directions of the Act of Assembly in that case made and provided, doth put, place and bind unto the said _Seth Hinshaw_ an orphan named _Henry Wise_ now of the age of _Nine_ years, with the said _Seth Hinshaw_ to live after the manner of an Apprentice and Servant, until the said Apprentice shall attain to the age of twenty-one years: during all which time the said Apprentice _his_ master faithfully shall serve, his lawful commands every where readily obey; _he_ shall not at any time absent _himself_ from _his_ said master's service without leave, but in all things as a good and faithful servant shall behave towards _his_ said master. And the said _Seth Hinshaw_ doth covenant, promise and agree to and with the said _Benjamin Marmon_ that he will teach and instruct, or cause to be taught and instructed, the said _Henry Wise_ to learn _the Hatters trade & to cypher through the rule of three & give him a freedom suit_ and that he will constantly find and provide for said Apprentice, during the term aforesaid, sufficient diet, washing, lodging and apparel, fitting for an Apprentice; and also all other things necessary, both in sickness and in health.

IN WITNESS WHEREOF, the parties to these presents have set their hands and seals, the day and year first above written. _Seth Hinshaw_ {seal}

Seth Harper

Benj Marmon {seal}

Apprentice Indenture for the nine-year-old orphan Henry Wise, the son of Naomi Wise and Benjamin Sanders, to be taught the hatter's trade by Seth Hinshaw, August 2, 1813, Randolph County, North Carolina (State Archives of North Carolina).

Naomi's daughter Nancy did not have an easy life. Her apprenticeship in Joseph Elliott's household ended by 1812. The reasons for the termination do not appear in court records. It is possible that Joseph's age or his wife Sarah's health may have influenced their decision to move her out of their household. Joseph's involvement in the 1812 trial of her mother's accused murderer, Jonathan Lewis, may have had an impact. In 1812, Nancy received a new apprenticeship and was bound to the Quaker Stephen McCollum to continue as a spinster, and was promised a feather bed, furniture, and a spinning wheel when she completed the apprenticeship.[20]

When she was 21 years old, Nancy was impregnated by Joseph Bulla (1785–1855) and gave birth to a child out of wedlock. The child, John Singleton Wise, was born either late in 1819 or early in 1820. On the bastardy bond dated January 8, 1820, Nancy named Joseph as the father.[21] On February 10, Joseph Bulla along with Henry Johnson and Solomon Wall, signed the guarantee for the £500 bond for maintenance of the child.[22] This is the same Joseph Bulla who had to be bound for £50 to assure his appearance at the Randolph County court in 1807, subpoenaed to give testimony for the state against Daniel Dawson and others who had guarded the Randolph County jail and allowed Jonathan Lewis to escape.[23] Joseph's father, Thomas Bulla, was a wealthy man and upon his death in 1809 had left his son Joseph the tavern house and courthouse lots consisting of 100 acres at Johnstonville. Joseph sold the courthouse tract in March of 1819 for $500.[24]

Joseph would seem to be a contemptable character, because despite his comfortable financial position, after signing the bastardy bond in February of 1820 he had no further documented connection to the Wise family—even two years after the birth of their son, when Nancy was indigent, sick, and became a ward of the county. In 1822 she would be auctioned off as cheap labor by the Wardens of the Poor.[25]

Through the offices of the Wardens of the Poor, who minimized public financial liability for the indigent by auctioning their labor, Michael Ramsower received the right to take in Nancy Wise. It was ordered in the minutes "that Michael Ramsour [Ramsower] be allowed $5 for the support of and attendance one Nancy Wise."[26] (Michael was the brother of Elizabeth Ramsower Craven, wife of jailer Joshua Craven, and his brother John Ramsower was the reputed husband of Hettie Elliott, whom Jonathan Lewis had courted.) It seems that Nancy became sick or was injured while under Ramsower's care, as the next entry concerned payment for her medical treatment: "Ordered Doctr. P. Nixon be allowed $20.70 for medical attendance on Nancy Wise."[27]

Nancy Wise bastardy bond naming Joseph Bulla as the father of her child, Randolph County, North Carolina, 1820 (State Archives of North Carolina).

Bond for £500 signed by Joseph Bulla taking responsibility for the maintenance of his illegitimate child, 1820 (State Archives of North Carolina).

Chapter 7. Family Hardship

William Dennis, the neighbor whom Mary Adams had first notified of Naomi Wise's disappearance, was one of the Wardens of the Poor, having been first elected sometime before 1812 and held the responsibility for more than one term through 1823.[28] William would have been apprised of Nancy's plight and been instrumental in overseeing assistance for her upkeep. Nancy appears to have been taken under the care of Joseph Newby after the onset of her ill health. According to the minutes, Joseph was allowed a payment of $15 for nursing Nancy Wise for 31 days.[29] The Newby family was Quaker and attended Back Creek Meeting located west of Asheboro, North Carolina.[30] While the Quaker family was attempting to nurse Nancy back to health, it seems probable her two-year-old son, John Wise, would have been with her.

Nancy's illness or injury and her association with the Newby family mark her disappearance from Randolph County records. After the February 5, 1822, entry, there is no mention of Nancy or her son in the minutes of the poor, other than records of delayed payments for her care by the county to the doctor and Joseph Newby.

What kind of illness or injury Nancy had is not known, but she may have died from the affliction. An 1899 biography of the Rev. James Needham, who had been a cabinetmaker in Randolph County as a young man, mentions that "he made the coffin in which [Naomi Wise's] sixteen-year-old daughter was buried."[31] While this reported age of Nancy's death is clearly incorrect, her disappearance from the records does coincide with the period when James Needham was working in the area as a cabinetmaker, between 1821 and 1824. If he did indeed make her coffin, Nancy would seem to have died around the age of 24.[32] There was no mention of burial expenses for Nancy in the minutes of the poor, however, if she died under the care of Quakers, members of the meeting would have provided for her funeral with a coffin and paid minor expenses.

Nancy's son, and Naomi's grandson, John Wise, was cared for by the Quakers in the Back Creek area of Randolph County, as witnessed by the Back Creek Friends Meeting records from February of 1839: "John Singleton Wise having been under the care of friends for some time past now requests to be received into membership with us which request this Meeting grants & receives him accordingly."[33] He would have been 19 years old in February 1839. John may have remained with the Newby family when young as he is listed directly below the name of Joseph Newby in a ca.1840 Randolph County tax list.[34] John was accepted as a member of Back Creek Friends Meeting and in 1844 married Elizabeth

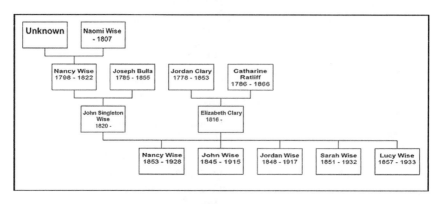

John Singleton Wise family tree.

Clary, the daughter of Jordon and Catherine Clary.[35] The Clary family were Quakers who had moved from Pasquotank County in eastern North Carolina to Randolph County in 1837.[36]

In 1845, at the age of 25, John reciprocated the care he was given as an orphan by apprenticing a free, four-year-old African American youth, Daniel H. Winslow, who was also an orphan. The apprenticeship specified the indenture would be fulfilled in 1862 when Daniel reached the age of 21, but noticeably contains an absence of the customary literacy requirements, which can be attributed to the effects of North Carolina laws discouraging the education of African Americans, both free and enslaved.[37] The agreement also lacks mention of a trade to be taught, but stated that when Daniel completed his apprenticeship he was to be given $50. A condition of the apprenticeship required a $500 bond to assure the child was not removed from the county.[38] Alfred Marsh, a merchant who was married to Benjamin Elliott's daughter, cosigned the $500 bond with John Wise. While the $500 bond offered protection from trafficking of free black children, it also allowed the children to be kept under the supervision of white county authorities.

By 1850 John Wise and his family had moved to Grant County, Indiana, where John was listed as a farmer in that year's census. The termination of Daniel Winslow's apprenticeship has not been found. The absence of county documentation leaves a broad spectrum of possible scenarios regarding Daniel Winslow's life. There is no mention of the apprenticed orphan in Quaker records or relevant census records. John and his wife Elizabeth raised five children during this time.[39]

State of North Carolina.
Randolph COUNTY.

THIS INDENTURE, made the *3* day of *November* in the year of our Lord one thousand eight hundred and *Forty five* between *H. B. Elliott* Chairman of the County Court of *Randolph* County, and State aforesaid, on behalf of the Justices of the said County and their successors, of the one part, and *John S. Wise* of the other part, Witnesseth, That the said *H. B. Elliott* in pursuance to an order of said County Court, made the *3* day of *November* and according to the directions of the Act of Assembly in that case made and provided, doth put, place and bind unto the said *John S. Wise* an Orphan named *Daniel H. Winslow* now of the age of *4* years, *February* with the said *John S. Wise* to live after the manner of an Apprentice and Servant until the said Apprentice shall attain to the age of twenty-one years: during all which time the said Apprentice *his* Master faithfully shall serve, his lawful commands every where readily obey: *he* shall not at any time absent *himself* from said Master's service, but in all things as a good and faithful Servant shall behave towards *his* said Master. And the said *John S. Wise* doth covenant, promise and agree to and with the said *H. B. Elliott* that he will teach and instruct, or cause to be taught and instructed, the said *Daniel H. Winslow* *of Caten* to learn *& when free to give him Fifty Dollars*

and that he will constantly find and provide for said Apprentice, during the term aforesaid sufficient diet, washing, lodging and appearel, fitting for an Apprentice; and also all other things necessary, both in sickness and in health; and give said Apprentice freedom dues according to law.

In witness whereof, the parties to these presents have interchangeably set their hands and seals, the day and year first above written.

John S. Wise (seal)

H. B. Elliott (seal)

Apprenticeship bond for the four-year-old African American youth Daniel Winslow to be apprenticed under Naomi Wise's grandson, John Wise, Randolph County, North Carolina, 1845 (State Archives of North Carolina).

Five-hundred-dollar bond to assure Daniel Winslow was not removed from Randolph County, North Carolina, 1845 (State Archives of North Carolina).

In 1870, the Wise family was living farther west, having moved to Neosho in Coffey County, Kansas. John had purchased an 80-acre tract with 15 acres of improved land, where he continued farming, raising cattle and hogs and growing Indian corn.[40] In the 1880 Census it was not documented where John's parents were born, perhaps his attempt to obscure his origins and reframe his family's legacy.

CHAPTER 8

Braxton Craven Revisited

Since 1807, the story of Naomi Wise has been told and retold—in oral history, in song, and in writing. The murder and its aftermath have become an enduring part of American folklore.

As is typical of the process by which a historical event enters into folklore, the many variants of Naomi's story have become an amalgam of verifiable fact, embellishments and misremembering, and age-old folkloric tropes. At one end of the spectrum, a local pejorative rumor whispered in male circles suggested that Jonathan Lewis may have contracted syphilis from Naomi, and that this had been the reason for her murder, and for his own supposed painful and early death. Since Lewis later married Sarah McCann, who remained healthy and had two apparently healthy children with him, this rumor appears to have been a fallacy with no basis other than conjecture, most likely simple victim-blaming. Alternatively, or additionally, it can be viewed as a blending of folk narratives about well-known murders. Perhaps the most famous of murder ballads, "Tom Dooley," tells the story of the real-life 1866 murder of a young woman, Laura Foster, by her lover Tom Dula in the foothills of North Carolina. In the oral history of Laura Foster's murder, a very similar tale has circulated, suggesting that she had infected Dula with syphilis, which he had passed on to the other women in his life.[1] (Like Naomi Wise, Laura Foster is said to have been pregnant at the time of her death.)

Another element of local oral history demonstrates the interconnectedness of community narratives and ancient folkloric traditions. Some accounts of the aftermath of Naomi Wise's murder tell how a community member—usually a female relative of the story teller—was present when the body was brought to the riverbank, and she observed that Naomi had been wearing a necklace. This elaboration appears to have originated around the turn of the 20th century when images appeared on the covers of printed material portraying her as a refined young lady in Victorian dress. Randolph County historian Laura Worth recorded a version of the story as told to her in September of 1938. "[A local resident] was the first woman to place her hand upon [Naomi's] brow. A strand of beads upon her neck broke and scattered. There were marks upon her throat where she had been choked." Though this seems at first to be an oddly obscure detail to have survived for centuries, its deeper significance can be found in the context of the cruentation ritual that took place when Naomi's body was recovered, when Jonathan Lewis was made to touch the corpse.

The "ordeal by touch" was based upon the belief that a murder victim's spirit would manifest indignation at her fate by causing her corpse to move, expel bodily fluids, or otherwise show emotion. Naomi's necklace breaking can be interpreted as the kind of sign the gathered observers would have been watching for. In British balladry and early northern European folklore, the breaking of jewelry or popping of buttons are a symbolic device that indicates great emotional turmoil. Folklorist Stith Thompson, in his Motif-Index of Folk-Literature, identified this device as Motif F1041.6.1, "Necklace bursts as a consequence of violent emotion," a sub-motif of F1041.6, "Buttons burst as a consequence of violent emotion."[2] The motif may trace as far back as the Norse Poetic Edda, to the poem Þrymskviða, in which Freyja's Brísingamen necklace breaks.[3]

> 12. Wrathful was Freyja, | and fiercely she snorted,
> And the dwelling great | of the gods was shaken,
> And burst was the mighty | Brisings' necklace

Precedents for the description of Naomi Wise's broken necklace can also be found in traditional ballads recorded both in the British Isles and in North Carolina, which tell of bursting buttons and jewelry of different kinds. Walter Scott transcribed the ballad "Annan Water" in the 1806 edition of his Minstrelsy of the Scottish Border, in which the hero's "waistcoat bursted aff his breast / He was sae full of melancholy."[4] In the 1960s, folklorist John Cohen recorded Berzilla Chandler Wallin (1893–1986) of Madison County, North Carolina, singing the ballad "Johnny Dial" (or "Johnny Doyle"), the story of a young woman abducted and forced by her family to marry a man she doesn't love; describing the moment of her abduction, the narrator tells, "And the very moment the squire appeared at the door / My earrings they bursted and fell to the floor."[5] As Naomi Wise was known by her community to be a woman who, like the narrator of "Johnny Dial," was "all crosséd in love," onlookers may well have interpreted the breaking of her necklace as emotional pain manifested even after death.

Front cover of *Naomi Wise or the Wrongs of a Beautiful Girl, A True Story, Enacted in Randolph County, N. Carolina about One Hundred Years Ago.* by William C. Phillips, Printer, Pinnacle, North Carolina, 1904 (Randolph County Public Library, Randolph Room).

Naomi "Omie" Wise

Running parallel to the oral history of Naomi Wise's murder has been its survival in written narrative. The earliest known version of the story outside of official documentation is the long narrative poem "A true acount of Nayomy Wise"—referred to throughout the preceding chapters of this book as the Woody poem—recorded in the commonplace book belonging to Mary Woody, a Quaker girl in Alamance County, North Carolina, sometime in the first quarter of the 19th century.[6] It was discovered in the 1980s by a colleague of the folklorists D.K. Wilgus and Wayland Hand, hidden away in the Special Collections of the UCLA Library in Los Angeles.

Mary Woody (1801–1861) was one of five children in the Quaker family of Hugh Woody (1770–1825) and Ruth Hadley Woody (1773–1810). Hugh and Ruth had five children, three boys and two girls; Mary was the second oldest. In 1812, after Ruth's death, Hugh married Mary Atkinson (b. 1771), with whom he had another three children. The Woody family were members of Cane Creek Friends Monthly Meeting in Alamance County, approximately 20 miles east of where the William Adams family lived in Randolph County.[7]

How Mary Woody ended up with the information contained in "A true acount of Nayomy Wise" is a mystery. It would seem to have been given to her as a writing or penmanship exercise, either copied or dictated, and perhaps also as a morality lesson. Given the specificity of the details, the poem's original author would seem to have been present at the inquest, or had access to the coroner's report or witness accounts. The use of the words "thee" (spelled "the" in Woody's book) and "thy" suggests that the author was a member of the Quaker community, by whom those words were commonly used. (Alternatively, the pronouns may have been changed to the Quaker style as the "Acount" was circulated in that community.)

Mary Woody's family was closely tied, by kinship and proximity, to many people directly involved in the story of Naomi Wise, so it is possible that the "Acount" was written by a member of her family. One possible author is Mary's aunt Hannah Woody Chamness (b. 1786). Hannah and her husband Edward Chamness lived near the Lewis and Field families at the time of Naomi's murder. Hannah's brother-in-law, the cabinetmaker Anthony Chamness, testified for the defense in Jonathan Lewis' 1807 grand jury hearing, and is said to have made Naomi's coffin. Her father-in-law was the brother to Martha Chamness Hussey, at whose home Lewis was apprehended the morning after the murder.[8]

The Woody poem is remarkable for many reasons. By recounting

Mary Adams' testimony, it gives a very detailed description and account of those involved, and of the locale of the murder, and offers an intimate look into Naomi Wise's life and details about what happened prior to and after her body was found in Deep River. Perhaps most significantly, it gives us a rare unfiltered view of morality through the perception of a woman in early 19th-century North Carolina. (The poem is transcribed in the Appendix as it was written in Mary Woody's book.)

Of all authors who have written about the murder of Naomi Wise, the most influential was Braxton Craven (1822–1882), whose romantic account, "Naomi Wise, or the Victim"—also quoted throughout this book—was published when he was 28 years old. That 1851 publication renewed interest in the murder, by then more than a generation past, and the associated ballad. In later years Craven referred to his story of Naomi Wise, along with other contemporaneous work, as "school-boy compositions," which he said "were crude and unpolished."[9] Nevertheless, "Naomi Wise, or the Victim" was republished many times over the years.

Braxton Craven, born in southern Randolph County, was in later life a prominent educator, ordained Methodist minister, and president of Union Institute, which would become Trinity College, and is now known as Duke University. Beginning in 1851, he and Reuben Brown published a literary magazine called *The Evergreen*, which was an offshoot of an educational journal, the *Southern Index*. *The Evergreen* was published in Asheboro, North Carolina, and ran for 12 issues, with "Naomi Wise, or the Victim" appearing in the third and fourth.[10]

The introduction to "Naomi Wise, or the Victim" mentions that Craven had formulated his version of the story based upon accounts that he had gathered

Braxton Craven (1822–1882), author of "Naomi Wise, or the Victim" first published in *The Evergreen* in 1851 (courtesy Stephen C. Compton).

from older residents of the area. Some of Braxton Craven's relatives were involved in the events, so he no doubt heard first-person accounts, as well as stories that had been handed down through the families over the preceding four decades. He would also have known General Alexander Gray, who in 1807 was a lieutenant colonel of the militia and figured prominently in the Naomi Wise story. The wealthy and influential Gray was president of the Union Institute Educational Society that was involved in the founding of Union Institute in northwestern Randolph County in 1839. During the time of Gray's presidency, Braxton Craven became an assistant teacher at the school and was eventually elected principal by the Educational Society. Union Institute became Normal College in 1851. Braxton Craven served as the president of Normal College and in 1859 when it became Trinity College he continued serving as president with a two-year hiatus in the mid–1860s.

Despite his undoubted access to first-hand witnesses to the murder's aftermath, parts of Braxton Craven's account of the events are heavily romanticized and theatrical. His portrayal of Naomi herself was heavily sentimentalized, presenting her not as she was—an experienced woman who had two children, and who had already seen more than her share of hardship from the men in her life—but, as Craven described her, a "gentle, confiding, unprotected creature" who was "just blooming in all the attractiveness of nineteen."

This insistence on Naomi's virginal innocence was no doubt due to Craven's affection for his own mother, Ann Craven (also referred to as Anna Craven), a contemporary of Naomi Wise to whom Braxton and his two siblings were all born out of wedlock. No copy of Braxton's bastardy bond could be found and it appears that Ann did not name the father, but chose to pay the bond for maintenance of her child. He must also have felt special sympathy for Naomi Wise because he too grew up as, in effect, an orphan from the age of seven, when he and his siblings were removed from their mother's care.

It was suggested by the Reverend Davidson V. York that Braxton Craven's father was Braxton York (b. 1798), a cousin of prominent North Carolina educator Brantley York.[11] Braxton York had married Mary Elliott (b. 1804) on January 17, 1821, which suggests that he would still have been a newlywed when he had an affair with Braxton's mother, Ann. Less than a year after Braxton's birth, Ann's cousin Lydia Craven swore in a separate bastardy bond that Braxton York was the father of her child as well.[12] York refused to pay the $500 bond for the baby's upkeep.[13]

Chapter 8. Braxton Craven Revisited

Like her son and like Naomi Wise, Ann apparently had to make her way through life without her parental care. The daughter of John Craven and Hannah Cox, she was said to have been disowned by her family. However, she was taken care of by her brother, the Reverend Jacob Craven, who gave her two acres of land and a cabin to live in.[14] Even with the help from her brother, it appears she was unable to care for Braxton, his younger brother Alston, and a younger sister, Sally. The usual solution to such problems was for indigent children to be bound out in apprenticeships, and it appears Ann had to give her three children up when they were very young. According to Braxton's autobiography, because of this duress, he had been sent to live with a Quaker neighbor, Nathan Cox, around the age of seven, and lived there for nine years.[15] Randolph County court records confirm in 1832 the sheriff was ordered to bring all three of Ann's children to the next court to be dealt with as it directed. Evidently, Nathan Cox was allowed to retain custody of Braxton, as there is no mention of the court ordering Braxton to be bound out in an apprenticeship.[16] Living in a community of Quakers who made it their responsibility to assist orphans, Braxton Craven was able to receive an education.

Nevertheless, the burden of illegitimacy would have influenced and limited Craven's options in life, as it had for Naomi Wise. Braxton, though, had the advantages of being a male child and bearing a locally influential surname. The Craven family was respected and had connections, which would have created opportunities for him. His sympathy for Naomi Wise, a fellow orphan, was clearly deeply personal, and it would seem that he understood how Naomi's particular circumstances—being female, and without family in the county other than her children—cast her to the bottom of the social order. In a baccalaureate sermon that Craven gave to a graduating class at Trinity College, he described the plight of orphans in impassioned terms.

That commingling of souls that now beguiles the passing hour may become a stranger to your heart; the day may come when you would give worlds for one—just one—to love you like a brother, when your soul reaches out the tendrils of affection only to be frozen to death; when your warm, inquiring eye sees nothing but the curled lip of disdain; when your great throbbing heart beats in a vacuum. It is so hard, so bitter, so torturing to a man of a great, loving heart, one that would embrace the world in its arms of affection, to find himself in a vast desert where none will call him friend or brother. Many a man, at such an hour, has learned to curse God and hate the world, and our only resource is in religion.

In all your ways, let me entreat you to remember the orphan by day and by night; his is a hard, oh, it is a bitter lot! There is much more poetry than truth in the world's pretended kindness to the poor, sorrowful-faced little boy that has no mother to love him and no father to protect him. He is sorely oppressed in his boyhood; he may dig himself a home in the mountain granite, but orphan haunts him like a midnight ghost. In his manhood, the lingering curse of his sad condition rests upon him. This world has no cavern to hide him from the opposition. I have seen his tears flow as if the fountains of his soul were broken up. I have seen him bow before God and ask for love to bind up his broken heart, and I have seen the cold combinations of this world grind him to powder. Always, my young friends, have a kind word for him, and treat him as a brother.[17]

In "Naomi Wise, or the Victim," Craven also gave voice to his concern for disadvantaged and isolated young women. In those pages he spoke out for his own mother, and for all women cast to the edges of society, when he wrote that

[t]here are many young men now moving high in society, that think violets were created to be crushed by haughty boot heels; that desert flowers should rather be blasted than waste their sweetness on the air; that pearls should rather adorn a Cyclops, than sparkle in their native deep. Not so, ye cannibals. If names must be blasted and character ruined, in the name of heaven, let your victims come from among the affluent and the honorable. Who will pity and protect the poor daughter of shame; who will give her a crumb of bread? The more wealthy victim might, at least, have bread to eat, water to drink, and wherewithal to be clothed. Ye fair, blooming daughters of poverty, shun the advances of those who avoid you in company, as you would shun the grim monster death.[18]

Craven's compassion for the disadvantaged extended only so far. He defended the institution of slavery and advocated white supremacy, commenting, "Slavery is not contrary to law, and is by no means as severe in practice as the law allows."[19] By the time he had written the story of Naomi Wise in 1851, he had owned at least three enslaved people, including a then-20-year-old man and 17-year-old girl who were enumerated in the 1850 slave census for Randolph County as belonging to him.[20] His pro-slavery stance no doubt put him at odds with the anti-slavery Quaker brethren in the area, and may partially account for his complete elimination of any mention of Quakers and the roles they played in his story of Naomi Wise. The harsh working conditions he himself was subjected to when placed as an orphan in Nathan Cox's home could have also played a part in his dismissal of Quaker influence.

Understandably, given its colorful style and emotional appeal, "Naomi Wise, or the Victim" was widely read in Piedmont North Carolina. Twenty-three years after its original publication in *The Evergreen*,

Chapter 8. Braxton Craven Revisited

The Greensboro Patriot reprinted the story (with the title shortened simply to "Naomi Wise," and under the pseudonym Charlie Vernon) in four separate Wednesday editions, between April 8 and April 29, 1874. When "Naomi Wise" appeared in *The Greensboro Patriot*, no one bothered to update the opening line from Chapter One of the original 1851 *The Evergreen* article stating the event had taken place "about 40 years ago." For better or worse, Braxton Craven's romantic and sometimes inaccurate story became the most influential printed account of the life and death of Naomi Wise.

CHAPTER 9

The Ballad Tradition

Without question, the main reason Naomi Wise is remembered around the world today, far from Randolph County, is the popularity of the ballad tradition that has perpetuated her story. Versions performed and recorded by musicians as prominent as Bob Dylan and Doc Watson, and dozens of others since the 1920s, come from a deep folk tradition that has kept Naomi Wise's memory alive for generations. Folklorist Frank C. Brown wrote, "Judged by the breadth of its diffusion," the ballad is "North Carolina's principal single contribution to American folk song."[1] Brown, among others, cited variants that had been collected not only in North Carolina, but in Tennessee, Kentucky, Florida, Arkansas, and Missouri. Though it clearly never lost its place in the folk tradition, the song gained renewed currency during the Folk Revival of the mid to late 20th century, and it remains popular among traditional musicians today. What is referred to here as the ballad (singular) of Naomi Wise is the most common family of songs, closely related both lyrically and melodically, to which such famous versions as Doc Watson's and G.B. Grayson's belong.

As is usually the case with folksongs, the ballads of Naomi Wise—often known as "Omie Wise" or "Poor Naomi"—have been through countless variations in lyrics and tunes as they have been passed from singer to singer in the oral tradition. Folklorist and ballad scholar Eleanor Long-Wilgus documented at least 147 various texts and fragments of the ballad. Of these, 133 were attributed to oral tradition and only 14 to commercial folios and sound recordings.[2]

Long-Wilgus posited that two melodies were associated with the Naomi Wise ballad. The first, she wrote, was in the Mixolydian mode, and the second in Dorian mode.[3] Others have suggested that the ballad was originally sung to the tune of the hymn "How Firm a Foundation."[4] In an interview in the 1950s, Randolph County historian Laura Worth suggested that while the original melody was similar to "How

Firm a Foundation," it was "unimitable." She wrote that she knew of no one who could sing it as mournfully as it had once been sung. The ballad as it existed in Randolph County into the 20th century was said to have sounded plaintive and dirge-like.[5]

The tune to which the ballad has most commonly been sung in field and commercial recordings is closely related to that of "How Firm a Foundation," although it is commonly transposed into a minor or modal key. Just as narrative traditions in folklore become associated with each other through similarities in story, familiar "floating" tunes can drift from one song to another because the songs share common elements, either thematically or in structure. In this way, the most familiar ballad of Naomi Wise is something of a cousin to the song "Poor Ellen Smith." Ellen Smith was a young woman whose 1892 murder in Winston-Salem, North Carolina, received wide press coverage. Though Naomi died at the beginning of the 19th century and Ellen at the end, both women were killed by their lovers in the northern Piedmont of North Carolina, and the themes of class, morality, and deception that made Naomi's story so compelling are mirrored in the oral history and press coverage of the later murder. It is no wonder that singers might find the tunes interchangeable, when the stories were so alike. This chain of associations is vividly demonstrated by a 1940 field recording of 86-year-old Logan County, West Virginia, singer Mary Jane Dyson. Dyson sang "Poor Omie Wise" to a variant of the tune of "How Firm a Foundation," with the upbeat timing and major key that usually characterize versions of "Poor Ellen Smith" sung to the same tune. (As if to underscore the association, Mrs. Dyson then—perhaps prompted by the field recorder having recognized the tune—sings a verse of "Poor Ellen Smith," and concludes, "That's all I know of it.")[6]

As is also true of most folk ballads, it would be difficult to impossible to establish definitively the original authorship of the lyrics. In Randolph County, though, local traditions suggest possible authors. George N. Hinshaw (1869–1935), an amateur genealogist, stated that his family tradition credited Elizabeth Pennington Beeson (1761–1823) and her son Levi (born ca. 1780) with writing the ballad shortly after the 1807 murder.[7] Elizabeth and Levi Beeson lived within two miles of the William Adams home and a mile from the murder site. They would certainly have known many of the individuals involved, and Elizabeth was listed as a witness for the prosecution in Lewis' murder trial in Guilford County.

Elizabeth Pennington Beeson was the daughter of Levi Pennington, Sr., and Martha Mendenhall. In 1790 Levi Pennington died leaving a 100-acre tract of land near William Watkins' residence, two miles south of William Adams' property in Randolph County, to his wife and daughter. The will stipulated that it was to go to his grandson Levi Beeson if Elizabeth later moved from the land.[8] Levi Pennington would have added Elizabeth's name on the will as a joint landowner with her mother Martha, because she had been deserted by her husband, Asahel Beeson, around that time, and abandoned with four children to support. Thirteen years later in 1803, Elizabeth went to court and in an appeal took it upon herself to be declared an "afem trader" in a court case against John Rich.[9] An afem trader or *feme sole* designation would have entitled her to be independent and to carry on business on her own responsibility and account. In court she testified that her husband had gone to countries unknown or was dead. Her case was tried with the resulting verdict that she had a right to law and to sue or be sued on her own contracts; however, she was not given the right to conduct business in her own name, but as a married woman or *feme covert*. This designation meant that her absconded husband was still considered her legal representative and she had fewer recognized rights as an individual. Not satisfied with the outcome in the Randolph County court, the next year in 1804, Elizabeth petitioned the North Carolina General Assembly for a divorce from Asahel Beeson requesting that "hereafter [they] may Acquire and give her the priviledges in her own name to buy and sell, Sue and be Sued, and in every respect transact business in as ample a Manner as if she had never been Married."[10] The General Assembly granted her *feme sole* request and divorce. Had Elizabeth filed for a divorce at an earlier date, when her children were younger, they could have been taken from her as orphans and placed in apprenticeships. Like Braxton Craven, Elizabeth would have understood some of the hardships Naomi Wise faced in life, and she would have had the inspiration to write the ballad. Elizabeth was educated, a feminist, and certainly ahead of her time in requesting freedom from societal norms, and successfully litigated to represent herself legally as an individual, Elizabeth Pennington.

Dr. Harold Meyer, a Chicago physician, came to North Carolina in the 1950s and 1960s researching the Beeson family. In 1960 he wrote a letter to Laura Worth in which he mentioned that it was the first time he had heard that it was a Mary Pendleton Beeson who had written the ballad of Naomi Wise. It is not known if he was confusing Mary Pendleton Beeson with Elizabeth Pennington Beeson, as again there was no supporting documentation in his letter concerning his information, nor any information Laura Worth had collected.[11] While connections such as these are tenuous at best, they should not be overlooked.

Elizabeth Pennington Beeson's oldest son, Levi, who was said to have helped her compose the ballad, was labeled by the county as being "in a state of insanity" because he suffered from seizures. The Randolph County court appointed William Dennis as Levi's guardian in 1806, with Joseph Elliott posting a £500 bond as security.[12] (William and Joseph were the neighbors who had searched for Naomi after she disappeared, and were witnesses at the coroner's inquest and trials of Jonathan Lewis.) As guardian, Dennis would have been in contact with Levi during the time that Naomi was living with the Adams family, and at the time of her murder and the resulting grand jury hearing. By 1808 William gave up guardianship because of the difficulty in dealing with Levi's disability. Levi Beeson was related to George Hinshaw. George's great-grandmother was Ruhana (Lorohame) Beeson Hinshaw (b. 1786), first cousin of Elizabeth Pennington's husband, Asahel Beeson and first cousin once removed to Levi Beeson. Later in life, Levi Beeson owned property adjacent to George Hinshaw's father and George's grand-uncle James Hinshaw became Levi's guardian.[13] Elizabeth and Levi also had a connection to the Lewis family, Asahel Beeson's aunt, Ann Beeson was married to David Lewis, the brother of Richard Lewis, which would make David, Levi's great uncle through marriage.

In 1929, the prominent western North Carolina folksong collector and folk music promoter Bascom Lamar Lunsford visited Randolph County to research Naomi Wise and the ballad about her. Lunsford wrote that, while visiting the neighborhood of Providence Friends Meeting, a "Miss Ava Chamness"—actually Alva Chamness (1862–1931)—presented him with a handwritten copy of the ballad "Poor Naomi Wise," which she said she had written down in April 1883, though she did not know its original author.[14] The same text, titled "Poor Naomi," was also found in the commonplace book of Alva Chamness' neighbor Elma Jane Barker, who had written down the lyrics on January 13, 1881.[15] Notably, the version that both women wrote down, which includes particular romantic and moralizing verses, seems to have originated from the lyrics published by Braxton Craven in *The Evergreen* in 1851 and reprinted in 1874 in *The Greensboro Patriot*.

Another version of the ballad was passed down through the Sarah Pugh Brown family in Randleman, North Carolina. Sarah Ellen "Sallie" Pugh Brown (1887–1966) was the daughter of Thomas Pugh, and was raised in the Providence area of Randolph County. Sarah married

Naomi "Omie" Wise

John Grover Brown (1885–1958). (Her sister Elsie Pugh married Claude Barker, whose mother was Elma Jane Barker.)[16]

In 1915, the Winston-Salem *Union Republican* newspaper printed a condensed version of Braxton Craven's story, and asked readers for their help providing additional stanzas to a ballad supplied by the author of the article, Colonel William A. Blair (1859–1948). As Blair was a native of Guilford County, bordering Randolph County, it can be assumed that his version of the ballad was probably local in origin.[17]

These three versions of the ballad are similar in poetic descriptions but contain material differences in the story they tell. The passage of time and the folk process account for some, but not all, of the variance.

Sarah Pugh Brown Version	*Craven/Barker/ Chamness Version*	*William Blair Version*
"Naomi Wise"	"Poor Naomi [Wise]"	"The Ballad"
Come all ye good People	Come all you good people,	Come all you good people,
I pray you draw near	I'd have you draw near,	I'll have you draw near,
A sorrowful story	A sorrowful story	A sorrowful story
You soon shall hear.	you quickly shall hear;	you quickly shall hear,
This story I'll tell you	A story I'll tell you	A story I'll tell you
Is about Naomi Wise	about N'omi Wise,	'bout Naomi Wise,
How she was deluded	How she was deluded	How she was deluded
By Lewis's lies.	by Lewis's lies.	by Lewis's lies.
		He was so good looking,
		so handsome and brave,
		And to many women
		his promise he gave,
		His horse was the finest,
		his clothes they were new,
		His bearing was knightly,
		his words were not true.
When he first came to see her	He promised to marry,	He promised to marry
The tales did he tell	and use me quite well;	and used me quite well,
He promised to marry her	But conduct contrary	But conduct contrary
And use her quite well.	I sadly must tell.	I sadly must tell,

Continued...

But now he has brought her
To shame and disgrace
Come friends and dear neighbors
And pity her case.

Come all you young ladies
As you go passing by,
Don't you be ruined
By Lewis's lies

He promised to meet her	He promised to meet me	He promised to meet me
At Adam's springs,	at Adams's spring;	at Adams' spring,
Some money to bring her	He promised me marriage	He promised me marriage
And other fine things.	and many fine things.	and many fine things,
But none of these he brought her	Still nothing he gave	Still nothing he gave
He flattered the case,	but yet flattered the case;	but flattered the case,
He says we'll be married	He says we'll be married	And brought his fine horse
It shall be no disgrace.	and have no disgrace.	he had won in the race.
Come get up behind me	Come get up behind me,	Come get up behind me
And we'll go to the town	we'll go up to town.	we'll go off to town,
And there we'll be married	And there we'll be married,	And there we'll be married,
And in union bound	in union be bound.	in union be bound.
She got up behind him	I got up behind him	I got up behind him
And away they did go	and straightway did go.	and straightway did go
To the banks of deep River	To the banks of Deep river,	To the banks of Deep River
Where the warter did flow	where the water did flow.	where the waters did flow:
Get down my dear Naomi	He says, now Naomi,	He says, "now Naomi
I'll tell you my mind,	I'll tell you my mind,	I'll tell you my mind.
I intend here to drown you	I intend here to drown you	My mind is to drown you
And leave you behind.	and leave you behind.	and leave you behind."
Oh! think of your infant	O! pity your infant	
And spare me my life	and spare me my life;	
Let me be full of shame	Let me go rejected	
If I can't be your wife	and not be your wife.	

Naomi "Omie" Wise

No mercy, No mercy,
This rebel replies,
In Deep River bottom
Your body shall lie.

No pity, no pity,
his monster did cry;
In Deep river's bottom
your body shall lie.

"Have mercy, have mercy,
Poor 'Omi," I cried.
"No mercy, no mercy,"
the monster replied,

"In Deep River's bottom
your body shall lie,
"I'll wed another,
I'll bid you goodbye."

This rebel he choked her

As we understand
And threw her in water
Below the mill dam

The wretch then did choke
her,
as we understand,
And threw her in the river,
below the mill dam

The wretch then did choke
her
as we understand,
She fell in the river
below the mill dam,

Be it murder or treason,
O! what a great crime,
To drown poor Naomi
and leave her behind.

Be it murder of treason,
oh! What a great crime,
To murder poor 'Omi
and leave her behind.

The river was muddy,
the water was deep,
And on its old bottom
poor 'Omi did sleep.

Young Lewis rode on
by night and by day,
Her spirit did follow
And haunt him, they say.

Naomi was missing,
they all did well know,
And hunting for her
to the river did go;

Naomi was missing
they all did well know,
And hunting for her
to the river did go,

They found her afloating
Where the waters were deep
Which caused her neighbors
And friends all to weep.

And there found her floating
on the water so deep,
Which caused all the people
to sigh and to weep.

And there found her floating
on water so deep,
Which caused all the people
to mourn and to weep.

102

Continued...

They took her from the water	The neighbors were sent for	The neighbors were sent for
It was a sad sight,	to see the great sight,	to see the sad sight,
On the banks of Deep River	While she lay floating	While 'Omi lay floating
She lay all that night.	all that long night.	throughout the long night,
Next morning quite early	So, early next morning	Early the next morning
A jury was held	the inquest was held;	the inquest was held,
And her good honest neighbors	The jury correctly	And the jury correctly
The truth they all tell.	the murder did tell.	the murder did tell.

The fourth and fifth stanzas of the Brown version are not found in the Craven/Barker/Chamness versions or in Blair's. These lines reveal a sympathetic attitude towards Naomi's situation, adding a moral warning for young ladies. The use of the word "treason" in the Craven/Barker/Chamness and Blair variants is notable in that it insinuates that Jonathan Lewis owed his victim allegiance—although the social norms of 1807 did not dictate that Lewis would have been socially obligated to his illegitimate child. The word is conspicuously absent from the Brown version.

Jonathan's virile appearance and the account that he had made promises to many women are mentioned only in the Blair version. The Blair version also departs from the others in its complete omission of any mention of Naomi's pregnancy. The line "And brought his fine horse he had won in the race" was substituted for "He says we'll be married and have no disgrace." Blair's variant would seem to have fallen victim to lingering Victorian codes of morality. In eliminating references to lack of sexual restraint, though, and substituting a reference to horse racing, the ballad exchanges one 19th-century moral infraction for another. Mention of the fine horse Lewis owned and won in a race has some historical merit. Horse races were common at fairs and other venues during that time, and there were racetracks less than one mile north of the William Adams property near the Centre Road. The "race paths" are mentioned in 18th- and 19th-century deeds, as well as in local Quaker records. They would become a bane to the later New Salem Friends Meeting, located nearby, because of their attraction for younger members.[18]

In his newspaper article, Blair requested that his readers submit any known additional stanzas. Four lines were added to Blair's published version that are not in other renditions, and are inconsistent in verse structure. "His horse was the finest / His clothes, they were new / His bearing was knightly / His words were not true." (The stanza's repetition of the word "his" at the beginning of each line is a pattern not found in the other versions, or anywhere else in Blair's song.)

The three variants agree that Naomi's body was discovered floating in the river. Only the Brown version accurately describes what actually occurred next. "They took her from the waters / It was a sad sight / On the banks of Deep River / She lay all that night." In the other two versions, the body is still floating in the river when neighbors are gathered to the scene.

The Brown, Craven/Barker/Chamness, and Blair versions affirm the very local detail that Naomi was choked and thrown (or that she fell) into the waters "below the mill dam." The milldam mentioned was said to have been built around 1800 when John Hinshaw purchased the property.[19] The 150-acre property was originally owned by Levi Pennington, Sr. In 1782 he purchased and received a North Carolina land grant for the tract. A 1786 North Carolina land grant to Levi for adjoining property mentions the 1782 tract as "his mill tract" suggesting there was a dam there at that time. The property changed hands six times prior to Hinshaw's ownership.[20] This is the same area on Deep River where in the 1870s the Naomi Falls Manufacturing Company placed their 300-foot-long, 13-foot-high dam to help generate power for their new mill. Remnants of these dams can be seen upstream when one crosses the modern bridge on East Naomi Street in Randleman.

All three versions appear to follow the murdered-girl narrative so familiar from such traditional songs as "Banks of the Ohio" and "Down in the Willow Garden," of the innocent young woman becoming ensnared by a dishonest lover, who eventually lures her to an isolated area and murders her. However, other than the moral admonition, likely added later and found in the Brown version—"Come all you young ladies / As you go passing by / Don't you be ruined / By Lewis's lies"—there is no mention or suggestion of Naomi being young or innocent. While the Brown version is the most closely aligned with the historical record, the other two ballads loosely follow the events as well. All three ballads end with the coroner's inquest. The Brown version tells of the neighbors revealing the truth at the inquest while the other two imply that the jury correctly accused Lewis of the crime. These are similar to the Mary Woody narrative poem, which also ends with the coroner's inquest. It also differs from the typical murdered-girl narrative, which often concludes with the apprehension of the lover and his trial and/

or confession of guilt. In several of the 144 other known variants of the Naomi Wise ballad, the murdered-girl narrative theme is followed more precisely, ending with Lewis being brought back to trial and justice, or confessing to the crime while on his deathbed. Stephen Canner, in "Unreliable Narratives: History and Folk Memory in the Southern Murder Ballad," suggests that the requirements of the narrative theme are reconciled in Craven's ballad, since the ballad follows historical events and in the people's mind Lewis is guilty.[21]

Four ballad variants from other areas of the United States offer clues as to the mystery of what may have become of Jonathan Lewis.[22] They are "Little Omie," Flossie Huddleston, Burkesville, Kentucky, 1956, AFC#5781; Alexander Moore, Austin, Texas, 1934, LC-AFS 5781; Hilliard Smith, "Poor Omie," Hindman, Kentucky 1909, Sharp-Campbell-Carpeles, vol. 2, 144–45, Pound, 119–20; Rob Morgan, "Little Anna," Bowling Green, Kentucky 1908, Berea HL-SC, Combs Collection. The ballads mention Jonathan being at Elk River and in prison for killing a man. In 1817 the Lewis family was living near Elk Run in Clark County, Indiana. One ballad, as sung by Hilliard Smith of Hindman, Kentucky, in 1909 not only mentions the location being at Elk River, but names another town with a further explanation.

> He has gone to Elk River, so I understand,
> They got him in prison for killing a man,
> They got him In Ireland bound down to the ground,
> And he wrote a confession and sent it around[23]

The community of Ireland, Indiana, was 65 miles west of Elk Run where Lewis was living.

For many years the survival of the ballads of Naomi Wise was dependent on their being passed down through written and oral traditions. The emergence of the commercial recording industry allowed for the ballads to travel more quickly and to a larger audience. Financial profit was a new addition to the equation, encouraging adaptations to appeal to the audience.

In 1925, 118 years after the death of Naomi Wise, the first commercial recording of a song about Naomi Wise was made, by the prolific Texas tenor Marion Try Slaughter, best known as Vernon Dalhart. His record—which was issued under the name Al Craver, another of his many pseudonyms—was recorded in New York for Columbia Records in 1925. The version Slaughter sang, titled "Naomi Wise," was credited to the early country musician Carson Robison, who played guitar on the record.[24] This version had all the classic elements of the murdered-girl narrative, from her "fair and handsome" face to the confession of John Lewis that he had "killed Naomi Wise" at the end. The music reinforced the song narrative, and what better way to sell a record than to tug at people's heart strings. The popularity of songs about Naomi Wise rose quickly, and shortly after the Dalhart song, Morgan Denmon performed the Robison version of "Naomi Wise" in 1926 for Okeh.[25]

In 1927 G.B. Grayson recorded "Ommie Wise" in Atlanta for Victor records, accompanying himself on fiddle.[26] He chose a version that told of John Lewis escaping justice by joining the Army. Grayson's is the first recording of the sad, slow ballad documented in the Piedmont and mountains that would eventually become the best-known song about Naomi Wise.

The ballads continued to be popular with the public, and in 1929 Clarence "Tom" Ashley recorded one with banjo accompaniment for Columbia records. Ashley's version, while related to Grayson's, broke from the standard murdered-girl narrative with the song ending with Naomi's drowning in Deep River.[27] In that same year the Red Fox Chasers, a group of four from North Carolina who had organized the band the previous year, put "The Murder of Naomi Wise" on a Gennet recording at Richmond, Indiana.[28] Their version, which was based on the Dalhart/Robison version, had Lewis confessing to the murder and added that Naomi's spirit hovers around the murder scene, "to warn some young girl of some villain's lies." In 1938 A'nt Idy Harper and the Coon Creek Girls, recorded the Dalhart/Robison variant with the title "Poor Naomi Wise" for Vocalion records.[29]

The Grayson recording "Ommie Wise" was reissued in 1952 in Harry Smith's *Anthology of American Folk Music*, which helped garner this version of the ballad wider recognition, and in the coming years it became a familiar song in the Folk Revival. In the liner notes, in which Harry Smith gave encapsulated synopses of the songs in headline form, Smith wrote of "Ommie Wise": "Greedy girl goes to Adam's Spring with liar; lives just long enough to regret it."[30] From then on, most versions recorded were descended from Grayson's recording.

In 1959 Shirley Collins released her album *Sweet England: A Collection of Love Songs and Ballads from Southern England* on the Argo label, which contained "Omie Wise," her rendition of the Grayson version.[31] A March 1960 review of the album from *Gramophone* mentioned "Omie Wise" as an American song and said the "mountain murder ballad— is given the dead-pan, faintly sardonic treatment it demands." However, the review added that the accompaniment of banjos and guitars "add an extra transatlantic flavor to the music" that purists might find objectionable.[32] Through her album, Shirley Collins introduced the song to British and international audiences. The *Gramophone* writer's assumption that "Omie Wise" was a "mountain murder ballad" shows how deeply the song had become embedded in the Appalachian-centered old-time music tradition; the writer would no doubt have been surprised, as others have been, to learn that the murder occurred in the Piedmont, far from the mountains.

Bob Dylan was recorded singing a song of Naomi Wise at Riverside Church Folk Music Hootenanny in 1961, and it became a popular bootleg recording.[33] In 1963 Judy Henske performed her own version, drawn from Dylan's arrangement, called the "Ballad of Little Romy," in the movie *Hootenanny Hoot,* and later that year she recorded it for the Electra release *Judy Henske.*[34]

The same year saw the release of the Folkways Record *Old Time Music at Clarence Ashley's: Part 2.*[35] Featured on the album was the ballad "Poor Omie," with Ashley singing and playing the banjo, and Doc Watson playing the guitar. Ashley was reprising his 1929 recording, which drew loosely from the Grayson version. (The album featured a discography in the notes for "Poor Omie," which even at that early date included recordings by 17 different artists.) Kentucky musician Roscoe Holcomb had been recorded by John Cohen around 1961 singing "Omie Wise," also vaguely derived from Grayson, perhaps via Ashley's 1929 recording.[36]

In 1964, Doc Watson released his self-titled Vanguard album, and it was his recording of "Omie Wise," the first song on the second side of this album, that would become arguably the best known.[37] According to the notes, Doc had heard his mother and grandmother sing the ballad, with the exception of one line which came from his father-in-law, Gaither Carlton. Watson's mother, Annie Greene Watson, and maternal grandmother, Mary Elizabeth Greene, were both born in Watauga County, North Carolina, as was Doc. The Watsons' version is very closely related to that recorded by G.B. Grayson, who himself was born in neighboring Ashe County. Despite the choice made by the Red Fox Chasers—from Alleghany County, on the other side of Ashe—to record the Dalhart/Robison song, the fact that the Watsons and Grayson sang the same ballad suggests that it was in circulation in the northwestern mountains of North Carolina in the late 19th and early 20th centuries.

In the 21st century, new recordings of the old songs and newly composed songs about Naomi Wise continue to introduce the story to a greater and more diverse audience. Elvis Costello has performed "What Lewis Did Last," with new lyrics that he set to the traditional tune, remedying what he described as the "dissatisfying" ending that told of Lewis' evading justice. (In a 2001 performance, Costello claimed that these new lyrics had been discovered on a parchment that was rolled up and hidden inside a wooden leg.)[38] Across the Atlantic, a rock band in Portugal chose Omie Wise for their name. According to the band, "besides the beautiful melody, her story is so tragically sad and moving we wanted to honor her memory by naming our band with her name," which, they wrote, conveyed both beauty and aggression.[39] In 2018, the progressive acoustic band Newtown introduced a version titled "Naomi Wise," which was written by Donna Hughes, a native of Randolph County. Hughes' song brought the tradition full circle, back to the county where Naomi Wise died more than two centuries ago.[40]

CHAPTER 10

Naomi's Legacy

In Randolph County, Naomi Wise's story survives in the oral tradition, daily reinforced by the sight of places associated with her life and death. Naomi's memory is preserved on the map, as well as in stories and songs. Beginning in the mid to late 19th century, interest in Naomi Wise rose to such a level that landmarks from her story became tourist attractions.

In the early 20th century, a shelter was built over Adams's spring (referred to as Naomi Wise spring) to accommodate visitors who came to see the spot where Naomi and Jonathan Lewis had their final rendezvous. The area around the nearby ford at Deep River, where she met her death, also became a destination for tourists. Many travelled to what was by then called Naomi Falls, and had their photographs taken at the dam above the ford where she drowned. The original dam, said to have been built by John Hinshaw at the turn of the 19th century, and mentioned in numerous ballad texts, had washed away years before. In the late 1870s, an impressive new 13-foot-high dam made of wood and rock, stretching 300 feet across Deep River, was constructed

Shelter covering Naomi Wise/Adams' spring, New Salem, North Carolina, 1926 (Randolph County Public Library, Randolph Room).

by the Naomi Falls Manufacturing Company. Built near the site of the old dam, it backed water half a mile upstream, running two wheels generating power for the soon-to-be-completed cotton mill.[1] The falls of the new dam made a perfect backdrop for visitors to have their photographs made.

On February 4, 1880, the Naomi Falls Manufacturing Company mill opened for business, and it was dedicated to the service of God by none other than Braxton Craven, who was invited to speak at the ceremony.

The romanticizing of Naomi Wise's story would continue for decades to come—epitomized by an 1883 article appearing in the Winston-Salem, North Carolina, *Union Republican.*

> For very many years it was the sorrowful theme on which the old, no less than the young and romantic often conversed, while sitting around their

Local residents visiting Naomi Falls dam on Deep River, ca. 1900. Photograph captioned "Where Naomi Wise Was Drowned, AD 1790, Naomi Falls, N.C., Wolfe Photos." Individuals identified on the back of photograph are (top left) Mack Stalker, (top right) Lizzie Winningham, (second row, left to right) Nell Spencer, Ed Clapp, Tom Swaim, Pauline Wood. Of the four other individuals, Jim Lineberry and Maude Barker are identified, with no location given in the photograph (courtesy North Randolph Historical Society).

The eastern side of the Naomi Falls dam, ca. 1900. Captioned "Where Naomi Wise Was Drowned, AD 1790, Naomi Falls, N.C., Wolfe Photos." Individuals are not identified (Randolph County Public Library, Randolph Room).

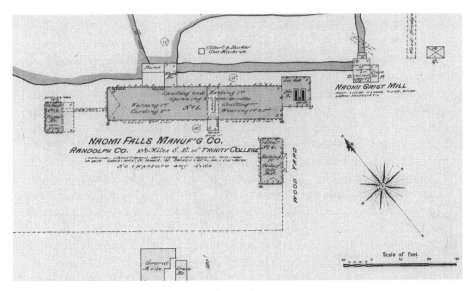

Part of an 1888 Sanborn Fire Insurance map showing Naomi Falls Manufacturing. "Sanborn Fire Insurance Map from Trinity College, Randolph County, North Carolina" (Library of Congress).

hearthstones; while the rustic poet summoning his saddest muse, wrote and sang in melancholy strains the tragic fate of the beautiful Naomi Wise; and sympathetic and sentimental maidens would often pause in their sylvan rambles; look sadly upon the rushing river, hear, in imagination the lamentations of the beautiful Naomi, as they seemed to mingle with the roar of the restless waters, and then drop into them a tear as a sad tribute to the memory of one who had experienced so hard a fate.[2]

In his 1890 book *Reminiscences of Randolph County*, J.A. Blair wrote that the village of Naomi, which grew up around the cotton mill, possessed "all the elements of a prosperous and flourishing village, and the tragic charms that cluster here, the romance of love and murder, the sorrowing sighs of the murmuring waves make Naomi the most inviting and attractive place on the river."[3] Twenty-five years later, a 1925 Greensboro *Daily News* article continued to sensationalize the story.

The spirit of Naomi Wise is the tragic muse of Randolph County.... At New Salem, just off the old Greensboro-Asheboro road, there is a spring now covered with a cupola. This spring has come in a way to represent Naomi Wise and the events that led to her death. The community built the cover and laid concrete blocks around the bubbling water and it has become known as the Naomi Wise spring. No one drinks the water and it is said to be hallowed ground.[4]

The truth is, the water was far from sacred. A gourd dipper hung at the spring, for the use of anyone stopping by. The spring was also a water source for the nearby New Salem Public School.[5] It had earlier been used to furnish water to a tannery owned by William Vickery in the 1860s; however, Civil War deserters stole the lead pipe used to transfer water from the spring to the tanyards, putting Vickery out of business.[6] After the Civil War, a steam mill and tanyard were rebuilt and the spring was again tapped as a water supply. An 1873 deed refers to the spring as simply the "tanyard spring," which would indicate that the later names of "Adams's Spring" and "Naomi Wise Spring" likely grew out of the publicity drawn by Braxton Craven's article.[7] In the mid–20th century, the spring was fitted with a pump and covered with a pumphouse to furnish water for a nearby residence.

Near the spring, there was for many years a stump which was believed locally to have been used by Naomi to mount Lewis' horse on the fateful night in 1807. The stump was first mentioned in 1851 by Braxton Craven, who said that it could still be seen by anyone visiting New Salem. A 1929 Raleigh newspaper article showed a photograph of the spring with an X indicating the stump.[8] By 1935, the stump was said to

Naomi Wise/Adams' spring, New Salem, North Carolina, ca. 1900. Caption on reverse of photo reads, "Adams spring where Naomie Wise mounted the horse and rode to the river—Photographs by O.E. Stuart- 20 cts apiece" (Randolph County Public Library, Randolph Room).

Naomi Wise/Adams' spring, New Salem, North Carolina, ca. 1960. A pump-house was placed over the spring to supply water to a nearby residence. Photograph looking east (Randolph County Public Library, Randolph Room).

be no longer visible, but children in the neighborhood still knew of its purported location.[9] While there may have been such a stump in 1807, it seems unlikely that it would have survived until the 20th century, so it appears a later one may have been identified to stand in as a relic of the story.

Another attraction was created for visitors when an enterprising local resident chiseled a footprint in the solid rock near the ford at Deep River. For a few cents he would escort people to see the spot where Naomi had supposedly stepped just before her death.[10] Bascom Lamar Lunsford saw the footprint when he came to Randolph County around 1929 to research the story and ballad. He wrote, "When I inquired the way to the 'Naomi Wise ford,' a young man volunteered to go down with me to the river bank and show me Naomi's barefoot track in the rock.... I went to the river and indeed found tracks resembling a barefoot woman's tracks."[11] A 1935 article in *The State* also mentioned the footprint, referring to it as a "ghostly footprint" that was "graven in the rocks" leading down to the bed of the river.[12] Lunsford got caught up in the romance of the story, taking a souvenir during his visit. "I visited the old Adams' home where Naomi had lived for several years as a dutiful house girl, and I have at my own home the latch which I took from the door. This is the latch Naomi pulled for the last time the night she met her lover at the old Adams' spring, where she took her last ride behind Lewis to Deep River. I visited this spring and drank from its cool, clear water."[13]

Before the Naomi Falls Manufacturing Company dam washed away, there was a legend, resurrected every few years, that the river was haunted close to the site of Naomi's drowning. For many years she was reportedly seen hovering above the mill dam and over the river near the ford. A clipping from the 1936 issue of the Asheboro *Courier-Tribune* carried a photo of the steel truss bridge across Deep River near the ford. It stated that for years people crossing the bridge at night "claimed to hear sounds that resembled the cries of this unfortunate maid as Lewis threw her into the deep waters."[14]

Today, while some physical remnants of Naomi's story are lost, others have survived, allowing a glimpse of history and life in the early 19th century. The village of New Salem still exists, alongside the city of Randleman. Modern-day New Salem Road generally follows the old Trading Road, which connected the homes of the Elliott, Dennis, and Adams families in the New Salem community area. What had been the River Way is now Brown Oaks Road, Fox Street, and East Naomi Street.

Adams's spring is overgrown and no longer visible, and the site of the schoolhouse on the knoll overlooking the spring, where Lewis waited for Naomi, is occupied by a modern residence. The house where Ann Davis and her sons heard Naomi's mournful screams "fifty perches from the dore" has succumbed to time and development, with a new residence taking its former place. Other houses remain standing, including the Joseph Elliott house, now moved from its original location.

For the nation's bicentennial in 1976, Randleman High School students in collaboration with other local citizens produced the "The Legend of Naomi Wise." More recently, in 2019, the North Randolph Historical Society with the City of Randleman, installed a marker honoring Naomi's legacy at Commerce Square in Randleman, near the street bearing her name.

While houses and tree stumps may gradually vanish, the Deep River is the most permanent reminder of Naomi Wise. The Deep River Nature Trail in Randleman allows a view of the remains of the dams, the site of the ford where Naomi was drowned, and the rock formation in the river where Naomi's body became lodged, as well as the flat rock, still known as "Naomi's cooling board," where her body awaited Jonathan's last touch at the coroner's inquest.

Here in Randolph County, we have never forgotten Naomi Wise. One of our most famous residents only lived here for a few years of her short life, yet it is her final resting place, and our community will forever be associated with her. Because of the global reach of the compelling ballad commemorating her death, people around the world have had occasion to imagine scenes from her life in a small Quaker community in

Marker placed in Randleman, North Carolina, commemorating Naomi Wise and the ballad bearing her name (authors' collection).

115

Appendix A

Dramatis Personae

George Adams Member of the militia; witness for the prosecution at Jonathan Lewis' murder trial in Guilford County Superior Court (1812).

Mary Adams Wife of William Adams; witness at the coroner's inquest into the death of Naomi Wise (1807) and Jonathan Lewis' murder trial in Guilford County Superior Court (1812); her testimony at the coroner's inquest was the basis for the narrative found in Mary Woody's commonplace book.

William Adams Husband of Mary Adams; landowner in Randolph County; employed Naomi Wise as a servant; witness for the prosecution at the murder trial of Jonathan Lewis in Guilford County (1812).

John Allred (d. 1792) Father of Lydia Allred; assaulted by Stephen and John Lewis.

Joseph Allred Clerk of Court for Randolph County (1813).

Lydia Allred (b. 1770) Daughter of John Allred; assaulted and raped by Stephen Lewis (1786).

William Allred Member of the grand jury indicting Jonathan Lewis for the murder of Naomi Wise in Randolph County Superior Court (1807); Randolph County Justice of the Peace (1813).

Obediah (Obed) Anthony (1765–1836) Witness for the prosecution at Jonathan Lewis' murder trial in Guilford County (1812).

Clement Arnold (d. 1842) Randolph County Justice of the Peace (1807).

Whitlock Arnold Member of the grand jury indicting Jonathan Lewis for the murder of Naomi Wise in Randolph County Superior Court (1807).

Enoch Barker Member of the grand jury indicting Jonathan Lewis for the murder of Naomi Wise in Randolph County Superior Court (1807).

John Beard Member of the grand jury indicting Jonathan Lewis for the murder of Naomi Wise in Randolph County Superior Court (1807).

Asahel "Sail" Beeson (1766–1840) Husband of Elizabeth Pennington; abandoned her for another woman.

Levi Beeson Son of Elizabeth Pennington and Asahel Beeson. He and his mother were said by family to have written the Naomi Wise ballad. Levi had epilepsy and was referred to as being "in a state of insanity" by the Randolph County court.

Appendix A

Henry Brown Witness for the prosecution at Jonathan Lewis' trial in Randolph County for escape from jail (1813).

Joseph Bulla (1785–1855) Placed under £50 bond to appear for the State in the prosecution of Daniel Dawson and others for aiding in Jonathan Lewis' escape, Randolph County (1808); named by Nancy Wise as the father of her child on a bastardy bond (1820).

Thomas Caldwell (1777–1859) Guilford County Clerk of Superior Court (1811–12).

Ann Carney (Karney) Witness for the prosecution at Jonathan Lewis' murder trial in Guilford County (1812); bastardy bond issued in her name in which she did not name the father of the child (1802).

Isaac Carns Member of the grand jury indicting Jonathan Lewis for the murder of Naomi Wise in Randolph County Superior Court (1807).

Anthony Chamness (1773–1858) Quaker married to Amy Reynolds; furniture maker; said by a descendent to have made coffin for Naomi Wise; witness for the defense at Jonathan Lewis' grand jury hearing in Randolph County Superior Court (1807); nephew of Martha Chamness.

Martha Chamness (1746–1830) Daughter of Anthony Chamness, Sr. (1713–1777) and aunt of Ebenezer Reynolds and Anthony Chamness (1773–1858); married Stephen Hussey.

Elizabeth Clary (b. 1816) Wife of John Singleton Wise, the grandson of Naomi Wise.

Joshua Cox Member of the grand jury indicting Jonathan Lewis for the murder of Naomi Wise in Randolph County Superior Court (1807).

Thomas Cox, Jr. (1763–1853) Married to Martha Hussey's sister, Sarah Hussey; moved to Ohio in 1807.

Elizabeth Ramsower Craven (1777–1847) Wife of Colonel Joshua Craven; sister of John and Michael Ramsower; witness for the prosecution at the murder trial of Jonathan Lewis in Guilford County (1812).

Joel Craven Guard at the Randolph County jail (1808).

John Craven (1752–1833) Randolph County coroner and Justice of the Peace who presided over the coroner's inquest into the death of Naomi Wise on the banks of Deep River and committed Jonathan Lewis to jail (1807); witness for the prosecution at Jonathan Lewis' murder trial in Guilford County (1812).

Joshua Craven (d. 1847) Randolph County jailer (1807); one of three men who went to retrieve Jonathan Lewis at the Falls of the Ohio (1811); witness for the prosecution at Jonathan Lewis' murder trial in Guilford County (1812).

Amos Davis Witness for the prosecution at Jonathan Lewis' murder trial in Guilford County (1812).

Ann Davis Lived near the ford of Deep River and was a witness at the coroner's inquest of the death of Naomi Wise (1807); witness for the prosecution at Jonathan Lewis' murder trial in Guilford County (1812).

Enoch Davis Private in the militia; charged as an accessory in Jonathan Lewis' escape from jail (1807); charges dropped (1808).

Joseph Davis Witness for the prosecution at Jonathan Lewis' murder trial in Guilford County (1812).

Appendix A

Joshua Davis Found Naomi Wise's body in Deep River the day after she was murdered; witness for the prosecution at Jonathan Lewis' murder trial in Guilford County (1812).

Ransom Davis Private in the militia; charged as an accessory in Jonathan Lewis' escape from jail (1807); charges dropped (1808).

William Davis Charged as an accessory in Jonathan Lewis' escape from jail (1807); charges dropped (1808).

Daniel Dawson, Jr. Son of Justice of the Peace Daniel Dawson, Sr.; private in the militia; charged as an accessory in Jonathan Lewis' escape from jail (1807); charged with aiding and abetting and giving a knife and sword to Jonathan Lewis (1808); tried and acquitted.

Daniel Dawson, Sr. Randolph County Justice of the Peace; co-signer of Naomi Wise's 1802 bastardy bond naming Benjamin Sanders as the father of her child.

William Dennis (1769–1847) The Quaker neighbor of William and Mary Adams; witness at the coroner's inquest into the death of Naomi Wise (1807); witness for the prosecution at the Grand Jury hearing for Jonathan Lewis in Randolph County Superior Court (1807) and his murder trial in Guilford County Superior Court (1812); elected official for the Randolph County Wardens of the Poor when Nancy Wise became ill (1822).

William Dobson Witness for the prosecution at Jonathan Lewis' murder trial in Guilford County (1812).

Joseph Dougan (1768–1830) Witness for the prosecution at Jonathan Lewis' murder trial in Guilford County (1812).

Jonathan Edwards Member of the grand jury indicting Jonathan Lewis for the murder of Naomi Wise in Randolph County Superior Court (1807).

Benjamin Elliott (1781–1842) Son of Joseph Elliott and brother of Hettie Elliott; Captain in the Randolph County Militia (1807); Randolph County Justice of the Peace; businessman and employer of Jonathan Lewis; witness for the prosecution at Jonathan Lewis' murder trial in Guilford County (1812); witness for the prosecution in Jonathan Lewis' trial for breaking jail in Randolph County Superior Court (1813).

Hettie Elliott Daughter of Joseph Elliott and sister of Benjamin Elliott; according to Braxton Craven, Jonathan Lewis was romantically interested in Hettie Elliott; thought to have married John Ramsower, brother of Elizabeth Ramsower Craven; witness for the prosecution at Jonathan Lewis' murder trial in Guilford County (1812).

Joseph Elliott (1755–1819) Neighbor of William Dennis and father of Benjamin and Hettie Elliott; apprenticed Nancy Wise as a spinster (1804); witness for the prosecution at Jonathan Lewis' murder trial in Guilford County (1812).

Samuel Elliott Witness for the prosecution at Jonathan Lewis' murder trial in Guilford County (1812).

Jinny Emery Wife of Stephen Emery; witness for the defense at Jonathan Lewis' grand jury hearing in Randolph County Superior Court (1807); divorced Stephen in 1813 for abandoning her and children.

Appendix A

Stephen Emery Husband of Jinny Emery; witness for the defense at Jonathan Lewis' grand jury hearing in Randolph County Superior Court (1807); was charged with raping an elderly woman in 1811 and fled the state, abandoning his wife and children.

Jeremiah Field Brother of Lydia Field Lewis; witness for the defense at Jonathan Lewis' grand jury hearing in Randolph County Superior Court (1807); uncle of Jonathan Lewis; paid half of the £250 bond (1812) for Jonathan Lewis waiting for his upcoming trial in Randolph County Superior Court for breaking out of jail.

Lydia Field (1762–1852) Wife of Richard Lewis and mother of Jonathan.

William Field Brother of Lydia Field Lewis; uncle of Jonathan Lewis; charged and sentenced in the Randolph County Superior Court to two months in jail and a fine of £20 for harboring aiding and abetting Jonathan Lewis in his escape out of North Carolina (1809, 1811); pardoned by Governor William Hawkins (1812).

Alexander Gray (1768–1864) Lieutenant Colonel of the Randolph County militia; was mentioned as the person to contact when Naomi Wise was missing; oversaw the guarding of Jonathan Lewis while in Randolph County jail (1807); one of the co-signers of Jonathan Lewis' constable bond.

John Green (b. 1779) Married Charity Swaim, the niece of Christopher Vickory; charged and sentenced in the Randolph County Superior Court to two months in jail and a fine of £5 for harboring, aiding, and abetting Jonathan Lewis' escape from North Carolina (1809, 1811); pardoned by Governor William Hawkins (1812).

Vachel Hancock (d. 1817) Captain in the militia (1804); Jonathan Lewis was reported to be at the Hancock's sale prior to being arrested at the house of Hancock's neighbor, Stephen Hussey; Vachel and family left North Carolina in the spring of 1807 and moved to the Indiana Territory below the Falls of the Ohio.

Archibald Harrison (ca. 1781–1823) Witness for the defense at Jonathan Lewis' grand jury hearing in Randolph County Superior Court (1807).

William Henry Harrison (1773–1841) Governor of the Indiana Territory (1800–1812).

Michael Harvey (1786–1856) Randolph County Justice of the Peace; married to Mary Hussey Cox, daughter of Thomas Cox, Jr., and Sarah Hussey.

William Hawkins (1777–1819) Governor of North Carolina (December 11, 1811–November 29, 1814).

Seth Hinshaw Quaker who apprenticed Henry Wise to the hatter's trade (1813).

Martha Hussey (1787–1845) Daughter of Stephen Hussey (1739–1812); married Alexander Underwood (1780–1857) December 1809; first cousin of Anthony Chamness; left North Carolina in spring 1807 and moved to Ohio.

Stephen Hussey (1739–1812) Married Martha Chamness; Jonathan Lewis captured in their house (1807); left North Carolina in spring 1807 and moved to Ohio.

Edward Jones (1762–1841) Solicitor General for the state of North Carolina; prosecuting attorney at the trials of Jonathan Lewis in Randolph and

Guilford County Superior Court; was responsible for the continued push to locate and bring Jonathan Lewis to justice after his escape from jail.

Tobias Julian (1779–1859) Witness for the prosecution at Jonathan Lewis' murder trial in Guilford County (1812).

Thomas Kirkman (1771–1850) Married to Tabitha Field, the sister of Lydia Field Lewis; uncle of Jonathan Lewis; Justice of the Peace (1812); paid half of the £250 bond (1812) for Jonathan Lewis awaiting his upcoming trial in Randolph County Superior Court for breaking out of jail; administered an oath of Insolvent Debtor for Jonathan Lewis so he could be set free from jail (1813).

John Lamb Witness for John Green at his trial in Randolph County Superior Court for harboring aiding and abetting Jonathan Lewis' escape from North Carolina (1809).

Isaac Lane (1768–1840) Randolph County Sheriff; one of three men who went to retrieve Jonathan Lewis at the Falls of the Ohio area (1811); charged with allowing Jonathan Lewis to break out of jail (1808), charges dropped (1812).

John Lawrence Member of the grand jury indicting Jonathan Lewis for the murder of Naomi Wise in Randolph County Superior Court (1807).

Jonathan Lewallen Member of the grand jury indicting Jonathan Lewis for the murder of Naomi Wise in Randolph County Superior Court (1807).

Jane Lewis (1796–1863) Daughter of Richard and Lydia Field Lewis; sister of Jonathan Lewis; said to have been able to handle a rifle equal to anyone.

John Lewis, Jr. (1763–1848) Son of John Lewis Sr.; brother of Richard Lewis; uncle of Jonathan Lewis; charged and sentenced in the Randolph County Superior Court to two months in jail and a fine of £5 for harboring aiding and abetting Jonathan Lewis' escape from North Carolina (1809, 1811); pardoned by Governor William Hawkins (1812).

John Lewis, Sr. (1720–1802) Married to Priscilla Brooks; father of Richard, John, and Stephen Lewis.

Jonathan Lewis (1783–1817) Son of Richard and Lydia Field Lewis; indicted for the murder of Naomi Wise in 1807; escaped jail and was hiding in the Indiana Territory and recaptured in 1811; married to Sarah McCann and had two children by her, Priscilla and Thomas Willis Lewis; brought back to North Carolina (1811) to stand trial for murder in the Guilford County Superior Court (1812); acquitted of murder (1812); convicted of breaking jail (1813) and freed under the Insolvent Debtor Act (1813).

Priscilla Lewis (b. 1812) Daughter of Jonathan Lewis and Sarah McCann Lewis.

Richard Lewis (1759–1826) Son of John Lewis, Sr.; husband of Lydia Field and father of Jonathan Lewis.

Stephen Lewis (b. 1757) Son of John Lewis, Sr., brother of Richard, and uncle of Jonathan Lewis; tried for the assault and rape of Lydia Allred (1786); according to Braxton Craven, Stephen was killed by his brother Richard.

Thomas Willis Lewis (b. 1816) Son of Jonathan Lewis and Sarah McCann Lewis.

William Lewis (1787–1844) Son of Richard Lewis; brother of Jonathan Lewis; was living in the Indiana Territory above the Falls of the Ohio as a hunter and trapper, where his brother Jonathan came after escaping jail in Randolph County, North Carolina (1807).

Francis Locke (1776–1823) Superior Court Judge; oversaw Jonathan Lewis' grand jury indictment on the charge of murder in Randolph County Superior Court (1807).

Catherine Maples Married to Marmaduke Maples; witness for the defense at Jonathan Lewis' grand jury hearing in Randolph County Superior Court (1807).

William Maples (1785–1858) Son of Marmaduke Maples; married to Mary Field who was a first cousin of Lydia Field Lewis; witness for the defense at Jonathan Lewis' grand jury hearing on the charge of murder in Randolph County Superior Court (1807).

Moses McCann (d. 1811) Father of Sarah McCann, who married Jonathan Lewis in 1811.

Sarah McCann Daughter of Moses McCann and wife of Jonathan Lewis; had two children by Jonathan, Priscilla (b. 1812) and Thomas Willis (b. 1816); married Hugh K. Howell in 1817; one known child by Hugh Howell, Tilman Clark Howell (b. 1819).

Simeon McCollum (1795–1855) Married to Mary Dennis, the daughter of William Dennis; apprenticed Henry Wise in the art of farming (1821) after Henry's release from apprenticeship with Seth Hinshaw.

Stephen McCollum (1756–1838) Quaker who was the father of Simeon McCollum; took control of and continued Nancy Wise's apprenticeship as a spinster (1812).

William McCrackin Member of the grand jury indicting Jonathan Lewis for the murder of Naomi Wise in Randolph County Superior Court (1807).

Return Jonathan Meigs, Jr. (1764–1825) Governor of Ohio (1810–1814).

Elisha Mendenhall (1749–1836) Foreman of the grand jury indicting Jonathan Lewis for the murder of Naomi Wise in Randolph County Superior Court (1807).

Harmon Miller Randolph County Justice of the Peace; called upon by sheriff Isaac Lane to view the condition of the jail for the safekeeping of Jonathan Lewis in 1807.

Robert Murdock The officer who arrested Jonathan Lewis at the Hussey house (1807); married Mary Elliott (1810); witness for the prosecution at Jonathan Lewis' murder trial in Guilford County (1812).

Archibald Murphy (1777–1832) Attorney for the state of North Carolina; involved in helping Randolph County issue the proper paperwork for Jonathan Lewis' apprehension in the Indiana Territory.

James Needham (1799–1899) Furniture maker said to have made Nancy Wise's coffin.

William Newby Charged as an accessory in Jonathan Lewis' escape from jail (1807).

Elizabeth Pennington (1765–1823) Married Asahel Beeson; divorced Asahel in 1804 after he abandoned her and married another woman; Elizabeth and son Levi Beeson were said by family to be the authors of the Naomi Wise ballad.

Appendix A

Eli Powell 1st Major in the Randolph County Militia; was with Robert Murdoch when he apprehended Jonathan Lewis at Stephen Hussey's house; witness for the prosecution at Jonathan Lewis' Grand Jury hearing in Randolph County Superior Court (1807) and murder trial in Guilford County (1812).

John Ramsower Brother of Elizabeth Ramsower Craven and Michael Ramsower; thought to be the husband of Hettie Elliott; constable (1814).

Michael Ramsower Brother of John Ramsower and Elizabeth Ramsower Craven; listed in the minutes of the Wardens of the Poor for Randolph County as receiving funds for support and attendance of Nancy Wise.

Amy Reynolds (1775–1829) Married to Anthony Chamness (1773–1858); first cousin of Ebenezer Reynolds.

Ebenezer Reynolds (1773–1824) Son of Jeremiah Reynolds and Susannah Chamness; married to Rachel Green; nephew of Martha Chamness Hussey; charged and sentenced in the Randolph County Superior Court to two months in jail and a fine of £5 for harboring aiding and abetting Jonathan Lewis' escape from North Carolina (1809, 1811); pardoned by Governor William Hawkins (1812).

Richard Richardson Witness for the prosecution at the trial of William Field and others for harboring, aiding, and abetting Jonathan Lewis' escape from North Carolina (1808); witness for the prosecution at Jonathan Lewis' murder trial in Guilford County (1812).

Benjamin Sanders Hatter; named in the bastardy bond as the father of Naomi Wise's son Henry Wise; married Jane "Jinny" Clark, daughter of William Clark and Eleanor Dougan.

Francis Sanders Member of the grand jury indicting Jonathan Lewis for the murder of Naomi Wise in Randolph County Superior Court (1807).

Micheal Shofner Husband of Sarrah "Sally" Shofner; filed a divorce petition to the General Assembly in 1811 accusing Sallie of having "criminal intercourse" with other men.

Sarrah "Sally" Shoftner [Shofner] Witness for the defense at Jonathan Lewis' grand jury hearing on the charge of murder in Randolph County Superior Court (1807).

Benjamin Smith (1756–1826) Governor of North Carolina (1810–1811).

John Spoon Member of the grand jury indicting Jonathan Lewis for the murder of Naomi Wise in Randolph County Superior Court (1807).

David Stone (1770–1818) Senator from North Carolina (1801–1807, 1813–1814); Governor of North Carolina (1808–1810).

George Swearingen (ca. 1779–1833) One of three men who went to retrieve Jonathan Lewis at the Falls of the Ohio area(1811); witness for the prosecution in Jonathan Lewis' trial for breaking jail in Randolph County Superior Court (1813); wife Elizabeth Swaim, niece of Christopher and Mary Vickory.

John Vernon Member of the grand jury indicting Jonathan Lewis for the murder of Naomi Wise in Randolph County Superior Court (1807).

Christopher Vickory (1737–1841) Married to Mary Lowe Vickory (second wife); daughters Ruhamah and Charlotte were married to the first cousins of Jonathan Lewis' mother Lydia Field Lewis; Christopher was a member of

Appendix A

the jury that acquitted Daniel Dawson Jr. for helping Jonathan Lewis break out of jail (1809).

Mary Lowe Vickory (1780–1826) Second wife of Christopher Vickory; hostile witness for the prosecution at Jonathan Lewis' grand jury hearing on the charge of murder in Randolph County Superior Court (1807); placed under a £50 bond and a capias issued for her arrest to be taken to testify at Jonathan Lewis' murder trial in Guilford County Superior Court (1807).

Peter Voncannon Member of the grand jury indicting Jonathan Lewis for the murder of Naomi Wise in Randolph County Superior Court (1807).

Seth Wade Randolph County Justice of the Peace (1807).

Bob Wall Witness for the prosecution at Jonathan Lewis' murder trial in Guilford County (1812).

William Watkins Witness at the coroner's inquest into Naomi Wise's death (1807) and Jonathan Lewis' murder trial in Guilford County Superior Court (1812).

William Wilkeson Member of the grand jury indicting Jonathan Lewis for the murder of Naomi Wise in Randolph County Superior Court (1807).

Joseph Windslow Member of the grand jury indicting Jonathan Lewis for the murder of Naomi Wise in Randolph County Superior Court (1807).

James Winningham (1756–1836) Cosigner on Benjamin Sanders' bastardy bond for Henry Wise in May 1803, and cosigner on Sanders' wedding bond to Jane "Jinny" Clark three months later in August 1803.

Henry Wise (b. 1803) Son of Naomi Wise and Benjamin Sanders.

John Singleton Wise (b. 1819/20) Son of Nancy Wise and Joseph Bulla; grandson of Naomi Wise; married Elizabeth Clary.

Nancy Wise (b. 1798) Daughter of Naomi Wise and unknown father. In 1819/20 gave birth to John Singleton Wise, whose father was named as Joseph Bulla.

Jebedia Wood Orange County sheriff, 1811.

Reuben Wood (ca. 1755–1812) Clerk of Court in Randolph County 1807 and 1809.

Zebedee Wood (1745–1824) Randolph County Justice of the Peace, attorney; co-signer of Naomi Wise's 1802 bastardy bond naming Benjamin Sanders as the father of her child.

Mary Woody (1801–1861) Daughter of Hugh Woody and Ruth Hadley; narrative poem *A true acount of Nayomy Wise* was found in her commonplace book.

Edmund York Member of the grand jury indicting Jonathan Lewis for the murder of Naomi Wise in Randolph County Superior Court (1807).

Appendix B
Transcribed Legal Documents

December 10, 1786

Stephen Lewis, charged with the beating and rape of Lydia Allred.
Criminal Action Papers, Box CR 81.326.2, 1780–87
State Archives of North Carolina (SANC)

State of N Carolina Randolph County.
December Term 1786

The Jurors for the State and County aforsd
upon their Oath present that Stephen Lewis
Late of said county Labourer on the tenth
day of December in the Eleventh year of American
Independence AD 1786 with force and arms in
the aforesaid County in and upon one Lidia Alred
then and there being in the peace of said State
did made an assault and her the said Lidia
then and there did beat wound and ill treat with
an intent her the said Lidia against her Will
then and there feloniously to Ravish and Carnally
know and other Wrongs then and there did to
the great damage of the said Lidia and
against the peace and dignity of said state.
Z Wood -atto-for-St

December 4, 1804

Divorce Petition for Elizabeth Pennington Beeson
General Assembly Session Records, Box 2, November–December 1804, Petitions (Divorce November–December 1804), SANC.

To the Honourable The General Assembly of the State of North Carolina,

The petition of Elizabeth Beeson of the
County of Randolph Humbly Sheweth,
That your petitioner amongst other misfortunes
in life, once had a Husband who lived with her

several years in the course of which time your petitioner
brought him four children; he then deserted his family
and your petitioner and removed to the State of South
Carolina and there Married another Woman.

Since his absence your petitioner has for upwards
of fourteen years by her care and industry supported
her said children and acquired some property which
will greatly assist her in maintaining them and herself.
She further represents that she is now rendred by age,
Hardships and infirmities unable to transact business
as formerly and has of late experienced some Dificulties
in recovering monies which was justly her due, she
not being authorized by law to Commence suits and make
recoveries in her own name _____.

She therefore prays your Honourable Body to
take her case under your consideration and secure to
her such property as she now has or hereafter may acquire
and give her the priviledge in her own name to buy and
sell, sue and be sued, and in every respect transact
business in as ample a manner as if she had never
been Married. Or grant her such other relief as you
in your Wisdom think best and your petitioner as in
duty bound will ever pray. Elizabeth Beeson

North Carolina
Randolph County   We the undersigned do certify that the
          Contents of the foregoing petition is true and pray
          That the petitioners prayer be granted.
          D. Dawson J.P.
          Eli Powell
          Thomas Bulla

April 8, 1807

Warrant signed by the coroner, John Craven, sending Jonathan Lewis to jail
without bond or mainprize for the murder of Naomi Wise. Randolph County
Criminal Action Papers, "State vs. Jonathan Lewis," C.R.081.326.10, SANC.

State of North Carolina} To Joshua Craven Jailor for the
          County of Randolph

I herewith send you the body of Jonathan
Lewis of said County Constable Charged with
the Murder of a Certain Omia Wise.
You are therefore Commanded to receive
him into you Jail & Custody and him there safely
keep without bail or Mainprise untill he is
from thence delivered by a due Course of Law.

Given under my hand & seal this 8th day of
April Domini 1807–John Craven Coroner

April 18, 1807

An order issued by three Justices of the Peace requiring the militia to guard
Jonathan Lewis as there was apprehension Lewis might be assisted in his
escape from jail. Randolph County Criminal Action Papers, "State vs. Jonathan
Lewis," C.R.081.326.10, SANC.

State of North Carolina   To Alexander Gray Lieutenant
Randolph County   Colonal Commt. of the said County

    Whereas it hath been represented to us
John Craven, Michael Harvey, and Benjamin Elliott
Justices of the peace for said county by Isaac Lain Sheriff
that there is a States Prisoner Committed to the Goal
of said County and that he is apprehensive that
there may be some danger of the said Prisioner's
being assisted by some persons to make his
escape from the said Goal it being remote from any
Dwelling—We therefore by Virtue of the power
and authority Vested in us by Act of Assembly
Require you to Order out from the Militia under
your Command five able bodied men well armed
to Serve as a Guard at the said Goal untill
our Next County Court to be held on the
first monday in May Next Given under our
hands this 18th day of April 1807 _____

           John Craven Jp
           M Harvey Jp
           B Elliott Jp

November 3, 1807
Arrest warrant for Daniel Dawson, Jr., Enoch Davis, Ransom Davis, and William Newby being accessories to the crime of murder for breaking Jonathan Lewis from Jail. Randolph County Criminal Action Papers, 1807–1808,
C.R.081.326.7, SANC

State of North Carolina
Randolph County

Whereas Edward Jones solicitor
General & Prosecuting Officer hath give
me information that he has reason to believe & doth
believe that Daniel Dawson Jr Enoch Davis
Ransom Davis & William Newby who were appointed
A guard at the Jail of said County for the safe

keeping of a certain Jonathan Lewis who was
confined therein on a Charge of having murdered
a Certain Omia Wise and that there is reason to
suspect & believe that the said Daniel Dawson
Enoch Davis Ransom Davis & William Newby
hath made themselves accessaries to the said
Crime of Murder after the fact by assisting the
said Jonathan Lewis to break Goal & make
his escape.
Then are therefore in the name of
the state to Command you to take the bodies
of them the said Daniel Dawson Jr. Enoch
Davis Ransom Davis & William Newby and them have
before me or some other justice of the peace
for said County to answer the said Charge
& be further dealt with as the Law directs given
under my hand & seal the 3rd Nov. 1807

        John Craven ___

October, 1808

Daniel Dawson charged with helping Jonathan Lewis escape by providing a
knife and sword.

Randolph County Criminal Action Papers, C.R.X. 240, SANC.

State of North Carolina }   Superior Court of Law
County of Randolph   October term 1808-

The jurors for the state upon Their oath presents that
on the ninth day of October in the year of our Lord
one thousand eight hundred and seven a certain
Jonathan Lewis Charged with Murder was in custody
of Isaac Lane Esquire sheriff of the aforesaid County
in the body of the Jail in said County and that the
said ~~Isaac~~ Jonathan Lewis so being in Jail in
custody as aforesaid for the cause aforesaid in the
county aforesaid one Daniel Dawson late of said
County labourer well knowing the premises and
intending and contriving to procure the Escape of the
said Jonathan Lewis out of the said Jail afterward
to wit on the Eleventh day of October in the year
aforesaid in the county aforesaid with force and
arms unlawfully and knowingly did bring and
cause to be brought and delivered to the said Jonathan
Lewis in the Jail aforesaid One knife and One
Sword to the Intent and purpose that the said
Jonathan Lewis might and should thereby be

enabled to make his Escape out of the said Jail
and that the said Daniel Dawson did then
and there without the license or consent of the
sheriff aforesaid did aid abet assist and
comfort the said Jonathan Lewis in Making his
Escape from the said Jail and Custody of the Sheriff
aforesaid against the peace and dignity of the state.

-E Jones

April, 1809

John Green, Ebenezer Reynolds, William Field, and John Lewis, Jr., charged for
aiding and assisting Jonathan Lewis in his escape out of the state of North Carolina. Randolph County Criminal Action Papers, C.R.081.326.10, SANC.

State of North Carolina
County of Randolph
Superior Court of Law
April Term 1809

The jurors for the state upon their oath
present that at a Superior Court of law and Court of Equity held
held for the county aforesaid on the first
monday after the fourth monday of September
in the year one thousand eight hundred
and seven a bill of Indictment was
preferred and sent to the Grand Jury
against One Jonathan Lewis for the
murder of one Omi Wise a single woman
and that the jury found the said
bill of Indictment and endorsed thereon
by their Foreman a True Bill and
that the said Jonathan Lewis
was then and there in the custody
of Isaac Lane esquire Sheriff-
of the said County on the body of
publick Gaol and prison of said
County—and that afterwards to wit
on the tenth day of October in the
year aforesaid the said Jonathan
Lewis broke the aforesaid Gaol & prison
and feloniously made his Escape there from
And the jurors aforesaid upon their
oath aforesaid do further present that
One John Green late of the county aforesaid
Yeoman Ebenezer Reynolds late of same county
Yeoman John Lewis Junior late of the same County

Appendix B

Yeoman and William Field late of same county
Yeoman afterwards to wit on the Tenth
day of October in the year aforesaid well
knowing that the said Jonathan Lewis
stood charged with the felony and murder
aforesaid in manner aforesaid and that
the said Jonathan Lewis had made his
Escape as aforesaid out the Gaol and
prison as aforesaid with force and arms then and
there in the County aforesaid him the
said Jonathan Lewis did then and
there receive harbour and maintain
and then and there did knowingly and
willfully did aid and assist to remove
and Escape out of the reach of the afore
said Isaac Lane Sheriff as aforesaid
and out of the limits of this state to the
great hindrance of Justice and against
the peace and dignity of the state.

Ed Jones
Sol Genrl

April 6, 1810

Edward Jones, the prosecuting attorney, letter to David Stone, the Governor of North Carolina. The attorney Jones requested the involvement of Governor Stone as he thought officials in Randolph County were not actively in pursuit of Lewis. Governor's Letter Books, David Stone, GLB17, 285, SANC.

To His Excellancy Governor Stone

Sir,

I think it may turn out to the benefit
of the Public If you will take the trouble
to request your Secty to advise John Craven
Coroner of this County by a line directed
to him at this Court House if any application
has been made to your Excellency to procure
an order under the act of Congress for the
taking a certain Jonathan Lewis against
whom a bill of Indictment has been found
some Courts ago for the worst murder I ever
heard of and who has made his escape from
Jail I have heard where he is and suspect
such application may be made not with
intention to take him. Your Excellency will
excuse the liberty I take, my reasons I cannot
now commit to paper.

I have the honor to be
your Excellencys Obt Serv
Randolph County   Ed: Jones
April 6, 1810

May 10, 1810

Governor David Stone reply to Edward Jones' letter of April 6, 1810.
Governor's Letter Books, David Stone, GLB17, 286, SANC.

Raleigh 10th May 1810

Sir,

Agreably to the intimation contained
in your letter of the 6th of last month I have
informed Mr. Craven the Coroner of Randolph
County that no application has been made
to me to demand Jonathan Lewis as a
fugitive from Justice. Indeed I have never
heard any of the case besides what is con
tained in your letter
I have the honor to be
with great respect—& Esteem
your Humble Servant
David Stone

Edward Jones Esq.

May 10, 1810

Governor David Stone to John Craven letter reminding him that no such application declaring Lewis a fugitive had been received by the Governor's office.
Governor's Letter Books, David Stone, GLB17, 287, SANC.

Raleigh 10th may 1810

Sir,

At the request of Edw. Jones Esquire
the Solicitor General that you might be
informed whether an application had
been made to me to demand Jonathan
Lewis charged with a murder in this
State as a fugitive from justice I now
inform you no such application has
been made.

And am very Respectfully
Your Humble Servant
David Stone

John Craven Esquire
Coroner of Randolph County

Appendix B

August 14, 1810

The 1807 bill of indictment for Jonathan Lewis by the Grand Jury in Randolph County for the murder of Naomi Wise (copy made by Thomas Caldwell, Clerk of the Guilford County Court) Governor's Papers: David Stone, Correspondence, GP. 34, 293–94, SANC.

State of North Carolina
Guilford County }
State
vs. }   Ind.d Murder
Jonathan Lewis   True Bill Eli. Mendinghall
        Transfer from Randolph

State of North Carolina
County of Randolph Superior Court of Law
       October Term 1807

The jurors for the State, upon their oath presents
that Jonathan Lewis late of the County of Randolph
aforesaid constable not having the fear of God before
his eyes, but being moved and seduced by the sin begotten
of the devil, on the fifth day of April in the year of
our lord one thousand eight hundred and seven , with force and arms,
in Deep River, in the county aforesaid, in and upon
one Omia Wise Single woman, in the peace of God, & the
State, then and there being feloniously, wilfully, and of his
malice aforethought, did make an assault, and that
the said Jonathan Lewis, with both his hands; the
said Omia Wise in and under the waters of said river
then and there feloniously wilfully and of his malice
afore thought did cast and throw, and the same Omia
Wise is in and under the waters of said river He the
said Jonathan Lewis with both the hands of him the
said Jonathan Lewis, the said Omia Wise, then and
there feloniously, wilfully, and of his malice afore thought
did press down, and hold,
of which pressing down and holding in and
under the waters of said river the said
Omia Wise then and there was suffocated and
drowned and then & there instantly died
and as the Jurors aforesaid upon their oath
aforesaid do say that the said Jonathan
Lewis the said Omia Wise in manner
and form aforesand feloniously wilfully and
of his malice aforethought did kill and murder
against the peace and dignity of the State
       Ed: Jones SolGl

State of North Carolina   Sup. Court of Law
County of Randolph }   Octr Term 1807
State
vs }   Ind.d Murder
Jonathan Lewis

Ed Jones Solicitor General and prosecuting officer
at this court maketh oath that in his opinion
there are probable grounds that the end of Justice
cannot be obtained in this county where this said
prosecution is now pending. Ed. Jones
           Sol. Genl.
Sworn to in open court
8th day of Octr. 1807

Where upon it is ordered that this prosecution be
transmited to the County of Guilford for trial -

State of North Carolina
    Guilford County   Sup. Court of Law
                   October Term 1807
State   Indicted Murder
vs   Transfer Octr. 1807
Jonathan Lewis

On information given to the court that Jonathan Lewis
had made his escape from the prison of Randolph County
the Witnesses bound on recognizance to this county were
discharged.

I Thomas Caldwell Clerk of the Superior Court of
law for Guilford County do Certify the foregoing to be
a true copy of the indictment and abstract of
the proceedings on the aforesaid prosecution. In
Testimony here of I have hereunto set my name and
affixed the seal of the aforesaid court.
this the 14th day of Augt.
      1810.
              Tho. Caldwell Clk.

September 26, 1810

Sheriff Isaac Lane to Governor David Stone. A physical description of Jonathan Lewis, along with a description of the location where he was thought to be
located. Governor's Letter Books, David Stone, GLB17, 313, SANC.

Randolph County 26th Sept 1810

Sir

I have enclosed all the papers that

Appendix B

I think neserey for to send on to have Jonathan
Lewis and William Aston apprehended on-
I take the Liberty of Describing the men and
where they are Lewis is a man under thirty years
of age near six feet high slim maid black hair
and Rather of dark Complexion he is said to live
with his father in the Indianna Teretory Clark County about twenty
miles from the falls of the Ohio his father is a verey Large
man & his name is Richard Aston is about twenty years
of age Slim maid and fair hair Strope shouldered & black
eyes and he is said to live in the Indianna near the falls
of the Ohio and his father is ther & his name is Richard.
Ther is a number of men that went from this County
that is well acquainted with both the men that live
near the falls. any men that shall be appointed to apprehend them
may redely find out the wright men by making enquiry.
I have not Recommended any person to be appointed
as a agent for the state as you will very redely
have it in your power to have some man of Respectabi-
lity Recommended that is willing to go & rid them if they
shold be apprehended.
I am with due
Rest— I Lane

January 8, 1811

Thomas Caldwell to Attorney Archibald Murphey concerning letters of Indictment against Jonathan Lewis being defective. Murphey Papers 1797–1817, Vol.
1, RC 33 Item 4, P.C.12.1, 73, SANC.

Guilford Jany 8th 1811

Dear Sir

Mr. Davis was so good as to show me a
letter you directed to him—I have
had the amount drawn off some time
past but had no good opportunity of
giving it to you I took it with me to
last Guilford County Court and you were
in the Bar. I inytiated giving it to you
I have sent the whole amount in all the counts
together with the amendment made by your
brother on the word as transmited as of ten shillings
for transmission.
I have sent two copies of the Indictment against
Jonathan Lewis to his excellancy Gov. Stone by I. Lane esq.
and all of the copies appear defective—as to the Bill

of Indictment I know that was verbatum the
Original and Mr. I Lane is again making applic
ation for another copy—I know not how to find
Better than I have done already—if you can find
any time at Caswell Court I will take the copies drawn out
and all the original papers for you inspection and
advice in forming a copy of said Record. I am sir
with Respect your most Obet. Hum—Servt.

Tho. Caldwell

March 4, 1811

Sheriff Isaac Lane to Governor Benjamin Smith, request to assist with the legal framework for obtaining the return of Jonathan Lewis to Randolph County. Governor's Papers, Benjamin Smith, GP. 35, 35–36, SANC.

Randolph County 4th march 1811,

Sir

I take the Liberty of enclosing a
Copey of a bill of indictment against Jonathan
Lewis who was Comitted to the jail of said
County in year 1807 on a charg of murder
Comitted on Omi Wiyse and in october 1807 he
broke Jail and escaped & I have not had it
in my power to Retake him since I have
found out whare he is and I got a Copey of the
bill of inditement & applied to Governer Stone
to make a Demand of him from the Governer
of State of Ohiho and on Examination it was
found impurfick & I have got a nother
drawn by Arcbald Murphy esqr. which is wright
I Request the favor of you to sind your
procklemation after him I will inform
you whare he is he is at this time at his fathers
about 20 miles from the falls of the Ohiho on the
other sid he is a man between 25 and 30 years of age
tall slim man five feet 10 or 12 inchis high black
hair and Reather of Dark skin his father is a Large
man six feet high & his name is Richard which
may be well to menshen that the governer may
Direct the officer how to find him Governer
Stone told me that the proper method to git him
was to Ishue a prockalemation to the Governer of
State of Ohiho & that he wod ishue his orders
to a officer & a gard to go and take him & confine him
in jail till he cud wright on to Exceptiture of

this State to appoint a agint for the State of north
Carolina
to go with a guard after him & if he should
be taken you can apply to me or som other
Gentelman in our County to Recomend a agint
for that purpus I trust you not fail.
I remain with Sentiments
of esteem I Lane

B the Reason that the copey of the bill of
inditement comes from the Clerke of Gilford
County Edward Jones atty general moved
the trial from Randolph. IL

March 28, 1811

Isaac Lane to Governor Benjamin Smith, continuation of the request for assistance with the apprehension of Jonathan Lewis. Governor's Papers, Benjamin Smith, GP. 35, 35–36, SANC.

Randolph County 28 March 1811

Dear Sir

I take the Liberty of troubelling you
I inclosed a Copey of the bill of inditment
agt Jonathan Lewis and fored to you with
a expectation that you wod send on to
governor of <u>State of Ohiho</u> & sinc I had
not heard any thing from it pleas to
forward me a line informing whether
you have red it or not & whether
you will set on it or not.
I am with due respect

I Lane

June 3, 1811

The North Carolina governor, Benjamin Smith, responded to Lane's inquiry approximately two months later. Governor's Papers, Benjamin Smith, GP. 35, 35–36, SANC.

Viz

Yours of the 28 of march
was received as also the previous
letter inclosing a copy of the file of murder
found against Lewis-
I deferred taking any procedure
or replying to your letter

untill I could see or hear from a
particular gentleman who I wrote
to consult on the Subject
but having been disap
pointed I now send the answers
requested & have taken
such steps as appeared proper to cause Lewis's apprehend-
sion
your very obd s BS

25th November 1811

Petition for Micheal Shofner asking for divorce from wife, Sarrah "Sally" Shofner. Sally was a witness for the defense at the 1807 Grand Jury Hearing for Jonathan Lewis. General Assembly Sessions Records, November–December 1811,
Box 3, Petitions (Divorce), SANC.

To the honorable the General Assembly of the State of North
Carolina now sitting at Raleigh

The petition of Micheal Shofner of Orange
County humbly Sheweth That he was intermarried
to Sarrah Smith in Said County on or about the 25th day
of December 1803 that the said Sarrah possesed beauty
and art sufficient to ensnare most men, and
particularly an inocent and unsuspecting youth
as was your petitioner at that time. In the state
of matrimony your petitioner calculated alone
on peace and happiness but unfortunatly for
him and to his great disappointment and sur-
prize he soon found what he looked upon as a
blessing to prove a curse—a demon. for dis-
-reguarding the sacred obligations of her marriage
vow—unmindfull of her duties as a wife, and
being insensible to shame—the virtue, or the
benefits of a clear conscience, She gave a look
to the barest Sensuallity and Guilty passions, throughing
off all appearance of modesty She saught Criminal
intercourse with every man who was wicked enough
to perpratrate the crime of Adultry with her.
It was in vain your petitioner endeavoured
to reclaim her from the paths of vice and debauchery
in vain did he offer her forgiveness on a promise
of her future good conduct, for no sooner was an
accommodation of this kind brought about than she
returned to her former ways of folly and wickedness

137

at length She abandoned his bed and board
without any cause by him given and absented
herself for many months, but after a length of
time by the persuation of friends and the willingness of
your petitioner to receive her, She returned to his
house and protection, and thence for a Short time
remained untill instigated by her ungovernable
lusts and wicked desires She again abandoned her
home and carried with her much of the property of
your petitioner which She sold and destroyed; Since
which time the said Sarrah Shofner has lead the most
abomnable course of life and Sensual pleasure, and
obstinately refuses to return to her home and discharge
the duties of a wife Tho often solicited to that effect.

Your petitioner therefore despairing of the said Sarah
ever returning and performing the duties aforesaid
and being anxious to be discharged from a woman
who is beyond the reach of reclaimation, and also
desirous to be secured against the fruits of her
criminal connections with other men, prays your
honourable body will take his hand case
into your wise consideration and after examining the documents herewith sent you, will grant
him a divorce from the said Sarrah or such
other relief as you in your wisdom may think
his condition deserves and your petitioner as
in duty bond will ever pray JB.

Micheal Shofner

Orange County
25th November 1811

Back of petition:

Petitions of
Micheal Shofner
Orange County
In H. Commons
Rejected   4 Dec 1811   Rejected
Read & refered
To the Committee on
Divorce & alimony

December 17, 1811
Pardon issued by Governor William Hawkins for William Fields, John Lewis, Ebenezer Reynolds, and John Green who were convicted of having aided and assisted Jonathan Lewis, charged with the murder of Omie Wise. Randolph County Miscellaneous Records Pardon File, C.R.081.928.11, 17. December 1811, SANC.

State of North Carolina
His Excellency William Hawkins Esquire
Governor, Captain General & Commander in Chief
To All to whom these presents shall come

Greeting

Whereas it has been represented to me that at a Superior Court of
Law held for Randolph County, William Fields, John Lewis, Ebenezer Reynolds
and John Green, were convicted of having aided and assisted, a certain Jonathan Lewis, (charged with the murder of Omie Wise,) to make his escape from
Justice, and were sentenced to imprisonment and fined; And whereas, I have
received sundry petitions, signed by many respectable persons, recommending
the said convicts to Executive clemency:

Now therefore be it Known, that by virtue of the authority vested in me by
the constitution of the state, and for many good reasons, I have pardoned
and remitted, and by these presents do pardon, the said William Fields, John
Lewis, Ebenezer Reynolds, and John Green, of the crime for which they stand
convicted, and remit their fine and imprisonment.

Of which the Sheriff of Randolph County and all others concerned are
hereby required and commanded to take especial notice.

In testimony whereof I have caused the Great Seal of the State to be
affixed to these presents and signed the same at Raleigh this seventeenth
day of December in the year of Our Lord One thousand eight hundred and
eleven and thirty sixth year of the Independence of the United States.

William Hawkins

By the Governor
A. G. Glynn
Private Secretary

December 31, 1811

Jonathan Lewis arrived back in Randolph County. The jail still remained in
a state of disrepair thus he was sent to the jail in Orange County. Randolph
County Criminal Action Papers, C.R.081.326.10, SANC.

State of No Carolina} to the sheriff of Said
Randolph County} County greeting I hear
with send you the body of Jonathan Lewis
how have been a fugitive which has bin
fled from justice on a charge of murder
Committed on a Certain Omi Wise in said
County & for wont of a jail in said
County I request the sheriff or jaler
of Orange County to Receive him in
to your jail & him safely keep until
he shall be discharged by a Due Case

of Law given under my hand
and Seal this 31 Day of December
1811-   Zebedee Wood JP

December 31, 1811

Jonathan Lewis was transferred to Hillsborough and placed in the Orange County jail to await his trial in Guilford County Superior Court . Randolph County Criminal Action Papers, C.R.081.326.10, SANC.

State of North Carolina   To the Keeper of the Publick
Orange County   Goal of Orange County

Agreeable to the within the said Jonathan
Lewis was brought before us the two justices of the
peace for the aforesaid County, upon examination
& we hereby Command you the said keeper
of the aforesaid Jail, to receive the body of
the said Jonathan Lewis into your custody &
Jail, there to be safely Kept untill discharged there
from by due course of Law.
Given under our hands & Seals this 31st December 1811

_____JP
AB Bruce JP

October 1812

Jonathan Lewis acquitted of the murder of Naomi Wise and placed on a £500 bond while awaiting trial for breaking jail in Randolph County. Randolph County Criminal Action Papers, C.R.081.326.10, SANC.

State of North Carolina } Sup.Cot Law October 1812
Guilford County

The State   Recognizance in the Sum of
Jonathan Lewis }   five hundred pounds for his appearance
                           at the next Superior Court to be
                           heldin for the County of Randolph
                           on the first Monday after the fourth
                           Monday of March next to answer a
                           a charge against him and not depart
                           without leave.

The State
    Jeremiah Fields &   Recogizance of each in the Sum of
    Thomas Kirkman }   two hundred and fifty pounds
                           for the appeerence of Jonathan Lewis
                           at the next Superior Court to be
                           heldin for the County of Randolph

To answer_____

I Thomas Caldwell Clerk of Said Superior Court of
Law and ye under my hand and the Seal of
Said Court that the above is a true copy of the
record in the Said Case-
Tho. Caldwell Clk.

August 1813

Petition by Sheriff Simeon Geren to Randolph County requesting payment for jailer's fees for Jonathan Lewis who was confined in Guilford County awaiting his murder trial. Randolph County Court of Pleas and Quarter Sessions, August Term 1813, RCPL, RR, 204.

The petition of Simeon Geren praying to be allowed
the sum of four pounds thirteen shillings & six
pence which was the Jailers fees against Jonathan Lewis
who was confined in the Jail of Guilford County
upon a charge of murder was presented to the
Court. And it is ordered that the same be allowed
& that the trustee pay over the said sum of
4.13.6 out of any monies in his hands not otherwise
appropriated.

October, 1813

Jonathan Lewis charged with breaking from jail.
Randolph County Criminal Action Papers, C.R.081.326.10, SANC.

State of North Carolina
County of Randolph
      Superior Court of Law begun and
      held the first monday after the
      fourth monday in September ad 1813

The Jurors for the state upon their oath present
that on the tenth day of October in the year of
Our Lord One thousand eight hundred and
seven a certain Jonathan Lewis was con
fined in the publick Gaol in Ashborough in
the County of Randolph aforesaid legally
charged and committed for the murder
of a certain Neomie Wise found dead
in Deep River in said County—And
that a certain Moses Smith was at same
time confined in the same Gaol legally
committed on a Charge of Horse stealing
and that the said Jonathan Lewis and the said Moses Smith were

then and there in the custody of Isaac Lane sheriff of said county in the Gaol
aforesaid
And the jurors aforesaid upon their oath
aforesaid do further present that the
said Jonathan Lewis and the said
Moses Smith being so in the said Gaol
in custody as aforesaid for the causes
aforesaid the aforesaid Jonathan Lewis
late of said county former well knowing
the premises but being a person of an evil mind
and wicked disposition and contriving and in
tending to procure the Escape of himself the said
Jonathan Lewis as also of the said Moses Smith
out of the said Gaol afterwards to wit on the day
and year aforesaid in the County aforesaid
with force and arms unlawfully the door of
the said Gaol did force and break by means
of which forcing and breaking of the said door of the
said Gaol he the said Jonathan Lewis and the
said Moses Smith afterwards to wit on the day and
year aforesaid in the county aforesaid then and there
being in custody of the said sheriff in the said Gaol
On the respective charges and commitments aforesaid
with force and arms against the will and without
the consent or permission of the said sheriff and
of the then Gaoler of the said Gaol unlawfully did
Escape and go at large out of the said Gaol and
from the custody of the said Isaac Lane sheriff
as aforesaid in contempt of the laws of the state
to the hindrance of Publick Justice and against
the peace and dignity of the state. Ed Jones
sol. Genrl

November 20, 1813

Release of Jonathan Lewis from jail as an insolvent debtor.
Randolph County Criminal Action Papers, C.R.081.326.10, SANC.

State of North Carolina
Randolph County
On the 20th day of November 1813
before us William Allred & Thomas Kirkman two of the Justices
of the Court of Pleas & quarter Sessions for Said County
At the Gaol of Said County personally appeared Jonathan
Lewis a Debtor confined therein, who besaught us to admit
him to the benefit of the Act of assembly for the relief of
Insolvent debtors & it appearing to us that Edward Jones

the Attorney General for the County & the Creditor at
whose suit he was confined, was duly summoned to
appear before us at the Gaol aforesaid & having not
appeared, the said Jonathan Lewis having No Vizable
estate real Nor Personal, to the knowledge of any person
We the Justices aforesaid Administered to the said
Jonathan Lewis the Oath of an Insolvent Debtor
in persuance of Said Act, a copy whereof subscribed
by him is hereunto annexed & ordered him to be discharged
from his Imprisonment, on account of the debt or
Costs, to the said Edward Jones Solicitor for which
he was imprisoned, given Under our Hands & Seals
this 20th day of November 1813—W Allred JP
    Ths Kirkman JP
I Jonathan Lewis do Solemnly Swear that I have
not the worth of Forty Shillings Sterling money-
in any worldly Substance Either in debts owing to me
Or Otherwise Lawsoever Over besides my wearing
apparel Working Tools Arms for Muster One Bed of Furni-
=ture One Loom One Wheel & One pr Chards & that I have
not at any time Since my Imprisonment or before
directly or indirectly, Sold assigned or otherwise disposed
of or made over in trust for my self or to defraud
any creditor to whom I am indebted—to the best
of my knowledge So help me God-
W Allred JP
Ths Kirkman JP   J Lewis

November 30, 1813

Petition of Jinny Emery for divorce from her husband Stephen Emery. Both
Jinny and Stephen were witnesses for the defense at the 1807 Randolph County
Grand Jury hearing for Jonathan Lewis. General Assembly Session Records,
November–December 1813, Box 3, Petitions (Miscellaneous), SANC.

To the Honourable the General Assembly of the State
Of North Carolina,
    The petition of Jinny Emery of the
County of Randolph humbly shewith, That in the
year 1811 Stephen Emery the husband of your petitioner
being Charged with having Committed a Rape on the
body of a poor Old decripted Woman, fled his
Country and has not been heard of since. Leaving your
Petitioner with two small children in a truely deplo-
-rable situation, the whole of his property being imediately
attacked to satisfy his creditors, your petitioner and

family must have starved had it not been for the
Humanity of her neighbours, who give her relief untill
she has become able to support herself and family by
her industry, she has also out of her small earnings
been compelled to satisfy debts contracted by her
said Husband before his elopement, and as many
of his debts remain unsatisfied every species of property
that your petitioner may hereafter acquire is Subject
to be Seized by his Creditors and may render it
impracticable for your petitioner to support herself
and family. And whereas there is not the least probability
that the Husband of your Petitioner will ever return
she Humbly prays your honourable body to take
her case under your Consideration and grant her
relief either by Divorcing her from her said
Husband; or securing to her such property as
she may hereafter acquire and your petitioner as
in duty bound will ever pray Jinny Emery

Alimony Granted

February 1815

Randolph County Court of Pleas and Quarter Sessions—Costs and Charges for prosecution of Jonathan Lewis for murder and acquittal in Guilford County, North Carolina. Randolph County Court Minutes, February Term 1815, RCPL, RR, 360.

February Term 1815

Ordered by the Court that the County Trustee pay the costs & charges
Attending the prosecution of Jonathan Lewis for Felony when
Trial was removed to the County of Guilford & the said
Jonathan there acquited, and since discharged from Jail
under the Insolvent Debtors Act. The Claim for the said
costs & charges appearing to be in the manner prescribed by
the Act of Assembly to wit -

To Edward Jones Sol. Genl.	£ 1.6.8
To Admr's of Reubin Wood } former Clerk of R. Sup. Court	3.2.0
To Isaac Lane Sheriff	6.0.0
To Clerk of Guilford Sup. Court	7.2.9
	17.9.5

To Witnesses

Elizabeth Craven	5.16.0	Obed Anthony	16.8
William Dennis	4.18.8	William Dobson	18.1

Appendix B

William Davis	4.5.0		Ann Davis	1.17.4	
Joseph Davis	1.14.0		Hettie Ramsower	1.0.8	
Amos Davis	1.14.0		Joseph Dougan	1.14.0	
Eli Powell	4.8.4	22.16.0	Elz. Pennington	1.2.0	
			Tobias Julian	2.4.0	
William Watkins	5.4.6		Robert Murdock	3.7.2	
Mary Adams	4.5.0		George Adams	1.12.0	
John Craven	6.18.10		Samuel Elliot	1.12.8	
William Adams	3.15.6			16.3.11	
Bob Wall	3.1.4			75.9.9	
Joshua Davis	2.18.1			£ 91.13.8	
Joshua Craven	2.0.8				
Ann Carney	3.7.1				
Benjamin Elliot	1.18.8				
Joseph Elliot	1.12.8	35.2. 4			
		£ 75.9.9s			

May 1815

Randolph County Court of Pleas and Quarter Sessions—Costs and Charges for prosecution of Jonathan Lewis for breaking from jail.

Randolph County Court Minutes, May Term, unmarked page, RCPL, RR.

May Term 1815
Ordered by the Court that the County Trustee pay the costs & charges attending the prosecution of Jonathan Lewis for braking Jail and Since discharged from Jail under the Insolvent Debtors Act. The Costs & charges appearing to be as follows. To Wit_____

Clerk fees	1.16.6	
Atto E.J.	1.6.8	
Shff. Lane	0.13.6	3.16.8

Witnesses			
Benjamin Elliott	0.12.8		
John Craven	1.14.8		
George Swaringen	1.10.8		
Joel Craven	1.16.8		
Henry Brown	1.18.8		
Isaac Lane	1. 8.0	9.1.4	£ 12.18.0

August 29, 1815

Orange County, Sheriff Samuel Turrentine requesting payment from Randolph County for the commitment of Jonathan Lewis from December 31, 1811, to October 21, 1812.

Appendix B

County Accounts and Claims, C.R.081.910, Box 1, Folder 1810–1819, SANC.

The County of Randolph
In Accounts With Samuel Turrentine

1811
December 31 To Commitment of Jonathan Lewis £ 0.3.0
      To keeping and maintaining said
      Lewis from 31st Dec. 1811 to 21st } £ 36.17. 6
      October 1812
      To Releace of Said Lewis–   .3.
      To Taking said Lewis to Guilford
      Superior Court With a Guard
      Of Men—& Irons that were never
      Returned—and the Hire of a } 5.0.0
      Chair—   42.3.0

         S. Turrentine

Appendix C

"A true acount of Nayomy Wise"

From the commonplace book of Mary Woody (1801–1861), in the Miscella-neous Manuscripts Collection, Special Collections, Charles E. Young Research Library, UCLA
Donated to UCLA in 1952 by Mrs. Thomas B. Williamson
(UCLA-URL-SC 100, Box 7)

To Such as here and Wants to know
A woman Came Some years ago
Then from a Cuntry namd by hide
In Randolph after did reside
And by Some person was defild
And So brought forth a basturd Child
She Told her name neomy Wise
Her Carnal Conduct Some did despise
It was not long till She another
That might be Cald a basturds Brother
And Being poor and Credit low
From hous to hous She had to go
And labors hard in tiol and pain
Herself and babes for to maintain
The Second Child neomy bore
Into think she a neighbors man Ben Sanders Swore
And now She seems give up to Sin
Too much neglecting grace within
In Eighteen hundred Six the year
She was over come a gain we here
And by a lewis was defild
And a third time became with Child
A Sprightly youth a lively man
Sutch was acounted Jonathan
He held himself of high degree
But too fond of Carnality
Although her case was Surely Sad
The girl it Seems apeard glad

147

Appendix C

That She had known So brave a man
Of So high Rank as Jonathan
She by a youngster was beguild
And pleasd to find herself with Child
And She So Sensless was of Shame
That She inclind to Spread the Same
She Seemd rejoiced and likd it well
And bold Enough the Sin to tell
And with the Scandel So Content
She told it mostly Where She went
Lewis then was offended high
To be exposed far and nigh
For his own Credit Such Regard
he promist her a grate Reward
If She Would keep it quite Conceald
And never let it be Reveald
To keep it Secret then Lewis Chose
And not the matter to expose
To his disgrace and open Shame
Nor bring dishonor to his name
Although Shed Caus to morn and weep
Yet She a Secret Cannot keep
So void of fear grief or Shame
What he Said She would proclaim
All Which inraged Lewis So
He thought Some further yet to do
He did not Choose her for a wife
But threatened Hard to take her life
Its guist he thought Vile work to Try
Join murder Carnality
So Carry on the massacre
And bring about the tragedie
Such tails She told against his Will
He threatened that he would her kill
She disregarded what he said
And of his threats Seemd not afraid
She liked her State So very well
She Still inclind of it to tell
And Lewis then with anger filled
We guis he Thought She must be Killed
She to the hous of adams Came
And Lived a While about the Same
A School hous to that place Was near
She promisd him to meet him there
A mournful Story to Relate
In 1807 date
the poor young woman ded was found

148

Appendix C

She deep River being drownd
The People Thought non more likely than
The angry Vexed Jonathan
Might in a Vile and Wickked fit
The Vile base murded might Comit
And under water force her head
Until he found that She was dead
Now look and See some reasone why
Thou think he made her drownd and die
I think he don't give reasone why
Theyd meet at a School house So nigh
And made naomy promiss well
Of theire apointment none to tell
When he was gone then soon behold
She of the Same to mary told
The went that night the both did go
But did not meet it happened So
Next day he Came a gain its said
And then a new appointment made
He told her then he thought he might
Apoint to meet next Sunday night
And Chargd her that She might Conceal
The mater unto none reveal
But she not fearful but was bold
To mary Adams Soon She told
And mary told her not to go
Least that he might some mischief do
He out of fury rage and spite
To her some private mischief might
Thare was no danger then she said
And seem'd of Lewis not afraid
Was tender hearted She believe'd
Tho by him She was mutch deceive'd
When night came on She took a pail
But to return did Shorely fail
She went with it towards the Spring
Just like She ment to water bring
That seemd a long and tedious night
Not knowing what there happened might
To mary long it Seemed to be
And tedious to that family
And when next morning plainly Came
Naomi wont returned home
Then mary went unto the Spring
And found her not a Shocking thing
But near the Same the pail She found
And Standing on or near the ground

Appendix C

So thare it was with water filled
And mary thought she was killd
And then She did to denis go
And thought Shed Let the neighbors know
about the matter and inquire
What he thought or did disire
Might yet be dun and further Said
There had been two apointments made
To meet there With Some intent
I realy think for mischief bent
And further more She also Said
He has murderd her I am afraid
But denis thought he would not killl
But he persuads against her will
To Sware the Child to other man
And Clear himself So if he Can
A Cunstable then Lewis Was
And Some aquainted With the Laws
A precept had he did prepare
To make the girl the Child to Sware
Before it was born What Could it be mand
Unless he went himself to Screen
Or that it might tend to his honor
to have the Crime laid all upon her
And dennis said or hoped Some
That soon she back again would Come
When mary thus Such thoughts are thine
And thy opinion is not mine
And then insisted he might go
To Joseph Elliotts for to know
If She was thare or had been seen
For thare some time her Child had been
And if She lives above the ground
Some there She thought She might be found
For denis Went but found her not
Then Came with him the said Elot
Then to the schoolhous Both Repair
And found his hors tracks plenty thare
Not many Sises grat and Small
The thought one hors had made them all
He Came and went plain to their Sight
and had Been there in both the nights
Or its to travel took the day
and one towards the River Way
The did Conclude and did agree
that She away must taken be
To tell about naomy Wise

[missing line]
And why on the morrow day
To hast away to Curnal gray
And then before the Curnal Sware
About Naomy as the are
And tell how She was missing too
Let him consider What to do
Which When he came to understand
He give a warent to Command
The Lewis to be taken why
That Justice might be done [?] thereby
But Scarcely home When mary heard
Naomy ded had then appeard
She in deep River being found
And most inhumanly She Was drowd
The neighbors Soon Collected Were
And many people being there
And men was Sent to Lewis take
And fetch him there a prisoner make
The brought him there firmly bound
Unto the place Where She was drownd
Next day the brought him Strongly tied
Unto the Bank or River Side
I guis to Lewis it was trying
For to be brought Where She was Lying
Was guarded here and Where he found
A Larg concors ware standing round
Would not the heart of any been
Much moved and pierced at Sutch a seen
If theyd but think and take a veiw
She was with Child and murder too
And the unhapy Victome See
Of Such a Wicked Cruality
then bound With Cord So fast and Strong
Which to Such people did belong
And then the orders the Ware Such
He Was requested her to touch
And So he did We understand
With a pale face and a trimbling hand
The Crowner then a Jury had
To try the mater which was sad
And divers people furder more
To what the knew the also Swore
And Mary adams did begin
And Swore to what is within
And William Wadkins did declare
That Lewis had been Surely thare

Appendix C

At his own house that very day
And in the evening went a Way
After the seting of the Sun
And he towards the Schoolhouse run
And also Wadkins did declare
That it was not two miles from thare
Ann Davis also Swore and Said
A noise was at the river made
Shrieking and a dofful Sound
In that Same night that She Was drownd
Shrieks Was awful two or three
A moaning then it Seemd to be
Supprising Shrieks a Shocking Crying
As if Some Woman might by dying
Which people Recond Was not more
That fifty perches from the dore
Some others might now mentioned be
Who Said the Same as Well as She
More Witnesses I mintion might
If I to tell it took delight
To them acounts men taking heed
The Crowners Jury all agreed
Neomy then was Carried by
Said Lewis Who had made her die
She in deep River being found
I(n) humanly and basely drownd
Amittance of Carnal gray

charity. Her size was medium; her figure beautifully formed; her face handsome and expressive; her eye keen yet mild; her words soft and winning. She was left without father to protect, mother to counsel, brothers and sisters to love, or friends with whom to associate. Food, clothing and shelter must be earned by the labor of her own hands, not such labor, however, as females at this day perform. There was no place for her but the kitchen, with the prospect of occasionally going into the field. This the poor orphan accepted willingly; she was willing to labor, she was ashamed to beg. She lived in an amiable family, still hers was a hard lot. The thousand comforts that parents can find for their children are never enjoyed by the fatherless. Fanaticism may rave over the chains of the Africans; the pity of sixteen States can be poured out for the southern Negro; great meetings are held to move on emancipation; but who pities the orphan? May the Lord pity him, for man will not.

At the time of which we speak, neighborhoods were nearly distinct; all that lived in the same vicinity, generally bearing the same name. To account for this, we have only to recollect, that most of our settlers migrated from Pennsylvania and Virginia; and that families generally came and settled together. Physical force being frequently necessary for self-defense, such families made a kind of treaty offensive and defensive. Sometimes, however, the most deadly feuds broke out among themselves. Such was the case with the Lewis family, that settled on Sandy Creek. Old David Lewis probably came from Pennsylvania; at least, an old gentleman by name Buchanan, told the writer so; Buchanan was personally acquainted with the Lewises. David had a considerable family of boys, all of whom were noted for their great size and strength. This was in every respect a very peculiar family, peculiar in appearance, in character, and in destiny. The Lewises were tall, broad, muscular and very powerful men. In the manner of fighting very common at that time, viz: to lay aside all clothing but pantaloons, and then try for victory by striking with the fist, scratching, gouging and biting, a Lewis was not to be vanquished. The family were the lions of the country. This character was eminently pugnacious. Nearly all of them drank to intoxication; aware of power, they insulted whom they listed; they sought occasions of quarrel as a Yankee does gold dust in California. They rode through plantations; killed their neighbors' cattle; took fish from other men's traps; said what they pleased; all more for contention than gain. Though the oppressed had the power, they were afraid to prosecute them; they knew these human hydras had no mercy; they dreaded their retaliating vengeance. For these men would follow their children while at work, and whip them from one side of the field to the other; they would compel them to stand in the yard during cold rainy nights, till the little creatures were frozen beyond the power of speech; and sometimes their wives shared no better fate. A fine colt belonging to Stephen Lewis, once did some trifling mischief, when the owner, enraged, shot it dead upon the instant. Anything, man or beast, that dared to cross them, periled its life. They neither sheltered themselves under the strong arm of law, nor permitted others to do so; they neither gave nor asked mercy. Yet these same men were unfailing friends, when they chose to protect. Their pledge was sure as anything human could be; if they threatened death or torture, those threatened always thought it prudent to retire to the very uttermost parts of the earth; if they vowed protection, their protege felt secure. Some of their remote relations are still in this country; they are among our most worthy citizens, but they never tamely submit to insult. Some inquire how such men as the Lewises could ever intermarry with other families; who would unite themselves to such cold-hearted creatures?

While such characters are in some respects to be abhorred, yet there is that about them that has in all ages been attractive. Ladies are accused, because they fall in love with fops, of wanting common sense, and of loving vanity rather than substance. The accusation is false. Except the love of a Christian for his Lord, the love of a woman is the purest and truest thing on earth; sweet as the incense of heaven, soft as the airs of paradise, and confiding as the lamb; it scorns the little, the vile and the treacherous. The tendrils of woman's affection despise the shrubs of odor and beauty to entwine closely and eternally around high forest trees that are exposed to howling storms and the thunders of Jove. The trees may be rough and crooked, but then they are trees. Find a man of great intellectual power, of iron will, of reckless daring, but of unshaken fidelity; in such you find a master magnet around which women's hearts collect by natural attraction. But how can a pure and good woman love a wicked man! Nonsense, thou puritan! She does not love his wickedness, but his soul. Did not the Savior love a wicked world, though he died to destroy its wickedness? Then a woman will love a wicked man better than a good one, will she? No, she will love a good man much the best, other things being equal. But you make daring deeds of wickedness the exponents of man's greatness. I do no such thing. I make actions that require power, energy, and firmness, test of greatness; that such actions should be tainted with evil, is a blot that mars them in no small degree; but still they are great actions, i.e., the products of powerful minds. There are certain philosophers in the world that would make all great actions cease to be great, when they ceased to be good; they would make their greatness directly as their goodness. These are evidently two different qualities, the one measuring the action per se, the other its moral character. Genuine love is as follows: woman loves the power, which is able to support and protect, and if that power be good she will love it the more; man loves the gentle, confiding one that leans upon him with confidence and trusts him with her destiny; if she be good, he will love her the more. This may be grossly misconstrued; but fools will not see, and the wise can see our meaning, it is therefore plain enough. We will hazard an axiom or two while on this point. No woman will or can really love a man who is intellectually her inferior. No man can love a woman that has not confidence in his fidelity and protection. If a powerful man be true to his wife, she being what she should, she will love him though he stain his hands in blood, and be guilty of the foulest deeds known in the catalogue of crime. But this is an unpardonable digression, let us return.

But few of the Lewises died natural deaths. Stephen Lewis was most unmerciful to his wife, he frequently whipped her with hobble-rods, and otherwise abused her almost beyond endurance. Finally by aid of Richard, a brother of Stephen's, she escaped from home and spent several months at an acquaintance's. Richard at length told Stephen that his wife would return if he would promise never more to abuse her, this he promised upon the word of a Lewis. He therefore told him to come to his house on a certain day, and he would find her. At the time appointed Stephen went, found his wife, and took her on his horse to convey her home. On the way, he made her tell the means of her escape, and the agents employed, the agent, as we have said, was his brother Richard. Stephen went home; kindly told his wife that he should henceforth treat her very kindly, but that he intended to shoot the scoundrel, Richard. Loading his gun, he immediately returned to his brother's. Richard, happening to observe his approach and conjecturing the object, fled upstairs with his gun. Stephen entered the house and enquired for Richard. Not learning from the family, and supposing him upstairs, he started up, and as his head came in view, Richard shot him, but did not kill him. Stephen was carried home and for a long time was unable even to sit up, still swearing, however, that when he recovered he would shoot Richard. His brother, knowing the threat would be executed, went to the house one day, and while

Stephen was sitting on the bedside having his wounds dressed through a crack of the house Richard shot him through the heart. It is said that the manner of men's deaths frequently resembles their lives. The fate of the Lewises seems to confirm the fact. They were heartless tyrants while they lived, and as tyrants deserve, they died cruel and bloody deaths.

Chapter II

> ... Like a lovely tree
> She grew to womanhood, and between whiles
> Rejected several suiters, just to learn
> How to accept a worse one in his turn.
> —Byron.

Naomi Wise was a lovely girl, just blooming in all the attractiveness of 19. Though serving as cook and sometimes as outdoor hand, she was the light of the family, and was treated better than such persons usually are. She was neatly dressed, rode to church on a fine horse and was the occasion of many youngsters visiting the house of Mr. Adams. New Salem was a place where the citizens of the neighborhood came to trade, and on Saturdays to try small cases before the magistrate, and to hear the news. The young men frequently went on such occasions without any excuse; their object was to see the fair Naomi, and perhaps have the pleasure of speaking to her. Among those who frequently found it convenient to call at Mr. Adams' was Jonathan Lewis. His father, Richard Lewis, the same that shot Stephen, lived near Centre meeting-house, on Polecat Creek, in Guilford County. Jonathan was clerking for Benjamin Elliott, at Asheboro, in Randolph, and in passing from Centre to Asheboro, it was directly in his way to pass through New Salem. Jonathan, like the others of the same name, was a large, well built, dignified looking man. He was young, daring and impetuous. If he had lived in Scotland he would have been a worthy companion for Sir

Appendix D

William Wallace or Robert Bruce; in England he would have vied with the Black Prince in coolness and bravery; in France he might have stood by the side of McDonald, in the central charge at Wagram; in our own Revolution his bravery and power would, perhaps, have saved the day at Brandywine. He was composed of the fiercest elements; his wrath was like whirlwinds and scathing lightning; his smile like sunbeams bursting through a cloud, illumined every countenance upon which it fell. He never indulged in tricks or small sport, the ordinary pastimes of youth had no attraction for him. The smallest observation would teach us, that such men are capable of anything; once engaged they are champions in the cause of humanity; but once let loose, like un-chained lions, they tear to pieces both friends and foes. The greatest men are capable of being the greatest scourges. Leonidas was a rock upon which Persia broke, but some provocation might have made him a rock by which Greece would have been ground to powder. Dirk Hatteraik was a daring smuggler, that in a low, black lugger, defied the power of England; if the government had treated this man wisely, he might have been an admiral to eclipse Nelson. Our daring, headstrong boys are generally given over as worthless; and here is the mistake; the world neither understands the mission nor management of such powerful minds. Bucephalus was pronounced a worthless animal by the whole court of Phillip. Alexander alone perceived his value and knew how to manage him; and in fact, Bucephalus was the greatest horse the world ever saw.

Jonathan Lewis saw Naomi Wise and loved her. She was the gentle, confiding, unprotected creature that a man like Lewis would love by instinct. Henceforward he was a frequent visitor at Adams's. The dark clouds that had so long hovered over the orphan were breaking away; the misty, dim vista of the future opened with clear light and boundless prospects of good; the fogs rolled away from the valley of life, and Naomi saw a pretty pathway bordered with flowers, and crossed only by little rills of purest water. Her young and guiltless heart beat with new and higher life; that she was loved by a man so powerful as Lewis, was sufficient recompence for the cheerless days of childhood. Day and night she labored to procure the indispensables of housekeeping; for in those days it was esteemed disreputable if a girl by the time she was 20, had not made or earned for herself a bed, some chairs, pots, tubs, etc. And a young lady then modestly displayed her things to her lover, with as much care as modern misses display their painting, needle-work, and acquirements on the piano. Instead of going to the piano, to the dance and other such latter day inventions, youngsters then went with the ladies to milk the cows, and displayed their gallantry by holding away the calves while the operation was performed; they then accompanied the damsels to the spring to put away the milk, and brought back a pail of water.

Time flew on, Lewis still continued as clerk, and had won the good opinions of his employer. Naomi was blooming in all the charms of early womanhood; her love for Lewis was pure and ardent; and the rumor was abroad that a marriage was shortly to take place.

But an evil genius crossed the path of Lewis in the shape of his mother. Her ambition and avarice projected for her son a match of different character.

Appendix D

She deemed it in the range of possibility that Jonathan might obtain the hand of Hettie Elliott, the sister of Benjamin Elliott, his employer. That mothers are ambitious everybody knows, and that they are the worst of matchmakers is equally well known. But Mrs. Lewis thought Miss Elliott a prize worthy an effort at least. The Elliotts were wealthy, honorable and in high repute. They have always stood high in this county, and citizens have delighted to honor them with public favors and private friendship-H.U. Elliott of Cedar Falls, son of Benjamin Elliott, and nephew of Hettie, is a man beloved and honored by those who know him, and is highly esteemed for his legislative abilities. Mr. B. Elliott, Hettie's brother, evidently prized Lewis highly; he regarded him as an honorable, intelligent and industrious young gentleman, and no doubt thought him a respectable match for his sister. Lewis made some advances to Hettie, which were received in such a way as to inspire hope. This was the turning tide in the fortunes of Lewis. The smile of one superior to Naomi Wise in every respect except beauty and goodness; the earnest exhortations of an influential mother; and the prospect of considerable property, bore down all obstacles. The pure love of Miss Wise, the native and genuine passion of his own heart, were not equal to a conflict with pride and avarice. Not but that Lewis, as any other man could and would love Miss Elliott. She was accomplished, beautiful, and of charming manners; an Elliott could not be otherwise. But these were not the attractions that won Lewis. Money, family connection, name and station, were the influences that clouded the fair prospects of innocence, opened the flood gates of evil, and involved all the parties concerned in ruin. Tupper has wisely said that nothing in this world is single, all things are in pairs; and the perfection of earthly existence consists in properly pairing all the separate elements. Two elements properly adapted have a natural attraction, and firmly adhere amid all circumstances of prosperity or disaster; but two elements improperly mated repel each other with natural and undying repulsion in spite of circumstances or calculations. The young instinctively and naturally love those that would make them happy; but pride, family interference and coldhearted calculation often interpose; sordid considerations tear asunder the holiest cords of affection, and vainly attempt to thwart nature's own promptings. Lewis loved Miss Wise for herself; no selfish motive moved his heart or tongue; this would have been a union of peace and joy; he wished to marry Miss Elliott, not because he loved her, but influenced wholly by other and base considerations.

An old adage says, "The better anything is in its legitimate sphere, the worse it is when otherwise employed." Lewis no doubt would have been an honorable and useful man if he had married Naomi; he would then have been using the highest and strongest principle of human nature in a proper manner. In an evil hour he listened to the tempter, he turned aside from the ways of honor and truth; his eyes became blinded, conscience, the star of human destiny, lost her polarity; and the fierce storms drove his proud ship into the maelstrom of ruin. Jonathan Lewis was no more the proud, manly gentlemen; he was henceforth a hard hearted, merciless wretch. He was a hyena skulking about the pathway of life, ready alike to kill the living, and to tear the dead from their graves. He not only resolved to forsake a lovely damsel, but first to ruin her fair name. His resolve was accomplished. He might have foreseen that this would ruin his prospects with the beautiful Miss Elliott; but the "wicked are blind and fall into the pit their own hands have digged." There are many young men now moving high in society, that think violets were created to be crushed by haughty boot heels; that desert flowers should rather be blasted than waste their sweetness on the air; that pearls should rather adorn a Cyclops, than sparkle in their native deep. Not so, ye cannibals. If names must be blasted and character ruined, in the name of heaven, let your victims come from among the affluent and the honorable. Who will pity and protect the poor daughter of shame; who will give her a crumb of bread? The more wealthy victim might, at least have bread to eat, water to drink, and wherewithal to be clothed. Ye fair, blooming daughters of poverty, shun the advances of those who avoid you in company, as you would shun the grim monster death.

Lewis, aware that a period was approaching that would mar all his hopes, unless they should immediately be consummated, urged his suit with all possible haste. Miss Elliott, however, baffled him on every tack, and, though she encouraged him, gave him but little hope of succeeding immediately. In the meanwhile, Naomi urged the fulfilment of his promise, that he would marry her forthwith, seconded by the power of tears and prayers. When these means seemed unavailing, she threatened him with the law. Lewis, alarmed at this, charged her, upon peril of life, to remain silent; he told her that their marriage was sure, but that very peculiar circumstances required all to be kept silent. But before he could bring matters to an issue with Miss Elliott, rumor whispered abroad the engagement and disgrace of Naomi Wise. This rumor fell like thunder upon Lewis; the depths of a dark but powerful soul were awakened, his hopes were quivering upon a balance which the next breath threatened with ruin. With a coolness and steadiness which innocence is wont to wear, Lewis affirmed to Miss Elliott that said rumor was a base, malicious slander, circulated by the enemies of the Lewis family, to ruin his character, and offered that time, a very fair arbiter, should decide upon the report, and if adjudged guilty, he would relinquish all claim to her, Miss Elliott's hand. For several days Lewis was apparently uneasy, appeared abstracted, neglected his business, and was not a little ill. Mr. Elliott assigned one cause, Miss Elliott another, but the true one was unknown to anyone. The kingdom was in commotion, dark deeds were in contemplation, and at length the die was cast. Mrs. Adams had frequently of late told Naomi, that Lewis did not intend to marry her, that he was playing a game of villainy, and that she should place no further confidence in any of his assertions; but the poor girl thought or hoped differently; she could not and would not believe that Jonathan Lewis was untrue. Woman's love cannot doubt. Lewis at length came to see Miss Wise, and told her that he wished not to delay the marriage any longer; that he had made all necessary arrangements, and that he would come and take her to the house of a magistrate on a certain day. She urged the propriety of the marriage taking place at the house of Mr. Adams; but he refused and she without much reluctance consented to his wishes. Time sped on, the last morn rolled up the eastern vault in his chariot, river, where we shall have a nice wedding." "Jonathan, I'm afraid everything is not right, and I feel so bad this evening, I had rather go home and put it off till another day." "No, no, that will not do. I tell you again, you need not fear anything. Just be perfectly contented, and fear no harm from him that loves you better than himself."

They were now on a high bluff that commanded an extensive view of the river and the country beyond. The bold, rocky channel of the stream was distinctly visible for a great distance to the southeast; whilst from the northwest came the river, now swollen by recent rains, roaring and tumbling over rocky ledges, and then moving calmly away. A blue crane was flying slowly above the bed of the stream, whilst amid the dwarfy pines and cedars that grew upon the crags, many ravens were cawing and screaming. This scenery, heightened by the dusk of evening, strongly impressed Naomi's mind. She remarked to Lewis:

"I am almost afraid to be in this lonely place; I wish we were away. O! how happy I should be, if we had a quiet home like yon from which that smoke is rising away over the hills. It may be foolishness, Jonathan, but I want you to be careful in going down these banks and crossing the river. I have so often feared something would happen to prevent the happiness we expect; and I am sure I never felt so bad in my life."

Lewis reined up his horse, stopped for a short time, then started forward, muttering, "I will though; I am a coward." Miss Wise asked him what he was saying, he replied that he only meant they should be married that night. The river was here tolerably wide and below the ford some little turf-islands covered with alders and willows, made several sluices. Lewis rushed his horse into the water, which came up to his sides, and plunged forward rapidly till he reached the middle of the channel, then stopping his beast and turning himself in the saddle, he said to Naomi in a husky voice:

"Naomi I will tell you what I intend to do; I intend to drown you in this river; we can never marry. I found I could never get away from you, and I am determined to drown you."

"O! Jonathan, Jonathan," screamed the victim, "you do not, cannot mean what you say; do not terrify me so much and make haste out of here."

"I mean," said Lewis, "just what I say; you will never go from here alive. You cannot move me by words or tears; my mind is fixed; I swear by all that's good or bad, that you have not five minutes to live. You have enticed me to injure my character, and you have made me neglect my business. You ought never to have been such a fool as to expect that I would marry such a girl as you are. You did not expect that I was taking you off to marry you, when you got up behind me; you no doubt thought I would take you to Asheboro, and keep you there as a base . Prepare to die."

"My Lord, what shall I do?" said Naomi, "You know I have loved you with my whole soul; I have trusted you, and when you betrayed me, I never reviled you. How often did I tell you that you did not intend to marry me! How many times did I beseech you to be honest with me! And after all, you certainly will not drown me. O, Jonathan, for heaven's sake take me out of this river! Do, O do. O, spare my life! I will never ask you to marry me, I will leave the country,

I will never mention your name again, and"—Lewis stopped short her entreaties by grasping her throat with his left hand; her struggles immediately threw them both from the horse. Being a tall, strong man, he held her above the water until he tied her dress above her head, and then held her under beneath his foot until he was alarmed by a glare of torches approaching along the road he had just come. He mounted his horse and dashed out of the river on the south side.

Mrs. Davis lived at no great distance from the river, and had heard the death screaming of poor Naomi. She had heard the startling cry as the villain caught her by the throat; then she heard the wild wail when she arose from the water, and lastly the stifled sobs as she was muffled in her dress. The old lady called her boys and bid them hasten to the ford, that somebody was murdered or drowned; but they were afraid to go; they hesitated and parlied; at last they set out with glaring torches, but it was too late. They arrived only in time to hear the murderer leaving the opposite bank. They neither saw nor heard Naomi. She was already dead, her last scream had died away, her last gasping groan had arisen through the rippling waters, and her body was floating amid the willows of a turf-island. A pure and beautiful damsel, she had attracted the admiration of a cold-hearted world without gaining its respect; her pathway had been waylaid by those who thought poor, unprotected beauty bloomed only to be blasted. Her pure and ardent affections having never enjoyed the sunshine of love, were ready to grasp the first support that offered. She had given her heart to a deceiver; she had trusted her life to a destroyer, and the murmuring waves that now bathed her lifeless form, and rocked her on their cold bosom, were the only agents, perhaps, that had ever acted inwards her without selfishness.

Early on the next morning the people of New Salem were searching in all directions for Naomi. Mrs. Adams had passed a sleepless night; a strange impression had instantly fixed itself upon her mind as soon as Naomi was missed; and in her broken slumbers during the night, she was aroused by sometimes imagining that Naomi called her, at other times by dreaming that she saw her dead, and again by thinking she heard her screaming. At early dawn she aroused the village, and going to the spring, the tracks of a horse were readily discovered and by the sign it was evident that Naomi had mounted from the stump. The company followed the track until Mrs. Davis and her boys were met coming to the village to tell the circumstances of the preceding evening. The old lady told the crowd of the screaming she had heard; that the boys had gone down with the lights and had heard a horseman galloping from the opposite bank.

"Ah!" said the old lady, "murder's been done, sich unyearthly screams can't come of nothing; they made the hair rise on my head, and the very blood curdle in my heart. No doubt poor Naomi's been drowned. O! ef I had been young as I wonst was, I would a run down there and killed the rascal afore he could agot away! What is the world a coming to?"

The company hastened to the river, and in a few moments discovered the body still muffled in the clothing. She was quickly borne to the shore and laid upon a rock; upon the fair neck of the dead were still to be seen the marks of the ruffian's fingers. The coroner was sent for, the jury summoned, and the verdict pronounced, "Drowned by violence." Some one of the vast crowd now assembled, suggested that Lewis should be sought and brought to the corpse ere it was interred. This was assented to by acclamation, but who would do it? Who would dare to apprehend a LEWIS? A firm, brave officer of Randolph accepted the task, and having selected his company from the numerous candidates, for every youth on the ground offered, proceeded to Asheboro.

So soon as Lewis saw the lights coming while he was at his work of death, as above said, he dashed out of the river, having no doubt that the water would bear the body into the deep pools below the ford, and render discovery impossible. We have seen that in this he was disappointed. Leaving the river, he rode rapidly round to another ford, and hastened to his father's near Centre Meeting House. He dashed into the room where his mother was sitting, and asked for a change of clothes. The old lady, alarmed, asked him why he came at that time of week, (for he usually came on Sunday) why he was wet, and why he looked so pale and spoke in such a strange voice. He replied that he had started home on some business, and that his horse had fallen with him in the river, and that his wet clothes made him look pale and altered his voice. His mother had too much sagacity to believe such a tale, but she could obtain from him no other explanation. Having procured a change of apparel, he departed and arrived at Asheboro early next morning. Riding up to Col. Cravens, he called at the door; Mrs. Craven answered the call, and exclaimed in astonishment:

"What's the matter, Lewis, what have you been doing; have you killed 'Omi Wise?"

Lewis was stunned, raising his hand and rubbing his eyes, he said, "Why, what makes you ask me that question?"

"No particular reason," said Mrs. Craven, "only you look so pale and wild; you don't look at all like yourself this morning."

Lewis made no reply, but the flushed countenance which he exhibited, would have afforded no small evidence to a close observer that something was wrong. So true is it "That the wicked flee when no man pursueth." Leaving Asheboro, Lewis went to a sale at a Mr. Hancock's at a place now owned by Thomas Cox. During the day, it was remarked by many that Jonathan Lewis had a cast countenance by no means usual. Instead of that bold daring independence that was usual to him, he seemed reserved, downcast and restless. By indulging freely in drink, which was always to be had in abundance on such occasions, he became more like himself toward evening; and even ventured to mingle with the ladies. For it should be observed, that in those days, the ladies attended vendues, elections, musters, etc., without derogation to their character. And in very many places, a young man showed his gallantry by collecting the fair ones whom he would honor, and conducting them to some wagon, where his liberality was displayed by purchasing cakes, cider, etc. Let it not be supposed that this custom was confined to the low or vulgar, for the practice was well nigh universal. Our lady readers must not think it beneath their dignity to read of such characters, for our mothers, and perhaps, theirs also, have received such treats. Lewis, on the occasion above named, seemed particularly attracted by Martha, the daughter of Stephen Huzza. After waiting upon her according to the manner of the times, Lewis accompanied her home. The manner of courting at that day, was very different from what now prevails; the custom then was, for the young people to remain in the room after the old people retired, then seat themselves beside each other, and there remain till 12 or 1 o'clock. Lewis had taken his seat and drawn Martha into his lap; rather a rude move even at that time, and not a little contrary to Martha's will—when a gentle rap was heard at the door. While the inmates were listening to hear it repeated, the door opened, and Robert Murdock, the brave officer who had pursued Lewis, entered, attended by a retinue that at once overawed the unarmed murderer.

He suffered himself to be quietly arrested and taken back to the river bank, where his victim still remained. He put his hand upon her face, and smoothed her hair, apparently unmoved. So greatly was the crowd incensed at this hard-hearted audacity, that the authority of the officer was scarcely sufficient to prevent the villain's being killed upon the spot. The evidence against Lewis, though circumstantial, was deemed conclusive. The foot-prints from the stump to the river exactly fitted his horse; hairs upon the skirt on which she rode were found to fit in color; a small piece torn from Lewis' accoutrement fitted both rent and texture; his absence from Asheboro, and many other minuter circumstances all conspired to the same point. In proper form he was committed to jail in Asheboro, to await his trial. A vast company on the next day attended the remains of Naomi to the grave. The whole community mourned her untimely death; the aged wiped the falling tear from their wrinkled faces; young men stood there in deep solemnity, and sighed over the fair one now pale in death; many, very many maidens wept over betrayed and blasted innocence, and all were melted in grief, when the shroud hid the face of Naomi forever. The writer knows not the place of her grave, else would he visit that lonely place; he would place at her head a simple stone, to tell her name, her excellence and her ruin; he would plant there appropriate emblems, and drop a tear over the memory of her who sleeps beneath.

> "Oh! fair as the wild flower close to thee growing,
> How pure was thy heart till love's witchery came,
> Like the wind of the South o'er a summer lute blowing,
> It hushed all its music and withered its frame,
> The young village maid, when with flowers she dresses
> Her dark flowing hair for some festival day,
> Will think of thy fate till neglecting her tresses,
> She mournfully turns from the mirror away."

Chapter IV

Though Lewis was confined in the strong jail that then towered in Asheboro as a terror to evildoers, his was not the character to yield without an effort; and such was his strength, skill or assistance, that he soon escaped. He broke jail and fled to parts unknown. Time rolled on, bearing upon its ever changing surface new scenes, actions and subjects of thought. Naomi was beginning to fade from the memory, and Lewis was scarcely thought of. The whole tragedy would, perhaps, have been nearly in the sea of oblivion, but for the song of

"Omi Wise," which was sung in every neighborhood. At length, rumor, the persecutor and avenger, gave tidings that Jonathan Lewis was living at the falls of Ohio, was married, had one child, and considered in prosperous circumstances. The murdered girl rose fresh in the minds of the people. Justice cried "Cut the sinner down"; Indignation cried, shame to the lingering servants of law. Col. Craven, Col. Lane and George Swearengain, properly commissioned, started in quest of the criminal. Many were the sighs and expressions of anxieties that escaped their friends, when these worthy citizens departed. All were aware that the enterprise was perilous. Most of the Lewis family had migrated to the same region, and one Lewis was not to be trifled with, much less a community of such personages. But brave men, especially of Randolph County, sustained by justice, never count the foe, or ask a parley. Having arrived in the neighborhood, or rather in the country, for they were yet many miles from Lewis' home, they made inquiry until they found the circumstances and positions of the families. Knowing that if they appeared in person their object would be defeated, they hired two sturdy hunters for a fee of $75 to take Jonathan, dead or alive, and deliver him at a certain town. "No work, no pay." The three officers went to the town to await the issue, and if it failed, to collect if possible, such force as might be necessary to wage civil war upon the whole offending tribe.

The hunters, unknown to the Lewises, having arrived in the immediate vicinity, learned that a great dance was to take place that night at a house in the neighborhood, and that all the Lewises would be there. They concluded that the occasion would either enable them to execute their object, or at least to make some useful observations; they accordingly rode to the place, in appearance and profession two wandering backwoodsmen. Arriving at a rude fence in front of the house, and seeing a considerable number already collected, one of the hunters cried:

"Hallo to the man of the house and all his friends."

"Hello back to you," said a voice within, "and maybe you'd light and look at your saddle."

"Apt as not," said the hunter, "if we're allowed to see our saddles on the peg, our horses eatin' fodder, and ourselves merry over hog and hominy."

"Ef you are what you look like," said the landlord, stepping into the yard, "and not Yankee speculators, nor bamboozled officers, nor Natchez sharpers, you are welcome to sich as we have."

"And spose we are not what we look like," replied the hunter, "what then?"

"Why, the sooner you move your washing, the better; we're plain honest folks here, and deal with all scatterlopers arter their deserts."

"Well, well, we'll light and take some of your pone and a little of your blink-eye, and maybe as how we'll get better acquainted." So saying, the strangers alighted, and having seen their horses supplied with a bountiful quantity of provender, they entered the house and mingled with the guests without exciting suspicion, or even much notice. They had previously agreed that one should do the talking, lest they might commit some incongruities. A glance convinced them that Jonathan Lewis was not there. The guests continued to assemble, women, men, and children; an old wrinkled-faced vagabond commenced tuning his violin, and the parties were arranging themselves for the dance, when a strong, powerful man entered. His hair was long, bushy and matted as if it had never known the virtue of a comb; his eyebrows were dark and heavy; his step was decided and firm; he wore a belted hunting shirt, in the band of which hung a long, double-edged knife, and under its folds were plainly visible two heavy pistols. His keen eye detected the strangers instantly, and forthwith he sought the landlord at the other end of the house, and engaged him for a time in whispers. Our hunters knew their man, and watched him with no small anxiety, nor was it long until he approached them and said:

"I reckon you're strangers in these parts."

"I reckon we are too, being we know nobody and nobody knows us; and we're perlight enough not to trouble strangers with foolish questions, and so I guess we shall still be strangers."

This answer to his implied question evidently displeased the interrogator; after eyeing them a moment, he continued, "But maybe we all come from the same land, and so might scrape an acquaintance easier than you think."

"As to that, it's no difference, without telling or asking names, we give the right hand to every honest hunter."

"Then you're hunters, I spose, and as we have a great deer hunt tomorrow, perhaps you'll join."

"That we will, if it's agreeable."

The dance passed off without anything remarkable, and early next morning the horns were sounding, the dogs yelping and everything alive for the hunt. In arranging the couples to stand at the crosses, it so happened that Jonathan and our talking hunter were stationed together, and the other stranger at no great distance. The drivers had departed, and the marksmen were reclining at ease or examining their firelocks when Jonathan discovered that he had no powder. As it would probably be an hour or two before the game would appear, Lewis proposed to his companion that they should go to the village and supply themselves with powder. They had no sooner started than the other hunter discovered his comrade to give the signal; he accordingly followed at some distance in the rear. Close by the village he met Lewis and his companion on their return. The hunters exchanged signs and agreed to make the effort; they were fully aware of their peril; for though two against one, they knew their antagonist to be much more powerful than either, and to be well armed. The hunter that met them pretended that he had become alarmed when he missed them, not knowing what might happen, and that he had come in search; then asking about the powder, requested to see some. While Lewis was pouring some into his hand, the other seized him from behind in order to hold his hands fast; while the front man grasping him by the legs, endeavored to throw him. Like a second Sampson, Lewis tore his arms from the grasp of the hunter, and with a back-handed blow sent him near a rod backwards, at the same time kicking down the man that was before him. But before he could level his gun the first hunter gave him such a blow with the barrel of his gun that he reeled and fell; but pointing his gun as the second hunter came, he would have shot him dead, if the other had not struck his arm; the flash of the gun, however, set fire to the powder, that in the melee, had been spilled upon the hunter's clothes and scorched the whole company not a little. Lewis, better capable of enduring such catastrophes than the others, taking advantage of the confusion, would have made his escape, had not the villagers arrived in sufficient strength to overpower him by force of numbers.

Col. Craven and his companions received Lewis bound with strong cords and immediately started for Carolina, nor did they travel at a moderate rate, well knowing that if the Lewis family with their confederates should overtake them, death would be the fate of the weaker party; nor did the hunters tarry in the vicinity, but hurried themselves far away in the western wilds. After Lewis found that further resistance would be useless, he seemed to submit to his fate and become tractable and social; so much so, that his hands were somewhat slackened and his captivity less strict. He awakened no suspicion by asking them to be less cautious, and seemed so much more social than they had ever known him, that his guards were almost tempted to free him from all restraint. One evening, while indulging their glee around the campfire, Lewis, unobserved, untied his bonds, and springing up, darted off with the agility of a youth. Craven and Swearengain pursued, but Craven was ere long left at some distance in the rear. They were now in a low bottom and the evening had so far advanced that Swearengain, who was close in pursuit, could only see Lewis by the whiteness of his clothes. So expert was Lewis in dodging that he constantly eluded the grasp of his pursuer and was now within a few paces of a dense thicket, Swearengain making a spring, struck Lewis with a blow so effectual that it felled him to the earth, and before he could regain his feet, he was overpowered by both his pursuers.

Lewis was finally brought to Randolph, from which county his trial was moved to Guilford, where he was finally tried and acquitted. Most of the material witnesses had died or moved away, and much of the minutiae was forgotten. After his release he returned to Kentucky, and died in a few years afterwards. After all hope of his recovery was given up, and his friends watched round his couch only to perform the last sad offices of life, he still lingered. He seemed to suffer beyond human conception; the contortions of his face were too horrid for human gaze; his groans were appalling to the ear. For two days the death rattle had been in his throat, and yet he retained his reason and speech. Finally he bid every person leave the room but his father, and to him he confessed all the circumstances we have detailed. He declared that while in prison Naomi was ever before him; his sleep was broken by her cries for mercy, and in the dim twilight her shadowy form was ever before him, holding up her imploring hands. Thus ended the career of Jonathan Lewis, for no sooner was his confession completed than his soul seemed to hasten away.

The following is the song so well known in this county as:

POOR NAOMI

Come all you good people, I'd have you draw near.
A sorrowful story you quickly shall hear;
A story I'll tell you about N'omi Wise,
How she was deluded by Lewis's lies.

Appendix D

He promised to marry, and use me quite well;
But conduct contrary I sadly must tell,
He promised to meet me at Adams's spring;
He promised me marriage and many fine things.

Still nothing he gave but yet flattered the case;
He says, we'll be married and have no disgrace.
Come get up behind me, we'll go up to town,
And there we'll be married, in union be bound.

I got up behind him and straightway did go,
To the banks of Deep river, where the water did flow.
He says now Naomi, I'll tell you my mind,
I intend here to drown you and leave you behind.

O! pity your infant and spare me my life;
Let me go rejected and be not your wife.
No pity, no pity, this monster did cry;
In Deep river's bottom your body shall lie.

The wretch then did choke her, as we understand,
And threw her in the river, below the milldam.
Be it murder or treason, O! what a great crime,
To drown poor Naomi and leave her behind.

Naomi was missing, they all did well know,
And hunting for her to the river did go;
And there found her floating on the water so deep,
Which caused all the people to sigh and to weep.

The neighbors were sent for to see the great sight,
While she lay floating all that long night.
So early next morning the inquest was held;
The jury correctly the murder did tell.

Note—It is said that in the dusk of evening, the following little song may
be heard about the river in accents sweet as angels sing:

Beneath these crystal waters,
A maiden once did lie;
The fairest of earth's daughters,
A gem to deck the sky.
In caves of pearled enamels,
We weave a maiden's shroud,
For all the foolish damsels,
That dared to stray abroad.
We live in rolling billows;
We float upon the mist;
We sing on foamy pillows,
"Poor N'omi of the past."

Appendix E
Naomi Wise Recordings and Discography

Recordings

Adams, Finley, "Omie Wise" (AFS 02796 B01, 1939).

Buchanan, Mrs. W.R., "Little Omie Wise" (AFS 02857 B03, 1939).

Cullipher, Ruth Clark, "Little Onie" (AFS 01031 A01, 1937).

Dyson, Mary Jane, "Poor Omie Wise" (WVU, #58, XIV, XVII, L-F4, 15-D, Disc 432, 1940).

Floyd, Minnie, "Naomi Wise" (AAFS 1301 A1, 1937).

Franklin, Cleophas, "Omie Wise" (AFS 02891 B2, 1939).

Gatts, Thomas, "Laomie" (Penn, 183, Bayard, S.P., T-82–00003–168–183).

Hagie, Mrs. Lloyd Bare, "Omie Wise" (AFS 02852 A02, 1939).

Hamilton, Goldie, "Little Omie Wise" (AFS 02829 A01, 1939).

Huff, A.J., "Omie Wise" (AFS 02877 B3, 1939).

Ison, Sarah, "Little Omie Wise" (AFS 02810 B01, 1939).

Jackson, Aunt Molly, "Oma Wise" (AFS 00824 B02, 1935).

Jackson, Aunt Molly, "Oma Wise" (AFS 03340 B02, 1939).

Johnson, Polly, "Poor Omie" (AFS 02760 A04, 1939).

Kilgore, Mrs. Esco, "Oma Wise" (AFS 02776 A02, 1939).

Kirkheart, Alexander, "Naomi Wise" (AAFS1700 A1, 1938).

Lunsford, Bascom Lamar, "Poor Naomi Wise" (AFS 01824 A, 1935).

Lunsford, Bascom Lamar, "Naomi Wise" (AFS 09507 B02, 1949).

Moore, Alec, "Poor Omie Wise" (AFS 00057 B01, 1934).

Price, Orrin, "Omie Wise" (AFS 07875 B01, 1943).

Reynolds, Mrs. Mary, "Naomie Wise" (WVU, #38, XIV, XVII, L-F31,6-D, Disc 284, 1939).

Shepherd, Johanna, "Omie Wise" (AFS 01405 B02, 1937).

Short, Lillian, "Naomi Wise" (AFS 05281 B01, 1941).

Sibert, Della, "Omie Wise" (AFS 01486 A02, 1937).

Temple, Lafayette Parker "Pick," "Naomi Wise" (AFS 08857 A01, 1945).

Temple, Lafayette Parker "Pick," "Naomi Wise" (AFS 08859 A03, 1947).

Wallace, Allie, and Virgie Wallace, "Little Omie Wise" (MSS 9936 Virginia Folklore Society records, 1932).

Wilson, Addina Palmore, "Omie Wise" (AFC1943023_6720B3, 1942)

Appendix E

Discography[*]

Vernon Dalhart (as Al Craver), "Naomi Wise" (Columbia 15053, November 24, 1925, New York City, 78RPM, U.S.).

Morgan Denmon, "Naomi Wise" (Okeh 45075, 78 RPM, October 1, 1926, Atlanta, Georgia, U.S.).

G.B. Grayson, "Ommie Wise" (Victor 21625, 78 RPM, October 18, 1927, Atlanta, Georgia, U.S.).

Cranford and Thompson (Red Fox Chasers), "Naomi Wise" (Gennett 6945, 78 RPM, June 13, 1929, Richmond, Indiana, U.S.).

Clarence Ashley, "Naomi Wise" (Columbia 15522, 78 RPM, 10", October 23, 1929, Johnson City, Tennessee, U.S.).

A'nt Idy Harper and the Coon Creek Girls, "Poor Naomi Wise" (Vocalion 04354, 78 RPM, May 30, 1938, Chicago, Illinois, U.S.).

Lillian Short, "Naomi Wise," *Folk Music of the United States, Album XII— Anglo-American Songs and Ballads* (Library of Congress AFS; on LC12, 78 RPM, 1947, U.S.).

G.B. Grayson, "Ommie Wise," *Anthology of American Folk Music Volume One: Ballads* (Folkways Records FP 251, Vinyl, LP, 1952, U.S. [Reissue of Victor 21625]).

Ed McCurdy, "Naomi Wise," *The Ballad Record* (Riverside RLP 12 601, Vinyl, LP, 1955, U.S.).

Ellen Stekert, "Omie Wise," *Ballads of Careless Love* (Cornell Recording Society CRS-10050, Vinyl, LP, 1956, U.S. & Canada).

Paul Clayton, "Naomi Wise," *Folk Ballads of the English-Speaking World* (Folkways Records FA 2310, Vinyl, LP, 1956, U.S.).

Cynthia Gooding, "Naomi Wise," *Faithful Lovers and Other Phenomena* (Elektra EKL-107, Vinyl, LP, 1957, U.S.).

Shirley Collins, "Omie Wise," *Sweet England: A Collection of Love Songs and Ballads from Southern England* (Argo Records RG 150, Vinyl, LP, 1959, UK).

Pete Brady and the Blazers, "Naomi Wise," *Murder Ballads* (ABC-Paramount ABC 310, Vinyl, LP, 1960, U.S.).

Obray Ramsey, "Omie Wise," *Obray Ramsey Sings Folksongs from the Three Laurels* (Prestige International INT 13020, Vinyl, LP, 1961, U.S.).

Pick Temple, "Naomi Wise," *The Pick of the Crop* (Prestige International INT 13008, Vinyl, LP, 1961, U.S.).

Clarence Ashley and Doc Watson, "Poor Omie," *Old Time Music at Clarence Ashley's—Part 2* (Folkways FA 2359, Vinyl, LP, 1962, U.S.).

Miss Judy Henske, "Ballad of Little Romy," *Judy Henske* (Elektra EKL-231, Vinyl, LP, 1963, U.S.).

Doc Watson, "Omie Wise," *Doc Watson* (Vanguard VSD 79152, Vinyl, LP, 1964, U.S.).

Roscoe Holcomb, "Omie Wise," *The High Lonesome Sound* (Folkways FA 2368, Vinyl, LP, 1965, U.S.).

---

[*]Arranged chronologically.

Appendix E

Dale Potter, "Omie Wise's Tragic Romance," *Hoe Down! Volume 1—Dale Potter* (Rural Rhythm Records RRDP 179, Vinyl, LP, 1967, U.S.).

Dock Boggs, "Little Ommie Wise," *Dock Boggs—Vol. 3* (Asch Recordings AH 3903, Vinyl, LP, 1970, U.S.).

Pentangle, "Omie Wise," *Reflection* (Transatlantic TRA 240, Vinyl, LP, 1971, UK).

Alex Campbell, "Naomi Wise," *This Is Alex Campbell, Vol. 2* (Ad-Rhythm ARPS-2, Vinyl, LP, 1971, UK).

Iron Mountain String Band, "Omie Wise," *An Old Time Southern Mountain String Band* (Folkways FA 2473, Vinyl, LP, 1973, U.S.).

Kelvin Henderson's Country Band, "Omie Wise," *Kelvin Henderson's Country Band* (Westwood Recordings WRS045, Vinyl, LP, 1974, UK).

Betty Smith, "Omie Wise," *Songs Traditionally Sung in North Carolina* (Folk-Legacy Records FSA 53, Vinyl, LP, 1975, U.S.).

John McCutcheon, "Omie Wise," *How Can I Keep from Singing?* (June Appal Recordings JA 003, Vinyl, LP, 1975, U.S.).

Jade, "Omie Wise," *Jade* (Not on Label PRA 824, Vinyl, LP, 1974, New Zealand).

Michael Melford, "Omie Wise," *Mandolin Fantasy* (Flying Fish 023, Vinyl, LP, 1976, U.S.).

Dolly Greer, "Omie Wise," *The Watson Family Tradition* (Topic Records 12 TS 336, Vinyl, LP, 1977, U.S.).

Addie Graham, "Omie Wise," *Been a Long Time Traveling* (June Appal Recordings JA 020, Vinyl, LP, 1978, U.S.).

Le Chéile, "Omie Wise," *Aris* (Inchecronin Records INC 7423, Vinyl, LP, 1978, UK).

Farmers Union, "Omie Wise," *Reunion* (Universe Productions LS-15, Vinyl, LP, 1978, Netherlands).

Clay Jones with Gail Gillespie Rogers, "Oma Wise," *Simple Gifts for the Dulcimer* (Sunny Mountain Records EB 1009, Vinyl, LP, 1979, U.S.).

Charlie Osborne, "Omie Wise," *Relics & Treasure* (June Appal Recordings JA049, Vinyl, LP, 1985, U.S.).

Morgan Sexton, "Omie Wise," *Rockdust* (June Appal Recordings JA0055, Vinyl, LP, 1989, U.S.).

Doc Watson and Family, "Omie Wise," *Treasures Untold* (Vanguard VCD 77001, CD, 1991, U.S.).

Doc and Merle Watson, "Omie Wise," *Remembering Merle* (Sugar Hill SH CD 3800, CD, 1992, U.S.).

Frank Proffitt, Jr., "Omie Wise," *Kickin' Up Dust* (Cloudlands CLC008, C-5489, Cassette, 1992, U.S.).

Atwater and Donnelly, "Omie Wise," *Like the Willow Tree* (Beacon Records BCN 10133–2, CD, 1994, U.S.).

Beacon Hillbillies, "Omie Wise," *More Songs of Love and Murder* (East Side Digital ESD 80882, CD, 1994, U.S.).

Bill Evans, "Omie Wise," *Native and Fine* (Rounder CD 0295, CD, 1995, U.S.).

Doug Wallin, "Omie Wise," *Family Songs and Stories from the North Carolina Mountains* (Smithsonian Folkways Recordings SF CD 40013, CD, 1995, U.S.).

Appendix E

The Rufus Crisp Experience, "Omie Wise," *Chickens Are A-Crowing* (Fellside Recordings, FECD113, CD, 1997, UK).

Carol Ponder, "Omie Wise," *Pretty Bird—A Cappella Ballads in the Southern Mountain Tradition* (Self-released EAN 06 6191 67001 2 7, CD, 1998, U.S.).

The Backstabbers, "Omie Wise," *The Backstabbers Country Stringband* (Run Mountain Records RMR 001, CD, 2000, Canada).

Burt Jansch, "Omie Wise," *Crimson Moon* (Castle Music CMAR683, CD, 2000, U.S.).

Debra Cowan, Acie Cargill, Susan Brown with Kristina Olsen, Ellen and John Wright, "Omie Wise," *The Songs and Ballads of Hattie Mae Tyler Cargill* (Folk-Legacy Records CD-128, CD, 2001, U.S.).

Wizz Jones, "Omie Wise," *Lucky the Man* (Scenescof SCOFLP1009, CD, 2001, U.S.).

Dyad, "Omie Wise," *Who's Been Here Since I've Been Gone* (Dyad Self-released CPS 724, CD, 2002, Canada).

Peggy Seeger, "Oma Wise," *Heading for Home* (Appleseed Recordings APR CD 1076, CD, 2003, U.S.).

Julie Doiron / Okkervil River, "Omie Wise," *Julie Doiron / Okkervil River* (Acuarela Discos-nois 1033, CD, 2003, Spain).

Tim Eriksen, "Omie Wise," *Every Sound Below* (Appleseed Recordings APR CD 1080, CD, 2004, U.S.).

The Lonesome Sisters, "Omie Wise," *The Lonesome Sisters* (Tin Halo Music EAN 08 2975 77432 2 6, CD, 2004, U.S.).

Rewolfinger, "Omie Wise," *In the Beginning* (Not On Label EP 2005, CD, 2005, Austria).

Emily Miller and Val Mindel, "Omie Wise," *In the Valley* (Yodel-Ay-Hee CD-0070, CD, 2006, U.S.).

Greg Graffin, "Omie Wise," *Cold as the Clay* (Anti–6809 2, CD, 2006, Australia).

Bruce Greene and Kore Loy McWhirter, "Omie Wise," *Come Near My Love (Mostly Quiet & Dark Songs)* (Hazeldog 507, CD, 2006, U.S.).

Kate and Anna McGarrigle with Elvis Costello, "Ommie Wise Part 1 & 2 (What Lewis Did Last...)." *The Harry Smith Project—Anthology of American Folk Music Revisited* (Shout! Factory 826663–10041, CD, 2006, U.S.).

Mountain Home, "Omie Wise," *Mountain Home* (Language of Stone LOS-002, CD, 2007, U.S.).

Mason Brown, "Omie Wise," *When Humans Walked the Earth* (Round Shining EAN 06 3942 90820 2 3, CD, 2008, U.S.).

Addie Graham, "Omie Wise," *Been a Long Time Traveling* (June Appal Recordings 0020D, CD, 2008, U.S.; reissue of JA 020, 1978).

Tom Godleski, "Little Omie Wise," *Fresh Preserves* (Not on label, CD, 2008, U.S.).

Tim Eriksen, "Omie Wise," *Northern Roots Live in Náměšť* (Indies Scope MAM451-2, CD, 2009, Czech Republic).

Emily Miller and Val Mindel, "Omie Wise," *In the Valley* (Self-Produced, CD/Album, 2009, U.S.).

J. Tex & the Volunteers, "Omie Wise," *Misery* (Heptown Records HTR044, CD, 2009, Sweden).

House Devils, "Naomi Wise," *Irish Folk: Adieu to Old Ireland* (ARC Music EUCD 2232, CD, 2009, UK).

Albert Hash, "Omie Wise," *Albert Hash Vol. 1* (Field Recorders' Collective FRC 411, CD, 2009, U.S.).

Naomi Burkhart, "Omie Wise," *Swallowed by the Sky* (Naomi Burkhart self-released, CD, 2011, U.S.).

The Tillers with Uncle Mike Carr, "Omie Wise," *Wild Hog in the Woods* (not on label—No. AABB1944, CD, 2011, U.S.).

Snakefarm, "Omie Wise (You Forget to Answer)," *My Halo at Half-Light* (Fledg'ling Records FLED 3086, CD, 2011, UK).

Ruth Gerson, "Omie Wise," *Deceived* (Wrong Records, CD, 2011, U.S.).

J.D. Wilkes, "Omie Wise," *Kitchen Tapes* (Arkam Records ARK 48, Vinyl, 7" EP, 2012, U.S.)

Chapel Hill, "The Ballad of Omie Wise," *One for the Birds* (Cosmopolite Records COS13011, CD, 2013, France).

Vandaveer, "Omie Wise," *Oh, Willie, Please...* (Quack! Media—QC, Vinyl, LP, CD, 2013, U.S.).

David Grisman Bluegrass Experience, "Omie Wise," *Muddy Roads—Old-Time Music of Clarence Ashley & Doc Watson* (Acoustic Disc ACD 80, CD, 2013, U.S.).

Hypnotic Sleep, "Omie Wise," *Hypnotic Sleep* (Static Age SA 14, Vinyl, LP, 2013, Germany).

John Allemeier, "Deep Water (Omie Wise) for Chamber Ensemble," *Deep Water—The Murder Ballads* (Albany Music Distribution TROY 1488, CD, 2013, U.S.).

Reverend John DeLore and Kara Suzanne, "Omie Wise," *The 78 Project: Volume 1* (The 78 Project 78P-001, Vinyl, LP, 2014, U.S.).

Eighth Blackbird, "Omie Wise," *Filament* (Cedille Records CDR 90000 157, CD, 2015, U.S.).

Doug Wallin, "Naomi Wise," *Classic American Ballads (From Smithsonian Folkways)* (Smithsonian Folkways SFW CD 40215, CD, 2015, U.S.; as on Folkways 40013).

The Skiffle Players, "Omie Wise," *Skifflin'* (Spiritual Pajamas—Spiritual 017, MP3, 2016, U.S.).

Crumbling Ghost, "Omie Wise," *Five Songs* (Withered Hand WHR012, WHR012LP, CD, Vinyl, LP, 2016, UK).

Kkkristinashleytomson VIII, "Omie Wise," *Toujours A L'Ancienne* (Old Timey Productions K7A2BAL004, Cassette, 2016, France).

Hasee Ciaccio with Kalia Yeagle, "Omie Wise," *Big Bend Killing: The Appalachian Ballad Tradition* (Great Smoky Mountain Association 200973, CD, 2017, U.S.).

The Cuckoo Sisters and Brother Owl, "Omie Wise," *Take Me Back* (The Cuckoo Sisters Self-released, CD, 2017, France).

Clarence Ashley, "Omie Wise," *Clarence Ashley—Live and in Person: Greenwich Village 1963* (Jalopy 004, Vinyl, LP, 2017, U.S.).

Appendix E

Newtown, "Naomi Wise," *Old World* (Mountain Home Music Company MH17202, CD, 2018, U.S.).

Julia Hobart, "Naomi Wise," *To Spill My Husband's Blood: Live at the Warming House* (Waterbury Music + Sound, Digital Album, bandcamp.com, 2019. U.S.)

Chapter Notes

Introduction

1. Vance Randolph, *The Ozarks: An American Survival of Primitive Society*, ed. Robert Cochran, (Fayetteville: University of Arkansas Press, 2017), 178; Henry M. Belden, ed., "Ballads and Songs: Collected by the Missouri Folk-Lore Society," *The University of Missouri Studies* 15, no. 1 (January 1, 1940), 323; Gerald Milnes, "West Virginia's Omie Wise: The Folk Process Unveiled," *Appalachian Journal* 22, no. 4 (Summer 1995), 376–389; John Burrison, ed., *Storytellers: Folktales and Legends from the South* (Athens: University of Georgia Press, 1989), 194–196.

2. In court records as well as in the folk tradition, Naomi Wise has been known variously as Omia, Omie, Omi, Oma, Ommie, Nayomy, Neomy, Neomie, Neomi, and Little Omie Wise.

3. Braxton Craven, "Naomi Wise, or the Victim," *The Evergreen* 1:3–4 (January–February 1851), 3:78–82; 4:111–16.

4. Mark Penny, ed., *Naomi Wise or the Wrongs of a Beautiful Girl* (Weldon, NC: Harrell Printing Company, August 1884); *Naomi Wise or the Wrongs of a Beautiful Girl* (Randleman, NC: W.C. Phillips Printer, 1888); *Naomi Wise or the Wrongs of a Beautiful Girl* (Pinnacle, NC: W.C. Phillips Printer, 1904); *The Life of Naomi Wise* (King, NC: King Publishing Company, 1911).

5. Charlie Vernon, "Naomi Wise," *The Greensboro Patriot* nos. 317–320, 1874.

6. *Danbury Reporter*, Danbury, NC, May 18, 1911, 5.

Chapter 1

1. Second United States Federal Census, 1800, Randolph County, NC.

2. J.A. Blair, *Reminiscences of Randolph County*, 1890 reprint edition (Asheboro, NC: Randolph County Historical Society, 1968), 50; *Laws of North Carolina 1818* (Raleigh, NC: Thomas Henderson, State Printer, 1819), 80.

3. Commonplace books were a kind of scrapbook, still used by some Americans in the 19th century, in which one would compile a variety of useful information—recipes, news clippings, letters, and the like.

4. Alvaretta K. Register, *State Census of North Carolina, 1784–1787* (Baltimore: Genealogical Publishing Co., 2001), 72.

5. Laura Stimson Worth Collection, ledger with handwritten notes, September 10, 1938, RCPL, RR.

6. Hyde County Register of Deeds, Deed Book B, p. 710, Deed Book C, pp. 284–85, Deed Book G, p. 130, Swan Quarter, NC.

7. Johanna Miller Lewis, "Women Artisans in Backcountry North Carolina, 1753–1790," *North Carolina Historical Review* 68, no. 3 (July 1991), 223–24.

8. Wardens of the Poor Minutes, March 28, 1796–May 4, 1832, RCPL, RR.

9. Craven, "Naomi Wise, or the Victim," 1:3, 80; Eleanor Long-Wilgus, *Naomi Wise: Creation, Re-Creation and Continuity in an American Ballad Tradition* (Chapel Hill: Chapel Hill Press, 2003), 29.

10. J.W. Cannon, "Spirit of Naomi Wise Drowned Over 100 Years Ago by

Her Lover Still Hovers Over Randolph," *Greensboro Daily News*, November 15, 1925.

11. Miriam Forman-Brunell and Leslie Paris, eds., *The Girls' History and Culture Reader: The Nineteenth Century* (Urbana: University of Illinois Press, 2011), 2–4.

12. Richard and Abigail Beeson letter, Randolph Co. Biography: Wise, Naomi file, RCPL, RR.

13. Joan Jacobs Brumberg, "Something Happens to Girls: Menarche and the Emergence of the Modern American Hygienic Imperative," in *Women and Health in America: Historical Readings*, second edition, ed. Judith Walzer Leavitt (Madison: University of Wisconsin Press, 1999), 152.

14. James Iredell and François-Xavier Martin, *Public Acts of the General Assembly of North Carolina*, Vol. 1 (Newbern: Martin & Ogden, 1804), 144.

15. "Ordered that Nancy Wise thirteen years old last March be bound to Stephen McCollum...," Minute Dockets of County Court of Pleas and Quarter Sessions, Randolph County (Randolph County Court Minutes), February Term 1812, RCPL, RR, 47.

16. John Haywood, *The Duty and Office of Justices of the Peace, and of Sheriffs, Coroners, Constables, & c., According to the Laws of the State of North-Carolina* (Raleigh: William Boylan, 1808), 27–28.

17. *Ibid.*, 27.

18. Randolph County Bastardy Bonds and Records, Benjamin Sanders to Omie Wise, May 1803, CRX. 407, State Archives on North Carolina (SANC). Cosigners of the bond were James Winningham and Thomas Yeargan.

19. Randolph County Court Minutes, February Term 1804, RCPL, RR, 84.

20. Long-Wilgus, *Naomi Wise*, 38; Polly Johnson, "Poor Oma" (Little Oma Wise), Wise, Virginia, 1939. UV-AL-WPA, 1150-C; LC-AFS, 2760 A4.

21. Land Patent Book 6, p. 149, Grant No. 43 issued December 6, 1761, for William Field, 200 acres. www.nclandgrants.com/ (accessed March 27, 2018).

22. Sueanne Field, "The Field Family in Pennsylvania and North Carolina,"

The Guilford Genealogist 20, #2, no. 60 (Winter 1993), 89–96.

23. Michael Lewis Cook, *Pioneer Lewis Families*, Vol. 1 (Evansville, IN: Cook Publications, 1978), 115–118; Rev. E.W. Caruthers, *Interesting Revolutionary Events: and Sketches of Character Chiefly in the "Old North State,"* Second Series (Philadelphia: Hayes & Zell, 1856), 313.

24. Craven, "Naomi Wise, or the Victim," 1:3, 78.

25. *Ibid.*, 1:3, 79.

26. Rev. E.W. Caruthers, *Interesting Revolutionary Events: and Sketches of Character Chiefly in the "Old North State,"* 314.

27. Criminal Action Papers, Box CR 81.326.2, 1780–87, SANC.

28. *Ibid.*

29. *Ibid.*

30. Criminal Action Papers, Box CR 81.326.1, undated; Box CR 81.326.2, 1780–87, SANC.

31. Criminal Action Papers, Box CR 81.326.1, undated; Box CR 81.326.2, 1780–87; Box CR 81.326.3, 1788, SANC.

32. *History of the Ohio Falls Cities and Their Counties: with Illustrations and Biographical Sketches* 2 (Cleveland: L.A. Williams and Company, 1882), 248; *History of Wayne and Clay Counties, Illinois* (Chicago: Globe Pub. Co., 1884), 332–33.

33. Deed Book 6, p. 81; Deed Book 9, p. 24, RCRD; Cook, *Pioneer Lewis Families*, 115–116.

34. Governor's Papers: Benjamin Smith, Correspondence, March 1811. G.P., SANC, 35–36.

35. Minute Dockets of County Court of Pleas and Quarter Sessions, Randolph County, May Term 1805, 151; May Term 1806, 217; February Term 1807, RCPL, RR, 267.

36. Allen Watson, "The Constable in Colonial North Carolina," *North Carolina Historical Review* 68 (January 1991), 1–16; François-Xavier Martin, *The Office and Authority of a Justice of the Peace, and of Sheriffs, Coroners, & c. According to the Laws of the State of North-Carolina* (New Bern: François-Xavier Martin, 1791), 100–107.

37. "1803 Tax List: Randolph County,

North Carolina," *The Genealogical Journal* XI:1 (Winter 1987), 4; Deed Book 11, pp. 92–93, RCRD.

38. https://randolphhistory.word press.com (accessed December 11, 2021). Benjamin Elliott was appointed a justice by the Governor of North Carolina in 1805. The appointment, as with all Justices, was a lifetime appointment. Randolph County Court Minutes, February Term 1805, RCPL, RR, 136.

39. Watson, "The Constable in Colonial North Carolina," 9–10.

40. Deed Book 6, p. 81; Deed Book 9, p. 24, RCRD; Cook, 115–116.

41. Second United States Federal Census, 1800, Randolph County, NC; Third United States Federal Census, 1810, Randolph County, NC.

42. Victoria E. Bynum, *Unruly Women: The Politics of Social and Sexual Control in the Old South* (Chapel Hill: University of North Carolina Press, 1992), 109.

Chapter 2

1. Randolph County Bastardy Bonds and Records, Ann Carney, March 1802, CRX. 407, SANC.

2. François-Xavier Martin, 105.

3. Randolph County Court Minutes, May Term 1806, RCPL, RR, 228.

4. Craven, "Naomi Wise, or the Victim," 1:3, 80.

5. *Ibid.,* 1:3, 81.

6. *Ibid.,* 1:3, 81–82.

7. Bynum, *Unruly Women,* 106–108.

8. Craven, "Naomi Wise, or the Victim," 1:3, 81.

9. Governor's Papers: David Stone, Correspondence, G.P. 34, SANC, Raleigh, NC, 293–94.

10. Edward W. Baptist, "My Mind Is to Drown You and Leave You Behind: 'Omie Wise,' Intimate Violence, and Masculinity," in *Over the Threshold: Intimate Violence in Early America,* eds. Christine Daniels and Michael V. Kennedy (New York: Routledge, 1999), 98–99.

11. Personal communication (1968), Virginia Wall Hayes (1892–1976). According to Mrs. Hayes, oral tradition

was that the Quakers had used a building as a school house at the location mentioned in the Woody narrative during the early 1800s and the later public school was built on the same site.

12. Apportionment for Randolph County Schools (January 14, 1914), "Randolph Co.—School Early History," RCPL, RR; "Randolph County Schools by Township (1750–1930)," *Randolph County School History C-7,* "Randolph Co.— School Early History," RCPL, RR. The school property was sold November 14, 1929. Deed Book 277, p. 231, RCRD.

13. Sunset data for Randleman, NC, April 5, 1807, https://www.google.com (accessed December 4, 2021). Phase of the moon for Eastern Time Zone, April 5, 1807, https://www.timeanddate.com/ (accessed December 4, 2021).

14. "Moon Phase on: April 05, 1807," https://www.moongiant.com (accessed December 4, 2021).

15. Based on a horse walking an average of four miles an hour, http://www.speedofanimals.com (accessed December 4, 2021).

Chapter 3

1. Howgill Julian, "Tragic Story of Naomi Wise Told by H. Julian," *The Asheboro Courier* Tuesday, September 2, 1879. Howgill Julian, whose father Tobias Julian was listed as a witness for the prosecution at the Lewis trial, stated it was Joshua Davis who was said to have found Naomi's body.

2. Adelaide L. Fries, ed., *Records of the Moravians in North Carolina,* Vol. VI (Raleigh: Edwards & Broughton Print Co., 1940), 2905.

3. Craven, "Naomi Wise, or the Victim," 1:4, 113.

4. In February 1807 Vachel released Patsy Stafford from her indenture with him, in preparation for the move to the Indiana Territory. Randolph County Court Minutes, February Term 1807, RCPL, RR, 263. Vachel Hancock purchased land October 7, 1807, in Washington Township, Harrison County, Indiana. http://genealogytrails.com/ind/harrison/

land_purchases-1807.html (accessed December 4, 2021).

5. "Martha Hussey," *The Family Puzzles—Demystified (Sort Of)*, http://rea-williams.com/getperson.php?personID=17613&tree=tree1 (accessed December 4, 2021).

6. Craven, "Naomi Wise, or the Victim," 1:4, 113.

7. D.G. McMasters, "Sketch of the Life of Alexander Gray Murdock," *The Courier*, October 3, 1912, 6. Local tradition was that a building in the Grant Township was said to be the Hussey house where Jonathan Lewis was captured. Lowell McKay Whatley, Jr., *Architectural History of Randolph County, N.C.* (Asheboro, NC: City of Asheboro and the County of Randolph, 1985), 144. In 1907, *The Randolph Bulletin* newspaper mentioned that W.H. Brower had brought by the newspaper office a piece of walnut from the old house where Jonathan Lewis was captured near the home of E. Brookshire in Grantville Township. "Local and Personal," *The Randolph Bulletin*, January 10, 1907, 3.

8. Haywood, *The Duty and Office of Justices of the Peace*, 60.

9. Martin, *The Office and Authority of a Justice of the Peace, and of Sheriffs, Coroners...*, 109–110.

10. Haywood, *The Duty and Office of Justices of the Peace*, 60.

11. Minnie McIver Brown, "Old Tragedy Deep River Still Fresh in Memory," *Raleigh News and Observer*, July 29, 1928. A photo in the newspaper article labels the rock where Naomi's body was found as being called "Naomi's Cooling Board." It was actually a flat rock in the same outcropping where her body was laid after being found that was referred to by that name locally. Laura Worth makes mention of the rock in her notes: "The large rock on which the body was laid and covered with Mrs. Davis sheet awaiting the Corner [Coroner] is still a sentinule [*sic*] on the river bank." Laura Stimson Worth Collection, RCPL, RR, Asheboro, NC.

12. William and Robert Chambers, "Exploded Follies: Ordeal by Touch," *Chambers Edinburgh Journal* 5, no. 240 (September 1836), 250.

13. Robert P. Brittain, "Cruentation: In Legal Medicine and in Literature," *Medical History* 9, no. 1 (January 1965), 82–88.

14. Craven, "Naomi Wise, or the Victim," 1:4, 113.

15. William Watkins, January 26, 1805, Book 11, p. 127, RCRD, Asheboro, NC.

16. Craven, "Naomi Wise, or the Victim," 1:4, 112.

17. Haywood, *The Duty and Office of Justices of the Peace*, 60.

18. Randolph County Criminal Action Papers, "State vs. Jonathan Lewis," C.R.081.326.10, SANC.

19. *Ibid.*

20. Craven, "Naomi Wise, or the Victim," 114.

21. L. McKay Whatley, "The New County Jail—1850," typed manuscript, RCPL, RR.

22. Randolph County Criminal Action Papers, "State vs. Jonathan Lewis," C.R.081.326.10, SANC.

23. *Ibid.*

24. "Report of the Committee to examine the Gaol Of the County of Randolph Report," 1807, RCPL, RR.

25. "Corrections to the Early History of Asheboro," *The Courier*, Thursday, December 1, 1921.

26. Randolph County Criminal Action Papers, C.R.081.326.10, SANC.

27. Richard and Abigail Beeson letter, Randolph Co. Biography: Wise, Naomi file, RCPL, RR.

28. Randolph County Criminal Action Papers, C.R.081.326.10, SANC.

29. Randolph County Superior Court Minutes, C.081.30008, Vol. 1, 1807–1833, SANC, 5.

30. Lawrence London, "Edward Jones," in *Dictionary of North Carolina Biography*, Vol. 3, H–K, ed. William S. Powell (Chapel Hill: University of North Carolina Press, 1979), 317; John H. Wheeler, *Historical Sketches of North Carolina from 1584–1851* (Philadelphia: Lippincott, Grambo and Co., 1851), 290.

31. Randolph County Criminal Action Papers, 1807–1808, C.R.081.326.7, SANC.

32. Randolph County Bastardy Bonds,

CR.081.102.1, 1807, SANC. Harrison was named in a bastardy bond by Fanny Curtace [Curtis] as being the father of her recently born son in 1807.

33. General Assembly Sessions Records, November–December 1811, Box 3, Petitions (Divorce), SANC. Sally as a nickname for Sarrah Smith Shofner, https://www.werelate.org/wiki/Person:- Michael_Shoffner_(3) (accessed December 4, 2021).

34. General Assembly Session Records, November–December 1813, Box 3, Petitions (Miscellaneous), SANC.

35. Randolph County Criminal Action Papers, 1807–1808, C.R.081.326.7, SANC.

36. Randolph County Superior Court Minutes, 1807–1833, SANC, 6.

37. Randolph County Criminal Action Papers, 1807–1808, C.R.081.326.7, SANC.

38. Sueanne Field, "The Field Family in Pennsylvania and North Carolina," *The Guilford Genealogist* 20, #3, no. 61 (Spring 1993), 165, 172.

39. Governor's Papers: David Stone, Correspondence, G.P. 34, SANC, 293–94.

40. Martin, *The Office and Authority of a Justice of the Peace, and of Sheriffs, Coroners...*, 111.

41. Randolph County Criminal Action Papers, C.R.081.326.10, SANC.

42. Randolph County Criminal Action Papers, 1807–1808, C.R.081.326.7, SANC.

43. Randolph County Criminal Action Papers, 1807–1808, C.R.081.326.7, SANC.

44. Randolph County Criminal Action Papers, 1807–1808, C.R.081.326.7, SANC.

45. Robert Roote, "The Historical Facts Behind the Celebrated Ballad 'Naomi Wise,'" *North Carolina Folklore Journal* 5, no. 2 (Fall–Winter 1984), 75–76; Joseph Bulla appearance bond copy, Naomi Wise File Folder, RCPL, RR.

46. Randolph County Criminal Action Papers, C.R.X. 240, SANC.

47. *Ibid.*

48. Randolph County Superior Court Minutes, 1807–1833, SANC, 28.

Chapter 4

1. *History of the Ohio Falls Cities* 2, 242.

2. William N. Logan, E.R. Cumings, Clyde A. Malott, Stephen S. Visher, W.M. Tucker, and J.R. Reeves, *Handbook of Indiana Geology* (Indianapolis: Wm. B. Burford, 1922), 90.

3. *Ibid.*

4. John E. Kleber, *The Encyclopedia of Louisville* (Lexington: University Press of Kentucky, 2001), 667; William N. Logan, E.R. Cumings, Clyde A. Malott, Stephen S. Visher, W.M. Tucker, and J.R. Reeves, *Handbook of Indiana Geology* (Indianapolis: Wm. B. Burford, 1922), 465–66.

5. *History of the Ohio Falls Cities and Their Counties: With Illustrations and Bibliographical Sketches* 1 (Cleveland: L.A. Williams and Company, 1882), 43.

6. Jane Sarles, *Clarksville, Indiana* (Charleston, SC: Arcadia, 2001), 7–9.

7. Daniel Waite Howe, "Laws and Courts of the Northwest and Indiana Territories," *Indiana Historical Society* 2, no. 1 (Indianapolis: The Bowen-Merrill Co., 1886), 11–12. That region of the Indiana Territory became Clark County in 1801. Lewis C. Baird, *Baird's History of Clark County, Indiana* (Indianapolis: B.F. Bowen, 1909), 46.

8. Francis S. Philbrick, ed., "The Laws of the Indiana Territory: 1801–1809," *Collections of the Illinois State Historical Library* XXI, Vol. 2 of Law Series (Springfield: The Illinois State Historical Library, 1930), clxxxiii.

9. *Ibid.*

10. Thomas Ashe, *Travels in America Performed in 1806: For the Purpose of Exploring the Rivers, Alleghany, Monongahela, Ohio, and Mississippi, and Ascertaining the Produce and Condition of Their Banks and Vicinity* (London: William Sawyer & Co., 1808), 246–47.

11. That region of the Indiana Territory became Clark County in 1801. Baird, *Baird's History of Clark County, Indiana*, 46.

12. Craven, "Naomi Wise, or the Victim," 1:4, 114.

13. Philbrick, "The Laws of the Indiana Territory," clxxxiiii.

14. Governor's Letter Books, GLB17, David Stone, 26 September 1810, SANC, 313.

15. Craven, "Naomi Wise, or the Victim," 1:4, 114.

16. Col. I.J. Brittain, ed., *Tragedy of Naomi Wise: How She Came to an Untimely End by Jonathan Lewis and Life of Andrew Jackson* (Winston-Salem, NC: Col. I.J. Brittain, 1910[?]), 22.

17. Flossie Huddleston, Cumberland County, Kentucky, 1956. WKU-FA, T-7-8, Western Kentucky University, Folklore Archives Collections, Bowling Green, Kentucky; Hilliard Smith, Hindman, Kentucky, 1909, in Olive Dame Campbell and Cecil J. Sharp, eds., *English Folksongs from the Southern Appalachians* (New York: Knickerbocker Press, 1917), 228–29.

18. U.S. Geological Survey Topographic Map, "Speed Quadrangle, Indiana," 7.5 Minute Series, U.S. Dept. of the Interior, 2013.

19. Randolph County Register of Deeds, November 20, 1809, Book 11, p. 400. Richard Lewis sold a remaining 125-acre tract of land to Francis Reynolds in 1810. See April 29, 1810, Book 12, p. 56, RCRD.

20. *History of the Ohio Falls Cities* 2, 244.

21. *Ibid.*, 248.

22. *Ibid.*, 237; "Indiana Marriages, 1811–2007," https://www.familysearch.org/search/collection/1410397 (accessed December 4, 2021). Sarah McCann's last name is often transcribed incorrectly as McCain or McCaun.

23. Richard Pangburn, "Moses McCan—frontier scout—Indians—PA KY VA IN," http://www.genealogy.com/forum/surnames/topics/mccann/1796/ (accessed December 4, 2021).

24. *History of the Ohio Falls Cities* 2, 167.

25. Sarles, *Clarksville, Indiana*, 7.

26. Gayle Thornbrough, ed., *Outpost on the Wabash, 1787–1791: Letters of Brigadier General Josiah Harmar and Major John Francis Hamtramck and Other Letters and Documents Selected from the Harmar Papers in the William L. Clements Library*. Indiana Historical Society Publications, Vol. 19 (Indianapolis: Indiana Historical Society, 1958), 128–29.

27. *History of the Ohio Falls Cities* 2, 430–31.

28. *Ibid.*, 431.

29. "Kentucky, County Marriages, 1797–1954," database with images, FamilySearch https://familysearch.org (accessed December 4, 2021); "Joshua Fleehart," in John Frost, Theo. Bliss, and H.C. Peck, *Heroes and Hunters of the West: Comprising Sketches and Adventures of Boone, Kenton, Brady, Logan, Whetzel, Fleehart, Hughes, Johnston & c.* (Philadelphia: H.C. Peck and Theo. Bliss, 1858), 118–126; Richard Pangburn, http://www.genealogy.com/forum/surnames/topics/mccann/1796/ (accessed December 4, 2021). See Lewis Collins, *Collins' Historical Sketches of Kentucky: History of Kentucky, Volume 2* (Covington, KY: Collins & Company, 1878), 351. By one account, Joshua Fleehart is said to have run off with a young woman, and was tracked down and killed by her brother. Her brother shot Fleehart through the cracks of a log cabin while his sister sat in Fleehart's lap with her arms around his neck.

30. Clarence Edwin Carter, comp. and ed., *The Territory of Indiana 1800–1810*, Vol. 7 of *The Territorial Papers of the United States* (Washington, D.C.: U.S. Government Printing Office, 1939), 705.

31. Clark County, Indiana, Wills and Executors Records, *Will Book A: 1801–1817*, pp. 39–41, Records Dept., Clark County Government Building, Jeffersonville, Indiana.

32. Craven, "Naomi Wise, or the Victim," 1:4, 114.

Chapter 5

1. Governor's Letter Books, GLB17, David Stone, April 6, 1810, SANC, 285.

2. Craven, "Naomi Wise, or the Victim," 1:4, 114

3. Governor's Letter Books, GLB17, David Stone, May 10, 1810, SANC, 287.

4. Governor's Letter Books, GLB17, David Stone, September 26, 1810, SANC, 313.

5. *The Revised Laws of Indiana: In Which Are Comprised All Such Acts of a General Nature as Are in Force in Said State; Adopted and Enacted by the General Assembly at Their Fifteenth Session,* Indiana General Assembly (Indianapolis, IN: Douglas & McGuire, 1831), 280–281.

6. According to the archivist at the Ohio Historical Society, in a letter dated 02, May 1997, the Works Progress Administration's Ohio Governor's Calendar of Papers, 1803–1878 was checked and a reference to a copy of a four-page indictment and record of prosecution dated 01 February,

1811 for Jonathan Lewis was included in the calendar, however the papers were not found. "In 1951, the Ohio Historical Society Manuscript Collections suffered fire damage. Some of the items from the Return J. Meigs Papers were damaged in the fire. It appears that the four-page indictment and record of prosecution in the Meigs papers were among them." Personal letter from Thomas J. Rieder, Reference Archivist, Ohio Historical Society, Archives/Library Division, Columbus, Ohio. 02, May 1997.

7. Craven, "Naomi Wise, or the Victim," 1:4, 114.

8. Craven, "Naomi Wise, or the Victim," 1:4114.

9. *History of the Ohio Falls Cities* 2, 167.

10. *Ibid.,*168, 239–40; "Silver Creek: A Historic Natural Treasure," *Clarksville Historical Society Newsletter.* Vol. 14, No.2 (2010).

11. *History of the Ohio Falls Cities* 2, 239–240.

12. Vachel Hancock and wife to H. McNary, 04 September 1815, Harrison County. Deed mentions Vachel being half-owner of the ferry in Clark County, Indiana, established in 1809. https://www.ancestry.com/mediaui–viewer/tree/1646386/person/-1906578707/media/5d918998–467c-494e-b353-a9d-a02c6c5b6 (Accessed December 4, 2021)

13. http://genealogytrails.com/ind/harrison/bios11.html (Accessed December 4, 2021); "Indiana Marriages, 1780–1992," database, *FamilySearch* https://www.familysearch.org/ark:/61903/3:1:S3HT-D4J9-

L72?cc=1410397 (Accessed December 4, 2021), Caleb Newman and Patsy Handcock, 08 Feb 1809; citing reference en 1; FHL microfilm 549,383.

14. History of the Ohio Falls Cities 2, 236–237.

15. Craven, "Naomi Wise, or the Victim," 1:4, 114.

16. David Christensen, "William Lewis," typed manuscript, 18. https://www.wancestry.com/mediauiviewer/tree/170509272/person/302210911776/media/5710b8ce-f273–4dba-a70b-8f1da3a107ed (December 4, 2021)

17. Craven, "Naomi Wise, or the Victim," 1:4, 114.

18. "Act of Congress: An Act respecting Fugitives from Justice and persons escaping from the Service of their Masters [Approved February 12, 1793]," *The Revised Laws of Indiana: In Which Are Comprised All Such Acts of a General Nature as Are in Force in Said State; Adopted and Enacted by the General Assembly at Their Fifteenth Session,* Indiana General Assembly (Indianapolis, IN: Douglas & McGuire, 1831) 281.

19. Craven, "Naomi Wise, or the Victim," 1:4, 115.

20. Randolph County Criminal Action Papers, C.R.081.326.10, SANC.

21. Randolph County Criminal Action Papers, 1808C, C.R.081.326.7, SANC.

22. Randolph County Criminal Action Papers, C.R.081.326.10, SANC.

23. Randolph County Superior Court Minutes, 1807–1833, SANC, 56.

24. Randolph County Superior Court Minutes, 1807–1833, SANC, 61.

25. Randolph County Miscellaneous Records Pardon File, , C.R.081.928.11, 17. Dec 1811, SANC.

26. Benjamin Swaim, *The North Carolina Justice: containing a summary statement of the statutes and common law of this state, together with the decisions of the Supreme Court, and all the most approved forms and precedents relating to the office and duty of a justice of the peace, and other public officers according to modern practice, the whole intended as a complete practical application of the new revised statues of North Carolina,* 2nd ed. (Raleigh: Henry D. Turner, 1846),

531; Randolph County Superior Court Minutes, C.081.30008, Vol. 1, 1807–1833, SANC, 73.

27. Randolph County Criminal Action Papers, C.R.081.326.10, SANC.

28. Randolph County Accounts and Claims 1784–1839, C.R.081.910.1, Folder 1810–1819, SANC.

Chapter 6

1. Colonel I.J. Brittain, *Tragedy of Naomi Wise*, 27.

2. Randolph County Court Minutes, February Term 1815, RCPL, RR, 360.

3. *Ibid.*; Fred Olds, *Story of the Counties of North Carolina with Other Data* (Oxford, NC: Oxford Orphanage Press, 1921) 33. The court records for the 1812 Jonathan Lewis murder trial may have been lost during an 1872 Guilford County courthouse fire, even though loss of records was said to be slight.

4. Randolph County Bastardy Bonds and Records, Ann Carney, March 1802, CRX. 407, SANC.

5. W.A. Blair, *Union Republican*, May 6, 1915.

6. Randolph County Wills, 1663–1978; Estate Papers, 1781–1928, Joseph Elliot 1819, SANC; Randolph County Criminal Action Papers, 1821-A, C.R. 081.326.16, SANC.

7. John Ramsower purchased several items at the estate sale of Hettie's father, Joseph Elliott, in 1819. Randolph County Wills, 1663–1978; Estate Papers, 1781–1928, Joseph Elliott 1819, SANC. Hettie and John Ramsower were subpoenaed as witnesses at the trial of John Ramsower's sister Elizabeth Ramsower Craven, and her son Wyatt, for the beating and murder of Rosetta Jo, enslaved in their household, in 1821. Randolph County Criminal Action Papers, 1821-A, C.R. 081.326.16, SANC.

8. Randolph County Court Minutes, February Term 1815, RCPL, RR, 360.

9. In 1813 Jinny Emery of Randolph County had filed for and was granted a divorce by the General Assembly from her husband Stephen Emery. General Assembly Sessions Records, Box 3, November–December 1813, Petitions (Miscellaneous), SANC.

10. General Assembly Sessions Records, Box 3, November–December 1811, Petitions (Divorce), SANC.

11. Minnie McIver Brown, "Old Tragedy Deep River Still Fresh in Memory," *Raleigh News and Observer*, July 29, 1928.

12. Craven, "Naomi Wise, or the Victim," 1:4, 113.

13. Randolph County Court Minutes, February Term 1815, RCPL, RR, 360.

14. Roote, "The Historical Facts behind the Celebrated Ballad 'Naomi Wise,'" 78.

15. *The Story of Naomi Wise or the Wrongs of a Beautiful Girl*, 30.

16. Roote, "The Historical Facts behind the Celebrated Ballad 'Naomi Wise,'" 78.

17. Randolph County Court Minutes, February Term 1815, RCPL, RR, 360.

18. Randolph County Court Minutes, May Session 1815, RCPL, RR, unnumbered page.

19. Randolph County Criminal Action Papers, C.R.081.326.10, SANC.

20. *Ibid.*

21. Haywood, *The Duty and Office of Justices of the Peace*, 205.

22. Lawrence H. Officer and Samuel H. Williamson, "Computing 'Real Value' Over Time with a Conversion Between U.K. Pounds and U.S. Dollars, 1791 to Present," MeasuringWorth, 2021, https://www.measuringworth.com/calculators/exchange/ (accessed December 4, 2021).

23. Randolph County Criminal Action Papers, C.R.081.326.10, SANC; Randolph County Court Minutes, May Term 1812, RCPL, RR, 52.

24. Randolph County Criminal Action Papers, C.R.081.326.10, SANC.

25. Randolph County Superior Court Minutes, 1807–1833, SANC, 82.

26. *Ibid.*

27. Randolph County Insolvent Debtors, 1812–1819, February 1814, C.R. 081.914.1, SANC.

28. Randolph County Criminal Action Papers, C.R.081.326.10, SANC; Randolph County Accounts and Claims, 1810–1819, C.R.081.910.1, SANC; Randolph

County Insolvent Debtors, 1812–1819. February 1814, C.R.081.914.1, SANC.

29. Brittain, *Tragedy of Naomi Wise*, 27.

30. *History of the Ohio Falls Cities* 2, 241.

31. *Will Book A: 1801–1817*, Clark County, Indiana Wills and Executors Records, 132,135.

32. Philbrick, "The Laws of the Indiana Territory," ccxxxv.

33. Craven, "Naomi Wise, or the Victim," 1:4, 115.

34. Communication with John Field Pankow, November 21, 2021.

35. *History of the Ohio Falls Cities* 2, 264.

36. Image of a page from Richard Lewis' daybook, Lewis File Folder, RCPL, RR; Field, "The Field Family in Pennsylvania and North Carolina," 167.

37. Indiana Marriages, 1811–2007, https://www.familysearch.org/search/collection/1410397 (accessed December 4, 2021).

38. 1870 U.S. Federal Census, Township 52 Range 19, Chariton, Missouri.

39. "Indiana Marriages, 1811–2019," database with images, *FamilySearch*, https://www.familysearch.org/ark:/61903/1:1:XX11–194 (accessed December 12, 2021).

40. 1850 U.S. Census, Clay County, Illinois.

Chapter 7

1. Mark Penny, ed., *Naomi Wise or the Wrongs of a Beautiful Girl, A True Story, Enacted in North Carolina 80 Years Ago* (Weldon, NC: Harrell Printing Company, August 1884).

2. Bryan Tyson, "Naomi Wise," *The Randolph Bulletin*, Asheboro, NC, January 30, 1908, 2.

3. Mrs. E.L. Cox, "Naomi Wise," *The Randolph Bulletin*, Asheboro, NC, February 6, 1908, 3.

4. The Museum of Early Southern Decorative Arts (MESDA), https://mesda.org/item/collections/table/21640/ (accessed November 26, 2021).

5. Communication with W. Calvin Hinshaw. Hinshaw said that Vera King (1899–1989) had specified that it was her great-grandfather Anthony Chamness who had made Naomi Wise's coffin; sales inventory papers from Anthony Chamness' estate listing cabinetmaking tools and lumber support that he was involved in cabinet making. North Carolina, Wills and Probate Records, 1665–1998, https://www.ancestry.com/search/collections/9061/ (accessed December 4, 2021).

6. https://www.findagrave.com/memorial/174721010/anthony-chamness (accessed December 4, 2021).

7. New Garden Quarterly Meeting, *Minutes, 1881–1933*, Collection: North Carolina Yearly Meeting Minutes, Guilford College's Quaker Archives; Greensboro, North Carolina.

8. The ballad "Poor Naomi" was dated January 13, 1881. Elma Barker, "Elma J. Barkers Book," April 11, 1880, private family collection, Providence, NC, 52.

9. Randolph County Court Minutes, February Term 1804, 81, RCPL, RR.

10. *The Old Discipline: Nineteenth Century Friends Disciplines in America* (Glenside, PA: Quaker Heritage Press 1999), 14.

11. Bascom Lamar Lunsford, "Notes from the Music Library," ed. John Lair, *Stand By Magazine* 29 (May 1937), 11; Bascom Lamar Lunsford letter to Donald Richardson, January 25, 1954, Richardson Collection, RCPL, RR.

12. Lunsford, "Notes from the Music Library," 11.

13. Personal communication, W. Calvin Hinshaw. Mr. Hinshaw stated that Allen Chamness had told him that the grave was nearer the road and showed him the vicinity of where it was. Ewart Pugh (1911–1973) stated in an interview with the authors that Mr. Allen Chamness as well as others in the Providence neighborhood had said the grave was nearer the road. Lunsford, "Notes from the Music Library," 11.

14. *The Old Discipline: Nineteenth Century Friends Disciplines in America*, 16–17. Dorothy Lewis, Williamsburg, Indiana, letter dated July 26, 1976, Lewis Family File, RCPL, RR.

15. Donald Ray Richardson, "The Birth of a Ballad: The Story of the Ballad of 'Poor Naomi,'" Senior Thesis, Department of English, Guilford College, 1957, 22. A photograph of the modern tombstone appears in "Randleman History Tells Story of Poor Naomi; Murdered Near There by Her Lover in 1808," *Burlington Hosiery News* 1, no. II, Greensboro, NC, August 1947, in the Richardson Collection, RCPL, RR.

16. *The Old Discipline*, 372, 462.

17. Randolph County Court Minutes, August Session 1813, 196; Randolph County Apprentice Bonds, C.R.081.101.02, SANC.

18. Randolph County Apprentice Bonds, C.R.081.101.02, SANC.

19. Randolph County Court Minutes, February Term 1821, RCPL, RR, 21.

20. Randolph County Court Minutes, February Term 1812, RCPL, RR, 49.

21. Randolph County Bastardy Bonds and Records, Joseph Bulla, 1820, C.R.081.102.2, SANC. Federal Census Records support the year of birth for John S. Wise. United States Federal Census 1860, Mill, Grant, Indiana; United States Federal Census 1880, Neosho, Coffey, Kansas.

22. Randolph County Bastardy Bonds and Records, Joseph Bulla, 1820, C.R.081.102.2, SANC.

23. Roote, "The Historical Facts behind the Celebrated Ballad 'Naomi Wise,'" 75–76. See Naomi Wise File Folder, RCPL, RR.

24. Robert A. Gennings, Ralph L. Bulla, and Juanita J. Kesler, *The Bulla Family* (Sequim, WA: R.A. Gennings, 1981), 30; Deed Book 20, p. 9, RCRD.

25. Wardens of the Poor Minutes, March 28, 1796–May 4, 1832, RCPL, RR.

26. Wardens of the Poor Minutes, February 5, 1822.

27. *Ibid.*

28. Wardens of the Poor Minutes, May 2, 1820.

29. Wardens of the Poor Minutes, February 5, 1822.

30. William Wade Hinshaw, *Encyclopedia of American Quaker Genealogy*, Vol. 1 of *North Carolina* (Baltimore: Genealogical Publishing Company, 1978), 727.

31. Rev. J.P. Rodgers, *Life of Rev. James Needham, the Oldest Methodist Preacher* (Pilot Mountain, NC: The Surry Printing House, 1899), 28.

32. MESDA Collections Database, Needham, James, http://mesda.org/item/craftsman/needham-james/26265/ (accessed December 4, 2021); Michael H. Lewis, "American Vernacular Furniture and the North Carolina Back Country," *The Journal of Early Southern Decorative Arts* XX, no. 2 (November 1994), 29–33.

33. Back Creek Friends Meeting, *Men's Minutes, 12/1792–1/1840*, Randolph County, NC, Guilford College's Quaker Archives, Greensboro, NC, 548.

34. Wally Jarrell, "A Partial ca. 1840 Tax List," *The Genealogical Journal* XXV, no. 1, Randolph County Genealogical Society (Spring 2001), 18.

35. *North Carolina Marriage Bonds, 1741–1868*, Bond #000115216, SANC. B.F. Hoover was bondsman.

36. William Wade Hinshaw, *Encyclopedia of American Quaker Genealogy*, Vol. 1 (Baltimore: Genealogical Publishing Company, 1978), 711.

37. Karen L. Zipf, *Labor of Innocents: Forced Apprenticeship in North Carolina, 1715–1919* (Baton Rouge: Louisiana State University Press, 2005), 26–27; William Jay, *Inquiry into the Character and Tendency of the American Colonization and the American Anti-Slavery Societies* (New York: Leavett, Lord and Co., 1835), 136.

38. Zipf, 26; Randolph County Apprentice Bonds, Daniel Winslow, 1845, C.R.081.101.4, SANC.

39. Back Creek Monthly Meeting (Grant County, Indiana), *Births and Deaths Mid–1800's*, vol. 2 or book B, Friends Collection and College Archives, Earlham, Richmond, Indiana.

40. U.S., Selected Federal Census Non-Population Schedules, 1850–1880, Neosho, Coffey County, Kansas, 1870.

Chapter 8

1. See, for example, the film *Appalachian Journey* (New York: Association for Cultural Equity, 1991).

2. Stith Thompson, *Motif-Index of Folk-Literature*, Vol. 6, Index (Bloomington: Indiana University Press, 1958), 110, 537.

3. http://www.voluspa.org/thrymsk vida11–15.htm (accessed November 26, 2021).

4. Sir Walter Scott, *Minstrelsy of the Scottish Border: Consisting of Historical and Romantic Ballads, Collected in the Southern Counties of Scotland; with a Few of Modern Date, Founded upon Local Tradition*, Vol. III (Edinburgh: James Ballantyne & Co., 1806), 72.

5. John Cohen, producer, and Peter Gott, recorder, *Old Love Songs and Ballads from the Big Laurel North Carolina*, Folkways Record FA2309, Vinyl, LP, Album, 1964.

6. Mary Woody's brother, Robert Woody, wrote his name and the date 1817 on a later page in her commonplace book containing the narrative poem "A True Account of Nayomy Wise," Charles E. Young Research Library, UCLA (UCLA-URL-SC 100, Box 7).

7. Hinshaw, *Encyclopedia of American Quaker Genealogy*, Vol. 1, 368–69, 430.

8. "James and Mary Laughlin Woody, Their Children and Their Grandchildren," Woody Family file, Randolph Room, RCPL; interview with historian Winford Calvin Hinshaw (1924–2016). See also North Carolina, Wills and Probate Records, 1665–1998, ancestry.com (accessed December 5, 2021).

9. Jerome Dowd, *Life of Braxton Craven, D.D., LL. D.* (Raleigh: Edwards and Broughton, 1896) 102.

10. Craven, "Naomi Wise, or the Victim," 3:78–82, 4:111–16.

11. Mattie U. Russell, "Craven, Braxton," *Dictionary of North Carolina Biography*, Vol. 1 of A–C, William S. Powell, ed. (Chapel Hill: University of North Carolina Press, 1979), 455.

12. Bastardy Bonds and Records 1820–1823, C.R.081.102.2, SANC.

13. William Rains, a relative of Lydia, accepted the obligation for her bastardy bond. Mary C. Purvis Craven, *280 Years with Peter Craven Family, 1712–1993, Randolph County, North Carolina, USA* (Asheboro, NC: M. Craven Purvis, 1995), 865.

14. Mary Craven Purvis, *Descendants of Peter Craven, Randolph County North Carolina, USA* (Asheboro, NC: M.C. Purvis, 1985), 378–79.

15. Russell, "Craven, Braxton," 455.

16. Randolph County Court Minutes, February Term 1832. "Ordered by the Court that the sheriff bring to May court next Ann Cravens 3 Children. Braxton 12 years old, Alston 7 years old, Sally 5 years old ... to be dealt with as the court may direct."

17. Dowd, *Life of Braxton Craven*, 111–12, 200–01.

18. Craven, "Naomi Wise, or the Victim," 1:3, 81.

19. "Connections to Slavery: Trinity College in Randolph County, NC," https://sites.duke.edu/trinityslavery/ (accessed December 4, 2021).

20. 1850 U.S. Federal Census—Slave Schedules, Northern Division, Randolph County, NC.

Chapter 9

1. Henry M. Belden and Arthur Palmer Hudson, eds., *The Frank C. Brown Collection of North Carolina Folklore: Vol. 2 Folk Ballads from North Carolina* (Durham: Duke University Press, 1952), 690.

2. Long-Wilgus, *Naomi Wise*, 21.

3. *Ibid.*, 21.

4. L. McKay Whatley, "Naomi Wise," *Notes on the History of Randolph County, NC*, June 3, 2009, https://randolphhistory.wordpress.com/2009/06/03/naomi-wise/ (accessed December 4, 2021).

5. Donald Ray Richardson, "The Birth of a Ballad: The Story of the Ballad of 'Poor Naomi,'" Senior Thesis, Department of English, Guilford College, 1957, 14.

6. Mary Jane Dyson, "Poor Omie Wise," WVU, #58, XIV, XVII, L-F4, 15-D, Disc 432, 1940. Mary Jane Dyson Collection, West Virginia and Regional History Center, West Virginia University.

7. L. McKay Whatley, "Naomi Wise," https://randolphhistory.wordpress.com/2009/06/03/naomi-wise/ (accessed December 4, 2021). According to Whatley,

local historian W. Calvin Hinshaw said that he was told by George Newman Hinshaw that the song first printed by Braxton Craven was written by Levi Beeson and his mother soon after the event. The authors were also informed by W. Calvin Hinshaw that the information had been passed through George's family, and in Hinshaw's notes he wrote, "Levi Hinshaw and mother wrote the song about Naomi Wise from papers of G. N. Hinshaw." Winford Calvin Hinshaw papers.

8. Wills, 1663–1978; Estate Papers, 1781–1928 (Randolph County), SANC.

9. Randolph County Court Minutes, August Term 1803, RCPL, RR, 48.

10. General Assembly Sessions Records, November–December 1804, Box 2, Petitions (Divorce), SANC.

11. Letter from Harold Meyer to Laura Worth, August 14, 1960. Laura Worth Papers, RCPL, RR.

12. Randolph County Court Minutes, May Term 1806, RCPL, RR, 217.

13. Deed Book 32, p. 252, RCRD.

14. "Tragic Death of Naomi Wise Is Told in Ballads Collected by Lunsford," *Asheville Citizen Times*, February 14, 1932, 6; "Poor Naomi Wise," Bascom Lamar Lunsford Collection, Box 72, Folder P, Southern Appalachian Archives, Liston B. Ramsey Center for Regional Studies, Mars Hill University, Mars Hill, NC, http://dla.acaweb.org/cdm/compoundobject/collection/Mars/id/458/rec/3 (accessed December 4, 2021).

15. Elma Barker, "Poor Naomi," 52–3.

16. The Pugh Brown ballad is similar to a ballad in the John Burch Blaylock Collection. Henry M. Belden and Arthur Palmer Hudson, eds., *The Frank C. Brown Collection of North Carolina Folklore: Vol. 2: Folk Ballads from North Carolina* (Durham: Duke University Press, 1952), 698.

17. Blair, *Union Republican*, May 6, 1915, 4.

18. Deed Book 15, p. 55, RCRD, Asheboro, NC.; State Land Grant Entry No. 288 to Levi Penington and Stephen Gardiner, December 3, 1787, SANC. The deed description mentions a corner near the "race paths." State Land Grant Warrant No. 2540 to Eli Whitney, February 10, 1825, SANC. "Salem preparative

Complains of William Dennis, Jr., for deviating from plainness, wagering on a horse race, taking too much strong drink and using bad language." See *Marlboro Monthly Meeting, Men's Minutes 1816–1853*, 161.

19. Blair, *Reminiscences of Randolph County*, 38; Levi Pennington, Book 1, p. 20, RCRD; Land Warrants, Levi Pennington, no. 285, Randolph 258–593, SANC.

20. Levi Pennington, State Land Grant, 1782, Deed Book 1, p. 21; Pennington to Thomas Dougan, 1784, Deed Book 3, p. 22; Dougan to William Bell, 1790, Deed Book 4, p. 101; Bell to John and Joseph Close, 1796, Deed Book 7, p. 154; Close to John Underhill, 1799, Deed Book 8, p. 194; Underhill to John Hinshaw, 1800, Deed Book 8, p. 194, RCRD.

21. Stephen Canner, "Unreliable Narratives: History and Folk Memory in the Southern Murder Ballad," *Folk Horror Revival: Harvest Hymns Volume I—Twisted Roots* (Durham, UK: Wyrd Harvest Press/Lulu, 2018), 77.

22. Louise Pound, *American Ballads and Songs* (New York: C. Scribner's Sons, 1922), 119–120, 247–248; D.K. Wilgus Papers #20003, Southern Folklife Collection, the Wilson Library, University of North Carolina at Chapel Hill.

23. Pound, *American Ballads and Songs*, 119–120, 247–248.

24. Vernon Dalhart (Marion Try Slaughter), Columbia 15053D, recorded November 24, 1925, New York City.

25. Morgan Denmon, Okeh 45075, recorded October 28, 1926, Atlanta, Georgia.

26. G.B. Grayson, Victor 21625, recorded October 18, 1927, Atlanta, Georgia; Tony Russell, *Country Music Originals: The Legends and the Lost* (New York: Oxford University Press, 2007), 105–106. E

27. Clarence Ashley, Columbia 15522-D, recorded October 23, 1929, Johnson City, Tennessee.

28. Cranford and Thompson (Red Fox Chasers), Gennet 6945, recorded June 13, 1929, Richmond, Indiana.

29. A'nt Idy Harper and the Coon Creek Girls, Vocalion 04354, recorded May 30, 1938, Chicago, Illinois.

30. Harry Smith, ed., *Anthology of American Folk Music*, Folkways Records FP 251, FP 252, and FP 253, 1952.

31. Shirley Collins, *Sweet England: A Collection of Love Songs and Ballads from Southern England*, Argo Records RG 150 LP, United Kingdom, 1959.

32. https://mainlynorfolk.info/shirley.collins/records/sweetengland.html (accessed December 4, 2021).

33. https://www.bobdylan.com/setlists/?id_song=27566 (accessed December 4, 2021).

34. Judy Henske, *Miss Judy Henske*, Elektra EKL-231, Vinyl, LP, Mono Promo, 1963.

35. *Old Time Music at Clarence Ashley's—Part 2*, Folkways Records FA 2359, Vinyl, LP, Album, 1963.

36. Roscoe Holcomb, *High Lonesome Sound*, Folkways FA 2368, LP, 1965.

37. *Doc Watson*, Vanguard VSD7 9152, LP, 1964.

38. Kate and Anna McGarrigle with Elvis Costello, *Shout! Factory*– 826663– 10041, 2 × CD, Compilation 2 × DVD, DVD-Video, NTSC Box Set, *The Harry Smith Project: Anthology of American Folk Music*, 2006.

39. Personal communication with Omie Wise band members, October 23, 2020.

40. https://donnahughes.com/naomiwise/ (accessed November 30, 2021).

Chapter 10

1. George F. Swain, J.A. Holmes, and E.W. Myers, "Papers on the Waterpower in North Carolina; A Preliminary Report," *North Carolina Geological Survey*, Bulletin No. 8 (Guy V. Barnes Public Printer, 1899), 166.

2. "Naomi Wise: A True Tale in Real Life," *Union Republican*, Thursday, May 24, 1883, 1.

3. Blair, *Reminiscences of Randolph County*, 38.

4. J.W. Cannon, "Spirit of Naomi Wise Drowned Over 100 Years Ago by Her Lover Still Hovers Over Randolph," *Greensboro Daily News*, November 15, 1925.

5. Communication with Ewart Pugh (1911–1973) who remembered a gourd dipper hanging at the spring allowing people to drink from the water. Communication with Talmadge Hayes (1910–1981) who attended New Salem School and could remember going to the spring to get water for use at the school house.

6. W.S. Lineberry, "New Salem," *The Courier*, Thursday, May 10, 1923, 3. The New Salem tan yards are shown on the 1885 Sanborn Insurance Map. See Sanborn Fire Insurance Map from Trinity College, Randolph County, North Carolina, Sanborn Map Company, July 1885, retrieved from the Library of Congress, www.loc.gov/item/sanborn06503_001/ (accessed December 4, 2021).

7. W.A. Woolen to James N. Caudle, Book 59, pages 54–55, RCRD.

8. Minnie McIver Brown, "Old Tragedy Deep River Still Fresh in Memory," *Raleigh News and Observer*, July 29, 1928; Susan Iden, "Among the Historic Hills of Randolph," *The State, A Weekly Survey of North Carolina* 3, no. 10, August 3, 1935, 17.

9. Iden, "Among the Historic Hills of Randolph," 16–17, 26.

10. Communication with Darrell Fogleman, April 11, 2018. The footprint was carved in the rock by an ancestor of the Jack Fogleman family living in the village of Naomi. The footprint was said to have been destroyed during a water main upgrade around 1960. See Bonnie Moore, "People Still Sing About Naomi," *High Point Enterprise*, Sunday, March 26, 1961.

11. Bascom Lamar Lunsford, "Notes from the Music Library," 11.

12. Iden, "Among the Historic Hills of Randolph," 17.

13. Lunsford, "Notes from the Music Library," 11.

14. J.W. Cannon, "Spirit of Naomi Wise Drowned Over 100 Years Ago by Her Lover Still Hovers Over Randolph," *Greensboro Daily News*, November 15, 1925; B.A. Botkin, *A Treasury of Southern Folklore* (New York: Bonanza Books, 1949), 323; Clipping from the Asheboro *Courier Tribune*, 1936, Randolph Co., Biography. Naomi Wise, Randolph Room, RCPL.

Bibliography

Books and Articles

Amster, Betty L. *New Albany on the Ohio: Historical Review, 1813–1963*. New Albany, IN: Sesquicentennial Com mittee, 1963.

Archive of Folk Song (U.S.). *Check-List of Recorded Songs in the English Language in the Archive of American Folk Song to July, 1940: Alphabetical List with Geographical Index*. Washington, D.C.: Works Projects Administration, 1942.

Ashe, Thomas. *Travels in America Performed in 1806: For the Purpose of Exploring the Rivers, Alleghany, Monongahela, Ohio, and Mississippi, and Ascertaining the Produce and Condition of Their Banks and Vicinity*. London: William Sawyer & Co., 1808.

Atkinson, David. "Magical Corpses: Ballads, Intertextuality, and the Discovery of Murder." *Journal of Folklore Research* 36, no. 1 (January–April 1999), 1–29.

Auman, William T. *Civil War in the North Carolina Quaker Belt: The Confederate Campaign against Peace Agitators, Deserters and Draft Dodgers*. Jefferson, North Carolina: McFarland, 2014.

Baird, Lewis C. *Baird's History of Clark County, Indiana*. Indianapolis: B.F. Bowen, 1909.

Baptist, Edward E. "My Mind Is to Drown You and Leave You Behind: 'Omie Wise,' Intimate Violence, and Masculinity." *Over the Threshold: Intimate Violence in Early America*, eds. Christine Daniels and Michael V. Kennedy. New York: Routledge, 1999.

Barker, Elma. "Elma J. Barkers Book." April 11, 1880. Private family collection, Providence, NC.

Belden, Henry M., ed. "Ballads and Songs: Collected by the Missouri Folk-Lore Society." *The University of Missouri Studies* 15, no. 1 (January 1, 1940), 322–324.

Belden, Henry M., and Arthur Palmer Hudson, eds. *The Frank C. Brown Collection of North Carolina Folklore: Vol. 2: Folk Ballads from North Carolina*. Durham: Duke University Press, 1952.

Blair, J.A. *Reminiscences of Randolph County*. 1890 reprint edition. Asheboro, NC: Randolph County Historical Society, 1968.

Botkin, B.A. *A Treasury of Southern Folklore; Stories, Ballads, Traditions, and Folkways of the People of the South*. New York: Bonanza Books, 1949.

Briles, C.R., comp. *1785 Tax List of Randolph County*. Typed manuscript, 1958.

Brittain, Colonel I.J., ed. *Tragedy of Naomi Wise: How She Came to Her Untimely End by Jonathan Lewis and Life of Andrew Jackson*. Winston-Salem, NC: Colonel I.J. Brittain, 1910[?].

Brittain, Robert P. "Cruentation: In Legal Medicine and in Literature." *Medical History* 9, no. 1 (January 1965), 82–88.

Brumberg, Joan Jacobs. "Something Happens to Girls: Menarche and the Emergence of the Modern American Hygienic Imperative." *Women and Health in America: Historical Readings*, second edition. Judith Walzer Leavitt, ed. Madison: University of Wisconsin Press, 1999, 150–171.

Bibliography

Buley, R. Carlyle. *The Old Northwest: Pioneer Period, 1815–1840*. Bloomington: Indiana University Press, 1950.

Burrison, John, ed. *Storytellers: Folktales and Legends from the South*. Athens: University of Georgia Press, 1989.

Burt, Olive Woolley. *American Murder Ballads and Their Stories*. New York: Oxford University Press, 1958.

Bynum, Victoria E. *Unruly Women: The Politics of Social and Sexual Control in the Old South*. Chapel Hill: University of North Carolina Press, 1992.

Camin, Betty J., and Edwin A. Camin, comps. *North Carolina Bastardy Bonds*. Mount Airy, NC: Betty J. Camin and Edwin A. Camin, 1990.

Campbell, Olive Dame, and Cecil J. Sharp. *English Folksongs from the Southern Appalachians*. New York: Knickerbocker Press, 1917.

Canner, Stephen. "Unreliable Narratives: History and Folk Memory in the Southern Murder Ballad." *Folk Horror Revival: Harvest Hymns Volume I—Twisted Roots*. Durham, UK: Wyrd Harvest Press/Lulu, 2018, 69–92.

Carter, Clarence Edwin, comp. and ed. *The Territorial Papers of the United States*. Vol. 7, *The Territory of Indiana, 1800–1810*. Washington, D.C.: Government Printing Office, 1939.

Carter, Clarence Edwin, comp. and ed. *The Territorial Papers of the United States*. Vol. 8, *The Territory of Indiana, 1810–1816*. Washington, D.C.: Government Printing Office, 1939.

Caruthers, the Rev. E.W. *Interesting Revolutionary Events: and Sketches of Character Chiefly in the "Old North State."* Second Series. Philadelphia: Hayes & Zell, 1856.

Caruthers, E.W., and B. Craven. *A Brief History of Col. David Fanning: Also, Naomi Wise, or the Wrongs of a Beautiful Girl: And Randolph's Manufacturing*. Weldon, NC: Harrell's Printing House, 1888.

Chaffin, Nora C. "A Southern Advocate of Methodist Unification in 1865." *The North Carolina Historical Review* 18, no. 1 (1941), 38–47.

Chaffin, Nora Campbell. *Trinity College, 1839–1892: The Beginnings of Duke University. 1900*. Durham: Duke University Press, 1950.

Chambers, William, and Robert Chambers. "Exploded Follies. Ordeal by Touch." *Chambers Edinburgh Journal* 5, no. 240 (September 1836), 250.

Christian Worker 8, no. 51 (December 20, 1883), 743.

"Clarksville Place Names." *Clarksville History Society Newsletter* 6, no. 10 (October 2001).

Collina, Lewis. *Collins' Historical Sketches of Kentucky: History of Kentucky, Volume 2*. Covington, KY: Collins & Company, 1878.

Comstock, Jim. *West Virginia Songbag*. Richwood, WV, 1974.

Comstock, Jim, ed. *The West Virginia Heritage Encyclopedia*. Vol. 23. Richwood, WV, 1976.

Cook, Michael Lewis. *Pioneer Lewis Families*. Vol. 1. Evansville, IN: Cook Publications, 1978.

Craig, James Hicklin. *The Arts and Crafts in North Carolina, 1699–1840*. Winston-Salem, NC: Museum of Early Southern Decorative Arts, Old Salem Incorporated, 1965.

Craven, Braxton. "Naomi Wise, or the Victim." *The Evergreen* 1:3–4 (January–February 1851), 3: 78–82; 4: 111–16.

Davies, Adrian. *The Quakers in English Society 1655–1725*. New York: Oxford University Press, 2000.

Dowd, Jerome. *Life of Braxton Craven, D.D., LL. D.* Raleigh: Edwards and Broughton, 1896.

Dowd, Jerome C. *The Life of Braxton Craven: A Biographical Approach to Social Science*. Durham: Duke University Press, 1939.

"1803 Tax List: Randolph County, North Carolina." *The Genealogical Journal* XI:1 (Winter 1987), 4.

Field, Arthur. "Why Is the 'Murdered Girl' So Popular." *Midwest Folklore* 1, no. 2 (1951), 113–19.

Bibliography

Field, Sueanne. "The Field Family in Pennsylvania and North Carolina." *The Guilford Genealogist* 20, #2, no. 60 (Winter 1993), 89–96.

Field, Sueanne. "The Field Family in Pennsylvania and North Carolina." *The Guilford Genealogist* 20, #3, no. 61 (Spring 1993), 163–175.

Forman-Brunell, Miriam, and Leslie Paris, eds. *The Girls' History and Culture Reader: The Nineteenth Century.* Urbana: University of Illinois Press, 2011.

Fries, Adelaide L., ed., *Records of the Moravians In North Carolina.* Vol. VI. Raleigh: Edwards & Broughton Print Co., 1940.

Frost, John, Theo. Bliss, and H.C. Peck. *Heroes and Hunters of the West: Comprising Sketches And Adventures of Boone, Kenton, Brady, Logan, Whetzel, Fleehart, Hughes, Johnston, & c.* Philadelphia: H.C. Peck & Theo. Bliss, 1853.

Gennings, Robert A., Ralph L. Bulla, and Juanita J. Kesler. *The Bulla Family.* Sequim, WA: R.A. Gennings, 1981.

Hastie, Christina Ruth. "'This Murder Done': Misogyny, Femicide, and Modernity in 19th-Century Appalachian Murder Ballads." Master's Thesis, University of Tennessee, 2011. https://trace.tennessee.edu/utk_gradthes/1045.

Hathaway, J.R.B., ed. *The North Carolina Historical and Genealogical Record.* Vol 1. Baltimore: Genealogical Publishing Co., 2002.

Haun, Weynette Parks. *Hyde County, North Carolina County Court Minutes.* Book I (1736–1756), Book II (1757–1785), Book III (1757–1788). Durham: W.P. Haun, 1985.

Haywood, John. *The Duty and Office of Justices of the Peace, and of Sheriffs, Coroners, Constables, & c., According to the Laws of the State of North-Carolina.* Raleigh: William Boylan, 1808.

Heads of Families at the First Census of the United States Taken in the Year 1790—North Carolina. Washington, D.C.: Government Printing Office, 1908.

Hinshaw, William Wade. *Encyclopedia of American Quaker Genealogy.* Vol. 1 of *North Carolina.* Baltimore: Genealogical Publishing Company, 1978.

Hinshaw, Winfred Calvin, ed. *1815 Tax List of Randolph County, North Carolina.* Raleigh: W.P. Johnson, 1957.

History of the Ohio Falls Cities and Their Counties: with Illustrations and Bibliographical Sketches. Vol. 1 and 2. Cleveland: L.A. Williams & Company, 1882.

History of Wayne and Clay Counties, Illinois. Chicago: Globe Pub. Co., 1884.

Howe, Daniel Waite. "Laws and Courts of the Northwest and Indiana Territories." *Indiana Historical Society* 2, no. 1. Indianapolis: The Bowen-Merrill Co., 1886.

Hudson, Arthur Palmer. *Folk Songs of Mississippi.* Chapel Hill: University of North Carolina Press, 1936.

Hutson, C. Kirk. "'Whackety Whack, Don't Talk Back': The Glorification of Violence Against Females and the Subjugation of Women in Nineteenth-Century Southern Folk Music." *Journal of Women's History* 8 no. 3 (1996), 114–142.

Iden, Susan. "Among the Historic Hills of Randolph." *The State, A Weekly Survey of North Carolina* 3, no. 10, August 3, 1935, 16–17, 26.

Iredell, James, and François-Xavier Martin. *Public Acts of the General Assembly of North Carolina.* Vol. 1. Newbern: Martin & Ogden, 1804.

Jackson, Rick. "Naomi Wise." *North Carolina Murder and Mayhem.* Charleston, SC: The History Press, 2019.

Jarrell, Wally. "A Partial ca. 1840 Tax List." *The Genealogical Journal* XXV, no. 1, Randolph County Genealogical Society (Spring 2001), 14–18.

Jay, William. *Inquiry into the Character and Tendency of the American Colonization and the American Anti-Slavery Societies.* New York: Leavett, Lord and Co., 1835.

Jones, Ruth Ann Marley. "The Story of Naomi Wise." Unpublished manuscript, Hackett Reunion, 2006.

Joshi, Jayant. "Poor Naomi Wise: The History behind the Folklore." *NC Friends Historical Society Newsletter* 36 and 37 (June and September 2009).

"Joshua Fleehart." *Heroes and Hunters of the West: Comprising Sketches and Adventures*

Bibliography

of Boone, Kenton, Brady, Logan, Whetzel, Fleehart, Hughes, Johnston, c. Philadelphia: H.C. Peck and Theo. Bliss, 1858.

Kalette, Linda Elise. *The Papers of Thirteen Early Ohio Political Leaders ... an Inventory to the 1976–77 Microfilm Editions.* Columbus: Ohio Historical Society, 1977.

Kemp, Mark Segal. "Down By the River." *Acoustic Guitar* 262 (October 1, 2014), 62–66.

Kleber, John E. *The Encyclopedia of Louisville.* Lexington: University Press of Kentucky, 2001.

Laws of North Carolina 1818. Raleigh: Thomas Henderson, State Printer, 1819.

Lea, Henry Charles. *Superstition and Force: Essays on the Wager of Law—The Wager of Battle—The Ordeal—The Torture.* 3rd ed. Philadelphia: H.C. Lea, 1870.

Lewis, Johanna Miller. "Women Artisans in Backcountry North Carolina, 1753–1790." *North Carolina Historical Review* 68, no. 3 (July 1991), 214–236.

Lewis, Michael H. "American Vernacular Furniture and the North Carolina Back Country." *The Journal of Early Southern Decorative Arts* XX, no. 2 (November 1994), 1–37.

Lindley, Harold, ed. *Indiana as Seen by Early Travelers: A Collection from Books of Travels, Letters, and Diaries Prior to 1830.* 1916. Indianapolis: Indiana Historical Commission, 1992.

Linn, Jo White. "Revolutionary War Claims, Abstracts from the Delamar Transcripts: Private Petitions in the North Carolina Legislative Papers." *North Carolina Genealogical Society Journal* III, no. 3 (1977), 165.

Lloyd, Glenda Gardiner. "Journal of Richard Lewis (1759–1833) of Randolph Co. NC and Floyd Co. IN." *North Carolina Genealogical Society Journal* II, no.4 (November 1985), 218.

Logan, William N., E.R. Cumings, Clyde A. Malott, Stephen S. Visher, W.M. Tucker, and J.R. Reeves. *Handbook of Indiana Geology.* Indianapolis: Wm. B. Burford, 1922.

London, Lawrence. "Edward Jones." *Dictionary of North Carolina Biography.* Vol. 3, H–K. William S. Powell, ed. Chapel Hill: University of North Carolina Press, 1979.

Long-Wilgus, Eleanor. *Naomi Wise: Creation, Re-Creation and Continuity in an American Ballad Tradition.* Chapel Hill: Chapel Hill Press, 2003.

Lunsford, Bascom Lamar. "Notes from the Music Library." John Lair, ed. *Stand By Magazine* 29 (May 1937), 11.

Martin, François-Xavier. *The Office and Authority of a Justice of the Peace, and of Sheriffs, Coroners, & c. According to the Laws of the State of North-Carolina.* New Bern: François-Xavier Martin, 1791.

Milnes, Gerald. "Poor Little Omie Wise." *Play of a Fiddle: Traditional Music Dance and Folklore in West Virginia.* Lexington: University Press of Kentucky, 1999.

Milnes, Gerald. "West Virginia's Omie Wise: The Folk Process Unveiled." *Appalachian Journal* 22, no. 4 (Summer 1995), 376–389.

Morris, Alton G. *Folksongs of Florida.* 2nd ed. Gainesville: University of Florida Press, 1990.

"Naomi Wise: Creation, Re-Creation, and Continuity in an American Ballad." *Béaloideas* 72 (2004), 259–262.

Naomi Wise or the Wrongs of a Beautiful Girl, A True Story, Enacted in Randolph County, N. Carolina about One Hundred Years Ago. Pinnacle, NC: W.C. Phillips, Printer, 1904.

The Old Discipline: Nineteenth Century Friends Disciplines in America. Glenside, PA: Quaker Heritage Press, 1999.

Olds, Fred. *Story of the Counties of North Carolina with Other Data.* Oxford, NC: Oxford Orphanage Press, 1921.

"Ordeal of Touch in Colonial Virginia." *The Virginia Magazine of History and Biography* 4, no. 2 (1896), 185–197.

Penny, Mark, ed. *Naomi Wise or the Wrongs of a Beautiful Girl, A True Story, Enacted in North Carolina 80 Years Ago.* Weldon, NC: Harrell Printing Company, August 1884.

Philbrick, Francis S., ed. "The Laws of the Indiana Territory: 1801–1809." *Collections of*

Bibliography

the Illinois State Historical Library XXI, Vol. 2 of Law Series. Springfield: The Illinois State Historical Library, 1930.

Polenberg, Richard. *Hear My Sad Story: The True Tales that Inspired Stagolee, John Henry, and Other Traditional American Folk Songs.* Ithaca: Cornell University Press, 2015.

Pound, Louise. *American Ballads And Songs.* New York: C. Scribner's Sons, 1922, 1972.

Purvis, Mary Craven. *Descendants of Peter Craven, Randolph County North Carolina, USA.* Asheboro, NC: M.C. Purvis, 1985.

Purvis, Mary Craven. *280 Years with Peter Craven Family, 1712–1993, Randolph County, North Carolina, USA.* Asheboro, NC: M. Craven Purvis, 1995.

Randolph, Vance. *Ozark Folksongs.* Vol. 2. Columbia: University of Missouri Press, 1980.

Randolph, Vance. *The Ozarks: An American Survival of Primitive Society.* Robert Cochran, ed. Fayetteville: University of Arkansas Press, 2017.

Randolph County, 1779–1979. Winston Salem, NC: Hunter Publishing Company, 1980.

Rankin, Robert. *The Government and Administration of North Carolina.* New York: Thomas Y. Crowell Company, 1955.

Redding, Sandra. *Naomi Wise: A Cautionary Tale.* Kernersville, NC: Alabaster Book Publishing, 2013.

Register, Alvaretta K. *State Census of North Carolina, 1784–1787.* Baltimore: Genealogical Publishing Co., 2001.

The Revised Laws of Indiana: In Which Are Comprised All Such Acts of a General Nature as Are in Force in Said State; Adopted and Enacted by the General Assembly at Their Fifteenth Session, Indiana General Assembly. Indianapolis: Douglass & McGuire, 1831.

Richardson, Donald Ray. " The Birth of a Ballad: The Story of the Ballad of 'Poor Naomi." Senior Thesis, Department of English, Guilford College, 1957.

Rodgers, Rev. J.P. *Life of Rev. James Needham, the Oldest Methodist Preacher.* Pilot Mountain, NC: The Surry Printing House, 1899.

Roote, Robert. "The Historical Facts Behind the Celebrated Ballad 'Naomi Wise.'" *North Carolina Folklore Journal* 5, no. 2 (Fall–Winter 1984), 70–81.

Russell, Mattie U. "Craven, Braxton." *Dictionary of North Carolina Biography.* Vol. 1, A–C. William S. Powell, ed. Chapel Hill: University of North Carolina Press, 1979.

Russell, Tony. *Country Music Originals: The Legends and the Lost.* New York: Oxford University Press, 2007.

Russell, Tony, and Bob Pinson. *Country Music Records: A Discography, 1921–1942.* New York: Oxford University Press, 2004.

Salmon, Marylynn. *Women and the Law of Property in Early America.* Chapel Hill: University of North Carolina Press, 1986.

Sarles, Jane. *Clarksville, Indiana.* Charleston, SC: Arcadia, 2001.

Schechter, Harold. *True Crime: An American Anthology.* New York: Literary Classics of the United States, 2008.

Schimd, David. *Violence in American Popular Culture.* Santa Barbara, CA: Praeger, 2015.

Sharp, Cecil, Olive Dame Campbell, and Maude Karpeles. *English Folk Songs from the Southern Appalachians.* Vol. 2. London: Oxford University Press, 1932.

"Silver Creek: A Historic Natural Treasure." *Clarksville Historical Society Newsletter* 14, no. 2 (April 2010).

Sokoloff, Kenneth L., and Georgia C. Villaflor. "The Early Achievement of Modern Stature in America." *Social Science History* 6, no. 4 (1982), 453–481.

The Story of Naomi Wise or the Wrongs of a Beautiful Girl. Randleman, NC: Randleman Rotary Club, 1944.

Stouten, Molly. "Omie Wise: The Ballad as History." *Old-Time Herald* 5, no. 7 (1997), 25–30.

Swaim, Benjamin. *The North Carolina Justice: Containing a Summary Statement of the*

Bibliography

Statutes and Common Law of This State, Together with the Decisions of the Supreme Court, and All the Most Approved Forms and Precedents Relating to the Office and Duty of a Justice of the Peace, and Other Public Officers According to Modern Practice, the Whole Intended as a Complete Practical Application of the New Revised Statutes of North Carolina. 2nd ed. Raleigh: Henry D. Turner, 1846.

Swain, George F., J.A. Holmes, and E.W. Myers. "Papers on the Waterpower in North Carolina; A Preliminary Report." *North Carolina Geological Survey*, Bulletin No. 8. Raleigh: Guy V. Barnes Public Printer, 1899.

Tait, Allison Anna. "The Beginning of the End of Coverture: A Reappraisal of the Married Woman's Separate Estate." *Yale Journal of Law & Feminism* 26, no. 2 (2014), 165–216.

Terry, Tanya Ann. *Murder Will Out: James Hogg's Use of the Bier Right in His Minor Works and Confessions.* Thesis. Provo, Utah, Brigham Young University, 2010.

Thompson, Stith. *Motif-Index of Folk-Literature.* Vol. 6, Index. Bloomington: Indiana University Press, 1958.

Thornbrough, Gayle, ed. *Outpost on the Wabash, 1787–1791: Letters of Brigadier General Josiah Harmar and Major John Francis Hamtramck and Other Letters and Documents Selected from the Harmar Papers in the William L. Clements Library.* Indiana Historical Society Publications, Vol. 19. Indianapolis: Indiana Historical Society, 1958, 128–29.

Underwood, Richard H. "Omie Wise." *CrimeSong: True Crime Stories from Southern Murder Ballads.* Lexington, KY: Shadeland House Modern Press, 2016.

Underwood, Richard H., and Carol J. Paris. "Crimesong: Some Murder Ballads and Poems Revisited." *Journal of Southern Legal History* 12, no. 1 (2004), 5–40.

United States Bureau of Labor Statistics. *History of Wages in the United States from Colonial Times to 1928.* Washington, D.C.: Government Printing Office, 1934.

Watson, Allen. "The Constable in Colonial North Carolina." *North Carolina Historical Review* 68 (January 1991), 1–16.

Wellman, Manley Wade. *Dead and Gone: Classic Crimes of North Carolina.* Chapel Hill: University of North Carolina Press, 1954.

Whatley, L. McKay, Jr. Lowell McKay. *Architectural History of Randolph County, N.C.* Asheboro, NC: City of Asheboro and the County of Randolph, 1985.

Whatley, L. McKay, Jr. "The New County Jail—1850." Typed manuscript.

Whatley, L. McKay, Jr. *Randolph County.* Charleston, SC: Arcadia, 2010

Wheeler, John H. *Historical Sketches of North Carolina from 1584–1851.* Philadelphia: Lippincott, Grambo and Co., 1851.

White, Geraldine, and Norman Curtis. *The Providence Pathfinders: The Story of a Special People.* Part One. Greensboro: Franklin's Printing, 1996.

Williams, Richard. "'Omie Wise': A Cultural Performance." *Kentucky Folklore Record* 23 (1977), 7–11.

Winick, Stephen D. " Reviewed Work: 'Naomi Wise: Creation, Re-Creation and Continuity in an American Ballad Tradition' by Eleanor R. Long-Wilgus." *Western Folklore* 64, no. 1/2 (Winter–Spring, 2005), 149–151.

York, Brantley, 1805–1891. *The Autobiography of Brantley York.* Durham: The Seeman Printery, 1910.

Zipf, Karen L. *Labor of Innocents: Forced Apprenticeship in North Carolina, 1715–1919.* Baton Rouge: Louisiana State University Press, 2005.

Documents and Records

Accounts and Claims, Randolph County
Apprentice Bonds, Hyde County

Bibliography

Apprentice Bonds, Randolph County
Asheboro, North Carolina
Asheboro, North Carolina
Back Creek Friends Meeting, *Men's Minutes, 12/1792–1/1840*, Randolph County, NC
Back Creek Monthly Meeting (Grant County, IN), *Births and Deaths Mid–1800's*. Vol. 2 or Book B
Bastardy Bonds, Craven County
Bastardy Bonds, Guilford County
Bastardy Bonds, Hyde County
Bastardy Bonds, Randolph County
Bastardy Bonds, Tyrell County
Bible and Cemetery Records
The Blue Ridge Institute & Museum, Blue Ridge Heritage Archives
Bowling Green, Kentucky
Catalog of Published Materials
Chapel Hill, North Carolina
Charles E. Young Research Library, UCLA
Clark County Government Building
Columbus, Ohio
Craven Family File
Criminal Action Papers, Randolph County
D.K. Wilgus Papers #20003, Southern Folklife Collection, the Wilson Library
Duke University, Rubenstein Library
Durham, North Carolina
Englehard, North Carolina
Estate Papers, Randolph County
Ferrum, Virginia
Field Family File
Folklore Archives Collection
Friends Collection and College Archives, Earlham
General Assembly Session Records: Divorce Petitions
Governor's Letter Books, David Stone
Governor's Papers, Benjamin Smith
Greensboro, North Carolina
Guilford College's Quaker Archives
Hyde County Historical and Genealogical Society
Hyde County Register of Deeds
Illinois State Archives
Indexes of Ohio History
Indiana Historical Society
Indianapolis, Indiana
Insolvent Debtors, Randolph County
James Taylor Adams Collection
Jeffersonville, Indiana
Land Warrants, Plats of Survey, and Related Land Grant Records
Laura Stimson Worth Collection
Lewis Family File
The Liston B. Ramsey Center for Appalachian Studies
Los Angeles, California
Marlboro Friends Meeting, *Minutes, 1816–1890*, Randolph County, NC
Marriage Bonds, Randolph County
Mars Hill, North Carolina
Mars Hill University
Minute Dockets of County Court, Randolph County

Bibliography

Miscellaneous Records, Randolph County
Murphey Papers 1797–1817
Naomi Wise File
Nashville, Tennessee
New Albany, Indiana
New Garden Quarterly Meeting, *Minutes, 1881–1933*; Collection: North Carolina
    Yearly Meeting Minutes
North Carolina Division of Archives and History
Ohio Historical Society
Raleigh, North Carolina
Randolph County Register of Deeds
Randolph Room, Randolph County Public Library
Richmond, Indiana
Southern Indian Genealogical Society
Springfield, Illinois
State Archives of Ohio Record Series 1322, Governors General Record
State of Illinois Public Land Purchase Records, 1813–1909
Stuart Barth Wrege Indiana History Room, New Albany-Floyd County Public Library
Superior Court Minutes, Randolph County
Swan Quarter, North Carolina
Tennessee / North Carolina Revolutionary War Land Warrants, 1783–1837
Tennessee State Library and Archives
University of North Carolina at Chapel Hill
Vincennes, Indiana
Vincennes University, Lewis Historical Library
Wardens of the Poor Minutes, Randolph County
Western Kentucky University
Wills and Executors Records, Clark County
Wills, Randolph County
Woody Family File
Works Progress Administration's Ohio Governor's Calendar of Papers, 1803–1878

Newspapers

Blair, William. *Union Republican*, May 6, 1915.
Brown, Minnie McIver. "Old Tragedy Deep River Still Fresh in Memory." *Raleigh News
    and Observer*, July 29, 1928.
Cannon, J.W. "Spirit of Naomi Wise Drowned Over 100 Years Ago by Her Lover Still
    Hovers Over Randolph." *Greensboro Daily News*, November 15, 1925.
"Corrections to the Early History of Asheboro." *The Courier*, Thursday, December 1,
    1921.
Danbury Reporter, May 18, 1911, 5.
Dibacco, Jerry. "Discovery Rekindles 1870 Murder Mystery; 'Ballad of Naomi Wise'
    Written to Chronicle the Murder." *The Inter-Mountain*, Elkins, WV, September 14,
    1992, 1, 14.
Julian, Howgill. "Tragic Story of Naomi Wise Told by H. Julian." *The Asheboro Courier*,
    Tuesday, September 2, 1879.
Lineberry, W.S. "New Salem." *The Courier*, Thursday, May 10, 1923, 3.
"Local and Personal." *The Randolph Bulletin*, January 10, 1907.
McMasters, D.G. "Sketch of the Life of Alexander Gray Murdock." *The Courier*, Octo-
    ber 3, 1912.

Bibliography

Moore, Bonnie. "People Still Sing About Naomi." *High Point Enterprise*, Sunday, March 26, 1961.
"Naomi Wise: A True Tale in Real Life." *Union Republican*, Thursday, May 24, 1883, 1.
"Naomi Wise—An Undying Legend." *Salisbury Sunday Post*, September 15, 1957.
"Randleman History Tells Story of Poor Naomi; Murdered Near There by Her Lover in 1808." *Burlington Hosiery News* 1, no. 11 August 1947.
"Tragic Death of Naomi Wise is Told in Ballads Collected by Lunsford." *Asheville Citizen Times*, February 14, 1932, 6.
Tyson, Bryan, "Naomi Wise." *The Randolph Bulletin*, January 30, 1908.
Vernon, Charlie. "Naomi Wise." *The Greensboro Patriot* nos. 317–320, 1874.

United States Censuses and Census Reports

1850 U.S. Federal Census—Slave Schedules, Northern Division, Randolph County, NC.
First United States Federal Census, 1790, Randolph County, NC.
Second United States Federal Census, 1800, Randolph County, NC.
Third United States Federal Census, 1810, Randolph County, NC.
Fourth United States Federal Census, 1820, Randolph County, NC.
Fifth United States Federal Census, 1830, Randolph County, NC.
Sixth United States Federal Census, 1840, Randolph County, NC.
Sixth United States Federal Census, 1850, Clay County, Illinois.
Sixth United State Federal Census, 1850, Grant County, Indiana.
Seventh United States Federal Census 1860, Mill, Grant County, Indiana.
Eighth United States Federal Census 1870, Chariton County, Missouri.
Eighth United States Federal Census 1870, Coffey County, Kansas.
Ninth United States Federal Census 1880, Coffey County, Kansas
U.S. Selected Federal Census Non-Population Schedules, 1850–1880. Neosho, Coffey County, Kansas. 1870.

Maps

Brazier, Robert H.B. "A New Map of the State of North Carolina." Fayetteville, NC: John Mac Rae; Philadelphia: H.S. Tanner, 1833. Retrieved from the Library of Congress, www.loc.gov/item/2006459002/.
Brooks, Jared, and John Goodman. " A Map of the Rapids of the Ohio River and of the Countries on Each Side Thereof : So Far, as to Include the Routes Contemplated for Canal Navigation." Frankfort, KY: Engraved by John Goodman, 1806. Retrieved from the Library of Congress, www.loc.gov/item/96687584/.
Davis, George W. Map of Clark County, Indiana. [Philadelphia: Chas. A. Mc. Cann & David S. Koon. Philadelphia: Printed by Braden & Burford, 1875] Retrieved from the Library of Congress, www.loc.gov/item/2013593193/.
"Map of Floyd County Indiana: showing the townships sections divisions and farm lands with the owners' names and number of acres, together with roads, rivers, creeks, railroads, &c &c." New York: P. O'Beinre & Co., Civil Engineers Topographical Surveys and Map Publishers, 1859.
"Map of the Falls of the Ohio and the Adjoining Countries From McMurtries' Sketches." N.p., 1819.
Munsell, Luke, and Hugh Anderson. "A map of the State of Kentucky: from actual survey; also part of Indiana and Illinois." Frankfort: [Publisher not identified], 1818. Retrieved from the Library of Congress, www.loc.gov/item/75653132/.

Bibliography

"Plan of the Rapids or Falls of the Ohio Latitude of Louisville." Paris: Arthus Bertrand. 1796. David Rumsey Historical Map Collection https://www.davidrumsey.com/luna/servlet/detail/RUMSEY~8~1~1278~100103:Plan-of-the-Rapids-or-Falls-of-the- .

Price, Jonathan, and John Strother. "Price-Strother Map; First Actual Survey of North Carolina." Philadelphia: Engraved by W. Harrison, 1808.

Thompson, Charles Nebecker. "Map Illustrating the Pioneer Periods in Indiana." *1932 Yearbook of the Society of the Indiana Pioneers.*

U.S. Geological Survey Topographic Map. "New Albany, Indiana." 7.5 Minute Series. U.S. Dept. of the Interior, 2013.

U.S. Geological Survey Topographic Map. "Speed Quadrangle, Indiana." 7.5 Minute Series. U.S. Dept. of the Interior, 2013.

Online Resources

"Activating History for Justice at Duke." https://www.activatinghistoryatduke.com/uploads/8/9/2/3/89234082/activating_history_for_justice_at_duke_lowrez.pdf (October 14, 2021).

"Alva R. Chamness." Find a Grave. www.findagrave.com/memorial/174761640 (December 4, 2021).

"An Autobiography from Press and Photography of Bascom Lamar Lunsford, Minstrel of the Appalachians, 1950, as compiled by his daughters Kern, Merton, and Jo." https://lib.digitalnc.org/record/106500 (January 29, 2021).

Berry, Grace. "Naomi Wise." Bascom Lamar Lunsford Collection, Box 71, Folder N, Southern Appalachian Archives, Liston B. Ramsey Center for Regional Studies, Mars Hill University. https://dla.acaweb.org/digital/collection/Mars/id/448/rec/2 (October 18, 2021).

"Calendar for year 1807." TimeandDate.com. https://www.timeanddate.com/calendar/?year=1807&country=1 (December 4, 2021).

Christensen, David. "William Lewis." typed manuscript. https://www.ancestry.com/mediauiviewer/tree/170509272/person/302210911776/media/5710b8ce-f273-4dba-a70b-8f1da3a107ed (December 4, 2021).

"Connections to Slavery: Trinity College in Randolph County, NC." https://sites.duke.edu/trinityslavery/ (December 4, 2021).

"Hancock Deed in Indiana." Ancestry.com. https://www.ancestry.com/mediauiviewer/tree/1646386/person/-1906578707/media/5d918998-467c-494e-b353-a9d-a02c6c5b6 (December 4, 2021).

"Harrison County Indiana Biographies." Genealogy Trails History Group. http://genealogytrails.com/ind/harrison/bios11.html (December 4, 2021).

"Harrison County, Indiana: Land Records." Genealogy Trails History Group. http://genealogytrails.com/ind/harrison/land_purchases-1807.html (December 4, 2021).

"Horse: Equus ferus caballus." Speed of Animals. http://www.speedofanimals.com/animals/horse (December 4, 2021).

Illinois Public Domain Land Detail Illinois State Archives. https://www.ilsos.gov/isa/landSalesSearch.do (December 4, 2021).

"Indiana Marriages, 1811–2007." FamilySearch. https://www.familysearch.org/search/collection/1410397 (December 4, 2021).

"Kentucky, County Marriages, 1797–1954." FamilySearch. https://familysearch.org/ark:/61903/3:1:3QSQ-G9SQ-C9MH-W?cc=1804888&wc=QD3Q-WBH%3A1300625411 (December 4, 2021).

"Levi Beeson, North Carolina Estate Files, 1663–1979." FamilySearch. https://www.familysearch.org/ark:/61903/1:1:QJ8L-11H9 (December 4, 2021).

Bibliography

"Mainly Norfolk: English Folk and Other Good Music." https://mainlynorfolk.info/shirley.collins/records/sweetengland.html (December 4, 2021).

"Martha Hussey." The Family Puzzles—Demystified (Sort of). http://rea-williams.com/getperson.php?personID=17613&tree=tree1 (December 4, 2021).

MESDA Collection. http://mesda.org/item/collections/table/21640/. August 4, 2018.

"Michael Shoffner, III." We Relate. https://www.werelate.org/wiki/Person:Michael_Shoffner_(3) (December 4, 2021).

"Moon Phase on: April 05, 1807." https://www.moongiant.com/phase/04/05/1807/ (December 4, 2021).

NC Land Grant Images and Data. www.nclandgrants.com/grant/?mars=12.14.107.220&qid=338966&rn=1 (December 4, 2021).

"Needham, James." MESDA Craftsman Database. http://mesda.org/item/craftsman/needham-james/26265/ (December 4, 2021).

"North Carolina, Wills and Probate Records, 1665–1998." Ancestry.com. https://search.ancestry.com/search/db.aspx?dbid=9061 (December 4, 2021).

Orricer, Lawrence H., and Samuel H. Williamson. "Computing 'Real Value' Over Time with a Conversion Between U.K. Pounds and U.S. Dollars, 1791 to Present." Measuring Worth. https://www.measuringworth.com/calculators/exchange/ (March 6, 2021).

Pangburn, Richard. "Moses McCan—frontier scout—Indians—PA KY VA IN." Genealogy.com. http://www.genealogy.com/forum/surnames/topics/mccann/1796/ (December 4, 2021).

"Poor Naomi Wise." Bascom Lamar Lunsford Collection, Box 72, Folder P, Southern Appalachian Archives, Liston B. Ramsey Center for Regional Studies, Mars Hill University, Mars Hill, NC, Digital Library of Appalachia http://dla.acaweb.org/cdm/compoundobject/collection/Mars/id/458/rec/3 (December 4, 2021).

Sanborn Fire Insurance Map from Trinity College, Randolph County, North Carolina, Library of Congress, www.loc.gov/item/sanborn06503_001/ (December 4, 2021).

Schechter, Harold. "The Murder of 'Omie Wise,' 1808." The Yale Review. https://yalereview.yale.edu/murder-omie-wise-1808 (December 4, 2021).

"Setlists at Riverside Church Hootenanny Special." Bob Dylan, 1961. https://www.bobdylan.com/date/1961-07-29-riverside-church-hootenanny-special/ (December 4, 2021).

Stolze, Dolly. "The ordeal of the bleeding corpse." Strange Remains. July 6, 2015. https://strangeremains.com/2015/07/26/the-ordeal-of-the-bleeding-corpse/ (December 4, 2021).

"Sunday, April 05, 1807 (GMT-4:56:02) Sunset in Randleman, NC." Google.com. https://www.google.com (December 4, 2021).

Völuspá—Norse and Germanic Lore. http://www.voluspa.org/thrymskvida11-15.htm (November 26, 2021).

Whatley, L. McKay, Jr. "Cedar Falls." Notes on the History of Randolph County, N.C. https://randolphhistory.wordpress.com/2007/06/06/cedar-falls/ (December 4, 2021).

Whatley, L. McKay, Jr. "Naomi Wise." Notes on the History of Randolph County, N.C. https://randolphhistory.wordpress.com/2009/06/03/naomi-wise/ (December 4, 2021).

Ballad Text Sources

Barker, Elma. "Poor Naomi." "Elma J. Barkers Book." Private family collection, Providence, NC, 1880.

Blair, William. "The Ballad." Union Republican, May 6, 1915.

Bibliography

Brown, Sarah. "Sallie" Pugh. "Naomi Wise." J. Brown, Private Family Collection. Randleman, NC, ca. 1915.

Chamness, Ava. "Poor Naomi Wise." Bascom Lamar Lunsford Collection, Box 72, Folder P, 4824A. Providence, NC, 1883, Mars Hill University.

Craven, Braxton. "Poor Naomi." *The Evergreen*, 1:4, Asheboro, NC, 1851, 115–116.

Dyson, Mary Jane. "Poor Omie Wise." WVU, #58, XIV, XVII, L-F4,15-D, Disc 432, 1940. Mary Jane Dyson Collection, West Virginia and Regional History Center, West Virginia University.

Huddleston, Flossie. "Little Omie." Cumberland County, Kentucky, 1956. WKU-FA, T-7–8, Western Kentucky University, Folklore Archives Collections, Bowling Green, Kentucky

Johnson, Polly. "Poor Oma" (Little Oma Wise). UV-AL-WPA, 1150-C. Wise, Virginia, 1939.

Moore, Alexander. "Poor Omie." Austin, Texas, 1934. LC-AFS 5781.

Morgan, Rob. "Little Anna." Bowling Green, Kentucky, 1908. Berea HL-SC, Combs Collection.

Smith Hilliard, "Little Omie." Hindman, Kentucky, 1909. Sharp-Campbell-Carpeles, vol. 2, 144–45, Pound, 119–20.

Discography

Ashley, Clarence. Columbia 15522-D, Johnson City, Tennessee, October 23, 1929.

Cohen, John, producer, and Peter Gott, recorder. *Old Love Songs and Ballads from the Big Laurel North Carolina*. Folkways Record FA2309. Vinyl, LP, Album, 1964.

Collins, Shirley. *Sweet England: A Collection of Love Songs and Ballads from Southern England*. Argo Records RG 150 LP. United Kingdom, 1959.

Cranford and Thompson (Red Fox Chasers). Gennet 6945. Richmond, Indiana, June 13, 1929.

Dalhart, Vernon (as Al Craver). Columbia 15053D. New York City, November 24, 1925.

Denmon, Morgan. Okeh 45075. Atlanta, Georgia, October 28, 1926.

Grayson, G.B. Victor 21625. Atlanta, Georgia, October 18, 1927.

Harper, A'nt Idy, and the Coon Creek Girls. Vocalion 04354. Chicago, Illinois, May 30, 1938.

Henske, Judy. *Miss Judy Henske*. Elektra EKL-231, Vinyl, LP, Mono Promo, 1963.

Holcomb, Roscoe. *High Lonesome Sound*. Folkways FA 2368, LP, 1965.

McGarrigle, Kate, and Anna, with Elvis Costello. *Shout! Factory*– 826663–10041, 2 × CD, Compilation 2 × DVD, DVD-Video, NTSC Box Set, *The Harry Smith Project: Anthology of American Folk Music*, 2006.

Old Time Music at Clarence Ashley's—Part 2, Folkways Record FA 2359, Vinyl, LP, Album, 1963.

Smith, Harry, ed. *Anthology of American Folk Music*. Folkways Records FP 251, FP 252, and FP 253, 1952.

Watson, Doc. *Doc Watson*. Vanguard VSD7 9152, LP, 1964.

Index

Numbers in *bold italics* indicate pages with illustrations

Index

Index

203

Index

204

Index

206

Index

Index

Acknowledgments

None of the stories in this book could have been written without the dedication of previous health professionals in uncovering the secrets behind how we are and how we function. My journey began with Dr. Shirley Sahrmann PT, PhD, FAPTA, whose textbooks, seminars and research provided me the foundation from which to help patients with difficult pain but also explore others' approaches as well. Thomas Myers' contribution to understanding fascial patterns has also been instrumental in my exploration of distant connections in our bodies. Lastly Thomas Hanna PhD and Eleanor Criswell EdD, C-IAYT, who together created the Hanna Somatics training, deserve my deepest thanks for developing their unique and powerful approach to solving pain.

Additionally I owe a debt of gratitude to Dr. Noah Charney whose advice helped make this book more readable.

I would also like to thank my medical illustrators, Martin Huber and Meghan M. Shoemaker, whose images help my readers see key relationships featured in *Solving the Pain Puzzle*.

Table of Contents

Foreword
by Elizabeth Sebestyen, M.D.

"Your pain is *not* incurable. It is caused by how you use your body. I'll help you identify and correct poor movement habits to end your pain. Even if nothing else has worked for you." This is the motto accompanying Rick Olderman's professional logo. And he holds true to his promise, whether your pain was caused by a recent injury or surgery or has been nagging you for years!

Over the next pages you will meet some of his patients and learn about their incredible recoveries. You will read about Rick's victories in unlocking contracted muscles and healing migraines, neck pain, shoulder pain and much more. Most importantly you will get to know Rick as he genuinely shares the ups and downs of his journey with all its frustrations and self-doubts. These hurdles are not uncommon in the life of a healthcare professional and can make or break him or her. They pushed Rick almost to the brink, only to make him the best physical therapist I had the pleasure to work with. They pushed him to find answers to the *whys*—the root cause of the problems; they pushed him back to the anatomy lab, to study nonconventional approaches and work out holistic solutions that are sometimes deceivingly simple.

My own story was not unique enough to make it to this book, and I am thankful for that. In medicine you never want to be an interesting case! Perhaps it was not unusual for Rick to help someone walk pain free after a complex ankle fracture and three surgeries. For me it was huge! And not only did I walk, but I was even able to handle the hilly, cobblestoned streets of Portugal shortly after my surgeon allowed me to walk!

Foreword by Elizabeth Sebestyen, M.D.

Without pain!

Rick helped me tremendously and I referred many of my patients, friends and family members to him.

Elizabeth Sebestyen, M.D., is an internal medicine physician integrating medical acupuncture into a busy primary care practice. She has always appreciated Rick Olderman's holistic approach and the lasting pain relief that his techniques and exercises offered to patients.

Preface

I've been interested in solving pain since I became a physical therapist in 1996. The problem I immediately ran into at my first job was that I clearly hadn't acquired the tools to do this. Over the years, as I unraveled how the body creates and solves chronic musculoskeletal pain, describing my emerging approach left me scratching my head. Only recently have I found the words to succinctly express how *I* solve pain, as distinguished from how I was *taught* to solve pain.

I describe it as a systems approach, as opposed to a component approach.

Through physical therapy school and today, evidence-based treatment has been the buzz phrase to describe how we should help others heal their bodies. Everything we do must have medical evidence to support it. To create evidence, it seems, we study and report on small pieces of our body puzzle—components. While this is an important process to unravel how we tick, this rule severely constrains creative thinking and the observation necessary to solve difficult cases. Had I restricted my treatment philosophy to only what was supported by medical evidence, none of the stories you're about to read would have had happy endings. At some point, we need to understand how to put the pieces of our puzzle back together to make Humpty Dumpty whole again—to help him function as a system (as much as a walking egg who chooses to sit on a wall can work as a system).

So, while evidence is important, synthesizing that information (adding a pinch of extrapolation here and of creativity there) to form concrete solutions becomes meaningful—especially to those who are suffering with chronic pain.

This book represents my efforts to create an evidence-directed, yet more holistic, approach to solving our body's pain puzzles.

Introduction

I would become Sherlock Holmes.

I'm probably not the first child to have concocted this master plan, but I'm likely among the few who actually made it happen. I solve mysteries. Not the kind involving butlers in the study with the candelabra.

They do, however, involve bodies.

⸺ ⸺ ⸺ ⸺

Let us consider the case of the Boscombe Valley Mystery, penned by Sir Arthur Conan Doyle, one of 58 short stories (as well as four novels) starring his famous character, Sherlock Holmes. After examining the site of a murder by bludgeoning in a forest, Holmes and Police Inspector Lestrade discuss the crime scene. Holmes hands Lestrade a rock.

"This may interest you, Lestrade," he remarked, holding it out. "The murder was done with it."

"I see no marks."

"There are none."

"How do you know, then?"

"The grass was growing under it. It had only lain there a few days. There was no sign of a place whence it had been taken. It corresponds with the injuries. There is no sign of any other weapon."

"And the murderer?"

"Is a tall man, left-handed, limps with the right leg, wears thick-soled shooting-boots and a grey cloak, smokes Indian cigars, uses a cigar-holder, and carries a blunt pen-knife in his pocket. There are several other indications, but these may be enough to aid us in our search."

Lestrade laughs and says, "I am afraid that I am still a sceptic." But Holmes is one step ahead of him. His friend, Dr. John Watson, is there to fulfill the role of reader, asking the questions we in the audience have but which are so basic that they would never occur to Sherlock to answer. Holmes explains how he deduced all the information about the murderer.

> "You know my method. It is founded upon the observation of trifles."
>
> "His height I know that you might roughly judge from the length of his stride. His boots, too, might be told from their traces."
>
> "Yes, they were peculiar boots."
>
> "But his lameness?"
>
> "The impression of his right foot was always less distinct than his left. He put less weight upon it. Why? Because he limped—he was lame."
>
> "But his left-handedness."
>
> "You were yourself struck by the nature of the injury as recorded by the surgeon at the inquest. The blow was struck from immediately behind, and yet was upon the left side. Now, how can that be unless it were by a left-handed man? He had stood behind that tree during the interview between the father and son. He had even smoked there. I found the ash of a cigar, which my special knowledge of tobacco ashes enables me to pronounce as an Indian cigar. I have, as you know, devoted some attention to this, and written a little monograph on the ashes of 140 different varieties of pipe, cigar, and cigarette tobacco. Having found the ash, I then looked round and discovered the stump among the moss where he had tossed it. It was an Indian cigar, of the variety which are rolled in Rotterdam."
>
> "And the cigar-holder?"
>
> "I could see that the end had not been in his mouth. Therefore, he used a holder. The tip had been cut off, not bitten off, but the cut was not a clean one, so I deduced a blunt pen-knife."

So much can be learned through thoughtful, proactive observation. We tend to forget that, especially today when we crave entertainment that allows us to think passively, to just watch, not to work too hard. It's not only Holmes' deductions that I admire but his confidence. He does not equivocate. This is a sign of years of study and application, consummate professionalism. This struck me as impressive when I read the stories as a child, and it is even more impressive to me now as an adult professional.

The deconstruction of Holmes' clues is a big part of the fun. In the end, I'm left with the obvious inevitability of his conclusions. The mysticism I felt at the beginning of the story is transferred from the deductions to the man making them. Holmes' powers of observation are extraordinary.

Yet for him, it's all in a day's work. His voice almost drips with boredom. Holmes understood that everything was important and so used all his senses. There was a reason those blades of grass bent like that. There was information in noting that the tip of the cigar had been cut, but not cleanly, rather than bitten off. Ash is not just ash, but a bi-product specific to a type of tobacco leaf from a certain place.

Everything is a clue. Details seem to wish to speak, yearning for us to understand them. The puzzle wants to be solved.

⇒⇐ ⇒⇐ ⇒⇐

I'm a physical therapist.

The term doesn't exactly ring with romance, and it certainly sounds less sexy than to call myself a detective. It's a medical field that doesn't get much attention. Fair enough that saving lives gets the headlines, but physical therapy (or physiotherapy elsewhere in the world) includes a wide spectrum of applications from brain injuries to wound care. My focus is on sports and orthopedics where I solve pain and help people return to their full potential. We may not be snatching patients back from the brink, but there is a lot to be said for fixing pain. There is a saying that goes "the healthy man has a thousand wishes, the sick man but one." The same could be said for anyone in pain. If you've felt physical discomfort for an extended amount of time, the one thing on your mind is how to stop it. There are types of pain that require medications and others that require surgical intervention. We help with those too, but my specialty is applying simple manipulations and shifts in habit, posture or movement which, almost magically, offer relief.

The mysteries I solve involve careful evaluation of patients. The moment I see them walk into my office I'm examining, evaluating, deducing. How they move, how they stand, how they sit can offer clues. Then there is what they say and any test results they bring, further shaking out puzzle pieces onto my desk, mysteries wishing to be solved. As we speak and as I examine them, I remain flexible in my deductions.

One of the "problems" with Sherlock's approach, as modern criminologists have pointed out, is that his deductions are always correct the first time around. If he sees a woman with a gold cross around her neck, he will deduce that she is religious. But what if her mother was religious and this was her necklace but the daughter is, in fact, agnostic? That doesn't happen to Holmes, but it happens all the time outside the borders of fiction. Holmes' murder suspect might have been left-handed, or might have been ambidextrous, or might have been carrying something in their right hand and so struck the victim with their left. Deductive reasoning requires flexibility and frequent resets and updates of hypotheses as new information comes forth. A patient might appear weak, and a doctor might suspect anemia, but a blood test shows that this is not the diagnosis, and so the hypotheses must shift. Holmes is a great inspiration but would not make for a good doctor.

A patient enters my office with baffling complaints of pain that have stumped other practitioners-as-investigators. They're looking for answers. If their pain is in the back or anywhere down to the foot, their walking pattern will be key to figuring out the mystery. The murderer in the Boscombe Valley Mystery might have limped because of a pain in his back, as much as being "lame," as Holmes concluded. If a patient's rib cage appears to slide down, or their knee points in or their hip juts out—it all has meaning. The body's ancient hieroglyphics are waiting to be read by someone who understands them.

If a patient's pain is above the waist, the clues I look for are found in how they use their shoulder blade, the shape of the thoracic spine, the rotation of the elbow. I find traces of rotations left at joints and study the lingering effects of their tension. The body and its movement (or lack thereof) paints a picture of behavior that has run amok and is now causing pain.

It all comes down to human behavior. That left-handed murderer had the habit of smoking his favorite brand of cigar, with a filter, and flicking his ash before discarding the butt. These are habits that are like tracks in the snow, leaving traceable trails if you know how to look.

With careful observation I can see these footprints, the ghost effects of the actual criminal I am hunting—the culprits behind pain.

After more than 25 years of practice as a physical therapist, the thrill of solving pain mysteries still excites me. I love seeing a patient who has baffled other practitioners. Our unique human construction demands that every case be considered differently. Even if I were to work with identical twins who lived together their entire lives, I would expect to see differences in their bodies. This is because the ultimate generator of pain and tension is the brain. Each person processes information differently, even if that information is identical. An early winter snowfall means different things to different people: one rejoices with thoughts of skiing, another weeps because they can't pay the heating bills, a third hopes school will be cancelled. Different reactions mean that tension patterns will differ too.

Like optical illusions in which some see a young woman and others an old hag, our brain "sees" in ways unique to an individual, like a fingerprint. Our brain senses and negotiates our environment through the five senses: smell, taste, touch, sight and hearing. These senses have a wide spectra of sensitivity and reach into our brain triggering domino effect repercussions in our minds and bodies. They result in behaviors. These behaviors are clues.

Although we are unique, pain is a shared experience. But rather than bringing us together in solidarity, we find ourselves separated in silent struggle to understand and rid it from our bodies. It is often lonely, especially without a cast or crutches to give us visible "permission" to hurt. It makes us feel that we are aging prematurely. It wakes us to our own mortality. In extreme cases, it can even make us wish to no longer live, if living means constant pain without promise of ebbing.

Pain is something we hide. We see it as a weakness, a failing of body, mind or spirit. In many cases, pain will resolve on its own. Sometimes it resolves because we've rested, bandaged, or avoided the activity that caused it. But in my more difficult cases, patients have robbed Peter to pay Paul. For instance, compensating for a flat foot by favoring the other foot leads to problems in the back. Subtle innocent compensations take their toll over time. Like taxes, inevitably they'll catch up to you.

None of these "criminals" show up on an MRI or x-ray. There are some suspects that would: a broken arm, a tumor. But when a doctor's arsenal of tests cannot locate the culprit, many medical practitioners are left scratching their heads in wonder and moving on to the next patient on their overloaded schedules. This is exactly the type of case a physical therapist is suited for—especially one who loves mysteries. And with about half of Americans seeking help for musculoskeletal pain, more than those who suffer from cardiovascular and chronic respiratory conditions combined, it looks like we're going to keep busy.

This book will help pull back the curtain to expose secrets of the body, debunk common medical myths and open your mind to new possibilities about pain and its relief. You'll learn to appreciate your body in a new way, pay attention to the clues it's trying to show you and become your own Sherlock Holmes.

≡ 1 ≡

The Reveal

The gentleman flew in all the way from New York to see me at my clinic in Colorado. It was the first time anyone had traveled extensively to see me, so I was taken aback. That's a long, expensive trip and I wanted to make sure I made it worth his time and effort. But the reason he'd come so far to see me was that his regular medical team was stumped.

In he walked or, rather, limped. He was in his late 60s, athletic of build. He loved to talk a mile a minute, and kept on smiling, punctuating his story with chuckles. He gave the impression that nothing could get him down. But here's the thing: he hadn't been able to straighten his knee for years. It all started after a minor surgery to fix a frayed piece of meniscus (a croissant-shaped piece of cartilage in the knee) that had been troubling him. But his problem was nothing you'd expect from a standard, simple surgery like that. He'd had x-rays, seen several doctors and physical therapists. There was nothing medically wrong with his knee, but no one had been able to help him.

There is a standard series of questions and basic but comprehensive examination techniques that I'll employ for every new patient, to get a sense of their baseline and to help identify what might be going wrong. A complete evaluation of the rib cage down to the foot is the starting point for any back or lower body problem at my clinic. Through the normal course of my exam, I would look at what I consider to be the usual suspects. I screen in a way that differs from most therapists, which can lead me to find things others don't. My basic screening distills the complex bio- and pathomechanics of the entire lower body system down to a few simple tests. A parallel is when a doctor orders a battery of blood tests, throwing out a large net to see if they can catch anything that shouldn't be there and could be a clue to the underlying problem. The clue then leads to further tests that home in on a diagnosis. I see my basic exam as a physical therapy version of this net. It's more comprehensive than most and I've found that it's well worth it to spend extra time on the initial screening.

I spent years developing my screening net. As I put together complicated connections in the body, I would add a new strand. After a while, it looked more like a big tangle than a proper net, perhaps reminiscent of a child's drawing of a spider web, instead of the elegant construction you might see nature produce. But each strand was a possible way to catch a clue that would lead to a diagnosis and helping the patient. Like a spider, if something touched a strand, I knew immediately where the insect—in our case, the cause of discomfort—must be. As I approached the cause, I had this idea that it would struggle more, touching more strands as it did, and my certainty that I was correct in my diagnosis would strengthen. But then, unlike a spider that would trap its prey, I would do the opposite. Once I'd homed in on the problem, I would set it free.

Even though I knew he was coming to me after seeing a flurry of other professionals, I started with the basics so that I could get to know his body. Anything that would restrict knee straightening, like the hamstrings, are the first thought. The hamstrings (there are three of them: semitendinosus, semimembranosus, biceps femoris) cross the knee joint in the back of the knee on both the inside and outside, originating further up the leg or even the pelvis. Short hamstrings would then restrict the knee, keeping it from straightening, like a rope that isn't quite long enough. Surprisingly, his hamstrings didn't appear short at all. When I discovered this, a small ember of dread began to smolder in the pit of my stomach. This must have been exactly what the rest of his medical team experienced when examining him. Our default usual suspects all had alibis.

But shortness isn't the only reason the hamstrings might prevent your knee from straightening. They could also be in a protective spasm, guarding the knee for some reason that is not actually necessary. But his muscles were relaxed. No protective spasm and no shortness. Another dead end. I was doing what I imagined all those who had examined him had done, failing to find the reason, and the embers in my gut became a small fire. I inwardly scratched my head (perhaps outwardly, too, but even when you're stumped, showing your puzzlement doesn't inspire confidence in the patient).

Because the calf muscles also cross behind the knee joint in back, they would also be a potential candidate to restrict the knee. Yet his seemed to be relaxed and spasm-free when I tried to straighten the knee. Another potential suspect cleared of involvement.

Then I moved on to the internal structures of the knee that might restrict motion. The meniscus is the first that came to mind because small pieces can tear or be sheared off. These can block the knee from straightening or bending, like the small blocks you see holding a jet airliner's wheels in place when it's parked at a gate— it doesn't take much. Since the issue arose after meniscus surgery, this seemed like the next most likely culprit. The problem is that he'd had his meniscus repaired by a top surgeon in New York and he'd been assessed by other top doctors and PTs via a battery of standard orthopedic tests, endless MRIs and x-rays. Surely something would have shown up. But I found nothing wrong here, either.

Was the temperature in the room rising? I could feel myself starting to sweat.

I also tested his internal ligaments: the anterior and posterior cruciate ligaments (ACL and PCL respectively). All clear. Through all this, he kept commenting, "Oh yeah, I've had this test before," or he'd critique my technique: "The doctors cranked on my knee a lot harder than that!" He couldn't have been friendlier, but it only piled on the pressure, since I wasn't coming up with anything new. He'd been through all the obvious choices, had all the right tests. This was a puzzle of a case, for sure. I felt sympathy for his other practitioners—I knew exactly how they felt.

I maintained my calm outward demeanor but inside I was screaming at myself, "I can't let this man fly all this way for nothing!" I desperately wanted to reward his faith in me, the confidence he had that I really knew what I was doing. I needed that confidence in myself too.

It would be easy to write this off as "simple knee pain." After all, it's just a knee. How important could that really be?

That attitude unfortunately seems pervasive in medicine. "Oh, well, if I can't figure it out, at least it's not life threatening," and the practitioner moves on to a case they can solve.

Clearly, though, it was of the utmost importance to this gentleman—he'd spent years and thousands of dollars trying to solve his problem. It was a dark cloud hanging over his otherwise happy existence. I've learned not to minimize anyone's pain, nor its repercussions.

In medical mystery TV shows, like *House*, the doctors are stumped until our protagonist thinks laterally, outside the box. There are checklists we're trained to work our way through, and for almost every case we encounter, we'll hit upon the solution before we've exhausted the checklist. But that 1 percent of cases that stubbornly refuse to be solved even when we've run the gamut of usual suspect approaches and ailments are the ones that stand out, and that I find most interesting—the zebras. Sherlock Holmes didn't get excited by open-and-shut cases. If it looked like the butler did it, and the butler did indeed do it, then it didn't stretch his mental muscles. Here was a case that Sherlock would have gone for.

It would be fun if my life were like a TV show, like *House*, miraculously providing answers to difficult cases for me if I only observe "the signs." Unfortunately, that's not the case. It's sometimes messy and haphazard and agonizing. No, I have to figure it out for myself—as do we all.

So no muscles or internal structures seemed to be the culprit. What were all of us missing? Then it hit me in a flash. We had forgotten about one very tiny, and often forgotten, muscle.

⇒⇐ ⇒⇐ ⇒⇐

It had been a long day, a longer week and an even longer month. I was exhausted from an overloaded schedule. For the past two months I'd been on double duty, as one of my therapists left the clinic and I hadn't found a suitable replacement. My own patient load was such that I extended my hours to absorb her schedule. This was not early in my practice. I'd already been a physical therapist for more than 20 years. At this stage, I was hoping to slow down a little. Off and on I've struggled with depression throughout my life, and this was a period when it was creeping back up on me. Being overworked and overtired certainly didn't help. I was even questioning my decision to remain

14

in this field. Sometimes things that you love and that you're good at can feel like a burden when life is getting the best of you.

Careers are supposed to have a constant upward trajectory. You start out modest and slope skyward, earning more money and accolades and solidifying your reputation until you plateau and then maybe take more time off and rest on your laurels.

Doesn't always work that way. Some careers just don't catch the public's attention, no matter how fascinating the people who practice them feel they are.

Although I owned a successful practice, the level of success, and especially my feeling of being successful, varied and swayed. I was in no danger of being invited on *Lifestyles of the Rich and Famous.* At the time, I drove a 20-year-old Subaru Forester that looked more like a golf ball on wheels than a car, its makeover courtesy of an apocalyptic hailstorm four years prior that gave its chassis a lunar look. I somehow had never gotten around to having it fixed or getting a new car. To be honest, at the time I couldn't afford it. My earnings went back into my clinic. I worked long hours, sometimes 12-hour shifts, to make sure everything ran smoothly. I was in danger of having a breakdown.

Anyone who runs a medical facility in the U.S. will know that helping patients is just one aspect of our workload. The most exhausting part is the labyrinth of frustrations and complexities that goes by the name of paperwork from insurance companies. There are many doctors who, when they reach a certain level, refuse to take patients who will pay through insurance because it's such a headache. The insurance companies try to pay out as little as possible, even when it's not in the best interest of the patient. A medical practice that relies on insurance payments can be like breathing through a straw—you just barely hang in there. It's a deal made with the devil: accept insurance contracts so you can see patients, but in doing so, you severely limit your income potential and play by the ever-shifting rules of insurance giants. Ask the insurance company to raise their reimbursement rate and they'll tell you to take a hike—there are plenty of other PTs itching for business.

So I breathed through that straw for years. I was burned out and starved for oxygen.

That's when Jeni appeared. She was a quiet, blonde-haired,

nine-year-old girl with oceanic blue eyes. In she limped, with her mother, Lisa, trailing behind. Jeni moved quickly, despite the limp, and it was clear she'd grown used to working around it. It was an odd injury. She couldn't straighten her left knee. It was frozen at a 30-degree bend. Imagine her leg straightening like clock hands: the upper part of her leg should point up at the 12 on a clock face, the lower part straight below it at the 6. In her case, her left leg was bent so that the lower part was stuck at 5 o'clock and couldn't make it to 6.

Jeni did her best to mask her limp. She walked on the tips of her left toes to make up for the length she'd lost due to her locked, bent knee. Her left hip was hiked high into the air to help unload the painful knee joint, which smarted when she put weight on that foot. She stared at me with a polite smile and steady blue eyes lacking confidence that I was her savior.

Jeni was an active girl who was involved in gymnastics, skiing, horseback riding and, at an informal level, wrestling with her twin brothers (she flexed her arm to show me her bulging biceps). She was precocious and had the firm handshake I might expect from a teenage athlete, not a nine-year-old.

Athletics had led to her current predicament. A month earlier she'd been running in gym class and had fallen, hitting her knee. The gym teacher reported hearing a loud, sickening "thump" when she hit the floor, and the whole room got quiet. An unnatural event in gym class. Not a good sign. Jeni was sprawled face down, unable to stand.

Her mother was called, and Jeni was taken to urgent care. X-rays confirmed that no bones were broken, but they found a bruise where the thigh bone met the lower leg bone.

At the knee, the long thigh bone splits into two lobes, called condyles. They are turned at slightly different angles. Through the magic of mechanical engineering, this allows for subtle rotation of the knee joint, as it bends and straightens. The inner condyle was bruised and would take time to heal. That wasn't her biggest problem at the moment.

The muscles around Jeni's knee had seized up and wouldn't allow her to straighten it. The hamstrings were most to blame. These muscles that run down the back of the thigh are very strong, designed for hard, constant work. When things go wrong, they can exert tremendous pressure on the knee joint. In Jeni's case, they locked her knee into that painful, bent position. She'd been stuck like this for just over a month with no change. Her method of accommodating had actually made it worse. Because she walked on the tips of her left toes, her left calf muscle, which crosses the knee joint, had also shortened.

I went through my examination, noting Jeni's elevated left hip and her inability to fully bear weight on her bent left leg. Throughout this process, I tried a few tricks, poking and prodding and gently massaging to find an open window that would lead to straightening her knee. All of my attempts were met with a silent grimace of pain. I was doing my best, my gentlest, but I was hurting this child patient of mine. She didn't make a sound or complain, but I could tell, and that, to me, felt like I was failing.

I was silently hoping that I wouldn't have to resort to forcing the knee straight. That would work, but it would be painful for her. And for me. I don't want to hurt anyone to help them.

Dramatically forcing a joint back into place is glamorized on TV but in reality it's a much different story. For example, with a dislocated hip, theoretically you should be able to pull the leg bone away from the hip socket to reset it back into place. Because of the size and strength of the muscles involved, a patient needs to be anesthetized to relax the muscles around the hip joint. Their spasm is actually preventing the hip from relocating, not to mention contributing to their pain. A knee would be a little easier as the muscles are smaller, but probably just as painful.

Jeni's case had echoes of a hip dislocation, due to the significance of the spasm involved in compressing the knee joint. The muscles just wouldn't let go until I said the magic word, whatever that magic word might be. But I didn't want to force the lower leg bone back into place. I would do all I could to avoid this traumatic last resort.

Jeni was my last patient at the end of that long day. The rest of the staff had gone home. Though it was mid–April, it was dark outside. Vivaldi's *Spring* played softly on the radio. It was the only positive vibe in the room. As my examination droned on, Jeni long lost interest in what I was doing. She rested patiently on her back and spaced out, staring into the patterns of plaster on my ceiling. Her mother Lisa's attention drifted away as she fiddled with her phone. I was on my own to figure this out.

I sat beside Jeni's left leg, keeping an eye on her face to see if anything I did caused discomfort. I needed to come up with something and I'd struck out so far.

Then I got an idea, more like a flash of inspiration. There's a muscle that is so small and unpopular and infrequently referenced that it's hard to believe it has any significance.

This is where my extensive training in anatomy from PT school must've kicked in. All those hours in the cadaver lab, month after month, teasing out the minutiae of muscles, nerves, ligaments and tendons. Where they run, their orientation relative to each other, how they interact with bones and so many other things that were lurking in the shadowy recesses of my memory, cobwebbed and waiting for me to find them again.

At that moment, I remembered having learned about this oft-overlooked muscle in school, but I couldn't recall the name. I did remember how it ran, its orientation and purpose. I held the lower leg bone, the tibia, just below the knee and gently pulled it towards me, away from her hip, to create a slight gap in the knee joint. I tried to exert only a pound or two of pressure, so as not to hurt her and trigger even more spasms in her muscles. I did this and included the slightest pressure to rotate the knee inward and offset the torque of this hidden, forgettable muscle the name of which, from that point on, I'd never forget.

The popliteus.

The popliteus is a thin strip of muscle that runs along the back of the knee from the inside lower leg bone, where it is thickest, to the outside thigh bone, where it is just a little tendon. It's small and deep and perfectly positioned to generate rotational torque in the knee joint. If I've learned anything in these past 20 years, it's that torque, or rotational force, often equals pain. While torque helps us translate power from one plane of movement to another, our bodies don't like to be stuck there. That's where Jeni's knee was, stuck in a torqued position that didn't show up on an x-ray.

Jeni's popliteus was locked in spasm and it had been for more than a month. This spasm, due to its rotational force, significantly increased compression at the knee joint which the muscles around were trying to guard against. It was like wringing out a rag: as you twist it, the distance between your two hands becomes smaller: compression.

The muscles around the knee didn't know they were contributing to the compression. They just knew that something was wrong and they were sentries on high alert. My rotation plus gentle massage released it, like letting go of one end of the rag. No more compression.

Jeni's thigh muscles and hamstrings began twitching softly like the fluttering wings of a moth trying to rise from the ground. And then they grew silent. Jeni's face gave no indication of pain as her knee slowly drifted down to the table, straightening. Was I imagining this? I maintained the pressure, cautiously tugging at her tibia while at the same time, unwinding the popliteus as her knee straightened further. Occasionally her thigh muscles quivered in weak protest and then silenced again. I almost heard them sigh as they gave up their fight completely, once the back of her knee touched down. Their long battle to protect her was over—their silent retreat gave no indication of the violence of their origins. They'd gone home to rest.

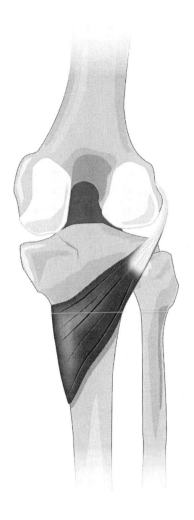

The popliteus, by virtue of its orientation, can twist the knee joint, creating pain.

Meanwhile, Jeni stared at the ceiling, bored and unaware of the quiet war we had just won.

Jeni's muscles had been caught in a reflex loop. Her knee was bent and slightly rotated, putting pressure on her bone bruise. This was painful and her muscles spasmed to protect the site of the pain. That was their job. But this caused more pressure on the bone bruise. Then her muscles responded with more contraction to protect the joint, which caused more bone bruise pain, which caused contraction to protect the joint and so on. I'd simply unloaded the site of the bone bruise to relieve the pain. This broke the reflex loop. The contraction was no longer necessary.

I looked up at her and whispered, "Hey, Jeni, check out your knee."

She lifted her head and did a double-take worthy of the Three Stooges. She stared in wide-eyed disbelief at her straight knee. I then saw a true smile on her entire face, not the half-smile indicating bravery in the face of adversity that she'd worn when she walked into my office. Her joy struck me like the soft brush of heat after you open an oven door on a cold February morning.

"Wow!" she whispered.

I turned to Jeni's mom. "Lisa, what do you think of this?"

Lisa had been immersed in her phone and only now looked up. Shocked by what she saw, she comically sputtered half-formed words, unable to utter a coherent sentence.

Finally, she said, "I can't believe it! What just happened? Is it really straight? Jeni! Can you see that? Oh my God, I'm about to cry!"

I almost teared up myself at their joy and relief. I felt like a magician who had just pulled off his big reveal to shock his audience. Voila! Except even I hadn't known how the trick would turn out.

Jeni got up from the table and, after a few tenuous steps, walked more confidently, with just a small limp that would go away in a day or two.

Lisa pulled me aside with moist eyes. "Jeni thought she'd never straighten her knee again. We weren't so sure ourselves. Thank you so much. What a session!"

My little magic trick for a nine-year-old girl and her mom proved to be just the thing. That moment, I was pulled back from a dark chasm. I felt my mind release. The reflex loop of my overwork and concern and depression let go. This didn't make everything right all of a sudden. I was still mentally limping. But it freed me from the

1. The Reveal

trap I was in and set me on the road to recovery. All was right with the world, and I was lucky to be a physical therapist. Helping little Jeni led to her helping me rise out of my lowest moment.

⇒⊂ ⇒⊂ ⇒⊂

There he was, the gentleman from New York, lying on my table like Jeni had so many years before. I'd learned more than one lesson from her back then. Not the least of which was how, when the usual suspects are not guilty, you've got to think beyond the boundaries. Turn to the improbable, but not impossible. By now I'd found that the popliteus was behind some of the cases that stumped other therapists. It was rarely the only culprit, but instead slunk around in the background, letting the major players do their thing.

I ran my hand along the gentleman's leg, found the popliteus and massaged it for about five minutes. Physical therapy is not massage therapy, but massage is a key technique to uncoil taut muscles. Somewhere around the fifth minute I felt a palpable unlocking, like a thief feeling the tumblers of a safe. Boom, his knee straightened out.

I kept an almost bored expression that my hero, Sherlock, would've been proud of.

"Well, that seems about it," I said coolly.

He sat up, shocked to see his knee straight on the table. "What the ... how did ... huh?"

I'll be honest: sometimes my own tricks as a therapist-cum-magician delight and surprise me nearly as much as they do my patients. It keeps me on my toes never knowing when the "big reveal" is going to happen.

21

≋ 2 ≋

Summiting Migraines

Debbie, a longtime friend of ours, had been involved in a pair of automobile accidents that left her with chronic migraine headaches. She'd suffered for a few years before my wife convinced her that I might be able to help. It hadn't occurred to her that migraines could be caused by a musculoskeletal problem. But medication wasn't working well enough and wasn't a long-term solution.

If headaches are mountains, then migraines are like K2, the second highest mountain in the world. They aren't your run-of-the-mill headaches. They're fraught with all sorts of additional symptoms, including throbbing, nausea and even vomiting. They can include changes in eyesight such as seeing auras or blind spots. Similarly, tingling on one side of the face can linger for several days. Interestingly, they often occur on one side of the head. To me this is a key attribute.

In my simple way of looking at things, I see migraines as being on a headache spectrum—something that isn't mentioned in most research on headaches. Of course, at one end are the people who rarely get a headache, perhaps once a year, and it passes rapidly. On my headache mountain analogy, these people are out for a little hike in the foothills—some up and down but nothing too strenuous. And then somewhere in the middle there are those with diagnoses of tension headaches which are more frequent, intense and longer-lasting. These can range from the Appalachian Mountains to Mt. Kilimanjaro—the third largest mountain in the world. Getting closer to the other end of the spectrum are migraines and finally the ultimate is trigeminal neuralgia—the Mt. Everest of head pain and one of the most painful conditions in the musculoskeletal system known to exist.

2. Summiting Migraines

Why do I see all of these on the same spectrum? Because my treatment approach to normal headaches also works very well for migraines. I've even helped the few cases of trigeminal neuralgia that have come my way. So the source of the problems seems to be very similar, if not the same. Instead, it's a matter of degree.

Migraines and trigeminal neuralgia both seem to happen mostly on one side of the head or face. Why would this be? In my experience, it's due to asymmetries in arm function due to handedness, past injuries that weren't adequately solved and posture patterns, such as having a rounded mid-back, faulty postural training and/or work-related postural issues. Of course, most medical practitioners will dismiss this interesting attribute as unimportant because they don't understand the connections between the arm and head or neck as a potential source of pain.

When I hear of musculoskeletal pain, no matter where it is in the body, as being unilateral, I automatically think I might be able to solve it. If it's on both sides this can indicate a more systemic origin such as a nervous system disorder, blood-borne disorder like a disease process, spinal disorder or some other issue not directly related to muscles, tendons and bone. That doesn't mean I won't try to help someone with bilateral symptoms; it just means my radar is turned to a high sensitivity in these cases to things that don't fit in to my treatment paradigm.

I was working out of our home at the time, so Debbie came by. After a few sessions her pain diminished significantly. She was pleased; I was pleased. This is where most physical therapists would stop. Quit while they're ahead, with a satisfied patient. Job well done, right? Well, sometimes I can't leave well enough alone.

I wanted to test to make sure she was truly better. So I got the bright idea to try to reproduce the stress of the accident. In our final session, I gently pressed on her left shoulder two or three times while she sat, mimicking the action of her seatbelt during those accidents. I used perhaps three to five pounds of pressure—not much. She didn't report any pain as I did this, so I figured all was well.

She called the next day to say her migraines had returned, and they were now worse than ever. I was dumbfounded. A delayed reaction, and now they were worse? I'm sure I spluttered something like "That's expected, don't worry." A classic stalling technique whereby

I hoped things just calmed down on their own somehow. Secretly I was completely stumped.

For three days I obsessed over her reaction. I could think of nothing else. Why had pressing her shoulder triggered her migraines? At the time I pressed her shoulder, I might've expected some shoulder pain or even some neck pain. But that it would trigger the worst migraine she'd had in years with such a gentle perturbation really threw me. Until that moment, I hadn't connected shoulders to headaches, only to perhaps neck pain at the most, which Deb had too. She could live with that, but the migraines were debilitating.

On the third day I had an epiphany. What if it wasn't her neck that was hurt after all? I still remember it clearly—it was almost like a religious experience. I was driving my car, vaguely paying attention to my surroundings, when a mental picture of the connections between the shoulder blade, neck and skull flashed into my mind. Once again, my extensive anatomical training in PT school came to the rescue. I instantly saw not only the physical connections but their implications for neck pain or headaches. I knew this was the answer—it explained it all perfectly to me. I couldn't wait to get home and look through my anatomy texts to confirm my vision! I was practically shaking with excitement and anticipation!

As far as car accidents are concerned, almost everyone has heard of the term "whiplash." Whiplash doesn't describe the tissues that are affected; it simply refers to the whipping motion of the head moving suddenly forward and back, as when a car abruptly comes to a halt, but your momentum continues to push you forward until the seatbelt stops you and throws you back into your seat. Rotation can be involved too, especially if the head was turned to see what that loud screeching noise was coming toward them. Considering that the human head weighs about 12–15 pounds, the physics of this type of accident becomes mind-blowing in terms of potential destructive power.

The problem is that the neck is a very complex and busy area of the body while also being vulnerable. The neck bones are the smallest in the spine because they need only support the head, instead of the entire upper body and trunk. The muscles and ligaments are smaller too and extensive, while balancing the head on top of the

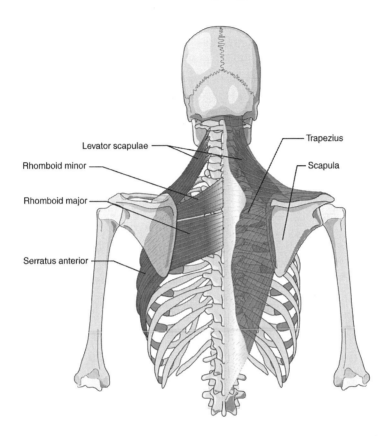

Levator scapulae

Rhomboid minor

Rhomboid major

Serratus anterior

Trapezius

Scapula

Connections between the shoulder blade, neck and head contribute to chronic headaches and neck pain.

neck. So a sudden jerk of the head can affect just about anything in this region.

Because there's so much happening in this area, up until that point, I hadn't considered that something other than the tissues found in the neck might have problems too. After all, everything below the neck is fairly stabilized with the seat and seatbelt.

Post-accident migraines can show themselves even many years after suffering whiplash. Treating her neck had soothed the migraines—my mistake was that I thought soothing meant solving. I had treated the neck and the symptoms went away, therefore the neck was the cause of her symptoms.

But the neck proved to be a red herring. By pressing on her

shoulder, replicating the force of the seatbelt upon her body during the accident, I unwittingly triggered the cascade of events at the root of her migraines—and they let us know loud and clear!

Current medical wisdom states that migraines are not completely understood but are caused by imbalances in chemicals in the brain, including serotonin, which regulates pain in the nervous system, and changes in the brainstem and how it interacts with the trigeminal nerve, which is the main highway for pain. The shoulder doesn't appear relevant to any one of the 10 most common migraine triggers named by the Mayo Clinic.

Fortunately, I didn't keep up with current medical wisdom as far as the causes of migraines. Not because I reject it, but because I'm engrossed in my little clinic identifying and following the strands of the web leading to pain. I generally don't accept "that's just the way it is." I've learned there's almost always a reason, even though nobody seems to have figured it out yet.

Going back to my anatomy books and studying the shoulder from a different point of view, I was able to see how the connections between the shoulder and the neck could lead to headaches and possibly migraines. The connections between our anatomy and their significance when it comes to pain and function were finally dawning on me. We learn this in a gross sense in school, which usually includes the actions of a muscle on a joint. But this new revelation went far beyond that for me, similar to the Butterfly Effect coined by the mathematician Edward Lorenz, which basically states that small changes in a system can have large ramifications further away from that source. These changes are often non-linear and therefore difficult to study or prove. But this understanding would forever change my approach to solving pain.

I thought I'd cracked the case.

I convinced Debbie to come in for one more treatment. Now that I looked at her differently, it was immediately evident that she couldn't hold her shoulder where it needed to be by herself. One of the things that tipped me off to this is that the dominant hand's shoulder should rest slightly lower than the non-dominant side. Debbie was right-handed but her left shoulder rested lower than her right. I hadn't thought this was significant because I didn't think the shoulder was significant. I was wrong. Reviewing the anatomical connections in my head, I visualized the stressors that must be acting on her skull.

Her doctors and I had been so focused on the neck that none of us had noticed her shoulder issue. I came up with a taping technique on the spot to hold it in place. She called the next day—no more headaches! Wow! It was as if I'd pulled off a magic trick, half-surprising myself. I thought it would work, but there's the lingering doubt until you try it, and then the delight in seeing that my theoretical mapping actually led to a real solution.

That was my first experience of the interplay between anatomy, movement and pain. The first of many. It strengthened my passion for finding the hidden pathways, ever expanding my knowledge so that I can reroute and solve pain.

≡ 3 ≡

Releasing Tigger

Years later, in my clinic, he was seated across from me, telling his story of eight years of sciatic pain. The man who sat in the wrong chair for 30 seconds and was in pain for a week after. His arms were folded across his chest, and his monotone voice ended with a drop in pitch, like Eeyore from *Winnie the Pooh*, saying, "If it is a good morning, which I doubt."

Al was a distinguished-looking 67-year-old in very good health, other than the feeling of numbness, offset by frequent stabbing pains, in his right leg. It was bad enough to send him to the emergency room on many occasions. His resigned, hopeless, Eeyore-like manner was the result of innumerable fruitless visits to a host of medical professionals. Cortisone shots to reduce a bulge they'd found in his spinal discs had failed to help him, as did surgery to remove some bone and part of a spinal disc. This offered relief for about six weeks. Then his pain returned, never to leave again.

Al struggled on. He had more tests to make sure the nerves exiting his spine weren't pinched. They were not. He was eventually told by a doctor that whatever it was would heal over the next two to three years. This is basically code for "We don't know what's going on. Let's wait and see if something shakes out." Another stalling technique from a stumped professional.

During those eight years, Al's lifestyle was negatively affected. He avoided things that triggered his pain, and that meant whittling down his life to keep pain at arm's length. The trade-off was that Al abandoned the small joys he once knew. This included spending time with his wife of 42 years, taking walks and shopping together. A simple trip to the grocery store was elevated to a serious review of the pros and cons of such an undertaking. He'd stopped working as a mechanical engineer. He couldn't lift, push or pull anything as a result of his sciatica. This included yard work, one of his favorite pastimes. Not only had he all but given up on medical professionals helping him, but he'd also given up on much that he enjoyed in life.

Al's pain pattern was typical of the sciatic nerve, a thick long cord that has its roots in the low back. Like an upside-down tree, the main trunk runs down the back of the leg, branching out along the way to supply the upper and lower leg muscles. This was the most obvious and most likely culprit for his suffering. When he walked, he felt pain and numbness in the toes of his right foot, the furthest branches of his sciatic nerve tree.

Lying on his back on my exam table, he lifted his leg while keeping it straight— Lasegue's Test. This looks for potential injury to the spinal roots of the sciatic nerve in his lower back. At my request, his eyes rolled, like my teenage daughter's do when my wife and I ask her to do something she'd really rather not.

"Okay," he sighed, knowing what we'd find. He raised his right leg a few inches off the table. "Oh my gosh, that hurts!" he said, through gritted teeth.

"Is that the pain you're complaining about?" I asked. "The pain you've been having all these years?"

"Oh yes, that's exactly what it is," he said, catching his breath after the lightning bolt that had just torn through his leg. His brow glistened with beads of sweat.

This confirmed that Al's nerve roots were pinched. No doubt other tests would also be positive for a source of problems in the spine.

But that was exactly the problem. Eight years' worth of various medical professionals had all come to the same conclusion. The simplest, most probable cause—the sciatic nerve. Therefore, to treat the sciatic nerve, you treat the lower back, and the problem would be solved. This was looking a lot like Debbie's problem. Her migraines and neck pain were assumed to be caused by a problem in her neck or head but were actually caused by her shoulder.

Likewise, it was assumed Al's pain was caused by his lower back. The question in my mind was "If not the lower back, where else?"

His treatment had focused on the spine the previous eight years. Certainly, if the problem was in the spine, the surgery, previous therapy, manipulations or cortisone shots should have cured it.

I've learned over the years that, while many of these tests or treatments may reveal irritation at the spinal level, they do not pinpoint *why* that spinal level is irritated. This, it turns out, is the key to solving pain. Medicine is great at identifying structures that might be damaged or cause problems, but we tend to forget about asking why it is happening in the first place. So yes, it may be a sciatic nerve causing the pain, and the lower back may actually be bothering the sciatic nerve, but the question is why.

I finished my initial evaluation and found several problems, but I decided to cut to the chase. He'd been through a long line of health care professionals, each one certain they could help him. Al had heard it all before. I needed to do something dramatic that would demonstrate that his time with me would be well-spent. I needed another big reveal.

I asked Al to lie down on his back and raise his right leg again—Lasegue's Test, Round Two. With Eeyore's resignation, he raised it a few inches off the table. The result was the same searing pain tearing down his leg.

"Okay, remember how far up you can raise that leg and how much pain you're feeling," I said.

"Got it," he said, testing it one more time, his leg shaking. "It shoots right down my leg."

"Now roll over and get onto your elbows and knees," I said. He gave me a weird look—this, apparently, was not something any of the other eight years' worth of health care professionals had asked of him.

I had him lift his right leg up in the air with the knee bent and perform two sets of little pulses, to activate his butt muscles, the gluteals. He did this with some effort on his part. Then I asked him to lie on his back again.

"Now lift your right leg," I said.

He looked at me doubtfully, took a deep breath...

And his leg shot right up, almost perpendicular to the ground.

He was completely perplexed. I confess that I love seeing that look on people's faces. But even I was surprised at the extent and speed of the correction. My bored Sherlock Holmes expression remained planted on my face, however.

He lowered it again and repeated the leg raising about ten more times—no pain.

3. Releasing Tigger

Al looked at me, no longer like Eeyore, but now incredulous. "Huh? What did you do?"

"I didn't do a thing," I said. "You did."

"I don't understand. How did that fix my back?"

"It's not your back that's the problem," I said. "It's your hip."

He pondered my words for a few moments. "But everyone's been telling me it's my back," he said. Then a longer pause before his inevitable next question: "Do you mean I didn't need to have that back surgery?"

"The back surgery may well have fixed problems in your back. But it seems those problems didn't relate to your pain," I replied. "It could be that the surgery removed a layer of problems that allowed this to work," I offered. The surgery may have been useless for the main issue. It may have been needed and useful for other reasons. It was difficult to say at that point.

"Then what's the problem?" he asked.

"You have a tracking problem in your hip joint that seems to be contributing to stress in your back."

Al had something called anterior femoral glide syndrome (AFGS), a fancy term meaning that the hip bone was moving around in the socket too much. When this happens, the bone usually moves forward, pinching tissue in the front of the hip. This is often diagnosed as a groin or inner thigh strain, or a labral tear. It can also cause hip bursitis, felt on the outside of the hip, due to the unruly thigh bone irritating a little lubricating sac called a bursa.

In the back of the hip, this often will be diagnosed as piriformis syndrome. The piriformis is a little muscle in the butt area that can irritate the sciatic nerve. Not surprisingly, this can irritate the entire hip joint, often attributed to arthritis. While these issues may be present, they are exacerbated by the poor movement of the thigh bone in the hip socket, causing them to feel painful.

AFGS is caused by poor butt muscle (gluteal) activity. The gluteals are primarily responsible for helping the thigh bone pivot correctly in the hip socket. When the butt muscles don't work well things get a little sloppy. I could tell just by watching Al walk to my table that his gluteals weren't working properly. This was confirmed during my exam.

In Al's case I believe the head of the thigh bone migrated forward when he moved his leg, causing the piriformis muscle in the back of the hip to spasm. This then pinched his sciatic nerve as well as stressed the lower back due to a poorly controlled pelvic bone, resulting in his debilitating pain. Al's mechanical engineer mind grasped the information quickly.

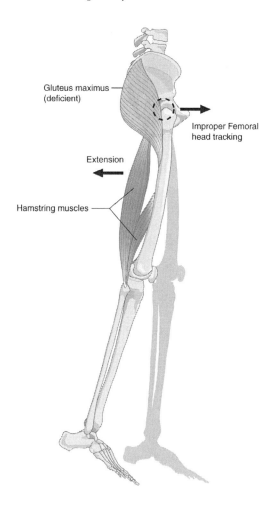

Gluteus maximus
(deficient)

Improper Femoral
head tracking

Extension

Hamstring muscles

Anterior femoral glide syndrome occurs when the gluteal muscles do not function properly, causing the head of the thigh bone to migrate forward in the socket.

3. Releasing Tigger

One of the things that tipped me off to his hip problem was something that Al *didn't* mention. Through all of my probing into his extensive history, Al never once mentioned he had back pain. Leg, yes. Back, never.

Al came back for his second visit a week later and was still pain free. But there was a second component to his issue that we hadn't addressed.

"But I still have this numbness in my lower leg when I use it a certain way, like moving something with my foot," he added. "What about that?"

"Show me," I said. I put an old phone book on the floor and Al slid the book with the side of his right foot. It produced numbness in his lower leg. He grimaced.

Al's sciatic pain was still gone. He'd been doing the exercises I assigned him to fix the weakness of his gluteals. Because his was a hip problem up to this point, I hypothesized that the origin of his lower body numbness wasn't coming from his back, either. So I performed a technique that used Al's own muscles to relax themselves around the right lower leg, foot and ankle.

The technique is called Hanna Somatics, a rather obscure approach that reduces muscle tension and reflexive spasming through controlled contraction and release. I spent three years studying this technique, which I like to say has become the jelly in my peanut butter and jelly treatment sandwich. The whole process took about five minutes. The result was like untying twine around a tightly wrapped Christmas tree and watching the branches fall loose again, assuming their natural shape. Al's muscles were able to move more freely, releasing compression of the branches of the sciatic nerve in his calf area.

"Test your numbness now," I said.

He moved the phone book—no numbness. I smiled at the look on his normally placid face. It was as if he'd just tasted chocolate for the first time.

He moved it more, scooting it across the floor. I held back a chuckle, watching this distinguished looking older gentleman express such delight at sliding a phone book around on the floor with his foot. Still no numbness. I added two more phone books on top of it. He moved those, too, without the feeling of numbness. He looked up at me.

"It's not my back," he whispered, half to himself. "After all these years, it's not my back."

As I watched Al's face, his eyes took on that unfocused look of someone who is thinking of something else while looking at me. I could almost see his brain synapses reconfiguring to align with this new reality. The image of a cocooned caterpillar that liquefies and reorganizes itself into a velvety butterfly came to mind.

To see those eight years of frustration and pain melt away from Al in that moment is one of the reasons why I love what I do. His face was a mixture of joy, relief and understanding. Imagine hurting for eight years. And then, suddenly, you don't. It can turn an Eeyore into a Tigger.

On Al's next visit I saw, in his relaxed confidence, the tone of his voice, his stride, that his new realization had settled in. Hope and understanding had been restored to his life. He was in control.

I then explained how Al got into trouble in the first place. This is important so patients don't slip back into bad habits. Remember, while Debbie had suffered a pair of car accidents, which were obvious precipitates for her migraines, Al had not been the subject of any particular trauma of which he was aware. I never learned of Al's precipitating event. For most it comes in the form of an auto accident, a fall, picking up a dirty sock, a yoga stretch, an extra mile of running that creates the dark solid pain.

His issue likely resulted from a slow burn of years of sitting at work in poor posture (and sitting too long), walking with poor technique and too little, performing the same exercise routine, sleeping in a slowly deteriorating bed, all of which enflamed very old injuries, causing joints to move a little less, muscles turning off just a little more. All of these tiny negatives accrue, like adding just a bit of a powder to a liquid until a solid pain precipitate emerges. So it is with how our bodies move. Problems crop up with a single severe incident (dumping a tablespoon of powder into a glass of liquid all at once) or very slowly (a few grains of powder at a time for decades). Either way, our movements have meaning and are often the keys to solving pain.

≋ 4 ≋

You'd Be Surprised

With something as finite as the human body, you'd think we'd know all there is to know about it by now. After all, our bag of skin has remained almost unchanged for tens of thousands of years. Yet our bodies are a never-ending source of investigation, wonder, pain, healing and exploration. Forget the infinite expanse of the cosmos or the unfathomable depths of the ocean. Just looking within ourselves will take us another thousands of years to unravel, so tightly are spooled our inner mysteries. We know so little about who we are. But we also know precious little of *how* we are.

My focus, as a physical therapist, is the musculoskeletal system. Most would think this the simplest system in the body to understand. It seems more finite than organs or neurons or cells, so we should have at least figured this part out by now, right? After all, we only have so many bones and so many muscles, don't we?

You'd be surprised.

Some people have an extra lumbar vertebra. Others are missing one. Some people have extra little rib nubs on their neck bones that most do not, called cervical ribs. Sometimes these are on one side, sometimes on both. Some have muscles that are absent in others. So, if you Google "how many bones are in the human body" and you receive the answer "206," or the number of skeletal muscles comes in at "650," just know that's not a definitive number.

Even if all the bones and muscles were known and constant, the variability in our bones' length and thickness means that some people have significant mechanical advantages (or disadvantages) due to the length of the lever arms their muscles act upon. And even if all of our bones were identical, where our muscles originate and insert into our bones has subtle differences rendering them stronger or weaker, depending on what you're testing. This is what allows one person to be a great swimmer while another is a great runner and a third is inept at sports altogether.

Of course, the master controller is the brain. If you think that there's variety in the body—in what should be our fundamental construction—then there are certainly infinite differences in our brains. These distinctions carry over to our control of our bones and muscles.

Consider a species of tree, say, an ash. Observe two different ash trees for even a few seconds and you'll see that no two are identical. Organisms are like snowflakes, each unique, even when they are the same species, even if they are twins. Within the same species of any living thing, you'll find variability. In humans, that variability creates differences in wear and tear on bones, muscles, ligaments and tendons.

At first glance, the musculoskeletal system appears as if we're all basically built the same. Well, that's what I thought upon entering physical therapy school in 1994. I assumed that everything had been worked out by researchers past, that there were no new mysteries to solve, at least about injuries and pain. After all, how hard can it be to understand how we move?

Turns out that the question may not have been how hard it is but instead where to focus our attention. As a profession, physical therapy over the years became more interested in defining the smaller parts of our body, like the forces delivered to the meniscus (a piece of cartilage in our knee) while pivoting, than how exactly we go about pivoting. Or the amount of compression felt by the discs between our vertebrae when bending forward, rather than *how* we're bending forward. To me, the "hows" of human movement feel more pertinent than knowing the exact newtons of force these tissues are experiencing or whether a millimeter of movement has occurred at a joint.

I'm an orthopedic physical therapist, and my job is to solve pain and improve function. Early on in school, it seemed to me that understanding how we move is central to this job. I learned, during school and most of my career, that this part has been largely skipped over. At the time I thought I'd simply missed this key information— that I had somehow fallen asleep during that class. This created significant anxiety in me as I prepared to graduate and land my first job as a PT. It didn't help that my classmates, all much smarter than me, appeared unconcerned to be released into the wild.

After some struggle, soul-searching and a significant battle with depression early in my career, I set off on a quest to learn how it is we fit together to create and solve pain. After reading some of the stories in my book, many of you might think, "But he hasn't included Treatment X"—you can pick any type of treatment that I do not touch upon. There are, indeed, infinite variations that can occur in our bodies, and there are myriad depths of problems at the roots of human pain. Not all cuts need stitches, even though stitches help cuts heal. Some people's problems might be shallow dips in a path, while others are deep holes they can barely see out of. This book is my way of showing how I helped people out of the deeper pits that they couldn't climb out of themselves, no matter how many medical professionals threw them lines to pull them up. Their issues required a deeper understanding of how and why we have pain. You don't call in Sherlock Holmes for an open-and-shut case. You call him in when you're stuck, when hope is at its dimmest. This isn't an encyclopedia of methods; it's a selection of stories of medical mysteries and how, with the right information, they unraveled. Most of the stories are now complete. With an understanding of their habits' role in their pain, these patients now think of the solutions as surprisingly simple, practically effortless. The common refrain from my patients is often "I don't feel like we really *did* much, but now I'm pain free." That's music to my ears. Education about why there is pain is integral to my program. Knowledge is power. It means that my patients almost never slip back into bad habits.

Some of you reading this enjoy medical mysteries. Others are aspiring health or wellness professionals interested in exploring some of the tougher cases of our field. But I'd guess that most of you reading this are doing so because you are a patient with some chronic or nagging pain that just won't to go away. You've tried your family doctor, maybe even a specialist or two, without luck so far. My greatest hope is that you think of the following stories of pain, diagnosis, therapy and relief as clues to solve your own pain. But they are not only clues. They are a whole new way of thinking about how your body operates. I hope to inspire you to take a lesser-known path and rekindle that inner fire to find your solution. The solution is there. It's just a matter of shifting your thinking, putting on your Sherlock Holmes hat, and looking where others have not. I'll be with you every step of the way.

I'll Have Mine
with a Twist

"Ride with your knees a quarter to a half inch further from the frame," I said, "and rotate your shoe cleats out about two or three degrees. Lastly, start walking with your feet turned out a bit."

"You mean walk like a duck?" Brian, my new patient, asked incredulously.

"Yes, if that's how you want to think about it," I answered.

"When can I ride?" asked Brian, a lean 31-year-old with the shredded thighs of an elite cyclist. He'd raced in many countries around the world and he was now training for the Colorado Classic, a multi-stage, multi-day road race ranging from about 90 to 130 miles of riding each day through the steep, winding valleys and passes of the Rocky Mountains. This was one notch that this Colorado native hadn't yet put in his belt, and he felt it was time.

Brian had been training for months for this race, but his efforts had ground to a halt due to stabbing right knee pain that developed three weeks earlier. He consulted Dr. Google (as the search engine is affectionately called by medical professionals) and had tried what the good doctor had suggested: rest, ice, stretches and various salves, ointments and over-the-counter medications. All to no avail.

All my patient examinations begin with them standing and facing me while I take in the big picture of the body they've brought in that day. Brian stood there in his shorts, with veined, shaved legs and bulging muscles around his knees. His feet pointed straight ahead, and he had high arches. This is referred to as foot supination, as opposed to foot pronation, which is low or flat arches. Like I do with all my patients, I examined him from rib cage to foot to understand his particular architecture as well as the stressors working on it.

Brian was an athletic specimen and, not surprisingly, had no discernible weaknesses or abnormally tight muscles. Everything tested out perfectly, as I suspected it would.

However, there was one twist (literally) in his structure that could explain his pain. Brian had retroverted femurs—thigh bones that were twisted outward a little more than normal. Like most things in the human body, there is a spectrum along which each person falls. In regard to thigh bone shape, some are twisted outward, like Brian's retroverted femurs, and some are twisted inward, called anteverted femurs, like those of Satori, a patient you'll meet later. This is a naturally occurring phenomenon. I've found that men typically develop retroverted thigh bones, while women typically develop anteverted thigh bones.

A common observation/complaint that I hear is that men typically sit with their knees apart. Often this is judged as unappealing. Women, on the other hand, sit with knees together—a more culturally acceptable manner. But I've come to believe that men and women have a general tendency to sit in these differing ways due to the shape of their thigh bones—it's natural for men's legs to spread apart because of this retroverted twist. Likewise, it's more natural for women to sit with their knees together, an act made easier by the anteverted twist in their thigh bones.

Of course, some women have retroverted femurs and some men have anteverted femurs. Some have one retroverted femur and one anteverted femur. This was the case of an NFL lineman, Carl, who came to me with chronic right-side hip pain that began during his college days and would manifest during his pass sets, when he would back up to create a protective pocket for the quarterback. He was a right tackle and was taught to slightly internally rotate his right leg (pointing his knee gently inward) while planting his right foot behind him, to create an unmovable post. The problem was that his right thigh bone was retroverted, rotated outward. This meant that he had less available inward rotation in that hip or knee joint, so asking him to slightly internally rotate his leg forced him to use up all his available internal rotation, which was very little anyway.

40

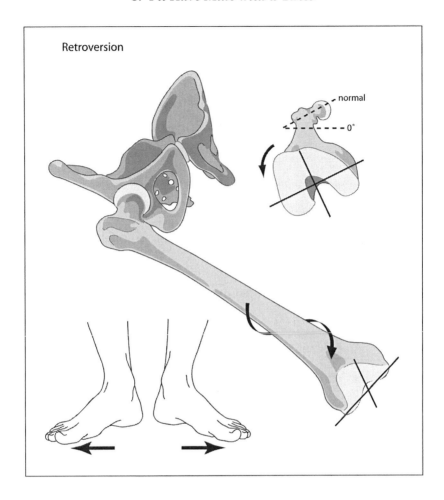

Retroversion

normal

0°

Femoral retroversion, where the thigh bone twists outwardly, occurs naturally. This is more common in males.

Internal rotation in any joint in the body, especially at the hip, knee and shoulder, increases joint compression, and therefore tissue breakdown and pain. Carl tested positive for a labral tear in his right hip joint—no surprise there given his profession and its necessary mechanics. But that wasn't the cause of his pain. It was the fact that his coaches had trained him to internally rotate his right thigh, unaware that this recommendation was actually weakening his ability to post that leg, rather than strengthening it. This, combined with the forces he was absorbing to protect his quarterback, was his recipe for pain.

Carl had three options. First, he could allow the right leg to remain slightly rotated to the outside, in order to maintain proper alignment based on the shape of his thigh bone. Second, he could strengthen his gluteal (butt) muscles. The gluteal muscles help externally rotate the thigh bone and therefore would reinforce his coach's instructions by countering or decelerating internal rotation of the thigh bone he was supposed to use in that situation. Or third, he could move positions, switching to the left side of the line, favoring his left femur, which wasn't retroverted, and consequently handle internal rotation better.

Due to his unique job, and the fact that he couldn't change sides of the line just based on the shape of his thigh bone, we decided to adopt solutions one and two. I gave him a gluteal strengthening exercise and tasked him with practicing his pass sets with less internal rotation of his thigh bone. On our next visit, a few days later, he complained of how sore his butt muscles were. He had never isolated them before. His training mostly included multi-joint strengthening exercises to prepare for the rigors of his job—not isolating specific muscles. He also reported his right hip pain was reduced by 75 percent.

Turns out that the remaining 25 percent was due to his tight soleus muscles controlling his foot and ankle. The soleus muscles lie deep to the calf muscles and originate about halfway up the lower leg bone in the back. Along with the calf muscles, they blend into the Achilles tendon to insert into the heel bone. The soleus muscles need length to allow the ankle to bend. Carl's were too tight, and therefore his ankle couldn't bend properly. In these situations, the forces trying to bend the ankle have two options: they can cause the foot to flatten excessively, contributing to a variety of foot ailments, or they can transfer the forces back up to the knee, which then has to deal with the problem. Carl's body chose to throw the problem back up to the knee, which was trained to follow the internal rotation of the thigh bone which, in turn, passed the forces into his right hip—another contributor to his right hip pain.

To tackle this (sorry, couldn't resist the pun), I gave him a soleus stretching exercise and we incorporated soleus lengthening into his training regimen to reinforce the new length we were asking of the soleus and foot and ankle. On his third visit, he reported that his hip pain was basically gone. A good thing, given that training camp started in two days.

⸻ ⸻ ⸻

"You can ride today if you want," I replied to Brian. "Let's see how it goes."

Brian left my clinic with a puzzled look on his face, after my recommendation to turn his cleats out a couple degrees and let his knees rest away from his bike frame another quarter to a half inch. He was especially confused when I said that, to top it off, he should walk with his feet turned out a little.

I'm used to those looks.

A big part of cycling is drafting, when the cyclist tries to remain in a streamlined position behind other riders, to avoid head winds. This involves tucking as much of the body into one's center as possible—internal rotation of most joints—a recipe for injury for those whose bones are not designed for internal rotation, like Brian's.

Allowing his knees to drift outward a little may not exactly change the amount of internal rotation of his thigh bones much, but it will certainly change the force he's using to keep them close to the bike frame. Sometimes a little decrease in force is all that's needed, especially when you're talking about tens of thousands of repetitions, as is the case with cycling. Turning the bike cleats out a few degrees would introduce a second layer of force reduction, stripping torque from the knees and hips by aligning the feet with the shape of his thigh bones.

Recall that Brian pointed his feet straight ahead when he stood and walked, but his thigh bones were rotated outward. People with retroverted femurs need to turn their feet out to match the rotation in their thigh bones. If they don't, torque is introduced into the system because one part of the leg, the thigh bone, is trying to rotate outward while another part, in this case Brian's feet, were rotating inward, relative to his thighs. In essence, he was trying to override the shape of his thighs to accommodate a socially acceptable ideal that all feet should point straight ahead.

They shouldn't.

Torque, in Brian's case, played out in his knee. It could've just as easily manifested as pain in his feet, ankles, hips, sacroiliac joint (the junction in the pelvis where the broad ilium meets the sacrum), pelvis or lower back.

Feet with high arches are uncommon. Brian's high arches, together with the fact that his feet were pointed forward, alerted me to the possibility that he was artificially adopting his current stance. This was confirmed when he commented that he would be "walking like a duck" by turning his feet out. This is a negative judgement about how he should be standing or walking, rather than an acceptance of how his body is built.

Brian came into the clinic a week later looking a little down. Prior to this, he complained that could ride only two miles before his stabbing knee pain began. I didn't have a good feeling. Had my approach failed?

"I did what you said and went out for a ride the afternoon after my last visit. At two miles, I had no pain, so I decided to try five miles. Still no pain, so I did ten miles—no pain. I ended up riding forty miles on hills and had no pain!" he said, smiling.

"Why the long face when you came in, then?" I asked.

"Oh, I was just messing with you!" he laughed. "I can't believe it! So simple! You solved it!"

⊐⊏ ⊐⊏ ⊐⊏

Understanding thigh bone rotation and its implications is critical to solving most lower body and back pain. At the other end of the spectrum, internally rotated thigh bones (femoral anteversion) cause problems too.

This was the case of Satori, a woman who flew in from Washington to see me. She explained that she had been born with a severe right hip deformity which caused her right leg to be three centimeters shorter than her left. She didn't want to stand out, so she'd tried her best not to limp ever since she was a young girl. As a result, she'd worn out her left hip and had a hip replacement 11 years earlier. Then, seven years later, her deformed right hip was replaced, a procedure complicated by a history of reconstructive surgeries for that hip. She reported that she'd had "crazy" left hip pain these last few months. She'd been through the usual host of tests and practitioners

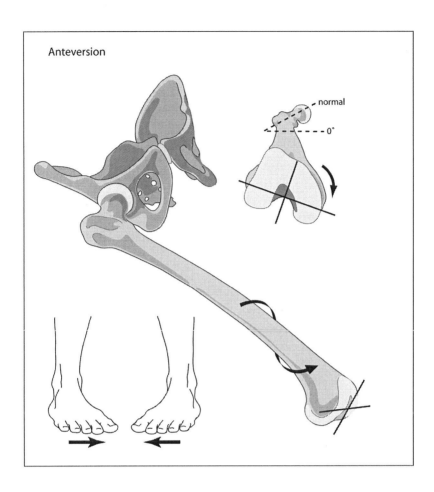

Femoral anteversion, where the thigh bone is twisted inwardly, is the opposite of femoral retroversion and is found more commonly in females.

and was desperate to stop her pain, which kept her up at night and lasted throughout the day. Her pain was in the front, back and side of her left hip.

I evaluated her as I did Brian and found that her knees rotated inward excessively, and she had flat feet. She walked by locking her knees straight. I discovered that she had an elevated left side of her pelvis and her left rib cage rested lower than the right side (I describe this as a "depressed rib cage").

Her walking pattern was unusual too. Her right rib cage shifted down when she stepped on her right foot and, at the same time, she hiked her left hip high into the air to swing her left leg forward. Based on her history, this could have been a very old pattern she adopted when she was young, to compensate for her right hip deformity. She had poor gluteal muscle activity and weakness. I also found she had internally rotated thigh bones (anteverted femurs). Lastly, I found that she had a problem with her new hip joints, which moved in their sockets incorrectly—Al's problem in Chapter 3.

After examining her, I was sure I could help.

Since she'd flown in from out of state, she blocked off the entire week to see me and we had three sessions to fix everything. I like to put at least a day in between sessions to give people a chance to try out my recommendations and see how they respond.

Our first job was to level her pelvis and rib cage. I use a powerful technique learned in my Hanna Somatics training to do this. It takes about 10–15 minutes and then I gave Satori exercises to maintain the level pelvis and rib cage. This is a key test for my patients. It's very easy to keep a pelvis and rib cage level once they've been corrected. If, when I see them next, they're not level, I know they haven't been trying hard to help themselves, at which time I become very stern. I prefer to work with people who will try to help themselves.

I also taped the backs of her knees to stop her from locking them. This is critical to establishing a therapeutic gait pattern. Locking the knees disrupts normal muscular activation throughout the lower body and back and is a habit that must be stopped.

Satori didn't disappoint me. Her second session began with my confirmation that her pelvis and rib cage were level. She reported that she felt about 65 percent better and had slept through the night with no pain. Great! When I see a large jump in pain reduction, it confirms that we're on the right track.

Next, I dealt with her butt muscle strength and timing by giving her a targeted butt strengthening exercise like Al's. I taught her to improve her walking pattern to turn on her all-important gluteal muscles too. This was critical because these muscles would prevent her thigh bones from rotating inward, help maintain a level pelvis, and improve how her hip bones were moving in her hip sockets. If the thigh bones can be controlled, then the knees won't collapse in excessively and this will unload foot flattening forces.

She was motivated, especially feeling so much better already. Her quick smile and laughter made working with her a pleasure—we were having fun.

Feeling hopeful, she then brought up that her left arm had been numb for several weeks and she wanted to fix that too. She hadn't mentioned it before, as she didn't think we'd make so much progress in a day. I took a quick look at her arm and taped her shoulder blade similar to how I taped Debbie's in Chapter 2. It is common for patients to start asking me about a bevy of other aches and pains once their main problem resolves. I don't mind at all: it's a sign that things are working better and that they trust me.

On our third day, she reported only a slight ache in her left hip—virtually no pain at all. Her left arm had just a small bit of tingling in it too. We fine-tuned her walking pattern to make it even better. I checked her hip joint motion and found that it had improved significantly. Finally, I confirmed that her pelvis and rib cage were still level. I then gave her an exercise to improve her shoulder blade strength, now that I knew that this was the source of her arm numbness.

She flew home later that day, but she still drops me an occasional email, thanking me and letting me know that she's still pain-free, now more than five years after her week-long visit, as long as she continues walking to control her rotating thigh bones and unruly hip joints. Her story is a valuable reminder that complicated problems don't necessarily need complicated solutions.

This underscores the reason that I'm sharing these stories. Chronic pain is rampant in the United States and around the world, resulting in an opioid crisis, lost wages, decreased productivity and, perhaps most importantly, lost family time. What if we could solve these problems before they ever became serious? What if coaches, gym teachers and trainers understood things like retroverted or anteverted femurs? Or dancers and gymnasts understood how depressed shoulder blades lead to chronic neck pain or headaches? Or doctors and physical therapists learned to understand how the legs are the primary stressors creating back, SI joint or sciatic pain?

The stories in this book often depict "miraculous" recoveries. That is not the exception at my practice; it is the rule there. We're in the business of miracle recoveries, but it's not due to miracles. It's about a deep, considered knowledge of the musculoskeletal system. Each body is a puzzle that I love to solve.

Knowing how quickly the body responds to the right things helps me move rapidly as a therapist solving pain mysteries. If I don't see at least a 30 percent or more decrease in pain after our first visit, I begin to think I might not be on the right track. If, by the second visit, someone's not 50 percent better, assuming there are no other extraneous medical complications, then I begin looking somewhere else for the potential source of pain. In my practice, I expect to solve body puzzles and ease pain in a way that patients consider miraculous, based on their previous experiences.

That's the beauty of understanding the human body from a systems standpoint, one that sees problems simultaneously from micro and macro levels: rapid identification of problems and rapid results. My method hinges on two core beliefs: First, pain is an indication that something is wrong right now, and second, our bodies have many self-repair mechanisms in place to assist us in healing. This is the only way I can explain why so many people feel better so rapidly once those obstacles are removed.

Hopefully, you're getting the picture that there may be answers for your pain too.

≡ 6 ≡

Ground Wires

When I was about 11 years old, growing up on our farm in Ohio, we had a cheap little toaster oven that sat on the kitchen counter next to the fridge. Every now and then we'd get to have an English muffin as a change from our usual Wonder Bread. I used to look through that half-burned glass to watch it toast, waiting to slather on the butter.

One day I came home from school and saw it sitting in the trash bin out in the garage.

"Why's the toaster in the trash?" I asked Mom.

"It's broken," she said.

Though I loved toast, this was the best news I'd heard in a long time.

I immediately snatched it from the bin and scuttled back to my bedroom. There I had an old red desk that served as my tinkering bench. It was like Christmas morning! Secretly I loved taking apart my toys to see how they worked. This was my first chance at a real adult appliance. I grabbed some of Dad's tools from the basement and set to work.

I removed the back panel and saw where the electric cord entered the toaster. After careful study, I noticed one wire suspended in the air. On the back panel, there was a weld spot with a little nub sticking out of it, just like the wire that was waving around. I lined them up and, sure enough, it was a perfect match. It was the ground wire.

My big sister had a phase then of making stained-glass ornaments. She'd set up a little studio for herself downstairs in the basement. I used to watch as her soldering iron magically melted metal, only for that metal to solidify again once the iron was withdrawn.

I was under strict orders not to touch it—ever.

In spite of this commandment, that afternoon her soldering iron dripped large gobs of solder on that broken metal tip inside our toaster oven, securing it back to the frame. That sucker was never going to come free again.

I then plugged in the toaster oven, flipped on the switch and saw the heating coils turn red—it worked!

I quickly put the panel back on and brought the refurbished toaster oven out to the kitchen counter. I stuck two pieces of bread in and turned it on.

Mom was sitting at the table reading a magazine.

"Hey, Mom, want some toast?" I blurted out.

For many months thereafter, every time I—or anyone else, for that matter—used the toaster oven, I would swell with pride.

That toaster was the beginning of my understanding that there's a logic to how things work. I saw that, while these connections were often hidden from view, with a little curiosity and work, I could figure them out and fix them if they were broken.

After I graduated from the Ohio State University with a degree in science education, I applied my fondness for tinkering to a broken-down motorcycle that I used to explore Australia in my early 20s. I couldn't afford a mechanic, so I would often camp by the side of the road in the Outback and practice taking apart the carburetor, memorizing where each screw went. At the time, I was reading *Zen and the Art of Motorcycle Maintenance* by Robert Prisig, which actually gave me a few clues as to how think about all this.

It was a time before mobile phones or the Internet, so it took me a while to understand things. I largely had to figure them out on my own—no instructional YouTube videos. Eventually, because my bike was so run-down, I relented and brought it into a bike shop. I explained that I was traveling around Australia and needed to learn how to fix this thing and that I wanted to watch what they did. I could only afford one visit to memorize everything. They were happy to oblige.

I discovered the role of floats in a carburetor and how to adjust them to keep the gas/oxygen mixture just right, to clean the gaskets that were prone to collect fine dust from the road and to remove and check the tubes feeding the carburetor. It was all very logical and satisfying to me on a deep level. That visit exposed the mystery of the engine and, from then on, I felt comfortable exploring further, knowing that I could put back together whatever I dismantled.

I managed to make it to Western Australia over the next several months tinkering with my bike along the way to keep it going. I needed to fix a new problem there, but I didn't have the right tools. So I found another motorcycle repair shop, this one in Perth, and I asked to use theirs. I removed my gas tank and carburetor within minutes while the owner watched.

"Hey mate," the owner said, "how long you been fixin' bikes?"

"Oh, about two months now," I said.

His eyebrows went up. "You serious?" he asked. His other two employees were listening now.

"Yeah," I said. "Had to figure it out cause this bike is such crap."

"Wait, you're not a mechanic?" he said.

"No, I'm just tooling around Australia," I replied.

After another minute of watching me, he said, "Mate, you want a job?"

I didn't imagine my future as a motorcycle mechanic in Perth, Australia (though, come to think of it, that sounds pretty sweet). But I was flattered and inspired by my ability to understand the inner workings of things, to recognize what wasn't functioning as it should, and to make it better.

I came home from traveling those many years and moved to Boulder, Colorado, where I worked various jobs. After some months there, a friend mentioned that her dad was in physical therapy for an ankle problem. I had never heard of physical therapy. I learned that it's a combination of medicine and exercise. I liked both of those fields and decided to check it out.

I volunteered at a sports and orthopedic clinic to learn more and fell in love. I saw therapists doing interesting things with people, handling different parts of the body in mysterious ways. People left feeling better. The therapists gave them exercises, critiquing or modifying them. I suppose on some level this spoke to my mechanical affinity for figuring out how things worked and fixing them.

My undergraduate grades at OSU weren't good enough to apply to PT graduate school. I had to take a few prerequisite courses to round out my application. But with my new enthusiasm, I received all As in my pre-req courses. Even so, I was happily surprised that University of Indianapolis let me in given the fact that the bulk of my science coursework was almost 10 years old and that my time off from school meant I was now a non-traditional older student. I was a risk.

While I wasn't the best student by a long shot at U of I, I enjoyed most of the classes. I learned so much and it all fascinated me. I often had to pinch myself to be sure I wasn't dreaming! I loved my anatomy classes best of all. To see our inner workings fascinated me. My classes in sports and orthopedic rehabilitation, while interesting, left me unsatisfied. I learned about strains, tears, broken bones, how they heal and what to do, but I had a nagging feeling that something was missing. I couldn't place my finger on it. I grew anxious as school continued.

There seemed to be a piece (or many pieces) missing for me. It was as if I were being taught the beginning of the equation—the anatomy, physiology, etc.—and then there was the end of the equation—progressing people through exercises—but there was a big chunk in the middle that seemed to be missing. Yet my classmates apparently understood this middle chunk or didn't notice the gap. How did that anatomy and physiology translate into pain or fixing that pain? Had I missed a key course in school?

Upon reflection, I think that I was missing the "why" behind it all. Today, this is the key to my approach. I search out and fix the why's—I find the butterfly whose wings are flapping causing a hurricane across the globe. Once the butterfly's wings are tamed, the hurricane hushes.

⸺ ⸺ ⸺

At graduation, one of my classmates came up to me and said, "Rick, I've never known whether you're the smartest guy in the class or the dumbest." I hadn't realized that it was so obvious to others.

I certainly never felt like the smartest which is why I often didn't express my concerns to my classmates—I didn't want to highlight the fact that I felt out of my depth. In fact, I was somewhere at the back of the peloton and, as graduation loomed, I was in a near panic. There was still so much I needed to learn! I felt unprepared to be a proper PT but I didn't know why. I simply had a general feeling that something was missing. It was like a secret had been passed to them that I'd somehow missed. What did they "get" that I hadn't?

I landed my first job as a sports and orthopedic physical therapist in the small town of Cortez, tucked into the southwest corner of Colorado. Luck seemed to dictate my patients' outcomes more than anything. I was basically on my own, with no mentor to show me how to help them. It showed. Every day I dreaded facing my patients, knowing that I didn't have the answers they were seeking. The fear I felt upon graduating bore out in the clinic. To put it simply, I felt I should be doing a better job.

It didn't help that I replaced a PT, Bret, who apparently worked miracles and whom everyone loved. I could never live up to his reputation.

In terms of my early failures in Cortez, there was a particular patient, Robyn, who stands out in my mind. Bright and full of smiles, young and athletic, she'd had ACL repair surgery. Things were going great until at about eight weeks, when she developed knee pain in her surgical knee. I assumed it was my fault: after all, I was her PT. No matter what I did, I could not get that pain to go away—I tried everything I knew. I asked other PTs and tried what they said. Her doctor confirmed that nothing was wrong with his surgery. She came back again and again for help but nothing worked. She haunted me.

Another patient with back pain was a young mother of two and very athletic. She could do back bends where her hands and feet were both on the floor. But nothing I tried helped. I drove six hours to Denver to take a back pain course one weekend, mostly with helping her in mind. I came back only to find none of the information I'd learned worked with her. Again, she looked to me for help, but I had none to give, despite my efforts.

These people and others looked to me for answers I didn't have. I thought of them daily, seeing their expectant faces searching mine for an answer. I could only stare back blankly—no answer, no wisdom, no understanding to offer them.

After that first year, I considered quitting physical therapy—clearly, I just didn't have what it took. But I had only recently graduated and spent so much time, effort and money on my education that I couldn't give up, at least not yet. I'd become a physical therapist to help people. It's what I felt I should be doing. I loved learning about how we worked. So I did what I did best at that time of my life and decided to travel, to think it all through. I bought a round-trip ticket down to Costa Rica for three weeks, which was fabulous.

I trekked through the mountains and volunteered for a leatherback turtle project in a small village without electricity on the country's east coast. Leatherbacks are huge, like oversized ottomans waddling around. My work involved patrolling the beaches during the night to ward off turtle egg poachers. While I explored Costa Rica, Spanish from a lifetime ago in college came back to me.

In spite of the beautiful beaches and gigantic turtles, there was a dark cloud hovering over me. "What will I do when I return? I'm not a good physical therapist." The very thought of working with patients again filled me with dread and anxiety.

My three weeks were up, and I was no closer to knowing what my next step would be. So I threw away my return ticket. Instead, I traveled overland through Central America and Mexico for the next six months. I didn't realize I was developing a mild form of PTSD. I would replay my failures in my head again and again with nothing else to think about. This sank me into a greater depression.

But there were many distractions from my quandary. The people of Central America were warm, friendly and tolerant of my Spanish. The markets were colorful with delicious foods, like plantains and a world of spices that reminded me of my world-wanderings when I was younger. My visits to ancient Mayan ruins like Chichen Itza helped put my problems into perspective. Right or wrong, a bigger picture started emerging of these once-thriving cultures being driven apart or simply melting away, absorbed by some other culture. I then felt the insignificance of my own life in the scheme of things. While this didn't help my depression much, it did help me step outside of myself and see my life as more than this moment, this month, this year. Things would change, I would learn or move on and go somewhere else. It wasn't the end, just a rock in the road that I needed to circumnavigate in some way. Some sweet, brief peace descended upon me, a levity I hadn't felt in months. I sat there in the shade, sweat trickling down my neck, bugs darting all around, and sighed. It would be okay. Eventually. I had no other option than to move forward, whatever that meant. That's life—moving, growing, hurting, recovering, thinking, feeling. Somehow through it all, I would still be me in the end.

6. *Ground Wires*

I lived with a family in Guatemala for a couple weeks while I studied Spanish and hiked the surrounding lush hills. I visited the white beaches of Nicaragua, Honduras, and Belize. Spent a few days on Isla de Mujeres, explored the pyramids of the Yucatan Peninsula and wove my way through central and northern Mexico.

Still, I was delaying "real life" and the question that came with it: "What am I going to do?"

No closer to an answer, I returned to explore the northwest of the United States, thinking I'd like to move there because I'd never been to that part of the country before. This was around Thanksgiving and Christmas. It was gray, cold and raining just about every day I was there. Being away from family and friends during the holidays is hard enough but, on top of that, I had a growing anxiety about returning to physical therapy. Add the miserable weather and I was pushed down into a hole.

By this time, I'd made it up to Seattle and was staying at a youth hostel. One early morning I woke up and couldn't remember who I was, not even my name. I didn't know where I was. I was in a bunk bed and sensed someone sleeping above me and others in the room. It was still dark. I remained still, trying to think. I lifted my hands to see if they were okay—no marks of damage. I remained still for what I think was an hour. Slowly, my name came back to me. Then I remembered where I was: in a youth hostel in Seattle. I remembered that I had a car. Then I remembered I had a family back east. I could get in my car and drive there. So I got up, found my car and left, driving east.

I didn't turn on the radio. I needed complete silence to orient myself and figure out what I was doing. I could barely drive the speed limit—it just seemed too fast. I thought then that I could find my parents and perhaps even live with them for a couple months. But what good would that do? I would still be me. I would still be in this quandary. And I didn't think I wanted to see the look of concern on their faces or to be asked the inevitable questions about what I planned to do. I was scared, though. This was really rattling me.

I then remembered that a friend of mine, Kristin, was in Denver. I drove to her place and told her I needed help. I just needed to sleep on her couch if I could. She let me stay there for four months. Denver is a bright, beautiful city, full of sunlight. This began lifting me.

I started a routine of stretching each morning and drinking tea—nothing else other than writing in my journal. No plans. Stretching, tea, journal, stretching, tea, journal. That was my day.

Kristin would cook dinner for me when she returned from work. We'd talk and she would just let me be. It was exactly what I needed. I realized, probably much later than I should have, that I needed purpose: to get a job and move out.

I had to do something. I thought that, if I wasn't good enough to be a PT, I at least enjoyed fitness. So I got a job at a prestigious downtown Denver health club and worked at the front desk—I was still too shaken to do anything more involved than that. For six months, I worked behind the front desk, checking people in and handing them towels.

Finally, my manager took me aside. "We hired you because of your PT background and expect you to work at least as a personal trainer. Why don't you get on the stick and start seeing clients?"

So I nervously became a personal trainer. Almost instantly my schedule filled with clients. They all had aches and pains they tried to exercise through. Because I was a PT, could I help them? It was as if there were a legion of walking wounded out there that I just discovered. These people looked healthy and fit but secretly many, so many, had chronic aches and pains. Almost all had been through a host of PTs, chiropractors, massage therapists, and doctors but were left with stubborn pain apparently no one could fix. They all had good insurance and expendable income to work with anyone they wished but, for one reason or another, couldn't find the answers.

They had fallen through the cracks of our medical system. Even in Denver, a fitness-oriented town where there are many elite health professionals, all these people had been unable to find solutions. If the cream of the medical community couldn't help them, then maybe I wasn't so terrible? When I realized this, I let out a deep breath I didn't know I was holding. I suddenly didn't feel so alone.

I had a fundamental belief that pain happened because of how we use our bodies. Much like my toaster or motorcycle, there should be a logic to the connections between function and the structures that are breaking down. But in PT school, I was only taught the separate parts—not how they all fit together from head to toe to create movement. For instance, anatomy class was focused on memorizing origins and insertions of muscles, nerve pathways and how those muscles moved a joint. Even in orthopedics, some of this was put together to demonstrate how it all worked to, say, raise your arm overhead or to walk forward. But there's so much more to it. School taught the basic mechanics of movement but not the significance or repercussions of movement or lack of it.

It was like learning that there's a ground wire in a toaster and how fix it but not about its relationship to the heating coils. Or in the case of my motorcycle carburetor, learning about the pin that guides the floats but not about how that makes the motorcycle move. Much later, I learned that it wasn't just my school that was missing these critical connections.

I realized, at this point, that I had three choices:

1. I could continue on as I was, helping to heal some people but not others.
2. I could quit being a physical therapist and try to reinvent myself.
3. I could try to figure out how it all fit together and become the best physical therapist I could.

Frankly, none of the three appealed to me immediately. The first choice was out of the question. That was why I was stuck in a deep depression in the first place. Choice #2 was not an option, at least not at the time. It had only been a couple years since graduation. If I followed that option, I'd sink into an even greater depression and feel that I'd wasted years and have to start from scratch without an alternative path in mind.

Number three was the only real choice left. But where could I begin to unravel the body's mysteries? Who was I to think that I could even do it? Far smarter people than I apparently either couldn't or didn't see the value in it. Yet this felt like my only real choice.

So I took stock of what I knew for sure. This was basically anatomy and physiology. I no longer had faith in the treatment side of my learning, as it didn't seem to work for me—at least not as well as I thought it should. And if there were so many people who hadn't been helped by doctors or PTs, then it seemed like it wasn't working for others either.

I began observing my clients, but I didn't know what I was

looking for. I simply noticed how they bent down, reached up, or sat. I started to experiment with some half-formed ideas and saw initial positive results.

The standard training states that you must lock your lower back into an arched position when squatting (lifting weights) from the ground, to protect the back. You see this in almost any ergonomic seminar or piece of advice on the Internet. I've even seen a little moving model of this on someone's desk once, where the back is locked while the model squats and stands up.

Yet many of the people I saw with back pain would lie on their back and pull their knees to their chest to ease their pain, rounding the lower back. This is the opposite of that bending advice. Who better to know if something eased their pain than the actual patient? So I began experimenting with allowing people to sit or squat down with a rounded back instead (with light squats only). Most reported that this felt much better for their back. Gradually many felt their pain melt away as they introduced this concept into the rest of their day.

Another personal training dictum was that the knees should not travel over the toes when squatting. I remember a lead trainer running up to me to point out my error when training someone with squats. "Then why are our ankles built to allow this?" I asked her, thinking of my extensive travels in Asia where people had been squatting for thousands of years, allowing their knees to move forward over their toes.

I started paying attention to peoples' shoulders when they lifted weights over their heads. I noticed some peoples' shoulder blades were asymmetrical when doing this. After some queries, I learned that almost all these people had had shoulder surgery at some point. While their surgery arm could reach just as high as the other arm, the shoulder blade acted very differently from one arm to another. I simply tried to get the surgical shoulder blade to move like the non-surgical shoulder blade, which seemed to help.

Definitely no miracles, just small wins. Clients were getting better. Soon I was the busiest personal trainer at the club and held that spot for the next three years, until I left.

Buoyed by my small successes, I drilled down deeper to discover more hidden connections. I began working out of my home, on the side, seeing people privately. I felt guilty charging people for my time. I was just experimenting with ideas, after all. I created a policy in which, if I didn't help someone, they didn't pay. That way I could explore relationships between movement, structure and pain without feeling pressure about how long it took me to figure things out. My wife wasn't happy about it, but I couldn't handle the guilt of someone giving me money when I hadn't helped them.

I remember telling one surgeon with back pain I had helped about my payment policy.

He looked at me and said, "Good PT. Bad businessman." Perhaps, but I felt that this was the right thing to do for me at the time. It was the only thing I could do that would allow me time to explore, without feeling pressure to solve a problem. Along with this approach, I began to feel better, about myself and about my life in general.

I hadn't thrown my education away. Instead, I looked at it through different eyes. I no longer held my instructors' knowledge as gospel. That slight shift in thought set me free.

I then remembered Lois, one of my classmates, talking about Dr. Shirley Sahrmann, a PT and PhD at Washington University in St. Louis. She, I was told, saw injuries and pain differently by connecting movements with pain. I attended Dr. Sahrmann's seminars.

Within the first hour of listening to her, I knew I'd found what I was looking for. It was like coming home after a long, arduous journey. She helped me create a system of evaluation and treatment that connected different parts of the body. I took all her courses. I was *that* student, always in the front row, raising my hand and taking enthusiastic notes.

Adopting Dr. Sahrmann's principles, I found my results with my clients at home became even more dramatic. More people sought me out for help, based on word-of-mouth recommendations. Over that year, my depression dissipated. I felt connected to my work. I stopped feeling that I was a failure and began to think that I was on to something special.

There's a saying that goes "When the student is ready, the teacher will come." The truth of that statement revealed itself by more patients with complex issues starting to show up at my door. Dr. Sahrmann had taught me the mechanics of pain but there was something else that was preventing these new clients from getting better. What I noticed was that, while I could correct the mechanics causing their pain, those mechanics would re-emerge, time after time. It was as if their bodies insisted on assuming these painful positions or habits. It was not conscious. This was something on a different level. There seemed to be an inner driving force creating these patterns of dysfunction that I was trying to correct. It was like rain falling on a windshield. Yes, the wipers would wipe it away but very quickly the rain would accumulate again. I needed to understand where this rain was coming from. My tectonic expectations and judgements were still working on me—I couldn't let it go. I had to figure out what this force was.

I received my answer in a phone call from a stranger who lived halfway across the country.

By this time, I had written my *Fixing You* books to help people solve their own pain. One day I received a call from a woman who was sobbing into the phone. She was wrestling with terrible back pain. She'd read my back pain book but couldn't seem to make it work. She even mentioned suicide. I spoke with her for more than an hour. She calmed down but, in the end, we were no closer to a solution for her. Her problem haunted me over the next month or so. It was similar to what I ran into with these new patients seeking help.

About two months later, out of the blue, I received a call from her again. She had fixed her pain.

"How did you do it?" I asked, dumbstruck.

"Have you ever heard of Hanna Somatics?" she asked. "You have to study this, Rick! It's exactly what I think you're missing. It's what you talk about in your book, but they fix it in a different way. I went to a practitioner and she reduced my pain by 75% in one treatment!"

I couldn't argue with her results. I jumped on the Internet to research Hanna Somatics. I immediately ran into a big problem—no research. My training as a PT dictated that all treatment should be evidence-based, meaning there must be research to support it, ideally published in peer-reviewed journals. But I did not dismiss it simply because it hadn't been researched. After all, much of what I had been doing to help people wasn't found in research. I was wary, but I couldn't get our conversation out of my mind. This just might be what I was looking for to help my more difficult patients. Whatever inner force was causing their bodies to assume these postures and to move in ways that caused pain was the rain, in my analogy. It was the nervous system responding to a problem, whether it be pain, anxiety, or something else. But I'd have to step out of accepted medical paradigm to track it down.

I took the leap and completed the training: nine-day sessions every six months for three years. The information was exactly what I was missing—a method of fixing mechanical problems by changing tension generated by our nervous system. The Hanna Somatics training, while complete, is drawn out and slow. It is designed to train a complete novice to become a very good bodyworker. So there is a broad spectrum of abilities of people who begin the training. Few have the tenacity to stick to it. I nearly quit a few times myself, but I knew that this was information that I needed to master, so I stuck with it. Not many medical professionals, or others, for that matter, will devote that kind of time to learning this system.

It wasn't until the fifth session that I realized that the instructors were trying not only to teach me but to *change* me. To make me into a more holistic practitioner. To be gentler and softer with my patients. To observe more and say less so that I could better perceive the problems my patients were facing.

It worked. It changed me as a practitioner and made me all those things and more. More because, in addition to that, I had other knowledge of which they weren't aware, the biomechanics and pathomechanics of movement that complimented their system so beautifully. When I tried to mention this aspect of pain to the organizers, they were dismissive. I get it. It was *their* system. So I quietly integrated the information myself.

With my new hires at my clinic, I try to pass on these Hanna Somatics principles as much as I can. Some of my associates are more receptive than others. In general, medicine focuses on intelligence as the primary prerequisite for inclusion at schools. But this can lead to excluding the softer characteristics that help people: compassion, caring, listening, gentleness. The Hanna Somatics training recognized this importance, too often overlooked for alpha, book-smart students. For many, me included, it was frustratingly slow—but worth it in the end. Not only for me but for my patients.

I updated my back pain book to reflect this new information. I saw even more success working from my home. My books sold well, and people got better faster than ever. I spoke at conferences, answered emails from readers, and had Skype sessions to help people around the world.

But nagging questions still hung over me. Would this work in a real clinical setting? Could this work for everyone, no matter what condition they had? Was it appropriate for surgical patients as well as those suffering from chronic pain? I had a feeling that the answer was yes, it really would work for all. But my inherent inferiority complex kept questions biting at my heels, questions that another person, endowed with an alpha, extrovert confidence, might not have thought twice about.

Working out of my home, I didn't see the volume or expanse of problems that are seen in a typical clinical setting. I didn't see post-surgical patients, I didn't see normal strains, sprains, broken bones or acute car accidents that are regulars in clinics. My clients' pain was chronic, often decades old. And they were motivated enough to pay cash to see me. That motivation helped them achieve their results.

In a clinic, some people come simply because their doctor told them to, even though they don't believe they can be helped. Some people's visits are limited by insurance restrictions, so they have maybe five visits to solve a 20-year-old problem. Some have just gotten out of surgery and are only coming to you because you're close by and in-network with their insurance. Some injuries are acute, some are chronic. Some are young, some are old. There is a whole spectrum of different types of patients seen in a clinic that accepts insurance as opposed to someone charging cash and working out of their home. I needed to know if this would work with the entire spectrum of problems PTs see in a clinic.

I didn't want to work at someone else's clinic because I knew that I needed to begin at my own pace. Many orthopedic clinics, in order to make ends meet, stack patients. So a PT could be seeing two to five patients at the same time, with an assistant or aide to help them. This maximizes billable time and revenue but is not good for the patient. I had done some temp work for one of these clinics and was constantly frustrated that I couldn't get down to the real problems behind people's pain. My intention was to run a clinic the way I wanted to treat patients, with income as a secondary consideration.

6. *Ground Wires*

My primary concern was seeing if my approach worked with all populations. Secretly, I'd wanted to own my own PT clinic for years. I thought it would be the pinnacle of my work as a physical therapist. But was I good enough? To even contemplate this was a 180-degree turn from where I was after my first years of practicing PT.

I found a PT about two miles from my home who was selling her small clinic. Would I like to buy it? Yes! After 16 years as a PT, my dream finally came true. I felt that my skills were at the point where I could really make a difference. I was ready to share what I had learned and perhaps even usher in a new way of practicing physical therapy.

It was a beautiful September morning. I had just signed the papers to purchase my new clinic. The keys were in my hand when I got a call from my receptionist—it was my first as a clinic owner. After seeing the caller ID, I thought to myself, "Will it be some difficult PT problem no one could answer?" I hoped so. I'd come so far—I'm ready to tackle the world!

"Is this Rick?" my receptionist said. "We're low on toilet paper. Can you pick some up before you come in?"

≡ 7 ≡

Big Man, Small Car

While in my 20s, living in Boulder and before attending physical therapy school, I volunteered for a Navajo hogan project promoting energy-efficient, solar-powered traditional housing as prototypes for reservations. Hogans were traditional homes of the Navajo. The president of the non-profit was an older Navajo man named Ernie.

Ernie was about 5'6" and in his 60s with long black hair punctuated by gray streaks. He had a perpetually serene expression. He was a friendly man of few words but whose broad face would break into a wide grin at the slightest provocation. His attention was often divided among larger concerns, but for some reason, one day I was lucky enough to be chosen to work with him alone. Our job was to tear down a stone wall dividing two rooms in a hogan to create more open space. I looked forward to spending time with him.

We had few tools to choose from but among them was a large sledgehammer and a smaller hammer. The wooden handles of both were pocked with chips and stains from years of service. I grabbed the sledgehammer, leaving Ernie with the smaller one.

I was younger and enjoyed physical work so immediately I pounded away at the wall with visions of it nearly exploding with the force of my sledge—kind of like the Kool-Aid man crashing through a wall bringing his drink to thirsty kids: "Oh yeah!"

For about 30 minutes I thrashed that wall, sweating and grunting with effort. At the end, I hadn't dislodged one stone—they were apparently set more firmly than I thought. I then looked back at Ernie. With a gentle tap, tap, tap of his hammer, he would loosen one stone, carefully place it on the ground and then begin on his next. He already had a small mound of stones while I had none.

Determined not to let him beat me, I went to work again, flailing away at the stone wall, hitting it right in the center. I pounded with furious energy, breathing hard, hands cramping as I gripped the sledge harder. The shock of each hit reverberated through my body like Wile E. Coyote after he ran into mountain. Twang! Again after 20 minutes of effort, not one stone loosened.

Catching my breath, I then looked back at Ernie, his placid face revealing his enjoyment of the work. Not a drop of sweat on his face. Tap, tap, tap went his small hammer and another stone gently dislodged; it was placed lovingly on the ground. He never looked up at me and seemed almost to be meditating.

I decided to observe him more closely and studied his gentle yet precise technique. I then turned with my sledgehammer, this time choking up on the handle, so my hand was near the head, and I gently tapped at the top layer of the wall. With just a couple taps and almost no effort, my first stone came free. I placed it on the ground and loosed my second stone just as rapidly with almost imperceptible effort. Before long I was enjoying the work in a different way, this time seeing my progress with little effort.

After our wall was finished, Ernie simply smiled at me and took drink of water. It wasn't until more than 20 years later his lesson finally drove home.

<hr />

Steve was a towering, athletic 6'3" tall man in his 40s, with close-cropped salt-and-pepper hair. He was an insurance adjuster who was out in his car most of the day traveling to sites when he wasn't at his desk writing up reports. Other than his height, his most prominent features were the perpetual laugh lines around his mouth and eyes. He had a booming voice and loved cracking jokes.

As Steve complained of chronic low back pain, I watched his laugh lines morph into a worried frown. It wasn't until his pain affected his job that he took it seriously. Each site he visited throughout the day required him to spend more and more time stretching his back. The pain had become worse over these last four weeks, and he finally decided to take action.

One of the most telling pieces of information I gather from patients is how their pain began. This holds clues as to the type of injury at the root of the problem. For instance, an injury that occurred after someone increased their running mileage may have to do with a strength deficit or shoe breakdown. Pain after a fall might indicate a tear or strain that needs to heal.

Steve was no help in this regard. His pain began out of the blue. He hadn't changed the number of hours he spent driving his car or working at his desk. He hadn't changed his exercise routine, diet, shoes or anything else. He was under no new financial or emotional stress. This line of questioning was a dead-end for me. The only thing that was clear was his desire to fix his problem. He recently began losing sleep too.

The next obvious issue was Steve's height. Tall people tend to slouch more so they don't stand out in a crowd. Steve did not slouch when standing but he did when sitting—he couldn't help it. Chairs are typically too short for most tall people. Because of their long legs and minimal space under desks, their knees tend to ride up too high which then tilts the pelvis backward, flattening the spine. While this feels good for most people with back pain, too much of a good thing can be bad. Unlike most people of average height, taller people rarely have an opportunity to get away from that constant flattening.

But Steve told me nothing had changed about his work habits. He drove the same number of hours and sat in the same desk chair as always. So it was unlikely this was the problem.

My examination found several problems that could explain his pain. Steve had flat feet which can affect knee and hip orientation and tight thigh muscles which would tilt his pelvis. One side of his pelvis was higher than the other and one side of his rib cage was lower than the other. His butt muscles didn't work as well as they should. He had poor posture when sitting.

Steve only saw me once a week due to our busy schedules. Undaunted and eager to get better, within three weeks he corrected everything we found wrong. He was an ideal patient who eagerly tackled his rehab homework. We even taped his feet to improve his alignment. I tried every trick I had. Nothing helped, though.

But not only had I not helped Steve, his pain was *exactly* the same as when we began. Like that wall I hammered with Ernie so long ago, I had thrown everything I had at Steve! How could all those corrections amount to nothing? The most obvious answer was they had nothing to do with his pain. Steve began losing faith in me. I saw it in his half-hearted participation with treatment. He was no longer eager. He came more out of habit than anything. Frankly, I was losing confidence too. It made no sense.

━━ ━━ ━━

During my first 20-plus years of practice, I hung my self-worth on the success of my patients. If they didn't get better, I was a failure and miserable. If they did, I was a success and on cloud nine. This led to an endless stomach-churning emotional roller coaster ride for me. Any doctor or therapist will tell you this is a really bad habit. But I couldn't help myself. I felt those old stirrings of failure once more.

Steve's case was like a splinter in my brain I just couldn't reach. What was I missing? Our most recent session left us with no more answers. On that overcast autumn day, he was my last patient and I followed him to the door to wish him a good weekend. My spirits were down but he was kind enough to stay chipper through another failed session.

I stood absently at the glass door and observed him walk away— with perfect balance and symmetry, I might add. Then I watched as he folded his 6'3" frame into his tiny two-door Subaru. It was almost comical. His knees came up on either side of the steering wheel. Then it hit me. I ran out and pounded on his window. He rolled it down.

"Do you have a different car you can drive?" I asked, breathless.

"Yeah, I have an SUV. My father-in-law's been borrowing it since his surgery a couple months ago. He can't bend his knee well," Steve said.

"Your homework is to stop driving this car and drive your SUV until I see you again," I said.

He looked at me quizzically. "Okay, if you say so." I'm sure he thought I was nuts.

Steve came back a week later. "My pain is gone! I haven't had it since I switched cars!" he laughed.

Ernie's lesson then came back to me clearly. I could only smile to myself as Steve walked out of the clinic that final appointment. I finally put words to what Ernie had shown me more than 20 years ago: A small effort directed precisely can have more impact than a big effort aimed broadly.

And my addendum: be more precise with my questions.

≋ 8 ≋

Naked and Afraid

I walked naked along a busy sidewalk. Sometimes I'd be up on stage with a guitar in front of a crowd only then realizing I couldn't play or sing. One time I was naked there too.

Bad dreams haunted me after my decision. I've always had thin skin, and I knew that if I were attacked, it would devastate me. Did I really have the constitution to put myself out there? I was just a guy working out of his house. What if I actually hurt someone? What if my license were revoked? I spent many sleepless nights leading up to that moment.

Eventually I put my fears aside.

≒ ≒ ≒

After a few years of working as a PT, I discovered workshops put on by Dr. Shirley Sahrmann, a professor of physical therapy at Washington University in St. Louis. With her information, my results got better and better. She helped me make sense of the connections I discovered in my patients.

There was a physical therapist I struck up a friendship with at the seminars and ran into him one day.

"How are you finding the information?" I asked him.

"Oh, I'm just taking bits and pieces," he said. "I'm more of a manual therapist and I don't see a use for a lot of it. I don't think patients will buy into it." A manual therapist is one who typically focuses on joint manipulations like a chiropractor.

"But it works really well," I said. "I'm getting great results. My patients seem to love it."

He shrugged dismissively. With that shrug I realized that Dr. Sahrmann's information was being filtered through therapists who might not embrace it. The full impact of her great work wouldn't be delivered to patients who needed it, many who live in rural communities like the one I grew up and worked in, and may only have access to one or possibly two therapists for help.

This is true of all professions—we tend to apply information that fits our training or personality and discard the rest. Because I had been so unsuccessful as a therapist, I had no allegiance to competing approaches I'd already tried, including manual therapy. They just didn't seem to work well, or at least as well as I thought they should.

I embraced Dr. Sahrmann's philosophy because it worked in the broadest populations and across a wide spectrum of injuries. It combined an understanding of the nuts and bolts of anatomy, neurology and biomechanics with movement habits. It was perfect for me.

Dr. Sahrmann's approach involves assessing movement dysfunctions causing pain. The roots of her brilliant work are in analyzing how the body moves to understand and solve pain. For instance, she came up with the concept of scapular depression as a system of dysfunction stressing the neck and head. I was only beginning to realize how pervasive it was, as well as grasping some of the causes, after attending her seminars. She broke back pain down into three primary patterns of dysfunction: Extension, Flexion and Rotation. This corresponded to what I was discovering with my patients as well, although I hadn't yet thought about rotation problems. She'd mapped out each type of problem and gave legitimacy to my discoveries by explaining why what I'd observed was happening. This helped me embrace what I'd been seeing as real patterns of problems in anyone with pain, not just in my own patients. In essence, her information provided the outline from which I could explore more rapidly and confidently those problems I was seeing and how to solve them. Knowing that she had been researching and experimenting with this information for decades prior to my discoveries helped me feel confident I was on the right track, that I wasn't making this up or that the cases I was solving using this information weren't aberrations.

My advantage at the time was that I worked out of my home and could take more time with people, tumbling down various rabbit holes of dysfunction until I reached an answer or a dead end, and then dive into another. I went further, linking foot, knee, hip and gait dysfunction to each pattern. Eventually I could identify the problematic painful pattern and several causes of it simply by watching someone walk into my home and sit down.

From here I developed a systematic evaluation paradigm testing key issues feeding different patterns of dysfunction. Initially it was full of tests, but I continued chasing down causes of problems, distilling them down to a few simple tests that revealed the chinks in people's systemic and functional armor.

The solutions were prescribing exercises to correct strength or tightness that resulted from poor function. It also required that I teach people how to use their bodies better to reduce strain (you'll see what I mean in the next chapter talking about walking better).

⇒⊏ ⇒⊏ ⇒⊏

Dr. Sahrmann wrote many research articles and two textbooks but, for some reason, her approach wasn't widely embraced in the physical therapy community. I wasn't about to attempt research of my own. I was just one therapist working out of his home, which made me feel that I was somehow incomplete as a professional. I let these thoughts fester in me for a while.

After a year or two more of using Sahrmann's techniques and unraveling deeper pain patterns, the idea came to me that perhaps I could reach people directly through a self-help book.

That's when I decided to write my first book about neck pain. I had a few "miracle" cures, and while the information was unique, it was also consistent. I helped most clients with neck pain or headaches. They were miracle cures to the patients because they solved chronic problems that they hadn't been able to figure out. They weren't miracles to me because I was gaining a better understanding of how the body works as ever-larger or smaller systems of function. The connections I was discovering, rather than being surprises, started making more sense. They became predictable.

So I buckled down and took the next several months to write my first book, shoot accompanying exercise videos, and hire an editor and illustrator.

Not a day went by in that period when I wasn't plagued with anxieties and doubts. "Who am I to write a book about neck pain? I'm no expert. I'm going to be ripped apart by the medical community. I'll be exposed as a fraud—I'm going to get sued!" I knew I wasn't a fraud, that I was doing my best, but this sort of catastrophic thinking has kept many a well-meaning idea away from those it might help.

I realize now that I was a very anxious person in those days although I never thought of myself like that. I think I was responding to pressure to support my family while discovering a better way to help people and get the word out. I was terrified of getting sued in our litigation-loving society. It was all very scary to me, but I felt it needed to be done. In the end, it turned out that no one really paid attention. All that worry was for naught. No PTs or doctors contacted me to tell me I didn't know what I was talking about. Nobody sued me. My license wasn't revoked.

I sent the book to more than 120 literary agents and publishers over the next few months. I received only one response. This good-hearted editor informed me that, because I don't work with celebrities or professional athletes, I had no basis from which to write a book. Essentially, I lacked a selling point. The content, it seemed, was a distant secondary consideration.

I was so thankful for that response! I'd convinced myself that no one wanted to publish it because the information was bad. Instead, it was simply because there was no marketing potential. This "no" actually propelled me forward. I'd already spent all the time and money to write it, so I might as well keep going.

That's why I decided to self-publish and sell the book on Amazon. Once uploaded, it was buried on page 27 of the search results for "neck pain" books. No one would ever find it. I took small comfort in that. I wouldn't be ridiculed. At least it was done. I could relax and let it go.

Three weeks went by. Then I received an email with the subject line "Your Neck Pain Book."

"Oh my gosh," I thought, "there are a lot of words in this email— this could be bad." Here's what they wrote:

Hello Rick,

...I was able to access the videos and found them extremely helpful. I am so glad I ordered your book. After two and a half years of severe pain on the left side of my head, around my left eye and a weird, extreme feeling of discomfort deep in my nose (a symptom I have not come across despite all my research, doctor's visits, etc.), I read your book, did all four rocking stretches numerous times just this past Wednesday and the hand on head position, and now Saturday I am on day 4 of living pain free. You have literally given me my life back. I had, in the fall of 2007, been on 3 antibiotics for what was assumed to be a sinus infection, then a negative sinus CT, visit to an ENT which included scoping up my nose, CT of my brain, an MRI and MRA of my brain, an MRI of my neck, onto a neurologist, who insisted I had migraines, despite my telling her it was not a headache I have but head pain (there is a difference), physical therapy appointments which caused increased pain due to aggressive massaging of trigger points, many chiropractic visits, which did offer some relief, 4 months of yoga, and acupuncture, which brings me to Dec. of 2009. I was just this past Monday suffering from depression and despair, thinking that this would be the rest of my life. I am 52 years old and before this in great health. Yours was the 4th book I have purchased on neck pain, but the only one that even mentioned the scapula and shoulder as being a probable cause. My husband is so happy that I have found an answer that he has actually mentioned flying me to Colorado to be seen by you. I anxiously await the film clips that I have ordered and intend to continue the exercises. I have never written any kind of testimonial before but felt I needed to express my thanks to you. Your book has become my bible! Thank you again.

Tears slid down my cheeks. My wife was at work, and I was home alone with the kids.

"It worked!" I screamed. I danced around. I gave the kids a piece of candy each. Until that moment, I'd never put myself out there to publicly fail.

I immediately called my mom and read her the email, choking up as I did so. She was so happy for me and listened patiently as I blathered on for the next 20 minutes.

I couldn't believe someone got such quick results with such dramatic debilitating symptoms. I'd certainly seen nothing like those symptoms in the patients I had treated when I wrote the book. It made me wonder what was going on with her. Later, I was to suspect a case of trigeminal neuralgia (the story of Lizzy, told in this book).

Her email lifted an enormous weight off my shoulders. All those years of failure (or at least what I perceived as failure), experimentation, work, time, cost and worry, those sleepless nights and nightmares had evaporated because of this woman's words. I thought, at that moment, that if I never sold another book or helped another person, it was worth it to help her. To change her life through words that I wrote meant everything to me.

In the end, I think she helped me more than I helped her.

≋ 9 ≋

The Case of the Shoulder Problem in Her Foot

In medicine, when someone's gone through a lot of practitioners without relief, they're often thought to be beyond help. Such was Sallie's case.

Past failures don't mean much to me, though. I know the types of treatments others have already tried. It doesn't surprise me that they've failed. I used those same treatment approaches in my first years as a PT which is part of the reason I sank into a depression. Most peoples' injuries have been approached by focusing on the joint or tissue that's painful. Medicine is good at that—isolating a structure that's damaged or irritated. We've got all sorts of sophisticated and expensive scans and tests to find these structural problems. So shoulder pain has been seen as a problem with the shoulder, neck pain is addressed by scrutinizing the neck, back pain blamed on the back. The problem is, if you're looking for a structure to blame pain on, you'll have plenty of opportunity to find it in the body somewhere. We're not perfect. Things break down all the time and we function just fine that way. Many people have disc bulges and even herniations with no pain at all. This is especially the case as we grow older. Blaming pain on a structural problem can be like assuming the heating coils were broken in my childhood toaster. Sometimes this is exactly what the issue is. But I don't believe it until I've had a chance to fix the functional and systemic problems that may be stressing those damaged tissues first.

By systemic, I mean the things that affect other things further away. For instance, if a foot is flat and the arch drops to the ground, the lower leg bone subtly rotates inward, following the foot. Since the lower leg bone includes half of the knee, it then rotates inward too, or at least experiences a force trying to rotate it inward. Since the other half of the knee includes the thigh bone, it also then follows the foot, shin and knee. Everything in the leg has a tendency to roll inward at this point, tumbling like a house of cards.

I've learned the body doesn't really like this kind of inward (internal) rotation. It tends to irritate joints, so now we get tissue irritation in the form of inflamed joints or cartilage breakdown or tears. Following this downward spiral further, the pelvis then experiences this internal rotation force. Over my years of practice, I've teased out the ways the pelvis will react to this phenomenon. For instance, that side of the pelvis can tilt forward, causing a height difference between the two sides. Because it's tilted forward, the back then may compensate by arching backwards, creating excessive unilateral arching on that side of the spine and relative side bending and rotation of the spinal bones. Another response could be that, since the pelvis is rotating forward and down, the waist muscles attaching to the pelvis then try to pull it up, creating tension on that side of the waist contributing, yet again, to a side-bending problem where compression results on that side of the spine. As you can imagine, this pattern is often a cause of sciatic or SI joint pain.

I think of functional issues as slightly different than systemic problems. Functional problems are more about behaviors feeding the systems issues. For instance, in the example above, perhaps all this is happening in part because someone isn't walking properly and therefore not activating their gluteal muscles. The gluteals, among their many functions, rotate the thigh bone outward (external rotation). This can also be thought of as putting the brakes on internal rotation of the thigh bone. If someone is walking correctly, it prevents the thigh bone from rotating inward too much, or at least slows it down a bit. This then prevents the knee from rotating in too much, which prevents the shin bone from rotating in too much. This then unloads the arch of the foot, preventing complete collapse and instead introducing controlled collapse. As you might imagine, this can have enormous ramifications on the tissues at any of these joints. Improving walking patterns is a powerful long-term fix.

Back up at the pelvis, if the butt muscles are activating properly, they also assist in stabilizing the pelvic bone from rotating forward.

In this case, the lower spine no longer has to arch to compensate for this movement, which then eliminates the side bending and rotational forces acting on the spine. The waist muscles can continue their reciprocal contractions because that side isn't trying to hold on to the pelvis for dear life, preventing it from dropping down or rotating forward too much.

You can see that a butterfly's flapping wings really do cause a hurricane in another part of the body. But the converse is true too: let the metaphorical butterfly rest happily on a flower, sipping nectar, and the hurricane melts away.

That's the relationship, in a nutshell, between systemic, functional and structural issues.

The patient perceives these results as miracles—for example, taping a foot arch up and resolving back pain. But like Sherlock Holmes, I've done my homework to understand exactly what the ramifications are to all sorts of idiosyncrasies of the body or behaviors. In that context, they are not miracles to me. The only miracle I'm left with is how rapidly pain melts away when a system and function are restored. It never ceases to amaze me.

It's also so much fun to hear the astonishment in people's voices that it works.

I remember a field of wildflowers I once visited in Utah while camping. I was simply overwhelmed by the beauty spread out before me like a purple ocean. After taking it all in, I scrutinized the area around me more closely and found there were actually small patches where no flowers grew. Closer examination revealed there were other types of flowers and plants interspersed throughout the sea of purple. Finally, I bent down to study a single flower. It took me back to my botany class as an undergraduate at the Ohio State University. I looked at the petal patterns and leaf shapes climbing the stem, and the pistil and stamen of the flower's purple center. Then I compared it to its neighbor to notice small variations between the two apparently identical flowers.

This type of scrutiny involving the whole as well as the parts and their interactions, most closely describes my approach to solving pain. As physical therapists, I think we've done a good job of looking at the parts. It seems we need to study more about how they fit together as a whole. The body is a system. It should be approached as such when the initial foray into dealing with one part at a time does not yield fruit.

⊐⊏ ⊐⊏ ⊐⊏

Sallie had bright blue eyes, a quick wit and big smile. She taught theater for years before retiring. Like my other theater friends, she had an extra volt of electricity to her personality. She practically glowed when she entered the room on this cold November morning.

At our first meeting, I watched Sallie walk toward my table and noticed several issues right off the bat: a pronounced limp with a leaning posture to the left, a left shoulder sitting just a little too low and unnaturally short steps that favored her right leg. They were subtle. Most people wouldn't even notice these things. It's just my job, like a forest ranger spotting a wild animal in the distance no one else can see.

Sallie had several problems consistent with my observations: chronic left shoulder and neck pain and left-sided low back pain for as long as she could remember. She had scoliosis, which was not so unusual given her age of 70. Sallie also had right knee pain which hurt most when walking and gardening—her pleasures in life.

Smiling, Sallie told me that her left shoulder was her top priority. She couldn't lift a bag of groceries without extreme pain. She couldn't get dishes from her cabinet or food from her fridge using that left arm. She had to use her right arm instead, which started to act up too. Her left arm was virtually useless and her back and right knee pain were so severe that she stopped walking and exercising. She lived alone and worried for her future independence. Her ever-present smile faded at this confession. I worried for her too.

Sallie's left shoulder problem was first up to the plate. Starting at her pelvis, I methodically assessed the major bones and muscles to understand what all the players were doing and who was misbehaving. Thankfully, I didn't detect any significant tears or other serious problems. After my examination, I explained to Sallie what I felt the issues were. She listened with polite acceptance and a neutral smile on her face—she'd been through it before.

Skepticism can be a dangerous thing. It goes hand in hand with hopelessness. When we don't have hope and have an abundance of skepticism, we tend not to take action. How can anything change if we don't take action?

I have a unique perspective on how the shoulder and neck function, as we will explore throughout this book. It is linked to my deeper understanding of body systems and how a problem in one area may need to be solved at another. This, added to two specialized techniques, Hanna Somatics and Dr. Sahrmann's approach, make my methodology distinct. My results are very consistent. So much so that, if someone does not respond to my treatment in two to three sessions, I suspect a larger problem, such as a tear. I call tears "structural problems" because they have to do with a breakdown of a physical component of a system, rather than a functional problem that speaks to how that system works.

This is a fundamental concept to this book and to my approach as a medical practitioner. I want to help re-frame the understanding of pain in terms of structural versus functional problems and how functional problems cause structural problems. It's easy to spot a structural problem (tears, disk bulges, arthritis and so on). What people and many medical professionals don't take into account is why those structural problems are occurring. They don't just happen out of the blue—there's a reason. This book is about those reasons that others don't seem to grasp.

So with my toaster analogy, the structural problem was the broken ground wire. No matter how we used the toaster, that ground wire would always be broken and so it would never work. The heating coils weren't really broken; they just appeared to be broken. This represents the systemic problem—a broken ground wire somewhere else causes the heating coil not to work (or, in humans, to be painful). The coils are actually fine. It's the ground wire that's not allowing the heating coils to do their job. That is the structural problem underlying the systemic failure.

The functional problem (or the reason behind the broken ground wire) would be that maybe people slammed the toaster door closed too hard too often, eventually breaking it. Or the toaster was continually jostled because it had to be moved to reach into the cabinet behind it. Functional problems are about how behaviors cause systemic problems and possibly structural problems.

If we don't change *how* we're slamming that door closed or

relocate the toaster to a different part of the kitchen that doesn't require it to be jostled, the ground wire will just break again and again. But if that ground wire isn't repaired, no matter how gently we learn to close the door or wherever we decide to move the toaster, it'll never work. Notice that I'm not even mentioning the coils— because there's nothing wrong with them. That's the relationship between structural, systemic, and functional problems. All are critical in understanding pain. This is the core lesson of this book and of how I teach PT.

I taped Sallie's shoulder blade into a position that would decrease strain to her neck and shoulder. It's the same method I developed to help Debbie with her migraines. The tape gave us a window of opportunity to see how her neck and shoulder would feel given ideal circumstances. Thankfully, Sallie responded rapidly and her left shoulder and neck pain were 80 percent improved in just a few sessions. We simply tinkered with those parts of her shoulder system that weren't working well.

As those improved, we weaned her away from the tape. Given this opportunity to function better, Sallie's body took care of the tissue repair. To me, that's where the magic is. I'm there to help the body realign and then the body handles the rest. The human body is the real hero of this book, and of the story of our lives. It's simply amazing how well designed it is, and how it heals itself when we allow it to.

Slowly, I saw the real Sallie peek out from behind the curtain of her pain. Like a fog had been lifted, she finally shone brightly. Hope was restored. That excitement is the part of my job I love most. Sallie was highly intelligent and caught on right away to how she was going to solve all these problems. I would point out the habits that were breaking down her system and she would fix them. Part of PT is my analysis of what is going wrong. Another part is my manipulation to help fix it. But the third component is teaching the patient how not to revert back to old patterns and how to fix issues themselves through proper movement and exercise.

"Well, since you told me that my shoulder pain was due to my habit of hunching down on that side, I started noticing that I did this when I brush my teeth too. And you know what? I was gardening and started feeling more shoulder pain and thought to myself, 'Now,

Sallie, what are you doing to make that shoulder hurt?' and then I remembered what you said about turning my arm in when I'm reaching, and sure enough...."

Soon she came to the clinic like an eight-year-old at Disneyland, brimming with excitement at the discoveries she'd made. Appointments from this time forward became fun.

My general rule for people who have multiple areas of pain is that we work with one area at a time until it's about 75 percent better. At that point, we know we have a handle on it and can move on to the next area. Otherwise, the benefits of treatment become diluted. This rule is harder to keep than you might imagine because most people want to fix everything at once. For some, it's a struggle to hold back until we reach this milestone.

Sallie was able to control herself and we next addressed her back pain. This time she was enthusiastic at the outset. In about four visits, she was around 85 percent better—she couldn't believe it. Then came her right knee pain, which we were able to improve by about 70 percent in just a few visits as well. This was partly because we needed to address many lower body problems to solve her back pain—so she was already well on her way with regards to her knee pain.

When Sallie came in for her next appointment, I could tell something was on her mind. In spite of our success so far, there was something else—a distant cloud that she could never catch. Sallie finally worked up the courage to tell me her biggest concern.

"I never thought we'd make it this far," she admitted, "and I'm so happy. If we can't do anything else, I'm still so grateful. But I have a problem no one has been able to help me with and, if it's possible, I'd like you to look at it." I could see the reticence on her face: would her request be too much to ask? Have we bumped into the limits of her ability to heal? It was her last hold out to the hope of really getting her life back.

"Well, what is it, Sallie?" I asked. "I'll do my best."

"It's my left foot," she said. "I had surgery on it eight years ago and it's been hurting me ever since. It was painful before but now it's just more painful," she said. "It really hurts to walk."

This came as no surprise, which surprised Sallie. I'd suspected the role of Sallie's foot in all this from the moment I saw her walk in for her first visit. I didn't know the extent of the damage, however. I needed to work through her other problems first before addressing what I felt was the ultimate cause. This gave us a chance to build trust and for me to see how well she would respond to my treatment approach. The more trust she had in me, the longer she would allow me to try to help her. Had we begun with her foot and stumbled with different approaches, she would never have come back for treatment elsewhere.

Sallie's left foot arch had completely collapsed. While I saw that her left foot was a major issue to address when we first met, this was actually the first time I closely examined it, as her upper body and back had kept us busy enough. The keystone of her arch, the large navicular bone, collapsed to the ground with each step. Actually, this isn't completely accurate. To say it collapsed to the ground would indicate that, at some point, it would rise back up. But Sallie's didn't rise up. It just remained down with no spring at all in her foot arch. I had only worked with one other foot like this, with minimal success. Sallie couldn't put her full weight on that foot and whatever weight she did put on it was brief. Imagine walking on a loose bag of 26 potatoes—one for each bone in the foot. It would be very unstable and you'd work twice as hard trying to control it.

The surgery on her left foot many years ago had only made things worse. It gave her foot fewer options to negotiate her root problem, her arch. She didn't have strong enough ligaments to hold it up anymore.

"Sallie, I've been working toward your foot this whole time. I think it's the reason you've been having all this pain. Don't worry, I have some ideas," I said. Secretly, though, I was concerned.

Her whole body slumped in relief at these words. I wasn't aware this had been weighing on her so much these past weeks. I was touched that she trusted me enough to bring up this enormous fear of hers. Sometimes it's easier not to address your fears and keep some little flame of hope flickering deep within than to voice the fear and find there's really no solution after all.

The trail of breadcrumbs from Sallie's foot to her other injuries went something like this: because Sallie's left foot was painful, her left waist and rib cage muscles worked overtime to hike her hip up to unload it. Those muscles then dragged her rib cage down. With the hip held up and the rib cage pulled down, excessive compression on that side of her spine lead to sciatic and low back pain.

The left shoulder blade, which is the foundation for all arm movement, rests on the rib cage and has muscle attachments to the neck and head. Because her left rib cage sat too low, the left shoulder blade followed, disrupting its normal movement. This created pain in her shoulder. Her neck pain resulted from strain of the muscular attachments between her shoulder blade and the neck and head on that side. Of course, the right knee broke down because it carried most of the load, thanks to that useless bag of potatoes she had on her left foot.

When I lay it out like this, it's all very simple. Well, at least it's logical to me, like my toaster on the farm or the carburetor on my motor bike in Australia. Our muscles and bones can be thought of like a Rube Goldberg device—a ball falling into a plastic cup can ultimately light up a Christmas tree at the far end of the room. It all seems haphazard until you take the time to tease out the logical connections along each step of the way. That's what I've been up to these past 25 years.

Yet there's more to it, because nothing in our body works without being told to work. How did the hip

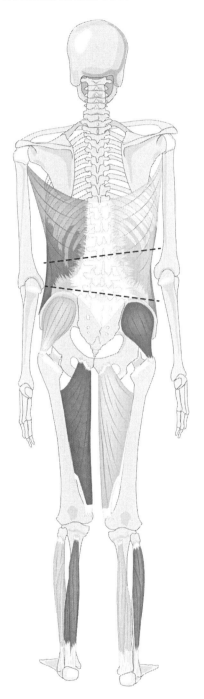

A series of compensations occur throughout the body in response to a foot problem, potentially even affecting the neck and shoulder.

know to lift or the rib cage to depress? How did the right leg know it needed to carry more load? Sallie's brain, of course, is the master controller. And, in her case, it had said, "Oh, now, don't be alarmed by this little obstacle. I'll quietly make this slight modification and we'll both be all right."

But this happened again and again, over a long period of time. Her brain had forgotten its way back to where it had begun, before the problems had come up. It simply adopted this new reality of compensation. These adjustments slipped under her radar while her cerebral cortex, in charge of higher-level executive functioning, worked on daily tasks and goals. What emerged was someone functioning quite differently than the young, athletic teen Sallie once was. The system had shifted to compensate and never shifted back.

Sometimes I feel like a tracker, reading the trail to find where it all began and where it's going. After I explain the trail of cause and effect behind a patient's pain, often I'm met with "I don't know how this happened. I used to be in such good shape when I was younger. I had no idea." Health care professionals can be similarly stumped if they look only at one component of the body at a time, rather than tracking through the system, noting everything that appears off, and tracing the links between errors and inconsistencies, wherever in the body they may appear.

Up to this point, we'd been able to restore better function to all Sallie's problem areas to decrease her pain. But they'd never remain pain-free and working properly if we didn't solve her left foot, which was the root of the collapse of the system—her ground wire.

The best and fastest way to address her foot would be to tape it. Like Sallie's shoulder, tape would give us an idea of how much pain would be relieved if everything were lined up correctly.

A collapsed arch is another matter entirely, though. At the foot, our body weight is multiplied several times with each step. Without an arch to help out, I wasn't sure how she'd respond. The arch in the foot functions like the arch in architecture—it's what holds things up (no wonder you can't spell "architecture" without "arch"). If you want to make a hole in a wall, for a door or a window, you can put in an arch above the opening, like the windows of Romanesque churches. The curve of the arch deflects and disperses the weight and allows for more pressure to be easily withstood. Each time we step onto our foot, the arch of the foot eases the pressure of our weight. Stepping onto a flat foot leads to a world of pain.

Sallie already wore custom shoe inserts made by her podiatrist. However, because she still had pain, I guessed that they weren't as effective as they could be. There are many reasons why inserts might not help people. But through all my experimentation over the years, I've developed a taping technique that works quite well to fix most foot problems associated with a flat arch.

My technique aggressively and precisely lifts the foot arch, holding the ankle in a more ideal position while walking. This is very unlike the taping you see happening on the sidelines for athletes. Tape in those situations is basically creating a snug, slightly mobile cast. That approach is not designed to precisely correct a problem. Instead, it immobilizes a foot and ankle so more damage isn't sustained, and the athlete can continue to play.

By contrast, my technique uses only one piece of tape to offset the spiraling line of force traveling down the leg, collapsing the foot. This single piece of tape allows for maximum mobility while elevating the arch and countering the rotational force traveling through the ankle. While it didn't lift Sallie's arch off the floor, it significantly unloaded the pressure when she walked.

"Okay, try that out, Sallie," I said after taping her foot for the first time.

She got up slowly and tentatively put her left foot down. She focused intently on her pain. Then she took a step with her right foot, weight bearing only briefly on the left, as usual. I worried then that the tape wouldn't help. She stepped with the left foot again and continued walking across the room, slowly.

She limped less with each step.

She turned to face me with tears in her eyes and the brightest wattage smile I'd seen from her yet.

"I have no pain," she said. "I can't believe it! I have no pain."

She still limped, however.

"Why are you still limping, then?" I asked.

She looked at me blankly. "I don't know; it doesn't hurt. I guess just out of habit."

"Then I want you to stop doing that," I said, "or all these problems will keep coming back."

Solving the Pain Puzzle

I once had a patient who limped for two years after he had a hip replaced, even though he was pain-free and had the strength not to do so. It was simply the habit he'd formed for the eight prior years of walking with hip pain. He was told by his surgeon to wait until he couldn't stand it any longer to have surgery. But several other secondary problems emerged because of his limping, as in Sallie's case. No amount of nagging on my part could change his habit—only time.

We weren't able to wean her from the tape, though—her foot was too badly changed. The good news is that I use the same approach to cast for shoe inserts—which she loved. Thus the shoe inserts replaced the tape.

When I tape, I manipulate the foot to lift the arch and improve the ankle alignment. I teach my patients to tape themselves or to have a partner tape them. However, if taping seems to be the permanent solution, if the patient can't fix enough other issues to allow us to wean them from the tape, then I recommend that they allow us to cast for shoe inserts. Because we cast for shoe inserts using the same technique we use when we tape, we're confident the shoe insert will work for them. This is important to me because shoe inserts are really expensive, and I see plenty of people who've shelled out lots of money for an insert that either wasn't needed or didn't do the job it was supposed to do.

Many come to our clinic asking for these pricy shoe inserts. Some clinics willingly oblige and just cast them and charge a lot of money. Shoe inserts are high profit centers. I'm always tempted to simply give people what they're asking for—we could certainly use the money. However, it's my responsibility to fix problems if I can, without shoe inserts. In most cases I can, which saves the person a lot of money and leaves them with a new appreciation for how their body works so the problem doesn't come back again.

Now that Sallie could finally walk on her leg without pain, I taught her to walk better.

Walking better is simple but describing walking better is complicated. First, we need to understand why it's important to walk correctly. This is where the butt muscles—the gluteals—come in. The goal of walking better is to naturally turn on and off your butt muscles at the right time and at the right intensity. They are the primary stabilizers of the hip joint. They also help orient the pelvis and lower spine to align them properly. They control rotation of the thigh bone which can affect the knee and shin bone and foot orientation, in terms of deceleration of pronation (flattening of the foot). Finally, proper activation of the gluteals helps relax the waist muscles on the same side of the body.

There is a huge payoff to walking better. In fact, no one leaves our clinic without first learning to walk better if they've been seen for back or any lower body pain. It's that crucial. The most common fault with walking is that of striking the foot on the ground ("foot strike" is how this is referred to in my world), while the pelvis is still behind the foot. Essentially this is a strong heel strike pattern. When the foot strikes the ground in this scenario, the knee tends to lock backward, irritating that small popliteus muscle discussed in Jeni's case. It also means that there is no reason for the butt muscles to turn on, because the foot and knee are absorbing the forces of walking, not the much larger and stronger pelvic muscles.

If you look at the classic Beatles *Abbey Road* album cover, you'll see they're all walking incorrectly. John Lennon, in white at the front, is the one closest to walking well. His pelvis and body are nearly aligned over the advancing foot when it is striking the ground. Paul, George and Ringo's bodies are lagging far behind their advancing foot strike. This is a recipe for damage to any structure in the foot up to the back. Some can get away with it, but those with chronic back and lower body pain cannot.

The waist muscles respond to correct gluteal activation by relatively turning off. If you're walking well and use your hands to squeeze your waist muscles, you'll feel that the muscles on the side bearing your weight will relax relative to the opposite side's waist muscles. This type of relationship happens all over the body. When one muscle group contracts, the opposing muscle group relaxes, to allow supple movement to occur. This at first seems counterintuitive, especially in our physical medicine culture of focusing on strengthening things in order to solve a problem. The body is fluid and needs to relax just as much as it needs to contract in order to move well. This is referred to as "reciprocal inhibition," meaning that the reciprocating muscle group (the one opposite the one you're trying to contract) is inhibited when that contraction occurs. If both groups are contracting on opposite sides of a joint, then excessive tension is delivered to that joint, eventually resulting in a breakdown of structures like cartilage, disks and ligaments. To me this is a beautiful, poetic manner of functioning. In order to move forward, sometimes we have to do less.

In most cases, stability isn't the issue (unless you're a hypermobile person with excessively lax ligaments—a different type of problem). Almost everyone coming to our clinic for low back pain has been told by someone (or some YouTube video) that their core is too weak. As a result, they've done thousands of sit-ups, planks, downward dogs or whatever to strengthen it. Yet they still have back pain. That should tell you, first and foremost, that your core strength isn't actually the problem.

I almost never focus on core strength because that usually isn't the problem. If I do focus on it, I certainly don't assign strengthening exercises to fix it, because those exercises have nothing to do with how that person is using their body. Instead, we teach them to activate the core naturally through changing posture. Correct posture, like walking better, or using your arms better, naturally turns on and off the muscles that should be turning on and off. No one should be walking around constantly tensing their core, or butt, or mid-trapezius—that's unnatural and it doesn't allow for reciprocal inhibition and suppleness of movement.

The combination of taping, shoe inserts and walking better eliminated the rest of Sallie's left shoulder, neck, back and right knee pain. The left foot could carry its own load from now on. The trail I'd followed was no longer there.

Except there was one more thing. A few months later, I caught Sallie limping again.

"Sallie, you're limping again. What's up?" I asked.

"Oh, it's just this callus on the outside of my little toe. It gets really painful. Don't worry, I'm going to the podiatrist to scrape it off today," she said.

"Well, why don't I take a look at it? You haven't mentioned this before," I said.

"Oh, well, that's because every two months for the last eight years, I've just gone to the podiatrist to scrape it off. It heals in a week and then I'm good for another couple months. There's nothing you can do about it. It's just the way it is," she said.

9. *The Case of the Shoulder Problem in Her Foot*

Nothing gets my hackles up more that someone saying there's nothing I can do about something. I always have to try.

"Let's take a look," I said.

She took off her shoe and sock and there on the outside of her left pinky toe was an enormous red callus.

"I don't remember seeing this before," I said.

"I had it scraped before we started on my foot," she said. "It was better for a while there but it's come back again."

I studied her foot and pulled gently on her little toe, distracting it from her foot. The swollen red callus disappeared and was replaced by a dent.

"Oh, that feels so good!" she said.

I remained there for a couple minutes, tugging on her little toe and moving it gently up and down. I discovered when I moved her toe up, the callus started coming back, but when I moved it down, it disappeared again. I suspected a mechanical cause of this callus.

"Try walking on it now, Sallie," I said

She walked about 20 steps. "No pain," she said, alarmed.

After another 20 steps the pain returned. Because we could interrupt her pain pattern, I felt confident I might be able to solve this last hurdle for Sallie. I asked her to stand in front of me while I observed her foot while weight bearing. The callus gradually returned. But I had discovered earlier that if I moved the toe down, it decreased the callus. I then got an idea.

"Sallie, hand me your left shoe insert," I said. She pulled it out of her shoe and I placed it on the ground and asked her to stand on it. I made a couple marks on her insert where her pinky toe began and ended. I got some scissors, and to her surprise, began cutting away a piece of her orthotic that supported her pinky toe.

"Stand on that, Sallie," I said. She did.

"Wow! That feels good!" she said. "And my callus is gone!"

I then asked her to put it back in her shoe and walk around. She had virtually no pain. I let her walk around for a few minutes.

"Now take off your shoe and sock," I said.

She did and her painful, swollen, red callus was half the size. We were both amazed.

"I'm gonna cancel my podiatry appointment!" she said.

What I think was happening is that there is more than one arch in the foot. There's one that runs side to side as well as front to back. Because Sallie's primary arch had completely collapsed, her big toe was level with or slightly below her pinky toe, upsetting the balance in her front arch. By cutting out a space into which her pinky toe could drop down, we re-established a more normal foot strike pattern between her big toe and pinky toe. This was a completely new concept to me—one that I won't forget. It's thrilling when I discover a new relationship in the body! It's one more piece to our amazing puzzle!

No longer will Sallie need to make visits to her podiatrist or limp.

≋ 10 ≋

Reading Hidden Signals: Three Pains in the Neck

My sophomore year playing high school football, I began to have frequent "stingers" in my left shoulder. Stingers are the result of a nerve getting pinched or stretched due to poor technique when tackling. These are no fun at all, as any young (or even pro) football player can tell you. They sent electric shocks down my arm. In the last part of our season, the stingers became a normal part of practice and games for me. I figured I'd have to live with them.

We had a weight training system in our basement at our farm that I would use three to four days a week. It was a Universal system, with weight stacks in the center and a bench press and pulleys on the sides. Slowly I lost the ability to hold the handles with my left hand. When bench pressing, I would twist my trunk in order to press weight off my chest on the left side—very bad form. Also while my right biceps could curl 30 pounds, I struggled with five pounds on my left. I could barely lift my left arm above my head.

I tried to ignore it, work around it, and I didn't tell anyone. Not my coaches, not my parents. This was not from some stoic standpoint; I just never thought that it rose to the level of importance to tell anyone. After all, my arm still moved and I had no loss of sensation to my knowledge.

Football merged into wrestling season. I managed to pin a few opponents, but I found that I couldn't use my left arm to leverage any holds or my left hand to grip. Wrestlers would pull my fingers apart as if they were cheap chopsticks. My left arm was only useful as a decoy—it really had no other value on the mat. It wasn't until I was knocked unconscious during a match that my parents realized there was a problem. They had no idea and were properly, grown-up concerned. They took me to a doctor.

"Lift your arms," he said. He placed a hand on each of mine. With a slight touch of his hand, my left arm fell down to my side like a wet noodle. He pressed harder and harder on my right. It didn't budge. I was shocked. I knew it was weak, but this simple test revealed just how weak.

"You've got extensive nerve damage," he said. I wasn't to lift anything, not even my schoolbooks, for the next six to 10 months. My wrestling coach was not happy and made occasional derisive comments. After all, I looked completely normal, especially when I wore a long sleeve shirt to hide my skinny left arm.

The coach was young, and I don't think he knew any better. After all, I wasn't in a cast and had no obvious injury. That's often how injuries went in those days and maybe to some extent today—people have a hard time empathizing with someone if they're not in some kind of cast or don't have a scar to show.

I also wasn't about to quit the team, as I might've lost the varsity letter I had already earned that year. Those were a big deal to me back in those days. So I went to practice every night and matches on weekends.

I was diagnosed at the Cleveland Clinic, which is a prestigious medical center. About a month or so later I was brought in for an EMG study, where they used needles to assess the muscle activity. I remember lying there on the table, the room full of doctors watching me, likely residents in training, observing the treating doctor's technique as he inserted and removed needles from my arms and back. The machine I was hooked up to would make a pulsing sound as it monitored a muscle. A fast, loud pulsing sound rang out when it hit healthy muscles. He demonstrated this on the right side of my upper body. It almost sounded like a race car video game.

Then on to my left side. The pulses were much slower, like someone exhausted slogging through mud. He would put the needle in various muscles throughout my back and left arm and then show the other doctors the same result on the right. They would ask questions I didn't understand.

It was after this test, hearing the differences between the two sides of my body, that I finally believed that something was wrong with me. Before, I hadn't understood the significance of what my doctor was saying. I just knew I was weak. Now I knew there was something broken inside that caused that weakness.

Then, many months later, at the end of my forced non-use period, I went in again for the needle testing. This time, the left was much faster than before and nearly as strong as the right. It was at this point that I could begin exercising again. I was very excited!

The strange thing was that none of this registered in my mind as it was happening. The weakness, the pain during practice, the uselessness of my arm had all happened gradually. I thought I just wasn't strong enough. That I needed to be tougher. That I had to lift more weights and not complain. My body was sending me clear signals I simply wasn't equipped to recognize, much less translate. Even if I had, my naivety might have led me to dismiss them as "to be expected," like the stingers that result from tackling incorrectly. Pain, weakness, and discomfort are not "to be expected." They are signs that something is wrong. My body had been shouting to me, waving for help, but I hadn't noticed or responded.

➤ ➤ ➤

Barb was an ER nurse with more than 30 years of experience. She was a no-nonsense, tough woman full of spunk. I could tell she laid down the law wherever she went. She related her story while locking my eyes with her steely blues, willing me to listen. I liked her immediately.

It was late March and Barb's recent bout of neck pain had begun in early February. She'd suffered from chronic headaches and neck pain for years, but it would gradually go away with massage or treatment. In this short interval of time, she'd already been to a chiropractor for several visits, had massage therapy, taken a strong pain reliever—hydrocodone—and tried trigger point injections, where lidocaine is injected into knots of muscles to make them go away. The volume of treatment she'd received in such a short period of time told me that she was in a lot of pain.

She hated to complain and felt that maybe "this ol' cowgirl just needed to pony up and tough it out," as she charmingly phrased it. No, Barb, not if I can help it.

When queried about past injuries, Barb denied ever having had any to speak of. I believed her. She was strong and so full of grit that no injury would dare come near her.

I'll believe my patients until I discover something that doesn't add up with their story—as happened with Barb. Even after I told her that I suspected a shoulder problem as the source of her headaches, she didn't recount the old shoulder pain she'd had 15 years earlier. It was a non-issue to her—she just didn't connect the two. But these old injuries almost always come out in my evaluation or treatment. We bump into a wall and I query the patient about it. Invariably, when I discover something that they hadn't mentioned, I'm met with "Oh, yeah, I forgot about that. It was such a long time ago...."

I remember that I was seeing a gentleman for back pain. He replied that he had no previous injuries. Then, during further questioning, it turned out that he'd played offensive tackle for the Oklahoma Sooners college football team back in the day.

My eyebrows shot up. "And no injuries?"

"Nope," was his response.

Then his wife, sitting beside him, chimed in. "Well, tell him about your surgeries."

He listed several surgeries on his ankles, knees and hips.

"I thought you said you didn't have any injuries," I said.

"Oh, well those are surgeries, they don't count," was his reply.

Once again, this was a reminder for me to ask more specific questions, as in the Big Man in the Little Car story. I need to actively listen but, most importantly, I need to verify, based on my examination.

At our initial evaluation, I determined that Barb's problem came from her shoulders. I treated them, which eliminated her neck pain and even her headaches. I taped her shoulder blades into a better position, just as I'd done with Deb to help with her migraines. I also have a technique where I lift the shoulder blade from the trunk, creating a small gap. Typically, the shoulder blade becomes adhered to the trunk in the case of shoulder injuries, preventing it from moving. Due to its inability to move well, stress then blooms away from this central problem, like dropping paint on a wet piece of paper and watching it bleed.

These two treatments are usually my go-to interventions to test my theory that the shoulder blade is the source of someone's pain.

When it is, in my experience their pain diminishes between 30 and 75 percent after just one treatment. The next question then is "why?" We've determined the systems problem, so now we begin searching for ground wires.

Barb's ground wires were found in her rotator cuff muscles. She was surprised.

"But I don't have shoulder pain," she said.

"That may be, but when I treat your shoulder blade, your headaches and neck pain go away," I replied.

"Well, maybe my shoulder problem is coming from my neck," she countered.

"That's unlikely, Barb. Your neck pain began again just a few weeks ago but the problems I'm seeing in your shoulders are much older than that." She'd had neck pain and headaches for years, on and off. This was just the latest bout.

"How can you tell? Maybe they happened because of my neck," she said, staring me down.

This was a fair question. How could I tell which came first, the chicken or the egg?

When Barb raised her arms up in the air, she sank her shoulder blades down toward her hips and pinched them together, like a dancer or a gymnast. Barb learned this in her yoga classes, which she'd taken for years.

In these classes, it's common to hear an instructor cue attendees to "bring your shoulder blades down and back into your back pockets," "squeeze your shoulder blades together" or "lengthen your neck" when raising your arms into the air. This is one of my biggest pet peeves of dysfunctional movement that's taught in exercise classes. It's a shorthand mantra called out in class by an instructor, and it can lead to damaging habits if incorrectly interpreted or implied beyond the boundaries of a yoga or Pilates series.

This isn't just taught in yoga classes. It happens in Pilates, dance and gymnastics too. The desire to create a long neck, which is aesthetically pleasing, is the core of the problem. People are ruining their shoulders and their neck to achieve this.

Creating a "long neck" is the opposite of proper shoulder blade function. Without going into all the biometric markers, the shoulder blades' general role is to rotate outward and lift as the arms move away from the body. This helps the shoulder muscles do their job: to lift the arm. Lifting the arms while creating a long neck essentially short circuits this whole process (to maintain our toaster analogy). Shoulder blade rotation and lifting also maintain a proper length and tension in the muscles connecting into the neck from the shoulder blades.

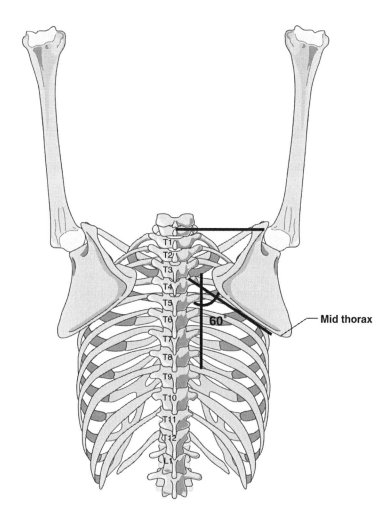

The shoulder blade's role is to assist with overhead motions and has specific landmarks to measure its function.

Barb was such an adept yoga practitioner that her critical shoulder blade muscles were turned off as a result. It took a bit of training to turn off these muscles so completely. Certainly more than a month. She had essentially trained, over an extended period of time, her shoulder blade muscles to no longer do what they were made for. The fact that Barb couldn't even activate them at all told me this was an old problem.

When basic rules of proper movement are broken, pain results. Like tackling with poor form in high school caused my pinched nerve. In Barb's case, the small muscles linking her shoulder blades to her neck became strained as a result of her habit of pushing her shoulder blades down toward her hips. Judging by her personality, Barb probably made it a point to beat everyone in the yoga room at it too.

I explained this to Barb and added, "If these were recent changes then you'd be telling me about shoulder problems too. But you haven't mentioned anything about your shoulders."

"That's because they don't hurt," she said.

I smiled. We went back and forth like this for some time. Some practitioners don't like to be challenged in this way, but I don't mind. It's actually kind of fun for me and can expose faults in my thinking or perhaps problems I hadn't considered. I was pretty sure about Barb, though—I'd seen this many times before.

Because yoga is an ancient movement art, the assumption is that it must be good for you. In most cases it is—except when it isn't. You need to remember that, hundreds of years ago, people didn't know about femoral anteversion or retroversion. They didn't understand how the gluteals control femoral rotation or the tracking of the hip joint in the socket. They didn't know that there were shoulder blade biometrics or what ideal movement was. Yoga was created out of the best information available at the time. But sometimes information needs to be updated. Just because your body *can* do something doesn't mean it *should* do something.

Sometimes, depending on what's wrong with you, yoga will not be the right solution and may even hurt you more, as in Lizzy's case in the next chapter.

I've noticed, over the years, that flexible people gravitate to exercise that rewards flexibility. They think they need more flexibility to solve their pain and typically avoid strengthening. Strong people tend to gravitate toward strengthening to solve their pain and they therefore avoid lengthening. We don't like to do things we're not good at. But sometimes when you find something you're not good at, it may be exactly what you need to be doing. On the other hand, there may be a very good reason why you're not good at it—because you shouldn't be doing it. That's where the value of seeing a physical therapist comes in: to evaluate your body, especially in relation to a desired activity. We can show you what might go wrong and how to make your mechanics better to avoid injuries.

But Barb's defensiveness didn't come from a conviction that yoga is a panacea. Barb was an old school emergency room nurse. She'd seen it all. She wasn't about to believe some story a random PT was telling her—especially after so many other failed treatments in the past. Even my attempts to show her how fixing the shoulder blade would fix her headaches didn't pass muster with her.

What I was saying was contrary to popular medical wisdom. Current wisdom is that all problems in the neck and head emanate from the neck, not the shoulder. This is because the nerves that feed our upper body system emanate from the neck, and so it follows that all problems must stem from this—except that it doesn't. That's too simplistic a way of seeing the body. In fact, the upper body system puts a strain on the neck, which then can feed back down into the upper body system. It's a negative loop.

Barb had never heard of such a thing. Her doctors had never heard of such a thing. And probably most impactful, in the era of Dr. Google, the Internet had never heard of such a thing. There's an assumption that Google will reveal all—if there's a treatment that hasn't been published extensively online, patients look upon it with suspicion.

But Barb was stubborn and wasn't about to have anyone pull a fast one on her. After all, no one had even looked at her shoulders before. She was a nurse who'd seen it all.

She insisted on a neck MRI.

"That's fine, Barb," I said. "Just know that many changes you might see on your MRI are normal and happen with age. They often have nothing to do with pain."

As we age, our spines naturally develop signs of wear and tear, like disc bulges, arthritic changes, thinning of the discs between vertebrae, even small fractures. These changes become less significant as we age because they are the simple result of normal wear and tear. Most people with these types of changes have no pain at all.

Barb's MRI revealed minor bulges in her discs and small arthritic changes too. Frankly, it wasn't very impressive—I'd seen far worse MRIs in people with less pain than Barb. Also, small world department, I noticed the name of her doctor. I happened to be treating him for a hip problem.

"I went to a neurologist with my MRI," she said a week later, when she came to the office. "He said there's no medical evidence supporting the shoulders creating neck pain."

"Yup," I said, "he's absolutely right. But let me ask you this, Barb. If your shoulders have nothing to do with your neck pain, then why is the neck pain relieved when we tape your shoulders?"

That stumped her for the time being. I used this opportunity to convince her to get a shoulder MRI. I wanted one because her pain would not decrease without the tape. Usually, after a week or two, people can fix their strength and range of motion problems and then wean off the tape. Not Barb. I was concerned that there was something more serious going on that I'd missed earlier.

She rolled her eyes. "Okay, I'll get a shoulder MRI."

Since her doctor knew me, and was my patient, he was not disarmed by my request for an MRI that seemed to have nothing to do with anything relevant.

The results shocked us all.

Barb had full-thickness rotator cuff tears in *both* shoulders! This means that the primary rotator cuff muscle was completely detached. On both sides.

When her doctor came to my clinic for his next visit, to work on his hip, he immediately brought up Barb's MRI. "I've never seen anything like this!" he said. "I'd never think to even look at her shoulders. How did you know?" I explained the connections and showed him a simple test I'd devised to figure it out.

I hadn't found Barb's rotator cuff tears in my earlier testing. This was likely because she was so good at compensating with her neck. Even after discovering the rotator cuff tears, I tested them

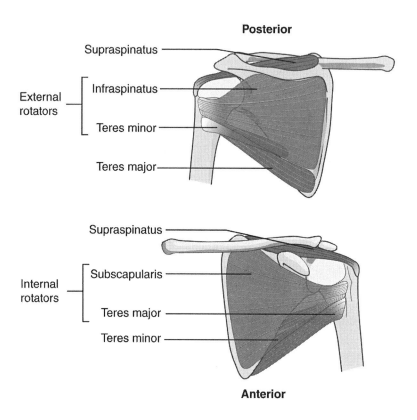

The most common rotator cuff muscle torn is the supraspinatus, which is responsible for assisting with raising the arm.

again. This time I saw how she did it. While her shoulder blade muscles were incapable of anything, she recruited her neck muscles and her shoulder muscles to compensate. This must've taken years to master.

"I thought you said you never had an injury to your upper body before," I asked her, mock-accusingly.

"Well, now that you mention it," she replied sheepishly, "I did hurt my shoulders about 15 years ago. This cowgirl just ponied up and, after a few weeks, the pain went away. I never thought about it again. By the way, my shoulder surgeon said there are no studies connecting shoulder problems to neck pain or headaches."

I smiled. "He's absolutely right, Barb. There aren't." But I think she was coming around to my way of thinking.

The only way to prove my theory correct was if Barb had rotator cuff surgery to repair the torn muscles. We were out of other options. Treating her shoulder blades eliminated her headaches. When we stopped, the headaches would resume.

The rotator cuff muscles, in this example, were the ground wires affecting the system. The headaches were the heating coils—the manifestation of something wrong with the system. The functional cause was likely her manner of using her arms that promoted scapular depression: postural cues to pinch the shoulder blades together and squeeze them down to create an erect spine. Over the years, this shut down her scapular positioning muscles, the trapezius and the serratus anterior. Sometimes when muscles shut down, they become neurologically weak, as in the mid-trapezius. This means the muscle isn't truly weak; it's just that the brain has forgotten how to engage the muscle well. This also happens to the gluteals with poor walking habits.

The serratus anterior is a weird muscle that begins in the side of the rib cage toward the front along many rib levels and inserts along the medial border of the shoulder blade (the flat border closest to the spine). This muscle is interesting in that, in the presence of anxiety, stress, or injury, it tends to contract, locking the shoulder blade to the thorax. I believe it's part of a larger pattern of muscles contributing to another deep reflex pattern, the startle reflex, which I learned about in Hanna Somatics training. That's another hard-wired reflex pattern we're born with.

You can watch YouTube videos of babies being startled and see the same pattern response. Typically, the arms come in, the shoulders shrug up and the eyes blink firmly. I think that the serratus anterior is responsible for the portion of the behavior involving the arms pulling in toward the body. I've found that, in order to separate the shoulder blade from the trunk, I need to relax the serratus anterior muscles with a gentle technique, getting them to let go of the shoulder blade.

The question of which muscles were locking the shoulder blade to the trunk stumped me for years. I thought it was the trapezius in the back. But a local PT graduate program, Regis University, opened up their cadaver lab to PTs interested in refreshing their anatomical knowledge. I jumped at the chance. I had so many questions about what I had seen clinically over the years. Because the university was using these cadavers for their PT program, they were already dissected to varying degrees. To test my particular question of which muscles were adhering the shoulder blade to the trunk, I needed to find a couple of cadavers whose shoulder blades had not been completely removed. There were a few.

While other PTs poked, prodded and observed, I sought out these cadavers, gently rolled them onto their sides and began mobilizing their shoulder blades, just like I did in the clinic. Holding the shoulder blade away from the body, I traced the muscles to see which had become taut. To my surprise, it was the serratus anterior, which I hadn't even considered before, due to its strange orientation.

Once I confirmed this with the other cadavers' shoulder blades, I sat at home thinking about this. If the serratus anterior are locking down the shoulder blade, what would be the best way to get them to let go? I studied the architecture of the muscle. It was thin and broad and lay right over those sensitive ribs. Whatever I would try, it would need to be gentle. I then reached to my own serratus anterior and experimented with different types of touch. I quickly settled on a broad palm technique that felt soothing.

I began experimenting with this technique with my shoulder blade patients and found it very quickly unlocked the shoulder blade from the trunk. I now alternate between this gentle massage and lifting the shoulder blade to release the blade from the trunk. I've also found significant trigger points in the serratus anterior that refer pain into the neck, head, face and hands. There are no direct anatomical connections to explain this. Instead I choose to think of it as massaging the center of a spider web of various tissues, which results in all points responding to that central massage.

After several more months of thinking about it, Barb eventually relented and had the surgery. Her neck pain and headaches disappeared and never returned—at least on that side. But rotator cuff surgery recovery is long and painful, so she only repaired one side at a time. We chose the side where her headaches were worst first. Later, she repaired the other rotator cuff. One of my other therapists worked with her post-surgery, but I would check in time to time to see how she was. To my knowledge, she hasn't had a headache since, or if so, they were a shadow of what they once were.

Shortly after I started with Barb, Sharon came to the clinic after enduring chronic neck pain and migraines on both sides of her head for many years. Like many patients who end up at our clinic, she had been through a lot of other practitioners. Often these people fall off their doctors' radar because they seek alternative care like chiropractic, massage, acupuncture, diet, etc. This can go on for years before they finally come back to their doctor again. I think this is how it was with Sharon. Her doctor had just recently learned of our clinic and sent her over. Sharon's right side was worse than her left, and when she was in pain, it was difficult for her to even lift her head to look up.

She had occasional numbness or tingling in her hands, which told me that the nerves in her neck were getting pinched. Her arms felt weak. She'd seen a chiropractor and massage therapist for years and decided to try something new. She couldn't remember any particular incident that marked the beginning of her problem.

Sharon was a young, athletic woman in her mid–30s who played softball, played cymbals in a band, took guitar lessons and worked in IT. Whenever anyone tells me they're in IT, my eyes glaze over. I'm mechanically inclined, which means I'm digitally declined: computer programming just seems about as tenable as shaping a soap bubble.

My examination found issues similar to Barb's. We set about strengthening Sharon's mid-trapezius muscle. This muscle is key in gaining control of the shoulder blade. Through the years, I've settled on a very precise technique to activate it properly. My strengthening is not like that of a typical PT. I don't begin with the classic rotator cuff strengthening exercises that are ubiquitous in shoulder rehab. Typically, with chronic shoulder problems, the middle portion of the trapezius has grown weak, so that's where I begin. I use just one strengthening exercise. Just like that Native American story of a well-placed focus is better than a broad-based effort. It seems to be key to long-term shoulder girdle strength and health, which means it's also key to the health of the entire upper body system. I also taped her shoulder blades to compensate for the weak trapezius, as I had with Barb.

We tried dry needling as well, using acupuncture needles to release key spasmed muscles. Dry needling is a physical therapist's application of acupuncture needles. If you've ever seen a picture of a person's body as understood by traditional Chinese medicine, you'll see that the body has lines that intersect all over it, like a grid. These are meridian lines which correspond to energy flow between different organs and parts of the body. An acupuncturist applies their needles according to this map. The system allows for what I've found to be true throughout my career: that points far away from a problem may have a relationship to the actual problem. This is similar to my thinking, but traditional Chinese medicine takes it much further, suggesting that acupuncture not only affects different parts of the musculoskeletal system but also internal functions, too, like digestion, breathing and the heart.

Dry needling uses acupuncture needles in muscles from which we would like to release pain-causing tension. There may be overlaps between the two systems, but the intent is very different. Applying the needles actually reduces reflexive spasms in the muscles. If you understand which muscles are in spasm and causing pain, dry needling can be very effective. But it's important not to forget to solve the "why," the reason a patient is in spasm. Once again, medicine is good at identifying a problematic tissue but not so good at identifying why that tissue is problematic.

Within a few weeks, Sharon's left neck pain vanished. That was the good news. The bad news was that her right neck pain remained.

I was suspicious.

Sharon's right neck and shoulder pain could disappear, too, but only when she wore the tape—like Barb. Once the tape was removed, her pain would swiftly return. It also rang alarm bells when we found that dry needling resulted in a heavy achy feeling in her arm the next day. This is not expected of healthy tissue. I've learned over the years that this likely indicates a tear or some other tissue damage. We continued trying to help her right shoulder but I'm ashamed to admit that her pain got worse. This was yet another red flag for me.

"I never noticed my shoulder pain until you started treating it," she said.

That didn't make me feel very good. But there was clearly a serious problem happening with her shoulder.

Finally, after a lot of back and forth, Sharon agreed to get an MRI. Shockingly for both of us, it came back normal. In fact, it was one of the cleanest MRIs I'd ever seen. A pristine shoulder. Some MRIs are more powerful than others. A 3T MRI is the most powerful on the market. The most common is the 1.5T, so the 3T is twice as powerful ... but also a lot more expensive. Most things show up well on a 1.5T, so most clinics use them. I think Sharon's MRI was a 1.5T. Also she did not use a dye contrast which exposes tears in tissues. Some surgeons, though, only trust 3T MRIs to get more detail—a 3T would likely have shown the issue.

MRIs also do less well with more chronic conditions, as scarring may obscure the actual tear. Finally, the shoulder is a complicated structure to image. The labrum is even more so, as it can be partially hidden deep in the shoulder socket. It's not uncommon for an MRI report to show that someone has a rotator cuff tear, only to find after the surgeon goes in that there are several other problems it didn't detect, like small tears in the labrum or biceps or other rotator cuff muscles, among other things. Whatever the reason, Sharon's MRI came out clean. Based on these results, her shoulder surgeon recommended she see a pain specialist. He also said that her shoulder probably had nothing to do with her neck pain or migraines.

I was upset about this recommendation. A pain specialist is primarily interested in controlling pain through medications or cortisone shots. Sharon was young and athletic. I refused to believe there was nothing wrong with her shoulder, which seemed to me to be at the heart of her neck pain. It didn't add up.

I sent her to another shoulder surgeon for a second opinion. He told her that if she didn't feel better after six more weeks of conservative care, he would perform exploratory surgery on her shoulder. We had worked with this surgeon before and he trusted our judgment. Six weeks passed and she went into surgery. She emailed me a week later to tell me that her doctor had repaired two massive labral tears in her right shoulder—the largest labral tears he had repaired to date.

The *labrum* is a piece of cartilage that surrounds the shoulder socket and deepens it, allowing the head of the arm bone to sit more securely in the socket. It also creates a vacuum within the socket and this suction helps hold the arm bone in place. With a torn labrum, this vacuum is disrupted, and the arm bone loses that nice secure fit into the shoulder socket.

Almost immediately after Sharon's surgery, her neck pain and migraines disappeared. Even through her rehab, she had no pain other than that associated with her surgery.

⇒⇐ ⇒⇐ ⇒⇐

Around the time Barb had her neck MRI, Alex came in for his chronic left-sided neck pain. He'd read my book and, with a little searching, found I lived near him in Denver.

Alex was 6'3" and built like a linebacker—I'm sure any NFL team would drool over him. He was solid muscle, weighing in at around 240 pounds. He practically filled the room.

Alex reported that, two or three years earlier, he'd had a mild left shoulder acromioclavicular (AC) separation. The *acromion* is a bony part of the shoulder blade which then connects to the collar bone (the clavicle), the junction of which, the AC joint, is held together by ligaments. The clavicle then articulates with the central bone of the rib cage in the front—the sternum.

The sternum is the only bony connection of the shoulder system to the trunk of our body. Essentially our shoulders and arms are floating objects. So a separation of the AC joint disrupts this already tenuous communication with our trunk.

Alex also admitted that he probably had some labral tears in both shoulders. Remember that the labrum is what Sharon had wrong with her right shoulder. Looking at his muscle bulk, I guessed there was more to the picture than he'd painted. You don't get that big and strong without damaging something. Alex worked out constantly and ignored these minor issues, which would be major to other people.

After he shared his history, we then went through our examination, from which I noted two significant findings. The first was that he had extraordinary range of motion in his shoulders. Usually with very muscular people comes a degree of tightness in the muscles. Exceptions to this rule are gymnasts, baseball pitchers and swimmers. Alex was none of these.

While having excessive range of motion is a blessing if you're involved in any of those sports, for ordinary people, too much motion can cause wear and tear in a joint. Because of this general looseness and his labral tears, I imagined Alex's shoulder joint was like a washing machine that was out of balance, careening off the sides of his socket. Unlike a washing machine, though, he didn't have an automatic shut-off when the system got out of control. He continued lifting high repetitions of very heavy weights. My general rule of thumb for heavy weightlifters is that those aches and pains are real and they add up. Get them checked out by a physician or a PT so you at least understand what you're ignoring.

In general, there is also a carryover for the range of motion you are strengthening. Most people don't need to strengthen the full range of motion to become strong through the full range of motion. I recommend strengthening through about 75 percent of your available range of motion. That last 25 percent or so that you're loading through is typically where damage is done to the tendons, ligaments or joint surfaces. While the body is made to go through that full range of motion, it's not made to do so under heavy loads repeatedly—something will eventually give. Better to avoid it all together.

Part of my exam involved testing strength. When I tested Alex, it was like that scene in *Rocky IV* when Apollo Creed is about to fight Drago, the Russian boxer. They bumped fists before the fight, but Drago's fists were like unyielding steel. Apollo's normally easy smile flickered briefly. I'm going up against him. I'm testing all the major muscles for weaknesses. I couldn't make him budge with any of the tests. Like the doctor did with me, testing my shoulder strength by having me hold both arms straight in front of me, then pressing down on my right (it didn't budge), then on my left (which collapsed immediately). It was like this with Alex, minus the collapsing—just unyielding strength, even as I increased the load to test for pain.

This was my experience with all of Alex's testing, except for one key muscle group that happens to be involved in stabilizing all shoulder and arm movements—the mid-*trapezius* muscle I mentioned in Sharon's case.

The trapezius is amazing in both its architecture and function. It's a very large, broad muscle that runs from the base of the skull down to the lower back bones of the thoracic spine, where the ribs attach. It then connects to the shoulder blade and collar bone. It's so big that we divide it into three zones when considering it, upper, mid, and lower, each of which has their own job to do.

With weightlifters like Alex, you tend to see bulging, over-developed upper trapezius muscles, which give the appearance of a thick neck. Alex's lower trapezius muscles were also incredibly strong, from all his lat pulldowns to create that classic V-shaped torso found in bodybuilders.

The mid-trapezius muscle is critical to proper shoulder blade strength and control. Alex could barely lift his arm against gravity on his left side during my testing. He was shocked to find a chink in his armor. He hadn't realized that he could possibly be so weak, especially with all his usual strength training targeting his back muscles. I'd found the same weakness with Barb and Sharon.

To his credit, Alex attacked his one weakness as if it were a personal affront. Strengthening that portion of his trapezius, together with my shoulder blade taping technique and a little bit of dry needling in his shoulder, completely eliminated his neck pain within a few weeks.

But then it returned again and again. Just like Barb and Sharon.

I asked Alex to get an MRI and see a shoulder surgeon. His MRI showed a variety of issues, including labral fraying, small tears in two rotator cuff muscles and scarring of a shoulder ligament.

Rotator cuff muscles are a group of muscles that create precision of the shoulder movements. Tears indicate the potential for larger problems. His shoulder surgeon wasn't concerned about any of this and did not recommend surgery to fix them. In my opinion, he was just looking at the shoulder as a shoulder—that's his training. He didn't understand that this was affecting Alex's neck. Also, because Alex was so incredibly strong, there was no reason to repair these apparently small issues because there was no functional breakdown in Alex's system. Lastly, partial rotator cuff tears can heal on their own, so I'm guessing that's what the surgeon was thinking. I didn't think this was likely, however, because of how much and how often Alex challenged his muscles with weight training. But the bottom line was, at least from the surgeon's point of view, Alex was functioning not only well but superiorly, so why operate?

Alex's issues concerned me, though, given the volume of his weight training and persistent pain. While any one of these findings may not raise a red flag, the spectrum of tissues showing damage indicated to me that his shoulder was in the process of breaking down. Alex needed as much stabilization as possible for that shoulder because he wasn't about to stop weight training—it was clearly his passion.

Alex asked his surgeon if the problems found in his MRI could lead to his neck pain.

"Highly unlikely," was the surgeon's brief response. But Alex asked him for a cortisone shot to the shoulder anyway.

Cortisone is a steroid that shrinks irritated tissue, calming it down. Often, it's accompanied by lidocaine, which numbs the area. Alex's shot to his shoulder completely cleared up his neck pain for several weeks. This confirmed to us that his shoulder was the true culprit behind his neck pain.

The doctor also gave Alex a set of simple rotator cuff strengthening exercises which, together with a few others, resolved Alex's neck pain as long as he continued them. I'd neglected to give Alex these basic exercises because he tested so strong initially. However, had I repeatedly challenged these muscles, I likely would have found that they had little endurance and needed some attention. I kicked myself for missing that.

Alex opted for strengthening his way to recovery. This played very well into his strengths (literally)—weight training. We stayed in touch via email over the next several months. He had few to no symptoms after the shot and strengthening plan. But I fretted over the long-term damage that might be happening to his shoulders.

These three stories of pains in the neck and headaches that were actually shoulder problems in disguise clearly show the connection between shoulder function and neck or head pain—the ground wires. I could relate many, many more. There are other connections in the body that are largely unknown to the medical community because they cannot be isolated in medical studies.

Why not? Our bodies' complexity of movement does not lend itself to double-blind studies—the gold standard for inclusivity in medical studies. At best, these stories would warrant a case study which has the lowest validity in the spectrum of research, and so are often ignored.

I don't fault surgeons for not knowing of these connections. Their training is focused on being the best surgeons they can be. This knowledge doesn't help them in that regard. Just as I don't read research on current surgical techniques. It's not pertinent to my success as a PT.

I suppose this really speaks to the specificity of medicine. After all, you wouldn't ask a cardiologist about a urinary tract infection. It's just not their specialty. This places a burden on the patient to understand who to ask for direction. Our body is trying to tell us something. But instead of it screaming out specific instructions, it sends coded signals that we medical professionals have to learn how to read.

≋ 11 ≋

Pain Is a Sandcastle

"It feels like a hook is in the left side of my mouth, pulling my lips to my ear," Lizzy offered softly, "and I feel like I have broken glass in my nose."

Lizzy was a 54-year-old mountain biker, runner, hiker, skier—all the typical sports we see here in Colorado. She was active and full of energy.

At least, that's how she should have been. The woman sitting in my office did not match that description. Speaking in a whisper and hunched over, she complained of left-sided head pain. But this was not a headache. It was stranger and more frightening. The muscles throughout her face, around her ear, eye socket, teeth, palate, jaw and the back of her head all hurt terribly.

She was highly sensitive to light and wore sunglasses even indoors. To accommodate, I shut off the overhead lights in the clinic. Sounds above a whisper grated on her and she complained of constant dizziness and nausea. These might have been signs of migraine, but the other symptoms suggested otherwise. Her sense of taste had been altered—she no longer enjoyed food. That wasn't a normal accompaniment of migraines. I couldn't imagine how miserable she must be.

She took medications every 30 minutes to keep her pain tolerable. But Lizzy didn't want to control it; she wanted to get rid of it. She was a photographer and these drugs interfered with her work, her life, and her well-being. She had already been to a slew of doctors and was desperate for help. Her doctor sent her to my clinic after another doctor in his practice had mentioned the good results I'd achieved for another patient. He figured he'd give me a try.

Her symptoms had been relentless for the several months since she'd attended a yoga class. The pain was constant in her jaw and face and spread to the other areas of her head too. She had to lie "just so" in order to finally fall asleep each night and would often wake from pain after just an hour or two. She was always tired. Sometimes she would have to wear a mask to keep breezes from touching her face, as even that would send her into waves of agony.

If this weren't enough, Lizzy's past history involved several car accidents, dating far back to her childhood, which left her with chronic migraines and general neck stiffness and pain. She told me that, since those accidents, she never liked having both arms raised over her head (which made me wonder at her enthusiasm for yoga). Several years earlier, she'd suffered a traumatic blow to her left shoulder which had dislocated it. It was "put back in" at the ER with no further treatment.

Contrary to Mel Gibson's portrayal of resetting a dislocated shoulder in *Lethal Weapon* by smashing it against a wall or pole, resetting a dislocated shoulder is not a violent procedure. Actually, it's quite gentle, involving supporting the arm and gently massaging the upper trapezius and deltoid until the head of the shoulder joint slips back into place—the Cunningham Technique. No pops, no cracks, no grunts. In fact, many people aren't even aware it's been relocated. The arm is then put in a sling with the hand resting near the belly to keep the system stable. There is a capsule that surrounds the shoulder joint to keep it in place. Repeated dislocations mean these tissues are likely becoming compromised.

Though it may sound strange, I was comforted after hearing Lizzy's history, fraught with traumas though it was, because there were clues in it that I might be able to help her. In fact, despite never having treated trigeminal neuralgia before, and knowing of its reputation for never going away, I was quite confident that I understood what was happening to her. I was excited to begin.

The consensus at the time I saw Lizzy was that she suffered from *trigeminal neuralgia* which was thought to be caused by a problem with the jaw. Today researchers have identified that the trigeminal nerve can get impinged by a blood vessel in the brain. This is a structural explanation. A ground wire is good, but my work focuses on the functional causes of pain, the reasons those ground wires are broken.

I had never seen a patient with trigeminal neuralgia before, much less encountered symptoms as severe as these. The trigeminal nerve is a cranial nerve, meaning that it originates in the brainstem, within the skull. Its tendrils reach into the eye sockets, sinuses and mouth. It's a sensory nerve, so it carries information, like temperature and pressure, from the face to the brain. This is distinct from a motor nerve that carries information from the brain to the facial muscles, to make them smile or wink an eye. Until that point, I was used to working with just about anything from head to toe. But I never thought I would actually work inside someone's brain.

During our evaluation, I found that I could press anywhere on Lizzy's left arm or hand and elicit pain in her face and head. This was news to her—no one had ever looked at this before. We also discovered that touching her right arm referred pain to her left face, also a surprise. Past evaluators had only looked at her neck and head, since that's where her pain was. This was mostly due to the belief that trigeminal neuralgia is solely a problem with a blood vessel in the skull. In their thinking, there's no reason to look elsewhere.

I approached her body as a network with triggers sometimes far from the pain itself. Additionally, I found that her left shoulder blade wasn't resting or moving correctly—no doubt from the shoulder dislocation years ago. Her trigeminal neuralgia pain was primarily on the left side of her head. To me, this was no coincidence. To someone who doesn't understand how the upper body system affects neck or head pain, this would appear to be an irrelevant detail.

When a medical professional interviews a new patient, it's similar to a detective interviewing a witness at a crime scene. And the patient (or witness, for patients are like witnesses to their own medical issues) may not realize what information will be most useful, will "solve the case." Lizzy might have dismissed or overlooked the fact that she began to suffer after yoga class because the connection didn't occur to her, or to any of the health professionals she'd seen to date, as significant. Largely this was due to the acceptance of current medical wisdom—that trigeminal neuralgia is caused by the blood vessel in the head. End of story. But Lizzy was telling me a different story.

My general view is that if a particular movement or incident triggered pain, then there's a good chance we can unravel whatever got tangled up and restore harmony in the body. But it was a big

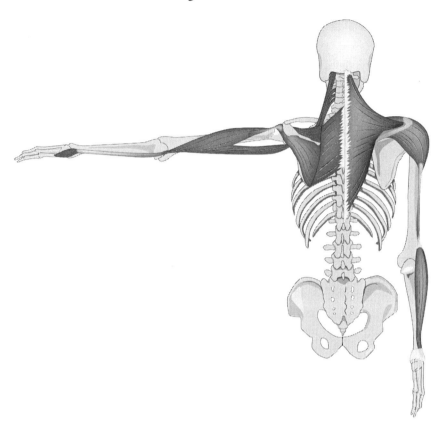

Muscles in the arm, shoulder blade and neck are connected via fascia creating a web of communication between distant tissues.

leap to suspect that I could apply this thinking to a problem deep in the skull. That was a connection I'd not yet considered, much less mastered.

There's a parable of a tugboat captain whose boat broke. He called a repairman who spent the next hour tapping valves and pipes, tugging on wires and pressing buttons as he evaluated the problem. Finally, in the end, he took out his hammer, tapped a small lever and the engine started up. He presented his bill to the tugboat captain: $1,000.

"But all you did was tap a lever!" the captain complained.

"Oh, it was $1 to tap the lever, $999 to know where to tap," replied the repairman.

11. Pain Is a Sandcastle

That's the value of understanding a system and how each component fits together. When you understand the system, interventions seem too simplistic—I hear that all the time. "I can't believe my back feels so much better just by unlocking my knees!" some would say. Or strengthening Al's gluteal muscles. Or taping Deb's shoulder.

That's me just tapping the right lever.

Anyone can learn to do what I do.

I needed to find Lizzy's lever and began by going after the biggest culprit, her shoulder blade. I moved it and massaged the deep muscle spasms that were locking it in an abnormal position. I read her face for signs of pain, but I thought nothing I could do would compare to the agony she experienced on a daily basis. Her pain tolerance had skyrocketed for the unfortunate reason of having suffered so much for so long. I then taped the shoulder blade into a better position.

After her first session with me, three new things happened with Lizzy. First, her pain decreased significantly and leveled off that day. Second, she slept through the night with no pain. Third, she forgot to take her pain meds for an hour and a half—she hadn't missed them for months.

The trigeminal nerve has a central portion called a subnucleus caudalis that extends all the way down through the brainstem and into the upper part of the neck around the second or third vertebra below the skull. I think of the nucleus like an egg yolk—it's the center of everything that happens in a cell. There's a portion of this nucleus that sends pain and temperature signals to the brain.

The shoulder blade has a muscle, the levator scapula, that attaches to the upper neck vertebrae at the same level as the trigeminal "egg yolk." I knew that Lizzy had a history of left-sided problems—shoulder dislocation and auto accidents left her with migraines and other symptoms. I'd had success fixing such things in the past by removing stress to the levator scapula. Maybe this would help release the nerve root fingers' hold on the trigeminal egg yolk?

It seemed to work. Simple, when you think about it.

As I mentioned, the trigeminal nerve has a unique architecture in that the nucleus that controls pain and temperature, subnucleus caudalis, extends down through the brainstem all the way to the upper cervical vertebral levels of C2 and C3. This nucleus also receives information from three other cranial nerves: facial (CN VII),

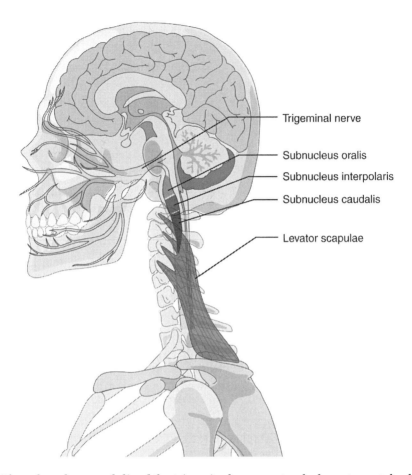

Trigeminal nerve

Subnucleus oralis

Subnucleus interpolaris

Subnucleus caudalis

Levator scapulae

The subnucleus caudalis of the trigeminal nerve extends down to vertebral levels C2 or C3 which allows it to be influenced by levator scapula inserting to those spinal levels.

glossopharyngeal (CN IX) and vagus (CN X). The vagus nerve has recently become a popular nerve to address due to its role in regulating internal organ functions. The facial cranial nerve helps control facial muscles but is also responsible for a large portion of taste receptors on our tongue. The glossopharyngeal cranial nerve also has a role in taste. Recall that Lizzy complained that her sense of taste had been altered.

So the trigeminal nerve is a big deal and communicates with

other cranial nerves too. I wasn't aware of this until long after my success with Lizzy.

When I first saw Lizzy, I vaguely remembered there was a trigeminal nerve. Cranial nerves are among the things we memorize in PT school and promptly forget afterward because we rarely deal with them—at least in orthopedics. So after meeting Lizzy, I gave myself a crash course in trigeminal nerve anatomy. The most important aspect of this, that the subnucleus caudalis extends down to C2 and C3, didn't come up in any of my searches. It was only after visiting the cadaver lab at nearby Regis University where I mobilized shoulder blades to understand exactly which tissues I was affecting during that maneuver that I was able to get an answer. Just before I was about to leave, the anatomy professor came in and I swooped down immediately, relating Lizzy's case.

"Why do you think I was able to help her by mobilizing her scapula?" I asked. "It must have something to do with the levator scapula,"

"Must be the subnucleus caudalis," he replied.

"What's that?" I asked, having never come across it.

"It extends down to C2 or C3."

I was terribly excited because my success with Lizzy was a few years before this conversation and I still couldn't get her out of my mind—I suppose I can be a bit obsessive about things.

I went back and searched "subnucleus caudalis" and pieced together the information you're reading today. I don't have this encyclopedic knowledge of the body in my head at all times. I remember the things that are meaningful.

The second idea I incorporated had to do with the points along her arms that triggered her symptoms. Nothing works in isolation in the body and one of the tissues that makes this a reality is fascia. Fascia is connective tissue that holds everything in place—muscles, blood vessels, nerve, viscera (our guts) and more. There are "highways" of fascia that run through our body. One runs from the hands to the head. This is why pressing anywhere on either arm elicited symptoms in her face—I was pressing her fascial web, delivering tension to the neck.

Think of that trigeminal egg yolk as the weakest and most irritated link in that web-chain. The fascia has a tendency to contract or become tight in the presence of injuries. Lizzy had quite a history of trauma from her car accidents and dislocated shoulder. So her fascia was already tighter than a drum before she headed into that fateful yoga class. The yoga simply added to her supersaturated condition, pushing it over the edge. Trigeminal neuralgia was the solid precipitate that fell from her concentrate.

In my simple way of looking at things, I figured that if this highway can irritate the trigeminal nerve, then it could also calm it down. So part of our treatment was gently massaging the main points along this fascial canal to reduce the tension in the web. It seemed to have worked.

During our third session, while I was working on her shoulder, she turned to me. "It's like when you have a sandcastle and pour water on it and see it melt away. That's what I feel like when you're working with me—my pain is melting away."

I loved that analogy. It meant that my approach was helping. I felt I was indirectly reaching up into her brain, visualizing the connections between her shoulder blade and the trigeminal nerve branches infiltrating her face.

Over the next few weeks, I watched a woman I had never met emerge from under her dark cloud of pain and misery. I wish I could say she was miraculously better in three visits, but to be honest, we had a lot of work to do because of her extensive history of car accidents and the shoulder dislocation, none of which had been addressed adequately.

What I noticed, though, was that she smiled more and lost that metaphorical heaviness she'd had been carrying on her shoulders. The face mask was no longer needed. She was sleeping better too. When we sleep, we heal—our mind clears, and we see the world a little differently.

Further into our work together, Lizzy began photographing again and going out with her friends. She slowly, steadily reclaimed her life. She had a new future ahead of her now, one that she thought she'd never see again, like a lost loved one taken for granted until they were gone. Except this time, she could have them back.

After a few more treatments, we'd eliminated almost all of her pain, including the fishhook in the face feeling, the broken glass in her nose, the sensitivity to light and sound. There was no more dizziness or nausea. She had weaned off her pain medications and she was sleeping much better.

She was about 85 percent better when she learned that her insurance wouldn't pay for any more sessions. I got on the phone to argue her case, but nothing on my part could convince them otherwise. It was a bureaucratic decision: the policy was that X number of sessions were covered and that was it, regardless of the situation. Before she stopped coming in, I taught her how to continue on her own so that she could achieve full recovery. I still think of her often, hoping she's out there laughing, enjoying the mountains and taking beautiful pictures.

≋ 12 ≋

Fear Can Be a Pain
in the Neck

I still have the silver dollar. On one side of it, my father inscribed the word FEAR. On the other side? FREEDOM. He pressed it into my hand when, long ago in my early 20s, I set off to travel the world.

"On the other side of fear is freedom," he would say. By this he meant that, if you face your fears, you can free yourself from them. Dad's silver coin reminded me to take time to think about my fears when deciding whether or not to move forward. Fear can inhibit but it can also empower. And fear is healthy. It makes you think before you act.

Well, now my daughter has my silver dollar. I gave it to her one night when she was having a bad dream and couldn't fall back asleep. I told her this story and said that her dreams were just in her head. Understand that they're only in your imagination and you're free of them. I wish I'd been told this about my own self-doubt. I still wrestle it, even though an objective observer would say that I've proven myself and I should be well past it. She clasped the silver dollar in her small hand and quickly fell asleep.

For my son's 16th birthday, my daughter and I bought him an identical silver dollar. She chose the coin and we took it to the engraver together. My son wants to see the world and I thought this would be a good companion for him, as it's been for me and my daughter.

I explored the world solo, with no companion save my journal and the occasional traveler whose path ran parallel to mine for a spell. Because I wandered alone, I became acutely aware of my thoughts and moods. Often I found myself worrying about something but I wasn't sure exactly what or why. I would then sit down with my journal and write about it. This would expose underlying fears that had snuck up on me. My journal allowed me to see them. It was like a lantern in the darkness. Seeing them helped me address them.

I was a budget traveler, and this was a time before the Internet or mobile phones. The transportation I took and the places I stayed were rarely in the safest parts of town. I was often squeezed into the humanity of the places I visited: Australia (where I celebrated my 23rd birthday), New Zealand, Japan (my 24th birthday), South Korea, China (25th birthday), Hong Kong, Indonesia, Thailand, Nepal, India, Egypt, Kenya (26th birthday), Uganda, Zaire, Burundi, Rwanda, Tanzania, Malawi. The smells, sounds, foods and livestock were constant sources of entertainment and wonder to me.

My fears were usually of things out of my control. Would there be a place for me to sleep? How would I get from the bus or train station to a hostel? If I was arriving in the evening, were there criminals waiting to relieve me of my money and passport? Could I trust the smiling taxi driver who offered to take me where I wanted to go?

These fears, if left unaddressed, would build to a raging whitewater of worry that washed through my mind and body. A sense of unease or a nagging feeling of dread would hang over me. I learned to identify them as soon as they appeared on my radar and to see them for what they were: circumstances I could be aware of but not control. The best I could do was to plan for whatever awaited me.

Because I couldn't understand what most people were saying, I learned to read their faces, gestures and body language. I developed a sense of intuition about people as a result. This helped me read situations, anything from buying food in a marketplace to crossing a border. I learned to trust in my ability to handle whatever was presented to me. As my confidence grew, my gnawing worries abated.

My silver coin, nestled in my money belt close against my skin, reminded me to face my fears. With my newly honed sense of intuition and awareness, I grew more comfortable with the unknown. Later, this would help me recognize fear and anxiety in others.

Solving the Pain Puzzle

Beverley drove an hour and a half to see me. I always feel more pressure when someone visits my clinic from far away. These people took the time to seek me out and have high expectations of my ability to heal them. I felt like I was being tested, like in PT school when an instructor would pull me to the front of the class to have me demonstrate an evaluation technique. I was on the spot. I thought I needed to pack in as much as possible for Beverley and wow her a little, so as not to disappoint.

Beverley had suffered from chronic migraines, neck pain and numbness in both hands for several years and was desperate for help. She was in her mid–20s and in excellent condition. She had been in a couple of car accidents in the past two years, each worsening her symptoms to the point where she was having a hard time functioning at school and work. She rarely smiled and had furrowed eyebrows. I imagined that these were a result of her war with pain. This was not the face of a carefree twenty-something.

While I was evaluating her, I noticed that she couldn't relax enough to allow her arms and hands to be floppy. I could see her wincing even with my light touch as I probed different muscles in her arms, shoulders and neck.

I performed all my usual tests, found the usual suspects that would contribute to her pain and we began working to untangle them. After a few sessions together, we saw little improvement. I felt terrible because she was driving so far to see me. But even more, I grew suspicious that something else was going on. This is one of the benefits of my approach; when I don't see a rapid change in pain, I can quickly move on to another potential source of it. Because my evaluation is comprehensive, I have a good idea of all the potential issues by the end of my exam.

"Beverley, I just want to look at something in your stomach," I said.

"Sure," she replied.

I asked her to lie down on her back while I slowly pressed down on her stomach until I reached what I thought was a deep muscle that lies along both sides of the spine, called the psoas.

To do this, I had to push through several other tissues, like the stomach muscles and digestive organs. At first blush, this might sound very aggressive and painful, but I can do it quite gently.

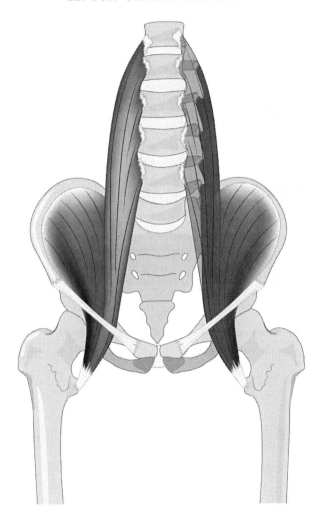

The psoas muscle lies deep to the viscera and connects the vertebrae of the lumbar spine to the hip bone. There are fascial connections traveling to the neck and head as well.

The key is to help the patient relax their stomach muscles. If they are tense, which many people are when I first touch them here, then I won't be successful. Beverley was no different.

"Okay, try to relax your stomach," I said. "I won't press hard here and, if you want me to stop, I will. I just need to check some muscles here that are a little deep."

She nodded and closed her eyes to help focus on relaxing her stomach. I slowly increased my pressure as she allowed me to go deeper. I watched her face to make sure she wasn't in pain.

I've learned over the years to pause just before I reach the psoas muscles. This is often a sensitive area for people even without chronic pain. As I get closer to my goal, patients tend to subconsciously contract their stomach muscles again. Pausing gives them a moment to relax and trust me and my presence there. As I paused with Beverley, I felt her mounting tension subside. This silent sign of trust allowed me to go just a little further toward my target.

I allowed my fingers to lightly brush the psoas muscles I was seeking. I looked for tissue that was a little too hard. I subtly allowed the ends of my fingertips to bend back, so I could use the softer pads of my fingers, rather than the bony tips, which can be painful. There are more nerve endings in my finger pads than the tips, which allowed me to sense the tissues better.

As I suspected, Beverley's psoas muscles harbored small knots of tissue. When I encountered one, I pressed slightly more firmly and waited for her response. She cringed and I noticed what seemed to be a fleeting look of nervousness on her face. I cautiously explored this muscle on both sides of her spine, feeling for knots, occasionally glancing at her face.

"I feel that up in my neck," she said. Her voice was just a half-pitch higher than usual. The words were slightly rushed, the eyebrows raised just a smidge.

My radar picked up something. I'd seen this before—in myself and other patients. Fear? Worry? Or was this more?

※ ※ ※

The Diagnostic and Statistical Manual of Mental Disorders (*DSM*) is a guide for health care workers to diagnose mental health disorders. It is periodically updated and, as I write, the *DSM* is in its fifth incarnation—*DSM-5*.

The *DSM-5* states that generalized anxiety disorder is characterized by "excessive anxiety and worry (apprehensive expectation), occurring more days than not for at least 6 months, about a number of events or activities (such as work or school performance)." Furthermore, "the person finds it difficult to control the worry."

12. *Fear Can Be a Pain in the Neck*

I had a lot of my own experiences of fear and worry, first while traveling and then when having a family of my own, as well as my perceived failures as a PT and my trepidation about writing and publishing my books, including this one.

Fear and worry abound, fed by the constant drone of news outlets and social media reporting new tragedies springing up apparently out of our control. If left unchecked, these fears and worries would induce anxiety even in people who are not prone to it. One of my patients described her anxiety as a physical expression of fear—something she could feel throughout her body.

I decided to gently query Beverley.

"Do you suffer from anxiety?" I asked.

Her eyes widened. "How did you know that?"

I explained that it was a lot of little things: her posture, the tension and tone of her muscles, her lack of progress and, finally, the irritation of her psoas muscles, together with her facial and voice cues.

She shared that she'd been dealing with anxiety for years.

The psoas muscles begin in the front of the lower back, deep to our guts, and insert into the tops of the thigh bones. They have connections to all five vertebra of the lower back and the discs between them. But why would I look to the psoas muscles for clues to Beverley's pain in her neck?

When we are born, we have reflexes hardwired into our brains and bodies that help us negotiate the world and develop as babies. One of these is the Landau Reflex that triggers our back muscles to contract, arching the back and lifting our heads. When we begin to move and crawl, we tap into this reflex so we can see where we're going.

It also comes into play when we need to be alert. Think of walking through a forest and hearing a loud snap of a branch near you. You freeze with your head up, back straight and eyes wide open, suddenly alert to every noise around you. That deep Landau Reflex is partially responsible for this unconscious response to help you assess a situation and be ready to respond to potential danger.

Another is a withdrawal reflex that, when our foot touches something unexpected or painful, triggers one side of our body to contract its muscles to pull that foot away from the stimulus. This happens in the blink of an eye. Imagine stepping, barefoot, onto a shard of glass. This hidden reflex helps you pull that foot away pronto, to keep you safe from further damage. This recruits waist and leg muscles to keep you safe.

Yet another is a startle reflex, in response to a falling sensation or loud sounds. This causes us to contract our arms and legs to protect our body. You can see this at work in pictures of people who are frightened. Their shoulders shrug up and they hunch over slightly to protect their vital organs and head. This pattern recruits many of the muscles in the front of our trunk, like the chest, abdominals and arm.

While these reflexes disappear at varying ages, the hardwiring remains. The reflex responses are overridden by our higher cerebral functions which allow us to deal with other concerns during the day. After all, we can't go through life reflexively responding to every event or sound.

I see the psoas muscles as part of the startle reflex pattern of contraction. They activate in response to fear stimuli, among other things. They are implicated in back pain, but I've found that they come into play with digestive issues, like gluten intolerance or Crohn's disease, and psychological issues, like anxiety, depression or trauma. These chronic issues seem to cause the psoas muscles to remain contracted and thus create the knots I was finding in Beverley.

This general description of the reflex patterns is part of the Hanna Somatics approach to solving pain. I tend to agree with it. Looking at the startle reflex pattern of contraction, to me the psoas seems to be an element of this. Interestingly, just as Dr. Shirley Sahrmann and Dr. Thomas Hanna describe three very similar patterns of dysfunction behind back pain, Thomas Meyers, a fascia expert, also identifies "super highways" of fascia running through the body that are virtually identical to Hanna and Sahrmann's description in his book *Anatomy Trains.*

There is no muscular attachment from the psoas muscle up to Beverley's neck that would account for her pain there. You might be wondering, then, why am I dragging you through Beverley's psoas muscles if there's no connection to her neck? For that, you need to understand just one more player in this mystery—fascia.

Fascia is tissue that holds everything together in our body like a web. Sometimes these strands are gossamer threads while others are broad, tough swaths of tissue, like bolts of fabric. These larger fascial tracts allow different areas and structures of the body to communicate with and influence one another. The brain is the spider constantly monitoring this web, unconsciously making small adjustments here and there.

The referral of pain from Beverley's psoas muscles to her neck told me that her anxiety issues, which were potentially causing her psoas muscles to contract, may be contributing to her neck pain, migraines and ultimately the numbness in her hands via these fascial pathways.

What this meant for Beverley was that we needed to calm her nervous system while also fixing the mechanical causes of her neck pain. Calming the nervous system helps reduce the effects of anxiety on the body by calming the muscles too.

While we hear about the mind/body connection almost daily, it's entirely another thing to manipulate that connection to achieve a physical outcome. Luckily, years ago, I learned a nifty technique that allows me to do just this.

Often, when working with the nervous system in this way, I remember when my son, Boone, was born. He was placed on a table, screaming, while the nurse tended to him. She monitored his heart rate while I gently placed my hand on his little head.

"He knows you," she said, "his heart rate went down when you touched his head."

We have billions of nerve endings that lie between one and six millimeters deep in our skin. These nerves are one way that our brain monitors the world around us. This means that we all are at least two millimeters away from directly impacting each other's brains through touch. That's less than 1/10th of an inch—a few sheets of paper. We're closer to making deep connections with each other than we might realize.

What this meant for Beverley and me was that, because our nerve endings were basically touching each other, she could read my nervous system just as I was trying to affect hers. I needed to remain calm to help her relax. I slowed my breathing, quietly exhaling longer than I inhaled. This stimulated a portion of my nervous system that promotes relaxation. I was also aware that Beverley would, on some level, listen to my breathing and pick up on those nonverbal cues subconsciously. I felt my heart rate slow, and my gaze soften, to take all of her in, scanning for signs of relaxation.

Having this time to be present with a patient is increasingly rare in medicine. Just ask any doctor, if you can slow them down enough, that is. The economics of medicine, particularly in the United States, drive doctors to reduce one-on-one patient time to just a few minutes. This often makes it difficult to connect meaningfully with patients. I'm always surprised that physicians do as well as they do, with the little time they have.

As a physical therapist, though, I have the luxury of establishing a relationship, taking in the non-verbal cues and interpreting them, tracing a pattern of problems to their source and generally getting to know my patients on a deeper level. This allowed me to make quicker connections with Beverley's problems. Being slower, more deliberate, actually sped things up in terms of identifying the problem.

The key to this technique was to stimulate the nerve endings in her skin. The funny thing about the nerves in our skin is that each responds to a different kind of stimulus. Some respond to light stroking, while their neighbors remain unaffected. But those same neighbors might respond to scratching or tapping instead, allowing the stroking nerves to remain calm and rested.

For this technique to work, there were five different types of nerves I was interested in stimulating: light stroking, tapping, vibration, deep pressure and light scratching. I devoted a few minutes to each for her arms and legs. This took about 30 minutes. I think of it as a long, slow reset of her nervous system.

While working with her, I watched and listened to her body. The tone of her muscles, the gurgle of her stomach, the cadence of her breath and the ease of her joint motions all suggested her parasympathetic nervous system, her rest-and-digest system, was coming online. This is what I hoped for.

When I finished, she groggily opened her eyes. "Oh my gosh," she yawned, "I can't remember when I've been so relaxed." Her speech was slower, she didn't move her body, and her voice dropped a couple of notes lower—more signs that she was calmer.

In spite of an hour-and-a-half drive back home that evening, she had no migraines or neck pain. Nor the next day. This hadn't happened in the previous two years. We both knew what this meant: her pain was caused, in a large part, by her anxiety, which was locking down her body in a particular pattern that triggered neck pain and headaches. The pathway seemed to be that the anxiety activated her psoas muscles along both sides of her lower spine, which then referred pain up to her neck and head via fascial connections.

The treatment I gave her helped release its hold temporarily—enough to see how much it contributed to her pain, which was a lot. Together we formed a plan for her to see a psychologist in parallel to my work on the mechanical problems.

Three months later, I was happily surprised to see Beverley on my schedule. She practically bounced into my clinic. No furrowed brow to be seen.

"I'm completely better!" she said. "I haven't had a headache in over a month! I just wanted you to check out my physical problems." She was beaming.

"That's great, Beverley! How did you do it?" I asked.

"I've been seeing a counselor who's been helping me while I did the PT exercises you gave me on my own. My anxiety is so much better. I feel like a new person. And no pain at all!"

"I'm so happy for you!"

Beverley chose to face her fears, worries and anxiety, and now she is free of them—along with her pain. I was not privy to her personal struggles, but I know that this was no simple task. Most of us would much rather work with a physical problem than a mental one. But, in Beverley's case, she had a chance to see exactly how much her psychological issues were breaking down her body.

The choice was clear.

She faced her fear and found her freedom.

≋ 13 ≋

Falling in the Same
River Twice

"No man ever steps in the same river twice, for it's not the same river and he's not the same man." Greek philosopher Heraclitus knew what he was talking about. But instead of stepping into the river, I fell in.

I prided myself on helping people quickly get out of pain and back to their lives. Andrea blew my average out of the water, though. And for one of the simplest problems I tend to see at the clinic—knee pain.

Andrea was a vibrant young woman in her late 20s, already with a young family. She lit up a room when entering and had a loud, infectious laugh. I could hear her from the next room as she waited, joking with my receptionist.

She came to see me for chronic knee pain which began a few years earlier. She had already had several knee surgeries. This was a little surprising for someone so young and who didn't play competitive sports. My radar was up a little—something different was happening here.

During my evaluation I found several problems common to knees such as hypermobility (ligaments and joints that are too loose), her knees locked backward when she walked or stood, and butt muscle weakness. We worked through these issues, but her pain remained the same. Even my miracle muscle massage to the popliteus behind the knee didn't work. Another red flag.

I then began my back-up plan. I looked further away from the knee into the foot and hip. I taped her flat feet to lift her arches. I attacked her hip weakness. I mobilized her hip joints to put them in a better position. No luck. Louder alarms went off in my head now.

On our seventh visit I tried some deep tissue massage to her legs. About 10 minutes into our session, I noticed a twitch in one of her arms. At the same time her eyes blinked hard as if a loud explosion had just occurred.

"I'm sorry, did I hurt you?" I asked.

"No, why?" she said.

"Oh, just that twitch in your arm and you blinked hard. I thought I hit a tender spot," I replied.

"I wasn't aware of any twitch," she said.

My alarm went off again. I hadn't picked up any signs of excessive muscle tension in her body during our evaluation but that could be because she was a hypermobile person. These people tend to be too loose rather than stiff so it's harder to pick up tension-related changes in muscle tone.

Hypermobility is a term I use for people whose joints move just a little too much. Joints are limited not only by their bony architecture but also by muscles and ligaments. Muscles contract to control joints but ligaments don't. They connect bone to bone and are the primary guides of our joint movements.

Think of Sallie's left foot that had collapsed. Her bag of potatoes was too loose. Hypermobile people have looser bags than the rest of us. We need some tension in our ligaments to hold the bones in place properly so our muscles can move them ideally. Ligaments in this way assist muscles so they don't become too strained and overworked. I think of ligaments as primary controllers of joints. Muscles are secondary controllers.

We tend to do more of the things we're good at. Hypermobile people gravitate to disciplines like dance, yoga, Pilates, gymnastics, and swimming. They believe stretching is the way to solve pain like a weightlifter thinks strengthening is the best way to fix a problem.

There are drawbacks to hypermobility, though. Muscles develop painful knots from overexertion of picking up the slack (so to speak) for ligaments that aren't helping them. These muscles are usually too long themselves. Joint surfaces become irritated because the ligaments and muscles aren't controlling them nicely and absorbing shock. That's why hypermobile people have their share of aches and pains too.

The contortionists you see performing for crowds at an outdoor mall, *America's Got Talent*, or Cirque du Soleil are extremely hyper-mobile people. I can't watch their performances without thinking about the pain they must be in. So if you find yourself competing to get that foot behind your head in yoga like your instructor, think again. It may not be the best thing for you, or them.

"I know this is a little weird, but have you had some kind of emotional trauma in your life?" I queried.

"Well, yes, some," she said, caught a little off guard. Her smile vanished.

I finished our visit with the deep tissue massage. I didn't expect her knee pain to change when she came in for her next session and I was right.

"Today, we're going to do something a little different, Andrea," I said. "I'm going to try to calm down your nervous system to see if that helps your pain. Is that okay with you?" I asked.

"Yeah, sure," she said, "but why did you ask about emotional trauma before?" She looked worried.

"Because you might be holding on to something that is causing tension in your knees. Today I just want to see if there's anything to that theory," I replied.

Pain from trauma can be expressed in a particular muscle or area of the body, similar to change to Beverley. I remember working out deep knots in a man's inner thigh muscles to resolve his hip pain. The tension and knots kept returning, though.

"Why are you holding so much tension here, Barry?" I said, half to myself.

"Do you mean because my mom abandoned us when I was five years old?" he said. Tears then gushed. "I don't know why I just said that," he confessed. "I haven't told anyone about that. Could that have something to do with it?"

"That very well could be the reason," I said gently after he calmed down. His inner thigh tension was much reduced after that session.

I applied my technique for calming Andrea's sympathetic nervous system (her fight or flight nervous system). It was the same process I used with Beverley earlier.

I began with her right arm then moved to her left leg. Both shoulders suddenly jerked forward off the table and back again. It was as if an electric shock just ripped through her body. It startled us both.

"What was that?!" she asked, rattled.

"I think you just let go of some of that trauma I was wondering about," I said. "When you relax more deeply, old patterns of trauma surface which have been held in your body and are released in the form of a large twitch."

"What do you mean?" she said, sounding anxious.

I explained to her there is a theory that when we experience trauma, our body will move into a freeze response whereby we are rendered incapable of moving. This happens especially in times when we feel we can't escape the event.

This can be seen in the animal kingdom when prey are caught. Typing in *trauma release animals* on YouTube will show some videos about this. They go into a deep trance-like state presumably to avoid the horror of being killed and eaten. Their sympathetic nervous system energy is overruled by a deeper freeze response from an older part of the brain. Dr. Peter Levine writes extensively about this in his amazing book *In an Unspoken Voice*.

Sometimes if the predator is distracted, has to fight off other predators for the kill, or walks away due to lack of interest, the prey snaps out of their trance and is able to get up and run away. Often the prey will later shake or tremble in parts of its body, releasing stored sympathetic nervous system energy.

This happens in humans too. The twitch is the body's way of releasing that deeper stored energy from trauma they haven't been able to release before. I often wonder if this is what happens with me, just as I'm falling asleep, when my arm or leg twitches, waking me up. Unfortunately, we're not always aware of the presence of this energy because our higher-level cognitive brain functions override that release.

"If you'd like to stop here, we can," I said. I was treading on shaky territory because I knew Andrea hadn't been seeing a therapist or counselor. I didn't know anything about the trauma she faced and wasn't equipped to handle that type of problem. She agreed to stop, but the next session she asked to do it again.

"I'm just curious if it was a one-time thing," she said. I was too.

I began the treatment again, and when I reached the left leg, she had a big twitch in her left arm.

"Keep going," she said, a little worried. "I want to see if it happens again."

I continued my treatment, and when I got to her left arm, it happened again. And then her right leg as well. She looked a little panicked.

"I don't understand. Why is this happening?" she asked, nearly sobbing.

"I think you've got some deeper trauma locked in your body. This might be why you're having chronic knee pain. Your body is experiencing tension from this trauma and your knees are the weakest links," I said.

"I don't like it," she said. After a few more moments, she added, "But I think you might be right."

"If I'm right, then you need to see a counselor if you want me to continue. You need a professional to help you deal with this. This isn't my specialty," I said.

Andrea found a therapist and they began their work while also continuing with me. One of my goals as a PT is to rapidly reduce pain and restore function. But this would take time. I had to adjust my expectations—I was in for the long term with Andrea.

We met once a week. Andrea would jerk in spasms while we released her tension. I was often uncomfortable being there with her, I'm ashamed to say. I focused on her experience, though. She needed this to happen. We were in the trenches facing it together.

Our time together helped me see the privilege of my job. To be deeply connected with another person is not common in most professions. That connection is possible through their willingness to be vulnerable.

Andrea was vulnerable with me in ways that perhaps she wasn't even with her family. This is, in my opinion, one of the gifts of being human, this ability to connect on many levels with another, in many different ways.

Eventually Andrea became less emotional about the spasms and started looking at them more objectively. We commented about the degree and timing of them as if they were things separate from her. Objectifying them helped calm her and conquer her fear.

At the end of the day, I returned home silent and tired, ate dinner and went to bed. Throughout our time together, I wondered if we were doing the right thing. This was uncharted territory for me. The human mind and body are vastly interconnected, and those connections are complex. I had to be comfortable not knowing where this was heading.

Almost a year had passed when we noticed her spasms began to occur later into the treatment. Eventually they became minor tremors. Finally, there were no tremors at all. Whether I had anything to do with it or not, I still don't know.

"I'm so excited about this!" said Andrea one day. "They're changing!"

On her own, Andrea worked on her strengthening and stretching exercises throughout our sessions together.

At the end of the year, she had virtually no knee pain. She was also a different person. The perky, vivacious young woman with a quick, loud laugh was replaced with a more self-assured individual. She seemed calmer, for lack of a better description. Content.

How did soothing her nervous system help with her emotional trauma? The short answer is I don't know. What I do know is that her pain seemed to be an expression of her trauma—the canary in her coal mine. Calming her nervous system had the effect of calming her mind by releasing the physical expression of that trauma. And vice versa.

I won't discount the fact that we developed a bond while working together that went deeper than most I have with my patients. I was one of the few people who saw her at her most vulnerable. Her loud, vivacious personality hung outside the door at each visit. As time went on, she seemed content to leave it there.

She taught me that being there for someone can be enough. I don't always have to do something. I now sit quietly when occasionally patients shed tears at my table, rather than rush to console them. They can let it out and I can be silent. They are quiet moments where we are fully human together.

I think about Andrea often and wonder how she's doing. I don't dare check in on her as I feel I might be a reminder of a painful time in her life that she'd rather put behind her. I hope she might see our time together, though, as a period where she shed her past and emerged a more aware person in control of her life.

≈ 14 ≈

The Three Pillars of Pain
(and How to Topple Them)

My three-year-old son ran across the playground, screaming with joy. I watched his chubby little legs occasionally misstep, almost tripping him up. Then he fell with what looked to be extraordinary force, hitting the ground hard. "How could that little body generate so much impact?" I marveled to myself. He looked up at my wife and me. She snapped into action.

"Boone, are you okay?! Oh my, are you hurt?" she yelled while running to him, her voice shrill.

His eyes then filled with tears, and he started crying. Make that screaming.

At this, I stood up and walked toward him slowly. My wife had him in her arms.

"Oh my goodness, what a fall. I bet that hurt! Let me look at you," she said to him while holding his sobbing body close to hers. "Oh my gosh, look at those scrapes. My poor boy."

"Let's take a look, Boone," I said when I got there. I looked at the scrapes on his forehead, elbow and knees. He was covered with dirt and his nose was running from crying.

"Wow, that was your best fall yet! Nice job, Boone!" I laughed. "Let's check you out. Man, I wish I had scrapes like that. You must be so proud of yourself. Can you move your arms and legs? Great! Ready to go again?"

And with that, he was up and running.

It took me a little while to help my wife change her reaction to our kids' accidents. I saw that our kids started crying only after checking on us parents to see how we reacted. If we waved them on, then they'd just get up and hop back to it. If we made a big deal of it, they reveled in, or fed off, our concern and started crying, welcoming the comfort we offered. It was up to us—they were fine.

Slowly but surely, my wife's reaction shifted from fear and worry to calm appraisal. First assess to see if any real damage was done. Give kids a chance to get up on their own. Hold them calmly, if that's what they need, and praise them for whatever they were doing when they fell. Let them know you love them. Then let them go.

To her credit, and against her instincts, my wife eventually mastered the idea. I think our kids were the better for it.

Later, when our kids had an accident, they would turn to us and be met with a "Nice job!" or "Whoa, that was a big one!" or "Wow, that was cool!" They would then get up and continue playing, happy that nothing was really wrong.

Many years later, my cousin, David, and I took my two kids canoeing and camping in Quetico National Park in Canada. It's a remote park with no amenities and great expanses of lakes and rivers.

Edie was 11 and Boone was 13. David and I paddled fiercely for about six hours our first day. We finally found a place to camp on an island after nearly capsizing from a sudden squall. Our campsite was a sloping slab of granite with small trees and grass growing out of it.

Freezing rain and wind pelted us for the two nights we camped. During the day it was windy. Our sleeping bags were drenched after the first night and remained cold and damp the entire trip. The wind and waves were so strong that we couldn't even get our canoe on the lake to fish the next day. Instead, I blazed a trail on our small island to get to the other side. I caught one walleye and we fried it up for dinner.

The second night, we listened to the cold, steady rain pelt our tent. Thunder and lightning rolled through all night long. A large branch poked into my back from below. I frequently awoke to cracks of thunder and watched my breath. My kids slowly slid toward the bottom of the slope on which the tent was pitched, inching down to the lower corner of our tent, where the water collected.

The next morning, Boone sat up in his sleeping bag. Water dripped from his zipper. That was the morning we were due to break camp to return home. My cousin and I cut our tarp into ponchos for the kids to keep them as dry and warm as possible for the journey home. Then we paddled through a freezing drizzle. Even covered, the kids shivered the whole way back. I could barely feel my hands. My cousin could hardly stand up once we hit shore.

That wasn't all. Mosquitos swarmed us after we landed. We had about a quarter-mile portage with our gear and boat uphill to get to the pick-up location. A small stream formed along the path, making the portage hazardous. Once all the gear was up from the lake, a van eventually arrived. We loaded our gear, and hungry, frozen and exhausted, we returned to our cabin in northern Minnesota four hours later. The cabin is owned by my Uncle Dave. I've taken the kids there for years, since they were small, to go fishing, eat s'mores and live on Kitchi Lake for about a week at a time. Growing up in urban Denver, they never had a chance to experience wilderness like that. It's one thing I felt I did right as a dad, taking them there every year. My cousin David's cabin was just 50 yards from mine and the kids would run between the two. It was here that they shot their first bow and arrow, BB gun and shotgun, caught their first fish, ate their first s'more, swam in their first lake, caught their first snake, got bitten by their first mosquito. We always went up on Father's Day each year and I was in heaven traveling with them, knowing they were going to have a wonderful time.

The fallout from the Quetico trip was divided. My son couldn't wait to go back. My daughter never would. In fact, that was the last time she joined us in Minnesota. Both had the same experience but internalized it differently.

There is an emotional component to pain. That aspect can be learned. Just like when my kids were small and looked to us for cues as to how to react to their accidents. If we screamed and acted panicky, they became afraid and cried, no doubt feeling their injury more.

But reactions are also hardwired in our brains, like my daughter refusing to return to Minnesota and my son chomping at the bit every year. Both had the same experience of childhood, the same parents, but they processed it differently. Pain becomes a stew comprised of learned reactions, hardwiring in our DNA, and physical problems. As a therapist, sometimes I need to tease these out to understand what's at the bottom of an issue.

I have had a surprising number of patients with chronic pain who have been resistant to the physical and psychological approaches I've tried with them. Surprising to others, who assume that anyone would be delighted to have pain alleviated. Not surprising to me. As a medical practitioner, I treat the human condition but live daily in the cloudy echo chamber of the human mind, seeing how it can powerfully affect the body, for good and for ill. Our minds are comprised of what we're born with mixed with what we experience, are taught and absorb as fact and truth.

There is one last ingredient to consider: things we ingest. Not metaphorically, like ideas, but literally. By this I mean the foods we eat and the air we breathe.

People have food allergies or sensitivities. Consuming these foods can cause the body to become inflamed, contributing to pain. I once had a client with chronic pain who discovered she was allergic to her favorite food which she ate all the time—watermelon. She cut this food out of her diet and her pain reduced by approximately 25 percent.

When patients stump me, I often suspect gluten intolerance as a possible source of irritation. Gluten is found in breads and pastas and can cause inflammation in those who are sensitive to it. It's the most obvious and easiest ingredient to eliminate from a diet. Anything beyond this I refer to a doctor or dietician. Diet and allergies aren't my specialty. But I see how often they affect physical therapy issues.

This category also includes things we breathe in, such as pollen and mold. Both can severely affect our bodies, creating an inflammatory condition. There are many books addressing these problems. It is more pervasive than you might think.

≡≡ ≡≡ ≡≡

Michelle was a longtime client of mine from my days working at a health club in downtown Denver. Although she didn't participate in sports, she was incredibly athletic and would quickly master any challenge I put to her. During our off days, she would spend hours working out in a home gym she'd built in her basement, outfitted with all the best equipment. Pound for pound, she was stronger and leaner than anyone at the club, which was filled with all sorts of elite athletes. She was simply amazing.

However, long ago, she developed some strange symptoms we

couldn't figure out. She would sometimes experience numbness and shaking of the left side of her body, which would pass after an hour or two. She would also complain of strange head pain and fatigue that might last a few days and then disappear. Additionally, her heart would sometimes race, even while she rested, and she sometimes had difficulty breathing.

Over the years we tried all sorts of ideas to help isolate the precipitating factors for these complaints. There was no discernible musculoskeletal cause or trigger, so we focused on her diet.

Michelle was also seeing a dietician and her food intake was pristine. No extra calories or processed foods. She was disciplined and would comply with whatever was recommended, 100 percent. This helped us quickly eliminate sources of triggers. The problem was that we ran out of ideas.

Michelle thought to visit a naturopathic doctor, an ND. NDs typically attend a four-year graduate program and are educated in basic sciences, like medical doctors. Their education also focuses on environmental and holistic medical intervention.

This doctor discovered that Michelle had, at one time, Lyme disease. Named after a small town in Connecticut where it was first discovered, Lyme disease is transmitted by a tick and can have far-reaching chronic effects on the body, including fatigue, headaches, muscle aches and more. I had heard of Lyme disease and knew it caused chronic musculoskeletal pain, but that was about the extent of it. To us, this likely explained Michelle's symptoms.

She received treatment and improved somewhat but never quite as much as we'd hoped. She decided to have further testing and her doctor found that she had traces of mold in her body. Mold spores are quite small and can be inhaled. At the time, I had no idea that mold could even be a factor in people's health. My focus was the musculoskeletal system and sometimes the mind-body connection. Mold was a completely new field for me.

Michelle's mold source was a mystery to us both; she lived in a very dry climate and her house was a relatively new build. Her workplace was also recently renovated, and no mold had been reported during the overhaul. She was a great cook and used only the freshest ingredients, so we didn't feel mold was coming into her body through her diet.

This mystery went on for years, as she continued to go to her ND for treatment. Then she and her husband decided to renovate their home. She wanted a new bedroom and bathroom, which took months to complete. During that renovation, she decided to change the flooring in her basement. When a worker pulled up a tile, it was completely black on the undersurface. Michelle literally screamed at the sight. She was mortified. They pulled up more tiles and found that her workout area was infested with black mold. Tracing it to the source, they discovered a gutter connection that had come loose and allowed water to stream down the side of the house. Over the years, it had migrated to the inside through small cracks in the mortar, above the dirt line, and traveled unseen behind the drywall, ending up in the basement.

Michelle wasted no time in tracing that leak, fixing it, and mitigating the mold. Within a few weeks, her symptoms abated and are overall about 90 percent improved, often 100 percent, she reports, unless her system becomes stressed by other factors.

To this day, Michelle's body is like a canary in a coal mine when it comes to mold. She has honed her awareness around this stressor. Recently, she went on vacation and walked into her hotel room. She instantly felt her sinuses begin to act up—there was mold in the room. She requested a new room in a different part of the hotel, one that was a newer construction, and had no symptoms at all.

⇥⇥⇥

Case studies like Michelle's helped me build up my overall Three Pillars of Pain theory. Think of pain as a line. Above that line, we experience pain. Below it, we do not. We want to stay below it. The line is our critical threshold.

There are three primary columns of issues pushing us up to this critical threshold of pain:

1. Physical problems like broken bones, muscle strains or the functional problems I've talked about causing strain to tissues, such as what happened to Al, Sallie and Jeni.
2. Psychological or emotional issues, like those of Beverley and Andrea.
3. Things we ingest like allergens, mold or gluten, as in Michelle's case.

Sometimes we reach our critical threshold from 100 percent of physical problems. Sometimes it's 40 percent emotional or psychological and 60 percent physical. And others its 50 percent things we ingest and 20 percent emotional or psychological and 30 percent physical. Everyone is different, each case a new combination of the Three Pillars.

There are myriad health and wellness books on the market. There are heal-your-back-pain books, like mine, anti-inflammatory diet books, and books that tout that all pain is from an emotional source. All of them are written by people who've had success using their approaches. All help some people and not others.

The Three Pillars of Pain explain why this is the case, why no one in medicine has a 100 percent success rate. There are just too many factors. Each patient brings their own recipe of genetics, history, psychology and physiology. Each medical practitioner brings their own recipe of training, experience, beliefs, successes and failures. It's great when the patient and practitioner line up and all runs smoothly, healing achieved. But that doesn't always happen. In terms of batting average, it probably doesn't even happen most of the time. The Three Pillars theory explains why.

Some might be put off by so many possibilities. But I write this to bring hope. I truly believe that there is an answer for almost all pain, even if it's not my answer.

That's an important thing for a medical practitioner to be able to say. We tend toward egotistical at times. We want to have all the answers, to heal all, to never disappoint a patient, to never disappoint ourselves. But it's critical, for our patients' sake, for us to remain humble and recognize our limits. We each have our strengths and specialties and we need to be willing to refer patients to others and admit when we cannot help.

≋ 15 ≋

The Well-Meaning
Mama Did It

"Her balance isn't so good. She has sensory processing issues," Diana urgently explained about her five-year-old daughter, Sarah. "Her legs are different lengths too. I have the same problem. Here," she continued, concerned, "I even brought her x-ray. See? One of her legs is clearly shorter than the other."

Usually, I received x-ray reports sent ahead of time. Diana carried Sarah's with her. This file was unusual, too, in that it was a full x-ray of both legs, from foot to pelvis.

I studied Sarah's image. Clearly her left hip was higher than her right.

"Yes, and is Sarah in pain?" I asked, a little confused.

"Not exactly," Diana said, "but look at her balance. It's hard for her to stand on one leg."

"Sarah, can you please stand on one leg for me?" I asked, turning to the fidgeting girl.

"Uh huh," she said as she stood on her left foot. She had to try several times before holding her balance on her leg for about 10 seconds.

"Can I see your other leg?" I asked.

"Sure," she said and stood on her right leg for about 30 seconds. She was much steadier.

"And watch her hop on one leg," Diana joined in. "Sarah, hop on one leg,"

Sarah hopped on her right leg. She landed in the same spot for about a minute.

"Now do your other one, dear," her mother said.

Sarah obediently hopped on the left leg. Sure enough, the foot landed in different places, like an amateur dart thrower trying to hit the bull's eye but only reaching the large outer ring of the board.

"Sarah," I said, "does it hurt to hop on your left leg?"

"Nope," she said, quickly glancing at her mother.

"I have the same thing," Diana said. "Ever since I was a girl, I've been accident prone and had weird aches and pains. Sarah has them too. She's just like Mama. Aren't you, sweetie?"

"Uh huh," Sarah nodded.

I studied Sarah's x-rays more closely. "So, Sarah's primary problem, as far as you can see, is that her balance is off, and she can't hop well on one leg?"

"And that one leg is longer. Yes, it's part of her sensory processing issues. We're seeing a specialist for them," Diana said with a worried look on her face.

"Well, I'm not well-versed on sensory processing issues, but if I could help Sarah with her hopping and balance, would you say that's what you've brought her here for?" I still wasn't clear about what the exact problem was, other than the leg length and balance issues.

"Yes, but you can't solve it. It's the way she's made. One leg is longer than the other. She needs shoe inserts to fix this. Hopefully that'll help her balance better and help her processing issues. I wear them too," she said.

"Oh, do you have a sensory processing issue as well?" I asked.

"Well, no one seems to know," she said. "But I think so."

"Okay, well, let me take a look at Sarah," I said, "and I'll see what I can do."

I evaluated Sarah and, sure enough, the left side of her pelvis was about an inch higher than her right. I showed her mother by putting my hands on the top of each side of Sarah's pelvis.

"So this is what you're talking about?" I turned to her.

"Exactly. That's why she needs shoe inserts. Just like Mama, right, Sarah?"

"I want to make sure you're seeing what I'm seeing," I replied to Diana. "Can you put your hands on top of Sarah's pelvis and confirm I'm seeing the right thing?"

I placed Diana's hands on the tops of Sarah's pelvis. "Now, kneel down so your eyes are at the level of her pelvis. That way you can see whether they're truly off."

Diana did as I asked. "I see it. You poor girl. We'll do our best honey, don't worry," she said.

I then asked Sarah to lie down on her back. "Sarah, I'm going to measure how long each of your legs are," I said. I grabbed my measuring tape from a nearby shelf and measured the length of her legs.

Practitioners measure the lengths of legs differently. Many measure them from a point on the pelvic bone down to the ankle bone or even the heel. If we measure from the pelvic bone to the ankle, that measurement crosses two joints: the hip joint and the knee joint. If we measure from the pelvis to the heel, that measurement includes three joints: the hip joint, knee joint and ankle joint.

It has long baffled me that some objective authority, a medical association, does not choose an optimal, universal way to measure. It would simplify matters to no end. I can imagine two reasons why it has not yet been done. First, medicine seems to proceed based on what's been done before. There are assumptions made early on that are never really challenged, so business carries on as usual until someone scratches their head and wonders about those precepts. You hear about this a few times a year, when a medical discovery turns our old ideas of how things work in the body on their head, paving the way for a more complete understanding of a phenomena. Second, leg length discrepancy is often something seen when standing and seeing one pelvis higher than the other. So naturally the pelvis should be included in the measurements. But I'd guess that this thinking occurred before anyone really understood how much a bone or joint rotates, contributing to the overall length of a limb. I've learned over the years that compensations occur through each joint in the chain which can contribute to the "appearance of a leg length discrepancy." After I realized how much the pelvic and ankle bones can be altered by muscle or ligament tightness or looseness, I realized I needed to take those out of the equation to get a true leg length measurement.

I've learned that the more joints you include in your measurement, the less reliable it becomes. This is because of subtle rotations that occur at each joint that make it appear that there are differences in length.

I measure from the top of the thigh bone to the ankle bone. This takes into account the length of the thigh and the lower leg bones and includes just one joint, the knee. The knee joint has less of a chance of rotation affecting the measurement.

Sarah's leg lengths were equal, according to my evaluation. She didn't have a leg length discrepancy. In my 20-plus years of measuring leg lengths in this way, I've perhaps come across just two or three patients who have more than a centimeter difference between their two legs. Yet I'd say 20 percent have been told by some medical practitioner that they have a leg length discrepancy.

I once gave a talk about this. A brave woman volunteered to come up for a demonstration. She told me she'd had a leg length discrepancy for years. I measured and found that her pelvis was uneven, but her legs were of equal length. I then corrected her pelvis, so it was level. Surprisingly, she wasn't happy with me. She'd had all her pants tailored to accommodate her uneven pelvis and would need to visit a tailor again—oops!

This confirmed to me that the differences in Sarah's apparent leg lengths were due to rotations at her joints. In Sarah's case, her left foot was flatter than her right, which would cause the left hip to drop down lower. Her left thigh muscles were tighter too. These attach to the front of the pelvic bone and rotate it forward, altering its appearance during measurements. Her left waist muscles tightened in an attempt to level her pelvis. They did too good a job at it. The left pelvis was held higher than the right by these muscles, similar to Sallie's case in Chapter 9.

I stretched Sarah's left thigh muscles, helped her left waist muscles release their spasm and taped up the arch of her left foot. I then measured her pelvic bones to see if they were level. They were.

"Diana, could you come over here and measure Sarah's pelvis for me? I just want to confirm what I'm seeing here," I said.

Diana came over, knelt down behind her daughter and measured the pelvic bones. "They're level," she said. "That's impossible. They can't be level. She has a difference in her leg lengths." She looked at me, perplexed. There was another emotion there I couldn't quite make out.

"Sarah doesn't have a leg length difference," I said, "Her foot is flatter on one side and a thigh muscle was tighter. This caused the

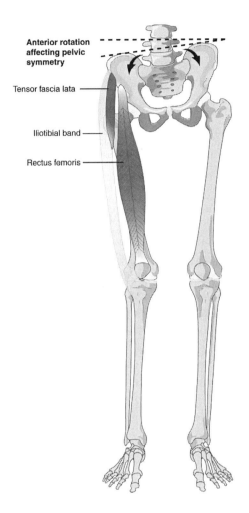

Anterior rotation affecting pelvic symmetry

Tensor fascia lata

Iliotibial band

Rectus femoris

A flat foot, together with tight thigh muscles, can make it appear as if a leg-length discrepancy exists.

waist muscles to lift that side of her pelvis, giving the appearance of a leg length discrepancy. My measurements show they are identical lengths. Sarah, can you please stand on your left foot?"

She did and stood for perhaps 20 seconds on that foot—definitely steadier than she'd been at the start of our session. This would improve even more if she practiced getting used to her level pelvis and having an arch that could help her.

"Sarah, can you hop around on your left foot?" I then asked.

Sarah dutifully hopped on her left foot. If the dart board distribution had been in the outer circle before, it was now in a much tighter formation, closer to the bull's eye. I then pulled out a miniature trampoline that we keep at the office.

"Sarah, can you hop on one leg on this little trampoline?" I asked.

This looked like fun, so she eagerly obliged, hopping first on her right foot for about 20 seconds.

"Now switch to your left foot, Sarah, if you would," I asked.

She then hopped on her left foot almost as well as her right. She was already learning from the improved alignment of her foot and pelvis.

Diana was flabbergasted and didn't seem all that pleased.

"How is this possible?!" she demanded. "She has a leg length discrepancy! She has x-rays to prove it!" She waved them in front of me.

"Well, it's true that it *looks* like she has a leg length discrepancy in the x-ray. But if you look closely, you can see that her left foot arch is slightly lower than the right. Now look at what that does to the ankle joint. Do you see how it's lined up differently than the right one? Look at the front of her lower leg bone. Do you see how it's pointing to the inside? Now look at the pelvic bone. See how that point is lower than the other side? These are all compensations occurring because of a flatter left foot and tighter thigh and waist muscles. We just corrected them, and she seems to be fine now. It's simple."

Diana became upset. I sensed that this might be her reaction, which is why I insisted that she measure Sarah's pelvis both times after I'd done so, so she wasn't just taking my word for it but saw it herself. She wasn't able to dispute the changes we made. Also, I made sure to have Sarah demonstrate her improved balance and coordination immediately after these changes, also so that her mother couldn't refute them.

You'd think that Diana would have been delighted. But a part of my job is psychology, not only helping people deal with problems but, occasionally, helping people digest good news when it goes against something they felt certain about. What I'd sensed from Diana's interactions up to this point was a need to validate her daughter's dysfunctions. I'm not sure why—that's for a full-time psychologist to weigh in on. Perhaps she was trying to validate her own problems by creating them in her daughter? Or perhaps she wanted her daughter to bond with her more closely by identifying so closely with her mother through a shared physical issue? There are many possible answers and working them out isn't my role, but it helps if I can sense them and ease the reception of news, whether that news is bad or good.

Whatever the reason, I felt it was my role to clearly show evidence that Sarah would be just fine—at least regarding the reasons Diana brought her into my clinic. There really was no leg length discrepancy and her balance improved significantly with just a couple of simple corrections.

I had not validated the story Diana was creating for her daughter. I showed her the truth of the matter. If Sarah was going to have a chance at a life in which her deficiencies weren't continually reinforced, then this was my opportunity to say no to that.

Diana and Sarah left and never returned.

Certainly, Diana was not intentionally trying to hurt her child. She was unaware of the psychological forces at work. Our beliefs and habits are deeply rooted in our experiences. We often pass those on to our children which can perpetuate that belief system. Patients will often say, "Well, I have a disc problem. My dad had it before me. My grandpa had before him. It's just how we're built."

Sometimes this is true. There may be some genetic issues behind this generational transmission of disc vulnerability, to give but one example. However, more likely it is an inherited belief system reinforced with learned behaviors, not an inherited physiological issue.

Children love to mimic their parents, especially when younger. They look up to them and want to be like them. They want their approval. I've seen them mimic their parents' walking patterns or gestures. They've learned how to walk (or bend or lift or run or work) the way their parents did.

But we need to consider someone's predisposition for a belief system too. For instance, my daughter was never interested in outdoor activities before our camping trip. She came with us to Minnesota and enjoyed herself, but not nearly as much as my son, who just loved every second.

She will likely have a revulsion to camping or outdoor activities because of her one bad experience. She will reinforce this by not trying it again. If she goes on a hike, she might notice the unpleasant things—bugs, heat or fatigue—and ignore the pleasant aspects, like the view, breathing fresh air and exercising. Therefore, she'll never have an experience contrary to her one event. The absence of anything to the contrary reinforces beliefs. She is already building her belief system and shoring it up with examples.

It was important that I show Diana a definitive result that was contrary to the story she was developing for her daughter, and which, by extension, her daughter was adopting for herself. My hope was to interrupt their belief and behavior cycle. I tried to create a different set of experiences and expectations for them both.

Andrea and Beverley's stories in the previous two chapters showed how trauma and anxiety can become expressed as physical pain. Our beliefs contribute to our experience of pain too. Just look at people who walk across fire pits at corporate events for team building. They're taught in a day or two to believe they will not be hurt.

In Diana and Sarah's case, I saw what I felt were the building blocks of a belief system that would ultimately lead Sarah into thinking she was vulnerable, that she was not in control. These beliefs lead to a life of chronic pain. I couldn't let that happen to that little girl. I saw an opportunity to change her subconscious programming and perhaps steer them both to a different path of pain-free lives. I don't know how successful I was. From an objective perspective, I had "solved" the issue in a single session. It was really up to Diana, then, to decide that the truth was an acceptable new narrative. Otherwise, she could inadvertently hammer a weakness into her child who did not have one.

≋ 16 ≋

A Case Is Never
Truly Closed

By now you'll know that I love a good mystery. She walked into my clinic at 8 o'clock on a cool September morning. Little did I know that I would become obsessed with this woman's problem for the next two years and counting.

Sandra was an elegant 50-year-old woman with chronic debilitating pain in the fourth and fifth fingers of her right hand. You might think that pain in these two fingers couldn't be *that* bad, after all, it's just her pinky and ring finger. We don't use those that often, do we? But Sandra described the pain as burning, stabbing, numbing, tingling, throbbing and sharp, rating the pain 10 out of 10. In medicine, we reserve a 10 out of 10 rating for pain that results in emergency room visits. But from past experience, Sandra knew there was nothing an emergency room could do to help her. Her pain would last anywhere from minutes to hours. It would come and go and she couldn't predict when it would strike, filling her with dread throughout her day. Sandra worked at a computer and her pain would stop her in her tracks—she could focus on nothing else while it raged in her hand like a cornered wildcat. Years earlier, her problem put a halt to her five-days-a-week exercise program. At night she would drift in and out of sleep, the smallest random movement triggering this stabbing pain that would last who knows how long.

As a teenager she'd played high school sports and had managed to escape without any serious injuries. Since then, she'd had breast implants 15 years before and had led a pain-free life with no other injuries or surgeries. Her pain gradually appeared more than 12 years before and worsened to the point where, after a plane flight, she would predictably have to sit doubled over and alone in the airport bathroom for 20 or more minutes waiting for it to subside. She didn't want anyone to see her in that condition. So she hid. The expansive possibilities of her life had constricted, squeezed by the pain. She was miserable. When she came to me, she said that her only hope to deaden the pain was through powerful medications which she hated to take, as they blunted her focus.

She also had swelling in her right hand, which had become slightly discolored as a result. This can happen when the arteries or veins are compromised, obstructing blood flow. Sandra's doctors concluded that she was suffering from thoracic outlet syndrome (TOS). The most common type of TOS involves squeezing all three nerves traveling down the arm and the blood vessels that accompany them too. That's why her hand was swollen—her blood circulation was impeded. The big squeeze usually happens somewhere between the neck bones and where the collarbone meets the shoulder. Symptoms of TOS typically involve pain in the shoulder area, forearm and/or hand and often cold or weakness in the hand.

In Sandra's case, pain in the fourth and fifth fingers indicated a problem with the ulnar nerve that feeds them. The nerves to the hand originate from the lower levels of the neck (C5-T1). There is one nerve exiting each spinal level. These then merge to form the brachial plexus, an area where they cross and combine like a bird's eye view of a particularly busy section of a Los Angeles overpass, finally distilling down to three larger nerves, the journeys of which end in the hand.

Think of the hand like a mountain lake into which three rivers flow. Each of those rivers carries water from five different peaks of the surrounding mountains. The three nerves feeding our hand are the ulnar, median and radial nerves, and each feeds a different part of the hand. The ulnar nerve only receives water from two of the peaks, C8 and T1.

These nerves have established pathways. They must contend with structures around which they wrap, under which they duck or through which they pierce—it's like a nerve obstacle course. It can be a perilous journey for those thin little guys getting messages to and from the hand to the neck and ultimately the spinal cord.

The ulnar nerve is no exception in this regard. Much like an action movie hero, the ulnar nerve valiantly carries his secret messages across hostile territory all day long without anyone suspecting his mission or paying attention to him—until he's hurt.

Its first hurdle is just getting clear of the neck bones which can become arthritic or shift to compress the nerve roots. Next, our little messenger travels through neck muscles (the scalenes), the grip of which can lock him in a chokehold. Then it passes between the collarbone and our first rib, a low cave he must shimmy through on his stomach before diving underneath a small chest muscle (the pectoralis minor) that could mash it into the rib cage like a WWF smackdown. At this point, our ulnar nerve has been accompanied by his brother and sister, the median and radial nerves, as well as blood vessels feeding the arm. But from here on, he becomes a lone hero to finish his job.

Our poor little ulnar nerve, alone but determined, runs down the inner part of the upper arm where, just like a bed sheet that's too tight, it can be bound by a layer of fascia. Our messenger then finds himself in a bony tunnel (the tarsal tunnel) at the elbow. If the ulnar nerve were flying on Elbow Airlines, he would always have a center seat on the plane. In a perfect world, our little guy would be sitting between two supermodels, so he would have plenty of room to move around and be happy. Sometimes, though, the bones of the tarsal tunnel thicken and his seatmates, now the size of NFL linemen, squeeze him unmercifully to the point where he can't even wiggle in his seat. That's what tarsal tunnel syndrome is like and it's no wonder that it could be responsible for Sandra's pain.

After he clears the elbow, our ulnar nerve hero happily runs down the inner forearm, before continuing across the wrist bones which, just in case he thought he was home free, could shift or fracture, wounding him.

If Sandra decided to rest on her palm a little too long in one position, she could inadvertently crush her ulnar nerve in its final leg of his journey to feed the fourth and fifth fingers.

I suffered an ulnar nerve crush injury by leaning on my hand over the course of three days while I varnished my front porch with a hand brush. Not an action that you'd expect would lead to injury! A typical ulnar nerve crush injury isn't painful: the fourth and fifth fingers simply become very weak. I had to stop playing guitar for months while the nerve regrew and strength returned. I now use a roller brush to varnish my front porch—not only does it protect my ulnar nerve but I'm done in an hour or two!

Thankfully, doctors can perform something called a "nerve conduction velocity test" to determine if the nerve is obstructed at any of these obstacles. Sandra had this done and it came back showing some minor obstruction, yes, but no definite points were evident.

Interestingly, through the course of her tests and images (x-rays and the like), the doctors found she had an extra rib in her neck. This is called a "cervical rib." Cervical ribs are found in about 1 percent of healthy people and about 30 percent of those diagnosed with TOS. She not only had one but two, one on each side of her neck, which is even more rare. A cervical rib is really just a nub of a rib—not like other ribs. But the presence of this "riblet" throws a monkey wrench into the whole brachial plexus machine. It tends to crowd an already busy area. That crowding can affect the nerves and blood vessels feeding the arm.

By the time Sandra arrived at my office for the first time, she'd had surgeries to shave those NFL linemen in her elbow down to size so her ulnar nerve had some more (pardon the pun but I just can't resist) elbow room. Her doctors also removed part of her first rib, to drop the floor of the cave at the collarbone, giving the nerve more room to scoot through. They also removed the cervical rib on that side of her neck and had one of her scalene muscles severed, to release the chokehold on the nerves passing through.

These last three surgeries solved one problem, the swelling and coldness in her right hand. But to everyone's surprise, none of them helped her hand pain. So, in exasperation, her doctor sent her my way.

I conducted her initial evaluation as gently as possible and found several potential suspects. I have a unique approach to helping people with TOS and thought this would be a slam dunk. But when she reported that her pain was much worse *after* our first session, I knew I had something different on my hands. I've worked with enough people with TOS or it's cousin, carpal tunnel syndrome, to know what to expect. Sandra didn't behave anything like these patients.

I was immediately suspicious—something unusual was going on here.

For her next visit, I decided to explore her forearm, since her symptoms only involved her hand and, occasionally, her forearm—perhaps the issue was lower down than anyone else had been looking? I gently massaged those muscles, paying particular attention to the pathway of the ulnar nerve. I was feeling for knots or restrictions that might trigger her hand pain but found none.

Sandra returned later in the week, reporting that her symptoms were much worse *after* our massage. Unfortunately, this became a common refrain in our work together as I tried to unravel her mystery.

Each visit I would focus on a different area to flush out our culprit. I explored her upper arm, then her shoulder blade, armpit, chest muscles, upper back muscles, and her neck. All my attempts over the course of several weeks resulted not only in no solution but in more pain for her. The Hippocratic Oath states, "First, do no harm." And here I was, with the best of intentions, but making my patient feel worse after each session than she had before.

I felt terrible—I couldn't remember the last time I had failed so thoroughly. All my go-to tricks had failed. Why was she even sticking with me?

Finally, I found a group of muscles that would give her the slightest bit of relief—the serratus anterior muscles.

The serratus anterior muscles are a funky group that begin along various levels of the upper and middle rib cage in the front and attach to the shoulder blade in the back. They lie along the side of the rib cage in the armpit area. Lightly massaging here would give her relief for perhaps a day, maybe two.

That's as far as we got. After several weeks of this, we both realized that this ultimately wasn't going to solve her problem.

She drifted off my schedule, while I guided her through various doctor appointments, testing other theories of potential sources of irritation. If my own sessions weren't leading to a definitive improvement, I wanted to at least assist her with finding another medical professional who might help.

One possibility was that her breast implant could have leaked, irritating the chest muscles, which was one of my discoveries during our initial exam. That turned out to be another dead end—her implants were intact. Then a cortisone shot to her pectoralis minor—the only muscle that wasn't operated on for her TOS. I pinned a lot of my hopes on this procedure. But, again, it failed.

What was I missing? My mind drifted to my visit about 10 years earlier to Regis University's cadaver lab to brush up on my anatomy. During my years as a PT, I grew to appreciate the uniqueness of each body I worked with, while also keeping in mind the general rules of the game. So, aside from my specific questions I came there to answer (why the shoulder was important to trigeminal neuralgia, what I was affecting when I mobilized the shoulder blade the way I did to create change), I slowly lingered over each cadaver, noting differences in muscle thickness, areas of muscle insertions, differences in bony architecture of the pelvis and shoulder blades, the lengths of Achilles tendons, the thickness of foot fat pads, the movement of hip joints in a cadaver with anteverted femurs versus retroverted femurs and how the joint capsule that surrounds the socket twists and untwists based on these differences, the relative thickness of people's suboccipital muscles at the base of their skulls and their insertions into the neck bones or the proximity of these insertions to the levator scapula—that muscle from the shoulder blade that causes so much pain.

No two were alike, of course, but I was thinking of these differences as they related to pain. How would this person's neck respond to my manual techniques if I were to perform a suboccipital release? I performed releases on the cadavers and noted exactly where my fingers were coming into contact with their necks or skulls. What tissues are taken up first if I were to add distraction to the equation?

I carried a notebook with me, which ended up being a bunch of scribbles even I had a difficult time decoding once I returned home. Textbooks make it seem like we're all built the same, with clearly defined borders of muscles, ligaments and bones—exploring a range of cadavers makes it clear that this is not so.

I learned there that I needed to be more patient with my patients and myself. I learned to keep in mind this variety when working with people, to be willing to experiment to accommodate their unique architecture with a slight rotation here or a gentle mobilization there to create the changes I thought were needed.

As I traced these variations, I began to speculate why one person might be good at an activity, say tennis, as opposed to someone else. Further, it appeared that the deeper, smaller muscles were more diverse than the larger, more superficial muscles. I'm sure this was pointed out when I was a student, but it was lost on me because I was too concerned at the time with memorizing the origin, insertion, innervation and action of the muscles—not their variability. I pondered their roles in stabilization and power generation. I wished, at that moment, that I could have sat down with each cadaver, have had a conversation about their life and watched them move, to test my ideas.

I received many valuable insights during that visit. Each person is unique, and medical practitioners would do well to remember that more often than we do. The presence of Sandra's cervical ribs was yet more evidence. What if Sandra had some type of anomaly that I'd never heard of? After all, this is the human body we're talking about. This potential variant would need to occur after the ulnar nerve separated from the rest of his family, the median and radial nerves, as well as the blood vessels. That would put it somewhere around the pectoralis minor muscle, deep in the chest near the armpit. But I'd explored these possibilities already. Where could it be? Had I missed something?

I searched for two hours on the Internet and found an interesting anomaly I'd never heard of before—an axillary arch. Axillary is the fancy word for "armpit." This is an extra portion of a big flaring muscle you see in body builders that gives them their trademark V shape—the latissimus dorsi, "lats" for short.

This muscle can shoot off a little extra runner, like a strawberry plant looking for new places to grow. That runner attaches further up the arm, closer to the armpit. The nerves traveling down the arm pass right through that arch which can constrict them. It's rare, occurring in about 7 percent of the population. That's enough of an anomaly that most doctors have never even heard of it. This means that radiologists who read MRIs also might miss it because they're not looking for it.

After further research, I found that a little runner can also emerge from our big chest muscle, the pectoralis major, our "pecs." Similar to the lats, the pecs send off a little slip of muscle, called the chondroepitrochlearis, to attach on the upper portion of the arm. This, likewise, forms an arch and can trap nerves or blood vessels.

I referred Sandra to a shoulder surgeon for a cortisone shot and an MRI. I hoped, like Justin (the big linebacker with neck pain), the cortisone shot would clear her pain temporarily and, in so doing, show that something was wrong in her shoulder joint. But she had no relief from her shot. I knew this was a long shot since my treatment hadn't picked up the shoulder as a culprit but I thought it was worth a try anyway. At least this let me rule out her shoulder joint as the problem.

We waited two weeks for her MRI appointment. In the meantime, I called the radiologist to inform him that I suspected an axillary arch or pectoral arch as the culprit. He hadn't heard of either of these anomalies, so I sent him some research articles. He promised he'd try to find them.

I was excited because these variations apparently cause neurological pain in at least 70 percent of the people who have them. I was running out of ideas for Sandra and needed to solve this mystery. This was the best lead yet.

I received Sandra's shoulder/armpit MRI report: negative. I felt like I'd been punched in the gut. The two arches seemed like the perfect solution. Additionally, she had another MRI of her brachial plexus region—where all the nerve and bone traffic congests near the neck. Negative. I was shut down at every turn.

I decided to go for gold and contact the author of one of the papers I'd found on the pectoral arch. He was a peripheral nerve specialist at a prestigious medical center, a specialist in nerves after they exit the spinal cord. I hoped I could pique his interest with a difficult case. Sandra said she was open to flying out to see him if he was interested. He responded that he had nothing to offer.

I could only think of one more test to order: a guided dynamic ultrasound. The benefit of this test is that the patient can move their body while the tester uses an ultrasound to "see" what tissues might be damaged or impinged during those movements. This is an especially good choice for someone who has intermittent pain or pain with a particular movement and whose MRI showed no problems. It seemed perfect for Sandra's case. I contacted Sandra's primary care doctor, who by this time was probably getting tired of all my special requests, to order one for her. My goal was to target the armpit and chest muscles, as well as to revisit the elbow tunnel, to see if something had been missed there.

16. A Case Is Never Truly Closed

Again, I contacted the radiologist prior to testing. He was part of a special group focused on more difficult cases. They were not familiar with either of the variants I was looking for and I sent them the research articles I'd uncovered. I'd even found one article describing the technique they used to "see" the chondroepitrochlearis they were looking for. This described the patient's arm position and had the patient exert some effort to cause the targeted muscle to contract, thereby showing up on the ultrasound better. I highlighted this for the radiologist and discussed the arm positioning and muscular contraction pattern we needed to achieve, in order to visualize either the axillary arch or its cousin from the chest muscle. He was very kind to listen to me and became excited at the prospect of looking for these variants if they existed, as he had not had a case like this before. My fingers were crossed. I finally had someone on my side interested in Sandra's case.

Unfortunately, all testing was put on hold due to the coronavirus. Sandra and I had to wait it out. While waiting, I continued to sift through her signs and symptoms. I found myself doubting her test results. Did the breast implant doctor really look well enough? Did the radiologist really get the image he needed to see these anomalies, and could he decipher one if he did, never having seen one before?

Eventually the testing was completed—no variants detected. All the wind was again knocked out of my sails. I can't imagine what Sandra must've been feeling at this news. So many dead ends, and I was the one leading her to most of them. I wouldn't have blamed her if she hadn't wanted to hear from me again.

Several months passed and I had no other leads. About this time, I had been helping one of my therapists with a shoulder problem. Finally, we decided she needed some imaging. She had a unique pattern of pain, and we thought that a dynamic ultrasound would be the best option.

She found a doctor to do it. It came back that she had a biceps tear. But she was really impressed with her doctor. He spoke excitedly about her shoulder and his work and had mentioned that he'd recently discovered a phenomenon in which the shoulder can leak fluid, irritating adjacent structures, including nerves. Neither of us had heard of this and I think he was having a hard time getting other doctors to listen. This sounded like a doctor who was willing to experiment and investigate unusual issues. My lightbulb went on. Could this be the doctor we needed for Sandra?

I got her on the phone and explained this new phenomenon to her. She agreed to see him for another dynamic ultrasound. I also wrote up a synopsis of her case, including surgeries, tests and conclusions. His office had never received this type of information from a physical therapist before—I'm not sure how they took it. Nevertheless, they agreed to look for the variants, as well as the possibility of a leaking shoulder joint. Sandra and I once again were very excited about the results.

But, once again, all tested negative.

The doctor traced out the entire ulnar nerve during the testing, from hand to neck, and found nothing wrong. He gave her a cortisone shot in her wrist to shrink tissues potentially impinging the ulnar nerve there.

Again, no change in her symptoms. I was baffled.

Soon after this, Sandra saw another doctor who injected three levels of vertebrae in her neck, her deeper chest muscle that could potentially trap the ulnar nerve (the pectoralis minor) and her forearm muscles. Once again, no change in her symptoms. She was fed up with all the testing and injections. I felt we had turned over every stone I and every other doctor could think of.

But there is never no answer. Walls are meant to be climbed. So many highly intelligent medical professionals with decades of experience between them trying to figure this out. So many tests. So many surgeries. All to no avail. What could it mean?

It meant I was looking in the wrong places. But what other places could there be?

I thought about all of this for weeks. I needed to shift my point of view. Then it struck me that we all were looking at the ulnar nerve pathway from a musculoskeletal perspective, as I described at the beginning of the chapter. The nerve had a certain obstacle course it must traverse to get to the hand. But what if there were another adjacent obstacle that wasn't part of the course, influencing the others?

I went back to my initial evaluation. One finding that never added up for me was her tender right chest muscle. That didn't fit with her complaints, because the larger chest muscle doesn't interact with the ulnar nerve. I'd put it aside to pursue more obvious solutions.

Not being an expert in breast augmentation complications, I assumed the only thing that could irritate that chest muscle was a leaking implant. We had pursued that idea and cleared it early on in our attempts to help her. But what if there were other issues of which I wasn't aware?

Once again, I went back to research for complications from breast implants. Most articles dealt with shoulder or chest pain as a result. Some indicated TOS complaints that resolved with surgery. Sandra had already had surgery for TOS which helped some symptoms but not this remaining painful symptom. Then I found one lonely blog article that described intermittent ulnar nerve pain that had stumped practitioners.

I discovered a phenomenon called "capsular contracture," where the breast implant hardens and scar tissue develops, constricting the capsule around the breast implant. This becomes like another hard surface pushing up against the TOS region of the neck and shoulder. This might explain why her right chest muscle was so tender. After all, this occurred three years *after* her implant surgery. That may be the amount of time it took for her body to build scar tissue enough to impinge upon nearby structures.

When I asked her to have her implant checked for leakage a year earlier, she told her doctor about her ulnar nerve pain and TOS issues. However, the doctor apparently assumed they were unrelated.

I called Sandra to talk about this possibility. It was only a few days after her last series of injections to multiple sites that bore no fruit. She was tired and fed up. This time I didn't hear the cheerful woman I'd been working with for two years. Instead, she sounded wary, doubtful and mistrusting of me.

"Maybe I just have to put up with it," she said.

"Sandra, I know I've said this before and you've no reason to believe me, but we've cleared everything that could be affecting the ulnar nerve. This has to be it! Hang in there just a little longer!" I urged.

I didn't want her to give up. I saw our past failures as clues to the real culprit—kind of like putting culprits in jail for a crime spree only to find the same crimes keep happening. They must not be the right culprits.

Now that we'd approached every possibility, we had to consider a new set of offenders. Maybe her sore chest muscle just a few years after her implant surgery was more than just a coincidence. It was a clue we'd all been ignoring but couldn't any longer.

As I sit here at my kitchen table writing this, I can barely contain myself. I haven't even had a cup of coffee, but I'm wired, buzzing with anticipation. This might be the answer, finally. This is a case I'm writing about in the middle of the action, not in retrospect. It's a thriller of a medical mystery for which I don't yet know the answer.

If this ends up being the source of her pain, how would this explain her most consistent irritant—traveling on a plane? It only takes a brief imaginary visit to your run-of-the-mill tight quarters on an airplane to come up with a theory. The seats are never wide enough, and throughout the flight, especially if you haven't won the battle for using the arm rest, your shoulder and chest must subtly work with the effort of holding your arm toward your body throughout the flight. If she had a contracture in her chest area, this would likely heighten it, thereby pressing the hardened tissue more firmly into the ulnar nerve space, compressing it ever so slightly. Sandra's report of her pain was that it occurred intermittently without any particular pattern. If we consider my three pillars of pain theory, this means that she must be very close to her pain threshold at all times. Any slight provocation will push her through the threshold. This is what prolonged chest contraction would do to her, such as trying not to touch the person sitting too close to her on a flight.

I asked her to return to her surgeon to explore this possibility. I'm waiting on pins and needles. Her story, as I complete this book, has not been fully resolved, which is difficult for me to accept. I still hold out hope that, prior to this publication, we will find her answer. While it seems strange to include an unfinished story in my book, it is also fitting. It illustrates the struggles that some people, and practitioners, have to find solutions. I see this as blessing and a curse of the miracle of our existence. The seemingly infinite permutations of form, function and response to some adverse element fascinates me. And this is only the musculoskeletal system. Thanks to this, I'm always kept on my toes.

⇒⇐ ⇒⇐ ⇒⇐

As a postscript to this chapter, Sandra's doctor confirmed there are no complications from her implants. I still haven't given up on her, though...

I hope that this book has expanded your understanding of your anatomy and pain. My greatest hope is that, if you are one of those who have been searching for answers to your pain, these stories perhaps offer a glimpse into new possibilities to solve your issue. I wish you success.

Index